IMPURITY AND PURIFICATION IN EARLY JUDAISM AND THE JESUS TRADITION

RESOURCES FOR BIBLICAL STUDY

Editor
Davina C. Lopez, New Testament

Number 98

IMPURITY AND PURIFICATION IN EARLY JUDAISM AND THE JESUS TRADITION

Thomas Kazen

Atlanta

Copyright © 2021 by Thomas Kazen

All rights reserved. No part of this work may be reproduced or transmitted in any form or by any means, electronic or mechanical, including photocopying and recording, or by means of any information storage or retrieval system, except as may be expressly permitted by the 1976 Copyright Act or in writing from the publisher. Requests for permission should be addressed in writing to the Rights and Permissions Office, SBL Press, 825 Houston Mill Road, Atlanta, GA 30329 USA.

Library of Congress Control Number: 2021945826

Contents

Preface vii
Credits ix
Abbreviations xi

1. Introduction: Purity Research and Resources 1

2. Purity and Impurity: A Short Summary 43

3. Levels of Explanation for Ideas of Impurity:
   Why Structuralist and Symbolic Models Often Fail
   While Evolutionary and Cognitive Models Succeed 51

4. Purity and Persia 79

5. The Role of Disgust in Priestly Purity Law:
   Insights from Conceptual Metaphor and
   Blending Theories 105

6. Disgust in Body, Mind, and Language:
   The Case of Impurity in the Hebrew Bible 137

7. Purification 155

8. Concern, Custom, and Common Sense:
   Discharge, Handwashing, and Graded Purification 181

9. Jesus and the *Zābâ*: Implications for Interpreting Mark 217

10. Skin-Disease Contamination and Exclusion:
    How Not to Reconstruct History for a Good Cause 251

11. Purity as Popular Practice: Erasing the Anachronistic
    Divide between Household and Cult 277

12. A Perhaps Less Halakic Jesus and Purity:
    On Prophetic Criticism, Halakic Innovation, and
    Rabbinic Anachronism 303

Bibliography 319
Ancient Sources Index 357
Modern Authors Index 368
Subject Index 374

Preface

It has now passed ten years since *Issues of Impurity in Early Judaism* (Eisenbrauns, 2010), a collection of articles and studies following up on *Jesus and Purity Halakhah* (Almqvist & Wiksell International, 2002; corrected reprint ed., Eisenbrauns, 2010). Since then I have tried to stay away from the topic and focus on other research areas, but in retrospect I have to admit that I have managed no better than the worst recidivist. Both *Emotions in Biblical Law* (Sheffield Phoenix, 2011) and *Scripture, Interpretation or Authority?* (Mohr Siebeck, 2013) contain substantial sections dealing with purity and impurity, and even in my recent Swedish book on same-sex activity in the Bible and the ancient world, *Smuts, skam, status* (Makadam, 2018), impurity forced its way through, though limited to a brief chapter.

During the last decade, I have also published some shorter essays in the field. In the present volume, nine of these are reprinted, occasionally with minor corrections. They have previously appeared in various types of publications, such as encyclopedias, journals, edited volumes, and memorial volumes, and some of them are not so easy for potential readers to locate. I frequently find fellow scholars referencing my books but missing my more recent and updated contributions to the ongoing discussions about purity practices in early Judaism and the emerging Jesus movement. In this volume, some of the more recent material is gathered and made easily accessible. Two new pieces have been added, together with an introductory chapter, discussing trends and tendencies in purity research.

The altogether twelve chapters range from phenomenological descriptions to methodological discussions. There are two foci: one is historical (origin, development, practice) and the other cognitive (evolutionary, emotional, conceptual). In relation to my previous books, I further develop a differentiated understanding of the evolutionary and emotional backgrounds to purity conceptions, the historical origins and developments of purity practices, and the metaphorical and rhetorical employment of purity language. I discuss details in the interpretation of ancient texts, the reconstruction of historical trajectories, and differentiation and diversity in practice, and also analyze various scholarly explanations and relate them to claims commonly made in purity debates.

Since each chapter stands by itself, there is an inevitable amount of repetition, more so in some chapters than in others. This, however, makes it possible for readers to use many chapters on their own, for example in courses on purity and ritual in early Judaism, on halakic development, on emotions in the Bible, and on the historical Jesus and the early Jesus tradition. Chapters range from short introductions to discussions of specific topics and detailed exegesis. There are overviews and there are methodological investigations. I hope that the chapters in this volume will be of use for students and scholars of purity alike.

There are so many people to thank for providing me with impulses and stimulating my thinking that I will refrain from mentioning names. Most of them are found in the footnotes. As always, Stockholm School of Theology (University College Stockholm) provides support for research, and Cambridge is a good hideaway with instant access to every resource when things need to get done quickly. Family is crucial, but although ancestors and progeny had their share, I never dedicated a book to my wife. However, as Birgitta prefers me over my books, that would be close to an insult. This book is for our garden, which provides an engagement very similar to that of research but supplies a very different type of food.

Alderkärret, Skinnskatteberg, June 2020
Thomas Kazen

Credits

The following chapters have been previously published and are reprinted here with permission:

Chapter 2: "Purity /Impurity." Pages 166–70 in vol. 3 of *Vocabulary for the Study of Religion*. Edited by Robert Segal and Kocku von Stuckrad. Leiden: Brill, 2015.

Chapter 3: "Levels of Explanation for Ideas of Impurity: Why Structuralist and Symbolic Models Often Fail While Evolutionary and Cognitive Models Succeed." *JAJ* 9 (2018): 75–100.

Chapter 4: "Purity and Persia." Pages 435–63 in *Current Issues in Priestly and Related Literature: The Legacy of Jacob Milgrom and Beyond*. Edited by Roy E. Gane and Ada Taggar-Cohen. RBS 82. Atlanta: SBL Press, 2015.

Chapter 5: "The Role of Disgust in Priestly Purity Law: Insights from Conceptual Metaphor and Blending Theories." *JLRS* 3 (2014): 62–92.

Chapter 6: "Disgust in Body, Mind, and Language." Pages 97–115 in *Mixed Feelings and Vexed Passions: Exploring Emotions in Biblical Literature*. Edited by F. Scott Spencer. RBS 90. Atlanta: SBL Press, 2017.

Chapter 7: "Purification." Pages 220–44 in *The Oxford Handbook of Early Christian Rituals*. Edited by Risto Uro, Juliette J. Day, Rikard Roitto, and Richard E. DeMaris. Oxford: Oxford University Press, 2018.

Chapter 8: "Concern, Custom, and Common Sense: Discharge, Hand-Washing and Graded Purification." *JSHJ* 13 (2015): 150–87.

Chapter 9: "Jesus and the *Zavah*: Implications for Interpreting Mark." Pages 112–43 in *Purity, Holiness, and Identity in Ancient Judaism and Early Christianity: Essays in Memory of Susan Haber*. Edited by Carl Ehrlich, Anders Runesson, and Eileen Schuller. WUNT 1/305. Tübingen: Mohr Siebeck, 2013.

Chapter 12: "A Perhaps Less Halakic Jesus and Purity: On Prophetic Criticism, Halakic Innovation, and Rabbinic Anachronism." *JSHJ* 14 (2016): 120–36.

Abbreviations

Primary Sources

11Q19	Temple Scroll[a]
1QM	Milḥamah *or* War Scroll
1QS	Serek Hayaḥad *or* Rule of the Community
4MMT	Miqṣat Ma'aśê ha-Torah (Some of the Torah Observations)
4Q266	Damascus Document[a]
4Q272	Damascus Document[g]
4Q274	Tohorot A
4Q277	Tohorot B[b]
4Q278	Tohorot C
4Q284	Harvesting
4Q414	Ritual Purity A
4Q435	Barkhi Nafshi[b]
4Q436	Barkhi Nafshi[c]
4Q51	Samuel[a]
4Q512	Ritual Purity B
4Q514	Ordinances[c]
4Q525	Beatitudes
Ag. Ap.	Josephus, *Against Apion*
Alc.	Euripides, *Alcestis*
Ant.	Josephus, *Jewish Antiquities*
Arakh.	Arakhin
b.	Babylonian Talmud
B. Bat.	Bava Batra
B. Qam.	Bava Qamma
Barn.	Barnabas
Ber.	Berakhot
D	Damascus Document

Deus	Philo, *Quod Deus sit immutabilis*
Die nat.	Censorinus, *De die natali*
DtrH	Deuteronomistic History
Exord.	Demosthenes, *Exordia*
Eruv.	Eruvin
Geog.	Strabo, *Geographica*
Gos. Thom.	Gospel of Thomas
H	Holiness source
Hag.	Hagigah
Hist.	Herodotus, *Historia* or Thucydides, *Historia*
HL	Hittite Laws
Hul.	Hullin
J.W.	Josephus, *Jewish War*
Ker.	Kerithot
Let. Aris.	Letter of Aristeas
LXX	Septuagint
m.	Mishnah
Migr.	Philo, *De migratione Abrahami*
Mikw.	Mikwa'ot
Mo'ed Qat.	Mo'ed Qatan
Morb. sacr.	On the Sacred Disease
MT	Masoretic Text
Murder	Antiphon, *On the Murder of Herodes*
Nat.	Pliny, *Naturalis historia*
Ned.	Nedarim
Neg.	Nega'im
Nid.	Niddah
Ohal.	Ohalot
P	Priestly Source
Pesah.	Pesahim
Pesiq. Rab Kah.	Pesiqta of Rab Kahana
Phal.	Lucian, *Phalaris*
Pss. Sol.	Psalms of Solomon
Quaest. conv.	Plutarch, *Quaestionum convivialum libri IX*
Quaest. rom.	Plutarch, *Quaestiones romanae et graecae (Aetia romana et graeca)*
S	Serek ha-Yaḥad (Manual of Discipline)
Shabb.	Shabbat
Shevu.	Shevu'ot

Somn.	Aristotle, *De somniis*
Spec.	Philo, *De specialibus legibus*
t.	Tosefta
T. Yom	Tevul Yom
Tehar.	Teharot
Vend.	Vendidād
Verb.	Festus, *De verborum significatione*
y.	Jerusalem Talmud
Yad.	Yadayim

Secondary Sources

AASOR	Annual of the American Schools of Oriental Research
ÄAT	Ägypten und Altes Testament
AB	Anchor Bible
ABD	Freedman, David Noel, ed. *Anchor Bible Dictionary*. 6 vols. New York: Doubleday, 1992
AcBib	Academia Bbilica
AIRRS	Acta Instituti Romani Regni Sueciae
ALGHJ	Arbeiten zur Literatur und Geschichte des hellenistischen Judentums
AnBib	Analecta Biblica
ANES	Ancient Near Eastern Studies
AOAT	Alter Orient und Altes Testament
ArchT	*Archaeology and Text*
ARSAT	Arbeiten zu Text und Sprache im Alten Testament
AYBRL	Anchor Yale Bible Reference Library
BA	*Biblical Archaeologist*
BAIAS	*Bulletin of the Anglo-Israel Archaeological Society*
BAR	*Biblical Archaeology Review*
BBR	*Bulletin for Biblical Research*
BCAW	Blackwell Companions to the Ancient World
BEFAR	Bibliothèques de l'École française d'Athènes et de Rome
BehBS	*Behavioral and Brain Sciences*
BETL	Bibliotheca Ephemeridum Theologicarum Lovaniensium
BibInt	Biblical Interpretation Series
BibSem	The Biblical Seminar
BibW	Bible World
BJS	Brown Judaic Studies

BM	Books of Moses
BN	*Biblische Notizen*
BNTC	Black's New Testament Commentaries
BS	Beer Sheva
BW	Bible and Women
BZABR	Beihefte zur Zeitschrift für altorientalische und biblische Rechtsgeschichte
BZAW	Beihefte zur Zeitschrift für die alttestamentliche Wissenschaft
ca.	circa
CAJ	*Cambridge Archaeological Journal*
CBQ	*Catholic Biblical Quarterly*
CBQMS	Catholic Biblical Quarterly Monograph Series
CD	Cairo Genizah copy of the Damascus Document
CE	*Cognition and Emotion*
ch.	chapter
CL	*Cognitive Linguistics*
cm	centimeter(s)
CM	Cuneiform Monographs
CMDJPH	*Classica et Mediaevalia: Danish Journal of Philology and History*
ConBNT	Coniectanea Neotestamentica
CQS	Companion to the Qumran Scrolls
CS	Contextualizing the Sacred
CurBR	*Currents in Biblical Research*
DHR	Dynamics in the History of Religion
DI	*Dine Israel*
DJD	Discoveries in the Judaean Desert
DSD	*Dead Sea Discoveries*
EBR	Klauck, Hans-Josef, et al., eds. *Encyclopedia of the Bible and Its Reception*. Berlin: de Gruyter, 2009–.
EHB	*Evolution and Human Behavior*
EJL	Early Judaism and Its Literature
ES	Emerging Scholars
ET	English translation
ETL	*Ephemerides Theologicae Lovanienses*
FAT	Forschungen zum Alten Testament
FRLANT	Forschungen zur Religion und Literatur des Alten und Neuen Testaments

GPIR	*Group Processes and Intergroup Relations*
H.F.	manuscript of Persian Rivayats (Revayats) collected by Hormazyar (Hormazdyar) Framarz
HAT	Handbuch zum Alten Testament
HBM	Hebrew Bible Monographs
HdO	Handbuch der Orientalistik
HL	Haskell Lectures
HR	*History of Religions*
HRR	*Human Rights Review*
HThKAT	Herders Theologischer Kommentar zum Alten Testament
ICC	International Critical Commentary
IEJ	*Israel Exploration Journal*
JAAR	*Journal of the American Academy of Religion*
JAbPsy	*Journal of Abnormal Psychology*
JAJ	*Journal of Ancient Judaism*
JAJSup	Supplements to Journal of Ancient Judaism
JANER	*Journal of Ancient Near Eastern Religions*
JAOS	*Journal of the American Oriental Society*
JBL	*Journal of Biblical Literature*
JCPP	*Journal of Child Psychology and Psychiatry*
JCPS	Jewish and Christian Perspectives Series
JCS	*Journal of Cuneiform Studies*
JEOL	*Jaarbericht van het Vooraziatisch-Egyptisch (Genootshap) Ex oriente lux*
JJS	*Journal of Jewish Studies*
JLRS	*Journal of Law, Religion and State*
JNES	*Journal of Near Eastern Studies*
JP	*Journal of Philosophy*
JPSP	*Journal of Personality and Social Psychology*
JPSTC	JPS Torah Commentary
JQR	*Jewish Quarterly Review*
JSHJ	*Journal for the Study of the Historical Jesus*
JSJ	*Journal for the Study of Judaism in the Persian, Hellenistic, and Roman Periods*
JSJSup	Journal for the Study of Judaism Supplement Series
JSNT	*Journal for the Study of the New Testament*
JSNTSup	Journal for the Study of the New Testament: Supplement Series
JSOT	*Journal for the Study of the Old Testament*

JSOTSup	Journal for the Study of the Old Testament: Supplement Series
JSP	Judea and Samaria Publications
JSPSup	Journal for the Study of the Pseudepigrapha Supplement Series
JSQ	*Jewish Studies Quarterly*
JSRNC	*Journal for the Study of Religion, Nature, and Culture*
JTS	*Journal of Theological Studies*
KS	Kernos supplement
l(l).	line(s)
LCL	Loeb Classical Library
LHBOTS	The Library of Hebrew Bible/Old Testament Studies
LIMC	Ackerman, H. Christoph, and Jean-Robert Gisler, eds. *Lexicon Iconographicum Mythologiae Classicae*. 8 vols. Zurich: Artemis, 1981–1997
LJLE	Library of Jewish Law and Ethics
LNTS	The Library of New Testament Studies
LSTS	The Library of Second Temple Studies
m	meter(s)
MdB	Le Monde de la Bible
MTSR	*Method and Theory in the Study of Religion*
MU.	Unvala, Ervad Manockji Rustamji, ed. *Dârâb Hormazyâr's Rivâyat*. 2 vols. Bombay: British India Press, 1922.
MUSJ	Mélanges de l'université Saint-Joseph
NCBC	New Cambridge Bible Commentary
NICOT	New International Commentary on the Old Testament
NovT	*Novum Testamentum*
NRSV	New Revised Standard Version
NT	New Testament
NTS	*New Testament Studies*
OBO	Orbis Biblicus et Orientalis
ORA	Orientalische Religionen in der Antike
ORCS	Oxford Readings in Classical Studies
OSAR	Oxford Studies in the Abrahamic Religions
OTL	Old Testament Library
P.Egerton	Bell, H. I., and T. C. Skeat, eds. *Fragments of an Unknown Gospel and Other Early Christian Papyri*. London, 1935
P.Oxy.	*The Oxyrhynchus Papyri*. London: Egypt Exploration Society, 1898–

PEQ	*Palestine Exploration Quarterly*
POC	*Proche-Orient chrétien*
PR	*Psychological Review*
Qad	*Qadmoniot*
RB	*Revue biblique*
RBS	Resources for Biblical Study
RelSoc	Religion and Society
RevQ	*Revue de Qumran*
RHPR	*Revue d'histoire et de philosophie religieuses*
RPP	Betz, Hans D., Don S. Browning, Bernd Janowski, and Eberhard Jüngel, eds. *Religion Past and Present: Encyclopedia of Theology and Religion*. 4th ed. 14 vols. Leiden: Brill, 2007–2013.
SAC	Studies in Antiquity and Christianity
SANT	Studien zum Alten und Neuen Testaments
SBE	Sacred Books of the East
SBLDS	Society of Biblical Literature Dissertation Series
SEÅ	*Svensk exegetisk årsbok*
SemeiaSt	Semeia Studies
SFSHJ	South Florida Studies in the History of Judaism
SHJ	Studying the Historical Jesus
SHR	Studies in the History of Religions
SIDA	*Scripta Instituti Donneriani Aboensis*
SIJD	Schriften des Institutum Judaicum Delitzschianum
SJLA	Studies in Judaism in Late Antiquity
SJT	*Scottish Journal of Theology*
SSAPDJJL	Series of Studies on the Ancient Period: David Jemima Jeselshon Library
SSEJC	Studies in Scripture in Early Judaism and Christianity
SSN	Studia Semitica Neerlandica
STAC	Studien und Texte zu Antike und Christentum
StBibLit	Studies in Biblical Literature
STDJ	Studies on the Texts of the Desert of Judah
STK	*Svensk teologisk kvartalskrift*
SymS	Symposium Series
TANZ	Texte und Arbeiten zum neutestamentlichen Zeitalter
TBl	*Theologische Blätter*
TDOT	Botterweck, G. Johannes, and Helmer Ringgren, eds. *Theological Dictionary of the Old Testament*. Translated

	by John T. Willis et al. 8 vols. Grand Rapids: Eerdmans, 1974–2006
TENTS	Texts and Editions for New Testament Study
TLJS	Taubman Lectures in Jewish Studies
TLOT	Jenni, Ernst, and Claus Westermann, eds. *Theological Lexicon of the Old Testament*. Translated by Mark E. Biddle. 3 vols. Peabody, MA: Hendrickson, 1997.
TynBul	*Tyndale Bulletin*
v(v).	verse(s)
VT	*Vetus Testamentum*
VTSup	Supplements to Vetus Testamentum
WAWSup	Writings from the Ancient World Supplement Series
WCD	Works of Charles Darwin
WUNT	Wissenschaftliche Untersuchungen zum Neuen Testament
ZAW	*Zeitschrift für die alttestamentliche Wissenschaft*
ZDPV	*Zeitschrift des deutschen Palästina-Vereins*
ZKT	*Zeitschrift für katholische Theologie*

1
Introduction: Purity Research and Resources

> The interest in ritual purity is not abating, and there is a continuous stream of research in the field. In this introductory chapter I provide an overview of important research and resources that are relevant to students of purity and impurity. I also discuss some recent publications, and I relate my own contributions in the subsequent chapters to ongoing discussions on purity-related topics.

Why is the topic of ritual purity, or rather, ritual impurity, continuing to engage scholars? Is it because of our fascination with that which we experience as archaic and obsolete? Or is it perhaps because the domain of dirt and cleanness still provides conceptual metaphors for various target domains and at various levels, a process I explore in some of the chapters in this book?

The essays gathered in the present volume are evidence for my own continuous engagement. My interest began more than two decades ago as an interest in historical Jesus research but soon turned into a much broader and more general interest in the topic of ritual purity for its own sake. I think my fascination is equally with purity's metaphorical relevancy as with its archaic conceptualizations and practices.

Instead of providing a traditional outline, chapter by chapter, of the present book, this introduction gives an overview of some important resources on the topic and a broad selection of publications that are relevant to the issues at hand. In doing this I will indicate where my own contributions in the subsequent chapters fit into the ongoing discussion.

Some of the material in this chapter is drawn from my annotated bibliography "Purity and Impurity in Ancient Israel and Early Judaism" (Kazen 2019).

A Pervasive Topic

To some, purity may seem a narrow field of research, but impurity is not a marginal issue in biblical and other early Jewish sources. In the Hebrew Bible, purity laws are mainly found in the book of Leviticus (Lev 11: impure animals and contagion by dead "swarmers" and carcasses; Lev 12: parturients; Lev 13–14: skin disease; Lev 15: genital discharges) and the book of Numbers (Num 5; 19; 31: corpse impurity). Another version of food impurity is found in Deut 14. Purification is also a prominent topic in the sacrificial laws (Lev 1–10) and the Day of Atonement ritual (Lev 16), particularly in relation to the ḥaṭṭā'ṯ and 'āšām sacrifices, which atone or effect removal (kipper).

But concepts of purity and impurity also figure in a number of other contexts. The Holiness Code (Lev 17–26) frequently uses purity language rhetorically in relation to various types of disapproved behavior, and some of the psalms and some of the prophets do, too, in particular in relation to sexual misconduct and worship of foreign deities (e.g., Hosea, Jeremiah, Ezekiel). Ezra and Nehemiah use purity language in relation to foreign influence and non-Israelites. Concepts of purity and impurity also surface in a number of apocryphal and pseudepigraphal texts: in narratives such as Judith and Tobit, in various apocalyptic texts, and in historical texts about and around the Maccabean revolt. A considerable number of Qumran texts, including the earlier-known Damascus Document, discuss issues of purity and impurity, in particular 1QS (Rule of the Community), 4QMMT (Some of the Torah Observations), and a number of fragmentary texts from Cave 4.

Turning our attention to texts from the Roman imperial period, we find purity issues discussed occasionally by Philo from Alexandria, by Flavius Josephus, in the New Testament gospels and Pauline Letters, and in some of the Apostolic Fathers and early church fathers. The Mishnah and the Tosefta deal with purity and impurity repeatedly, especially in the tractates of the sixth order, Tohorot, and purity issues are conspicuous in the Sifra to Leviticus and the Sifre to Numbers.

Although various sources differ enormously as to their interests and emphases, we find by merely listing the most important texts and passages that purity is hardly a subject to be downplayed or ignored.

Where to Begin?

Dictionary and encyclopedia articles often provide good introductions. David Wright's *Anchor Bible Dictionary* article "Unclean and Clean (Old

Testament)" from 1992 is still an excellent place to begin, even though the categories of permitted and prohibited impurities are somewhat unsatisfactory.[1] The corresponding New Testament article by Hans Hübner, however, is less helpful, not only by being barely a third in size (including a few lines on Qumran) compared to Wright's, but, most importantly, by being clearly outdated with regard to its interpretation of Jesus's stance (e.g., disregard for food laws separating clean from unclean animals and tax collectors and sinners being equated with the unclean).

Considering other not so recent encyclopedic material, entries on pure and impure in the *Theological Dictionary of the Old Testament* and the *Theological Lexicon of the Old Testament* are valuable, especially for their lexical aspects, which include conceptual discussions as well.[2] Several dictionaries, such as the *Theologische Realenzyklopädie* article on "Reinheit" and the *Religion Past and Present* articles on "Pure and Impure" and "Purification" also include comparative sections, discussing purity conceptions in ancient West Asia, Greece, and Rome as well.[3] An important but often overlooked resource is the book-length French article "Pureté et impureté" in *Dictionnaire de la Bible: Supplément*, which despite the fact that it was published half a century ago is still very useful, as it contains a wealth of comparative material and engages in a careful mapping of all important texts and text groups.[4]

Other evident resources, but usually less systematic due to their genre, are biblical commentaries to Leviticus (and to a lesser extent to Numbers). The commentaries of Jacob Milgrom, Erhard Gerstenberger, and Thomas Hieke all contain substantial discussions on purity and impurity;[5] Gerstenberger views the purity laws as mainly focused on daily and domestic life, while the other two are mainly sanctuary focused. (This is a topic I will discuss especially in chs. 11–12.) Among these, Milgrom is the most comprehensive. In his seminal commentary, he incorporates many of his previous writings on purity issues, including comparative material and further developments in Qumran and rabbinic interpretation.[6] He acknowledges

---

1. Wright 1992.
2. André and Ringgren 1986; Ringgren 1986; Maass 1997. For *ṭhr* there is also Theodor Seidl's (1997) thorough linguistic study.
3. Maier et al. 1997; Stausberg, Seidl, et al. 2011; Stausberg, Cancik, et al. 2011.
4. Henninger et al. 1979.
5. Milgrom 1991; 2000; 2001; Gerstenberger 1996; Hieke 2014.
6. See also Milgrom 1990, which contains several excursuses on purity issues.

the common ancient West Asian roots for ritual practices and demonic conceptions, but with the Kaufmann school, he views the Israelite cult as thoroughly purged from the demonic. Milgrom assumes that the Holiness source redacts the Priestly source,[7] but his dating is early preexilic, which is far too early for most scholars and fits poorly with the predominant trend at least in European research to date both the Priestly source and the Holiness source to the Persian period (see ch. 4 in this volume for further discussion and references). Milgrom closely associates purity with the cult and develops a particular understanding of defilement of the sanctuary "from afar," both of which have been criticized.[8] Hieke, on the other hand, situates Leviticus within the context of Persian-period Yehud and discusses purity practices from this perspective. Here we should also mention Christophe Nihan's magisterial study on the composition of Leviticus, which, although not a commentary, discusses the text systematically and contains a wealth of material on purity laws and purification offerings.[9]

Besides Milgrom's commentary, there are certain monographs that have become classics, some of which were published in the 1970s. Wilfried Paschen's *Rein und Unrein* is one of the earliest and most thorough contributions to the field.[10] Paschen discusses the Hebrew Bible, Qumran, and the New Testament, but since this was years before the wealth of material from Qumran Cave 4 was published, the work has obvious limitations in that area.

Most works focus on the Second Temple period and early rabbinic texts. Jacob Neusner's *The Idea of Purity in Ancient Judaism* provides a sort of baseline for many of the infinitely repetitive books that followed through the years.[11] Here Neusner argues that although the Priestly source portrays purity as primarily a cultic concern, this is true neither in earlier Israelite culture nor in Second Temple or rabbinic Judaism. After discussing biblical occurrences of *ṭm'* and *ṭhr*, Neusner provides an overview of purity in the biblical writings, extracanonical texts, and the Talmud, giving special attention to the ways in which the idea of purity changes and develops. In many regards, this remains Neusner's most valuable work on purity, as it

---

7. Following Israel Knohl (1995).
8. See, e.g., ch. 11.
9. Nihan 2007. In addition to these resources, one should also look out for the second volume of James Watts's commentary on Leviticus, not yet published.
10. Paschen 1970.
11. Neusner 1973.

opens up to a number of topics that are still discussed. (Purity as a cultic versus domestic concern is further discussed in ch. 11.)

In contrast, much of his later work, focusing on purity in rabbinic Judaism, takes a markedly ahistorical approach. In *Purity in Rabbinic Judaism: A Systematic Account*, two decades after *The Idea of Purity*,[12] Neusner summarizes his view of rabbinic purity laws as a systemic discourse, an alternative to myth and theology for expressing a system and a worldview. He discusses sources, effects, and loci of impurity, followed by rites of purification, but since the rituals were not supposed to be carried out, he argues that their purpose was to establish boundaries to sacred reality. Statements of law are understood as dealing with metaphysical reality—the ritual has become the myth.

Also in the 1970s we find Gedalyahu Alon's *Jews, Judaism and the Classical World* appearing in English.[13] This collection was originally published in Hebrew in the 1950s, and the most important articles for dealing with purity and impurity were first published in *Tarbiz* in 1937–1938. Alon suggests that during the Second Temple period, purity was practiced not only in relation to the cult, and that the eating of ordinary food (*ḥullîn*) in purity was not just restricted to a few sectarians but a much more general phenomenon. On this issue Alon argues against, among others, Adolph Büchler, whose study *Der galiläische 'Am-ha'areṣ* from the early twentieth century reappeared in 1968.[14] Büchler claims, contrary to Alon, that during the time of the temple, handwashing was practiced generally for sacrificial food only but not for ordinary food, except as a voluntary undertaking by a few individuals, mainly Shammaites. We will return to these issues below (see "Scope of Purity and Archaeological Evidence").

Büchler, Alon, and especially Neusner constitute an important part of the background to Ed P. Sanders's work on purity and impurity during the early Roman period. Sanders is of most interest to New Testament scholars and perhaps best known from his books on Jesus. His major works dealing with purity issues are from the early 1990s. In *Jewish Law from Jesus to the Mishnah*,[15] he continually argues with Neusner, as he focuses on Jesus and the Pharisees. One of the studies deals with whether the Pharisees ate ordinary food in purity, and another focuses on purity and food in

---

12. Neusner 1994.
13. Alon 1977.
14. Büchler 1968.
15. Sanders 1990.

the diaspora. Two years later, Sanders systematized some of his previous discussions in *Judaism: Practice and Belief*.[16] There will be more on Sanders in chapter 8, where I engage in an extended discussion with him (see also ch. 11).

Another major contributor from the same period is Hyam Maccoby, whose overview of the purity system, *Ritual and Morality*,[17] engages in conversation with Milgrom, Neusner, and Mary Douglas (more of Douglas in a while). Maccoby claims, among other things, that impurity ascribed to idols and evil deeds is metaphorical only, and he argues (successfully, in my view) against Milgrom's understanding of sanctuary defilement "from afar." Like Sanders, however, he takes a minimalist view on the scope of purity (see further below), and in some regards his study says more about rabbinic interpretation and rabbinic development than it does about the interpretation of biblical purity rules during the Second Temple period, as he often reads the Hebrew Bible through a rabbinic lens.

Methods and Perspectives

Through the years, many scholars have related their work on purity and impurity to the perspectives of anthropologist Mary Douglas. In *Purity and Danger* (1996), Douglas applies a structuralist model for interpreting the food laws in Lev 11, explaining them as anomalies in relation to zoological taxonomies. In her view, food functions as a code, and by being embedded in a system of social relations, it carries messages about hierarchies and boundaries.[18] She understands conceptions of impurity to focus on the body, its emissions, and its borders, indicating a concern over social boundaries and the unity of the social group. "Where there is dirt there is system" is an oft-quoted statement, whether praised or criticized.

Although biblical interpretation played a very minor role in Douglas's anthropological research to begin with, she increasingly came to focus on biblical purity laws, and her new approach was theological and quite apologetic.[19] She claims that, in contrast to other cultures, Israelite impurity conceptions were not used to separate categories of people. The priests, in fact, tried to restrain popular xenophobia, and Israelite laws

---

16. Sanders 1992, ch. 12.
17. Maccoby 1999.
18. Douglas 1972.
19. See Douglas 1993; 1999.

had little in common with taboo systems of other peoples. Consequently, she argues that the Israelite (priestly) purity system was unique. She also denies that these rules in effect would have given privileges and power to the priests. Israelite religion is seen as entirely different from the surrounding cultures.

Douglas's views, both the early and the late, have influenced many scholars. Neusner, Milgrom, Maccoby, and Jonathan Klawans are all influenced by Douglas and in dialogue with her.[20] Walter Houston, for example, depends on Douglas and her structuralist approach for his interpretation of the food laws, the emergence of which he associates with the development of monotheism.[21] Seth Kunin takes her interpretation even further, in his neo-structuralist approach to Israelite practices.[22] Catherine Murphy partly follows Douglas in her interpretation of John the Baptist as a prophet of purity.[23] Jerome Neyrey applies Douglas's approach in his textbook article on purity as a core value in the New Testament and its world.[24] Darian Lockett adopts her symbolic approach in his study on purity language in the letter of James, suggesting a taxonomy with categories such as natural, ritual, moral, and figurative purity.[25] Purity language is understood as a boundary marker, evoking identity and suggesting separation from the world, although not sectarian withdrawal.

The list could go on. Douglas's great influence on biblical scholars has, in my view, been disproportionate, considering that her approach is not particularly suited for the historical interpretations that many exegetes engage in. Tracy Lemos has, for example, criticized Douglas for her understanding that the Israelite purity system was different from others and that Israelite purity ideas did not create social hierarchies, and her tendency to collapse Israelite religion and the priestly system with Judaism. She also points out that the kind of interpretation Douglas has inspired often attempts to find one underlying rationale for all biblical texts and tends to schematize, treating ritual as secondary to belief and the body as

---

20. Klawans 2000. For the first three, see above. In fact, Douglas's new turn seems to a large extent to have been triggered by interaction with Milgrom.
21. Houston 1993.
22. Kunin 2004.
23. Murphy 2003.
24. Neyrey 1996.
25. Lockett 2008.

secondary to the mind.[26] I offer a more detailed discussion of structural-functionalist as well as theological "explanations" of impurity, including Douglas, in chapter 3.

It is common to distinguish between various types of impurity, but classifying purity according to categories is a contested issue. At the core lies the fact that purity language is used in the Hebrew Bible in a number of contexts: ritual purifications, food taboos, animals, sacrifices, sexual acts, murder, sin in general, worship of other gods, non-Israelites, and intermarriage. Tikva Frymer-Kensky distinguishes between major and minor pollutions and also between pollution beliefs (ritual pollution) and danger beliefs (danger of divine sanction because of wrongdoing).[27] Wright differentiates between tolerated and prohibited impurities. Prohibited impurities, in turn, are divided between intentional and unintentional impurities, while tolerated impurities are sorted into four classes: death related, sexual, disease related, and cultic.[28] The preponderance of death and sex as keys for understanding or explaining impurity conceptions is conspicuous. But although they are stated or assumed by many interpreters,[29] they are neither comprehensive nor convincing, and I will return to this several times in the following chapters.

Klawans has been particularly influential by the way in which he distinguishes between ritual and moral impurity. He suggests that certain types of moral impurity should be understood as real and literal, rather than metaphorical. He also argues that while the Bible and the rabbis generally kept the two types of impurity apart, the Qumran sectarians conflated them.[30]

More categories have been added. Christine Hayes distinguishes genealogical impurity from ritual and moral impurity. All sources understand gentiles as capable of generating moral impurity, says Hayes, but Ezra introduced a concept of genealogical impurity, which makes assimilation/conversion impossible. This concept became prominent in some Second Temple groups. Both Paul and the rabbis are understood to have broken with this genealogical emphasis, even though we still see some remains in rabbinic sources, as well as in the notion that gentiles defile rit-

---

26. See, for example, the criticism in Lemos 2009; 2013.
27. Frymer-Kensky 1983.
28. Wright 1991.
29. See, e.g., Wright 1992; Marx 2001.
30. Klawans 2000.

ually.³¹ Aspects of "moral" impurity have also been construed in different ways. Mila Ginsburskaya separates "sin-impurity" from physical impurity.³² Eve Feinstein suggests a specific "sexual pollution concept" and contrasts technical with rhetorical usage of pollution language. She investigates why the idea of pollution is associated with particular domains and explores the rhetorical function of disgust.³³

In the subsequent chapters, especially 3, 5, and 6, it will become clear why I take a different approach from that of Klawans, as I base my argument on conceptual metaphor theory and evolutionary considerations, in which emotions, disgust in particular, play a decisive role. It will also become clear why I do not think that we need to expand the growing taxonomy and construe even more types of impurity, but rather acknowledge that almost every use of purity language is at some level metaphorical and best analyzed with conceptual, emotional, and rhetorical tools. There are several examples of scholars going in that direction. Although suggesting one more category, Feinstein does emphasize the emotional and rhetorical function of pollution language. Joseph Lam discusses metaphorical representations of sin as impurity and suggests that these are rhetorical tools, evoking visceral feelings.³⁴ Yitzhaq Feder explores the interrelationship between human experience, folk conceptions of infection, and concepts of pollution.³⁵ I think these are fruitful directions in which to go.

Comparative Efforts

The development of purity conceptions and the interpretation of purity rules in Israelite religion, in Second Temple and rabbinic Judaism, and in the early Christian movement took place in continuous interaction with surrounding cultures. Purity and impurity are concepts found with all or most of Israel's neighbors and mapped to varying degrees. But much research remains to be done regarding the extent to which Mesopotamian, Egyptian, Hittite, Canaanite, and especially Persian ideas and practices influenced or related to the evolving Israelite priestly purity system. This applies to the role of Greek and Roman influence on the development of

---

31. Hayes 2002.
32. Ginsburskaya 2009.
33. Feinstein 2014.
34. Lam 2016, ch. 4.
35. Feder 2013; 2016.

purity practices during the late Second Temple and early rabbinic periods, as well.

A couple of fairly recent multiauthored collections must be mentioned: *How Purity Is Made*, including also medieval and modern issues, and, in particular, *Purity and the Forming of Religious Traditions in the Ancient Mediterranean World and Ancient Judaism*.[36] The latter covers purity concepts all over ancient West Asia and the Greco-Roman world, including ancient Mesopotamia, Egypt, Anatolia, Phoenicia, Iran, Greece, and Rome. It also contains separate chapters on Leviticus, Numbers, Deuteronomy, Ezekiel, Ezra-Nehemiah, Hellenistic Judaism, Qumran, and archaeology of the late Second Temple period.

This is not the place to list studies on purity and impurity in various regions and cultures in general.[37] But some interesting comparisons have been made, besides those found in commentaries such as Milgrom's and encyclopedia articles such as those in the *Dictionnaire de la Bible*, already mentioned above.[38] For example, Henri Cazelles compares Ugaritic and Israelite purity concepts, Carsten Colpe suggests a relationship between Vendidād and Leviticus, and Reinhard Achenbach argues for Persian influence on Israelite purity conception, particularly with regard to corpse impurity.[39] In *The Disposal of Impurity*, David Wright compares Hittite and Mesopotamian literature with disposal rites described in the Bible, beginning with the scapegoat ritual but continuing with impurities of the body, and Yitzhaq Feder studies the role of blood for purification in *Blood Expiation in Hittite and Biblical Ritual*.[40] Moshe Blidstein does some comparison between Greco-Roman conceptions and Jewish purity practices in the late Second Temple period, in his study of early Christian purity issues during the first three centuries of the common era.[41] But in spite of several studies of purity conceptions in Greek and Roman culture,[42] there

---

36. Rösch and Simon 2012; Frevel and Nihan 2013.

37. See my bibliography on purity and impurity in *Oxford Bibliographies Online* (Kazen 2019).

38. Henninger et al. 1979.

39. Cazelles 1977; Achenbach 2009; Colpe 1995. But Colpe's claim for a literary relationship based on an analogous structure between *Vendidād* and Leviticus is highly exaggerated.

40. Wright 1987; Feder 2011. See also Christiansen 2013 for an overview of possible influences from Hittite purity conceptions on biblical traditions.

41. Blidstein 2017.

42. See, e.g., Parker 1983; Lennon 2014; Meinel 2015; Petrovic and Petrovic 2016.

is a lack of major comparisons between these and Israelite or early Jewish practices. One should also mention linguistic studies, such as Jan Wilson on holiness and purity in Mesopotamia, and Feder on Hittite and Akkadian terms.[43]

In chapter 7 I do some general comparisons, and in chapter 4 I engage in a more detailed discussion of possible Persian (Zoroastrian) influence on emerging purity practices during the early Second Temple period. I also touch on linguistic data in several chapters and relate them to discussions about metaphor.

Comparisons with other cultural and religious systems are meaningful in order to understand the historical development of purity concepts in early Judaism, but so are internal comparisons. Already before the publication of all the Qumran Cave 4 fragments, some of the peculiarities of the probably Essene group associated with the Scrolls were studied, and their purity halakah was being compared to that of the Pharisees, as well as to the practices of early (especially Pauline) Christ-believers.[44] An important study by Hannah Harrington compares Qumran purity conceptions with those of the rabbis on all major sources of impurity.[45]

Comparisons continue, especially between the *yaḥad* and the Pharisees on issues such as oil, stone, and the *ṭəbûl yôm*. The latter category, in particular, has given rise to many arguments. Twenty-five years ago, Lawrence Schiffman argued that the rulings in 4QMMT, the Temple Scroll, and the Damascus Document texts resemble the position of the Sadducees, in their debates with the Pharisees, according to rabbinic texts. He suggests that a legal analysis of the Qumran texts gives us access to a growing body of Pharisaic halakot.[46] Joseph Baumgarten had earlier suggested that the Qumran texts, like the Sadducees, reject the *ṭəbûl yôm*.[47] Comparisons have continued. Magen Broshi suggests six categories of purity laws in which the Qumran community differed from the Pharisees/rabbis.[48]

However, several scholars have warned against too rash conclusions.[49] Martha Himmelfarb advises against a sharp dichotomy between priestly

---

43. Wilson 1994; Feder 2016.
44. Cf. Baumgarten 1967; 1980; Newton 1985; García Martínez 1988.
45. Harrington 1993.
46. Schiffman 1994.
47. Baumgarten 1980.
48. Broshi 2006.
49. See, for example, Fraade 2011, 70 n. 4, for more references.

and rabbinic halakah, suggesting there is no reason to assume that the Scrolls are reacting against a Pharisaic version of the rabbinic interpretation of *ṭəbûl yôm*.⁵⁰ Cana Werman takes the discussion a step further as she tries to reconstruct the halakic disagreement between priestly circles (as in Qumran) and the Pharisees. Their differences did not concern the concept of the *ṭəbûl yôm* but his role in the red-cow ritual, she argues. While the Qumran texts reserve the preparation and sprinkling of purification water for priests, the Pharisees did not think that intercession and mediators were necessary.⁵¹

More generally on corpse impurity, Vered Noam compares Qumran texts with parallels in the halakic midrashim and discusses the mechanisms behind the rabbinic development toward leniency.⁵² She also compares Josephus's understanding of the exclusion or isolation of impure persons with that of the Temple Scroll and rabbinic legislation, finding that in spite of differences, all regard corpse impurity as very severe, and simultaneously all display leniency toward corpse-impure persons.⁵³

I address some of these issues in chapters 8–10 and also in chapter 3 of my 2013 book on halakic conflict and development in relation to the Jesus tradition.⁵⁴

Purity and Qumran

Research on purity conceptions in the Qumran texts is, in fact, a whole field of its own.⁵⁵ The texts from the Dead Sea have been subject to intensive research for decades, and especially after the publication of all the

---

50. Himmelfarb 2010.
51. Werman 2011.
52. Noam 2010b.
53. Noam 2012.
54. Kazen 2013a.
55. The present section has room only for the broad issues and ignores a number of interesting details, for example the question of whether the Qumran sectarians regarded scrolls as defiling the hands (Magness 2010; Mizzi 2019), their view on excrement as impure and defecation as defiling, as compared to other Jewish views, resulting in distinct toilet practices (Magness 2012), their understanding of oil as defiling stone vessels (Eshel 2000), the susceptibility of glass (Mizzi 2017), and their view on foreigners and intermarriage (Harrington 2008; 2012). A recent feminist analysis of purity practices in the Qumran community is Keady (2017), who uses masculinity studies as a framework with the help of embodiment theories and theories of space.

fragments from Cave 4 in the 1990s, purity became a major topic. The *Halakhic Texts* volume in the Discoveries in the Judaean Desert (DJD 35), which incorporates many of Baumgarten's arguments from previous articles, is of course an important resource.[56]

Harrington's *Currents in Biblical Research* article and bibliography from 2006 is an excellent resource, together with her more comprehensive overview in *Purity Texts*, which discusses all of the Qumran texts that deal with purity issues and includes a thematic discussion of the three main sources of bodily impurity, as well as the impurity of outsiders.[57]

The extent to which purity conceptions and purity practices in Qumran can be systematized is a contested issue. Harrington, who at an early stage established herself as an expert in this field, takes a rather systemic approach.[58] This has been challenged by, among others, Ian Werrett, who attempts to analyze texts and groups of texts separately and emphasizes internal differences. He concludes that we should not talk of a "system."[59] But even though *system* might be the wrong term to use, I cannot see how the minor variations that certainly can be found could invalidate the major similarities that together suggest a specific tendency.[60]

Others, too, assume a basic tendency. Himmelfarb, for example, argues that the purity laws in 4QD take the Torah's laws as a system and thus organize them more clearly in order to make explicit connections.[61] Laura Quick suggests that without a demand for coherence, it is possible to trace some differences between the Community Rule and the Damascus Document to the scriptural paradigms they preferred (the Priestly source for S and Deuteronomy for D).[62]

A most interesting question, then, is not only *how* interpretations and practices represented by the Dead Sea texts differ from those of the Pharisees or later rabbis (on comparison, see above) but *why*. What are the often-implicit principles behind Torah interpretation and customary behavior—that which we somewhat anachronistically call halakah—as reflected in the texts from Qumran? I discussed such issues in more

---

56. Baumgarten 1999a.
57. Harrington 2004; 2006.
58. Harrington 1993; 2004.
59. Werrett 2007.
60. Kazen 2009. See also the recent critical discussion in Snyder forthcoming.
61. Himmelfarb 2004.
62. Quick 2017.

detail in *Scripture, Interpretation, or Authority?* back in 2013, inspired by Aharon Shemesh and several others,[63] and I refer more to this in chapter 11. The relationship between popular custom, close reading of Scripture, and views on divine revelation is key to this discussion. Legal interpretation in Qumran, including purity halakah, can often be characterized as realist, or with the terminology strongly recommended by Aryeh Amihay, "legal essentialist."[64] The results are at times innovative and often tend toward stringency.

Closely associated with the question of halakic development in Qumran and the principles behind it is the issue of graded impurity, which has been subject to vigorous discussion for a long time. This applies in particular to the development of an extra first-day water rite during the late Second Temple period. A first-day immersion evolved in order to mitigate corpse impurity and was arguably also employed in other contexts, particularly for discharge impurity.

The discussion surrounding this topic is based in particular on a number of studies by Baumgarten, as well as Milgrom, and involves interpretations of especially 4Q414 (Ritual Purity A), 4Q512 (Ritual Purity B), 4Q514 (Ordinances^c), and 4Q274 (Tohorot A). Already in 1992, in an analysis of the purification rituals in 4Q512 and 4Q514, Baumgarten discussed evidence for a first-day immersion and compared with rabbinic tradition, noting the penitential theme that distinguishes the Qumran instructions.[65] At the same time, Milgrom argued for first-day ablutions being employed for initial purification both from corpse impurity and from other severe impurities, finding support in an analysis of the then–recently discovered 4Q514.[66] Soon thereafter, both Baumgarten and Milgrom published on 4Q274, relating it to the previously mentioned texts and to the issue of graded purification and an extra first-day ablution for other than corpse impurity. The discussion also includes the question whether discharges by themselves were considered more impure than the people suffering from

---

63. Kazen 2013a; in ch. 3 of that study I discuss purity from this perspective. See Shemesh 2009 (see also Werman and Shemesh 2011). Others include Schwartz 1992; Schremer 2001; Noam 2006; 2010a; 2010b.

64. Amihay 2017, 19–30. Amihay suggests that instead of "realism" and "nominalism," which originally belong to a different discourse, we use "legal essentialism" and "legal formalism."

65. Baumgarten 1992; cf. 1999b, where he, in addition, analyzes 4Q284 (Harvesting).

66. Milgrom 1992; cf. Baumgarten 2000.

them.⁶⁷ This would have been different from rabbinic understanding but reflecting Second Temple period practice, as argued by Hanan Birenboim.⁶⁸ I took part in this debate in 2010 with a new reconstruction and translation of 4Q274 1, arguing that the text discusses various categories of *purifying* persons, giving evidence for a first-day ablution not only for the corpse-impure but also for genital dischargers. I return to the issue of graded impurity several times in the present book, especially in chapters 8 and 12.⁶⁹

As already mentioned, Klawans suggests that in contrast to the Bible and to the rabbis, the Qumran sectarians conflated ritual and moral impurity.⁷⁰ The way in which some Qumran texts deal with moral impurity has puzzled more than one scholar, and strategies to solve this puzzle are diverse and sometimes speculative. Already in 1980, Barbara Thiering suggested two different objects for purification in 1QS, two instruments for purifying, and, thus, two different rituals for these purposes.⁷¹ Casey Toews argues that 1QS is the first example of a literal adaptation of what was originally a metaphorical washing for moral impurity, which the prophets considered as a less harsh alternative to the death penalty.⁷² Eyal Regev thinks that purification from moral impurity is ritualized and that the author of 1QS sees ablutions "in the holy spirit" as the purifying ritual for moral impurity.⁷³ Yair Furstenberg comes close to Klawans in suggesting that "sin impurity" was reified during the Second Temple period so that the distinction between ritual and moral impurity was blurred. He thinks that practices for purification from ritual impurities were applied

---

67. Baumgarten 1995a; Milgrom 1995. Milgrom suggests that initial first-day ablutions were required for all who were impure for more than one day, that impure people were considered to defile other impure people further, and that even in such cases, ablutions were required before eating. Baumgarten (2000) also argues that purification water with ashes from the red cow came to be used for other purposes than purification from corpse impurity. I rather think that 4Q274 refers to further defilement of *purifying* persons and doubt that there is evidence for Baumgarten's generalized suggestion.

68. Birenboim 2012.
69. Kazen 2010b; cf. 2013a, ch. 3.
70. Klawans 2000.
71. Thiering 1980.
72. Toews 2003.
73. Regev 2007.

for purification from sin and that both Qumran and early Christians give evidence of this.[74]

Others are more skeptical. Himmelfarb argues against Klawans's idea of conflation. Based on 4QD, 1QS, and 4Q512, she suggests that in the former text, impurity is a ritual category with no moral significance, and that in the two latter texts the association between sin and impurity is "primarily evocative rather than halakic."[75] She thus implies an emotional-rhetorical understanding. Ginsburskaya suggests that there was no conflation between "sin-impurity" and physical impurity: the sin-impure were denied right of counsel but allowed at communal gatherings, while the opposite was the case for the ritually impure.[76] In addition, Benjamin Snyder has recently refuted Klawans's arguments for conflation and argued that the relevant texts "do not provide evidence of conflation, they simply assert that one cannot be morally delinquent and expect ritual purification to function mechanically."[77] I find Snyder's arguments convincing and think that evocative and rhetorical aspects of purity language must be taken seriously. With the perspective on language and metaphor that I discuss and develop in this book, for example in chapters 5–6, there is little need to talk of conflation or to suggest forced explanations. Thereby I do not deny that conceptual metaphors and their rhetorical use have the capacity to trigger ritual inventions.

John's Immersions as Purifications

The water ritual of John the Baptist and its development into the Jesus movement's entrance rite is often seen as such a ritual innovation or mutation. Risto Uro has recently emphasized the innovative character of John's baptism, as John turns a basically self-administered and repeated purificatory washing into a once-and-for-all, or at least a less frequent, special agent ritual, with high sensory pageantry.[78] (I discuss water purification and baptism in relation to theories of ritual in ch. 7.)

Opinions differ widely about the character of John's immersions. Robert Webb, who follows Morton Smith's understanding of John's baptism

---

74. Furstenberg 2016b.
75. Himmelfarb 2001, 37.
76. Ginsburskaya 2010.
77. Snyder forthcoming.
78. Uro 2016, 84–87.

providing an alternative means of forgiveness, besides the temple cult, also points to his administering the ritual as a crucial difference compared to ordinary purification.[79] Webb suggests that repentance and baptism were closely intertwined and that God responded with forgiveness of sins. Sins were understood as a moral contagion, from which the person was cleansed through baptism.[80]

Joan Taylor, on the other hand, suggests that John's baptism was for physical purification and denies that it effected forgiveness—forgiveness was thought to come as a result of repentance, which preceded baptism. Taylor thus gives priority to Josephus's account of the Baptist and distinguishes between inner and outer cleansing, but her interpretation requires a forced reading of Mark 1:4 (*baptisma metanoias*). She has a strong argument, however, for understanding baptism as basically a purification ritual and for claiming that this is the way people would have naturally interpreted John's activity in its historical context.[81]

Klawans agrees with Webb that John's baptism was probably not repeated, at least not very often. He doubts that it was thought of as purificatory: it does not seem to have been repeated often enough for maintaining purity, and he finds no evidence for sin being viewed as ritually defiling in the context. He suggests that if repentance alone could account for forgiveness, John's special type of baptism would not have been necessary.[82] Klawans concludes that John's baptism was a distinct development "by which he concretized the metaphors one finds in passages such as Isaiah 1:16 and Psalm 51:9."[83] His ritual was associated with purification but enacted its metaphorical use for the forgiveness of moral sins.[84]

An earlier understanding of a Jewish "proselyte baptism" being part of the background to John the Baptist's practice is more or less abandoned today; there is simply no evidence for the first century CE.[85] A baraita

---

79. Webb 1991, 214.
80. Webb 1991, 214–15.
81. Taylor 1997.
82. Klawans 2000, 138–43.
83. Klawans 2000, 143.
84. Cf. Toews 2003.
85. The best-known defense for an early proselyte baptism is perhaps offered by Joachim Jeremias (1949; 1960), but most scholars today agree that his arguments are flawed (an exception is Marcus 2018, 74–80). For a convincing discussion of the evidence, see Webb 1991, 122–30, and especially Snyder forthcoming (ch. 5). See also Furstenberg forthcoming.

from the Babylonian Talmud explicating Num 15:15 is often referred to, listing circumcision, immersion, and sprinkling with blood as entrance requirements for the covenant.[86] Webb agrees that proselyte immersion is a post–temple period development, and although he suggests that it functioned primarily as an initiatory rite, he also thinks it was understood as a purificatory rite, at least by some, although it remains unclear from what it would have purified: moral contagion or gentile impurity.[87] The third alternative would be from ritual impurity, and Snyder's recent dissertation provides strong support for this view: all sources confirm that the immersion of a gentile in the context of conversion was for the purpose of ritual purification.[88]

Snyder consequently suggests this for John's immersions, too. He argues that if John's baptism took on an initiatory role, it was only in retrospect. Whether John performed these immersions or his audience self-immersed under his supervision, says Snyder, there is no reason to deny the character of these immersions as being ritual purifications. While John's context was eschatological, this need not mean that his immersions were not for ritual purification. In Jewish tradition, ritual purity was required in view of encounters with the holy, and Snyder understands John's baptism as a ritual purification in view of God's coming in judgement: "it is neither the messiah nor the end times that require immersion, rather it is human-divine interaction."[89]

I am giving some attention to Snyder here, because his suggestions combine the strengths of several previous suggestion and open up for

---

86. The text from Numbers says: "There is one statute for the congregation, for you and for the *gēr* [in the rabbinic period *gēr* was interpreted as 'proselyte'], a statute for eternal times. The *gēr* will be like you before Yahweh." In b. Ker. 9a this is explicated: "'like you' means like your forefathers. As your forefathers did not enter the covenant except by circumcision and immersion and the sprinkling of blood, they cannot enter the covenant except by circumcision and immersion and the sprinkling of blood." I am inclined to think that just as the sprinkling with blood does not refer to a unique ritual but to a sacrifice that may be repeated in many contexts, so the immersion refers to ritual purification being integrated in the conversion process. Only circumcision is a unique rite. To remove one's ritual impurity by purification in water as part of a conversion process does not necessarily turn this immersion into a specific type, different in character and unique, compared to other purificatory washings.

87. Webb 1991, 129–30.
88. Snyder forthcoming, ch. 5.
89. Snyder forthcoming, ch. 6 and conclusion.

interesting perspectives on the purificatory character of baptism in the early Jesus movement.[90] Here is a trajectory I have often wished to pursue but never had time for, and there is nothing in the present book either, except that I briefly touch on agency in baptism in chapter 7.

Scope of Purity and Archaeological Evidence

According to a rabbinic saying in the Tosefta (t. Shabb. 1:14), purity "broke out" (or perhaps rather "spread") in Israel at the end of the Second Temple period. There is an ongoing debate among scholars about the extent to which purity practices and purification rituals were engaged in by the Jewish population in general or restricted to elite or extremist groups in Roman Palestine. Was adherence widespread or mainly limited to Jerusalem, or at least to Judea, and primarily related to the temple and to temple visits? Or was purity kept as a natural and self-evident part of life in general, regardless of the temple cult?

These issues have been discussed all along, by many of the people already referred to (Büchler, Alon, Neusner, Maccoby, Sanders, etc.). They are also involved when the relatively strict rules found in many of the texts from Qumran are compared with the stance of the Pharisees and that of the later rabbis. During recent years, there has been an increasing interest in the archaeology of purity, usually confirming a more expansionist interpretation of the evidence.

John Poirier has been an important voice in this debate, with two seminal essays. In a 1996 article on the Pharisaic handwashing custom, he argues, against both Neusner (imitation of priests) and Sanders (only for temple visits), that the explanation is found in diaspora practice and an understanding of the ritual divisibility of the body. Pharisees washed their hands before meals to avoid defiling their insides.[91] In "Purity beyond the Temple," from 2003, Poirier criticizes the minimalist views of Sanders and Maccoby, claiming there is no evidence from the Second Temple period for the supposed temple orientation of purity laws. He finds evidence in the many *miqwa'ot* and the widespread use of stone vessels, in handwashing practices, and in purity practices in Qumran

---

90. For interesting examples, see Furstenberg forthcoming; Weiss 2017.
91. Poirier 1996. Whether or not one accepts Poirier's interpretation (interior defilement), his rebuttal of Neusner's and Sanders's arguments is valid.

as well as according to Hellenistic Jewish texts. The minimalist view is blamed on Maimonides.[92]

In a similar vein, Regev argues that "nonpriestly" purity was commonly observed between the second century BCE and the second century CE. He understands this as resulting from an increasing tendency to individualism, with the aim of attaining a spiritual relationship with the holy.[93]

The tendency to interpret all purity practices and purification rites as mainly related to the sanctuary has dominated for long.[94] Archaeological evidence, however, has come to change the picture. In his 2006 study *Washing in Water*, Jonathan Lawrence compares ritual bathing in the Hebrew Bible, Second Temple literature, and the Dead Sea Scrolls, relating the textual evidence to material remains. He discusses the historical development of ritual bathing practices together with the archaeological evidence and attempts a chronological reconstruction of the development of ritual bathing and *miqwa'ot*. Lawrence suggests that ritual washings begin as preparation for theophanies and take on their purificatory function as part of an evolving priestly and postexilic purity system. The Maccabean period comes with a number of developments and innovations, including the *miqweh*. Lawrence finds an "expansion of ritual washing to new uses not known in the Hebrew Bible."[95]

The identification of stepped water basins as *miqwa'ot* during Yigael Yadin's excavation of Masada in the mid-1960s initiates what today may be termed the archaeology of purity. Although Roland de Vaux had discovered many water installations in Qumran a little more than a decade earlier, he did not believe they were purification pools but needed for water supply in the desert. Since then we have learned to know more and better: the *miqwa'ot* from Hellenistic and early Roman times that have been excavated to date are found in all parts of Roman Palestine and count around nine hundred.[96] Ronny Reich's Hebrew dissertation in 1990 was published in revised form in 2013, but was not enough updated in relation to Yonatan Adler's research from 2011.[97] I discuss the details and implications in several chapters in this volume, especially in chapter 11.

---

92. Poirier 2003.
93. Regev 2000a; 2000b.
94. See, e.g., Maier 2001.
95. Lawrence 2006, 189.
96. Adler 2011; 2014a.
97. Reich 1990; 2013; Adler 2011; 2014a.

The Hellenistic context for the boom of stepped pools for ritual washings seems to be confirmed by archaeology, too.[98] Regev has even argued that Herod the Great integrated *miqwa'ot* as part of his Jewish ideology.[99] Further discussions have focused on the purpose of various water installations and the requirements for a stepped pool to function as a *miqweh*.[100] They will not be rehearsed here, but some of them will surface in the subsequent chapters. Many of these debates are summed up in Stuart Miller's *At the Intersection of Texts and Material Finds* from 2015.[101] Miller discusses research history, archaeological findings, the development of immersion practices, the debate about the *'ôṣār*, stone vessels, and other issues. He warns against assuming that pools have to meet later rabbinic requirements in order to be identified as *miqwa'ot*, and he emphasizes the pervasiveness of purity practices and the widespread popular adherence to purity rites as part of "domestic Judaism."

The interest in *miqwa'ot* was followed within a few years by a similar interest in chalkstone vessels, which caught the attention of archaeologists when Jerusalem's Jewish quarter was excavated after 1967. Since then, stone vessels and stone vessel factories, mainly from the first century BCE and the first century CE, have been found all over the country. Jane Cahill published a comprehensive catalogue and discussion of chalk vessels in 1992, as part of the final report of the excavations at the city of David, directed by Yigal Shilo between 1978 and 1985. Cahill categorizes the vessels according to morphology and mode of production, suggesting a production center in the city of David, because of the number of cores and unfinished vessels. She also includes a survey of chalk vessels found all over regions inhabited by ancient Jews.[102] Soon after, Roland Deines published a thorough and detailed study of stone vessels, mapping out sites and findings, as known by then. Deines discusses these finds in relation to the stone vessels in John 2 and suggests a widespread concern for food, including ritual handwashing, at the time of Jesus.[103]

---

98. Adler 2018; cf. Fatkin 2019.
99. Regev 2010.
100. See, e.g., Reich 1981; Netzer 1982; Reich 1984; 1988; Eshel 1997; Wright 1997; Adler 2006; 2008a; 2008b; 2009; 2014b. Gibson (2005) argues that during festivals the large pools in Jerusalem were also used for purification.
101. Miller 2015.
102. Cahill 1992.
103. Deines 1993.

Also in the 1980s, both Yitzhaq Magen and Shimon Gibson excavated the stone-vessel production site at the Ḥizma caves. In their publications they describe and illustrate production methods for stone vessels and discuss their distribution, dating, and place in relation to Jewish halakah.[104] A full report in English on this and other related excavations did not appear until 2002. Here Magen includes chapters on the quarries and workshops, the finds, typology, production methods, the ossuary industry, stone vessels in written sources, and their distribution and chronology. He concludes that there were three different types of production technique and sees stone vessels as a typical first-century CE phenomenon, associated with halakic purity concerns.[105] In a recent article, David Amit, Jon Seligman, and Irina Zilberbod report on the excavations of stone-vessel workshops discovered in two caves on the eastern slope of Mount Scopus. The article includes a discussion of production methods and a typology of vessels (product list).[106]

However, stone vessels have been found all over the country. Adler collects data about chalk-stone vessels from more than 250 sites and has recently uncovered two stone-vessel workshops in Galilee.[107] Archaeological finds attest to widespread observance of purity not only in Jerusalem and Judea but far from the temple and apart from cultic concerns. An earlier view of concerns for purity as predominantly a Jerusalem phenomenon focused on the temple is no longer possible to uphold.[108] I return to this repeatedly, and chapter 11 deals with this issue specifically.

Archaeologists have contributed to a better understanding of purity practices as part of Jewish life in the Second Temple period. Jodi Magness's *Stone and Dung, Oil and Spit*, from 2011, is a good example.[109] Here an experienced archaeologist discusses practices and circumstances in which impurity conceptions and purity rituals play a crucial role, such as various impurities of the body, impure foods, the impurity of vessels, dining, oil, and burial customs, within a broader context. Another example is Adler's forthcoming book on the emergence of Judaism during the Hellenistic period, which looks at evolving purity practices against a wider background.[110]

---

104. Gibson 1983; Magen 1994 (based on previous publications in Hebrew).
105. Magen 2002.
106. Amit, Seligman, and Zilberbod 2016.
107. Adler 2011; 2019.
108. Miller 2015; Adler 2016.
109. Magness 2011.
110. Adler forthcoming.

Archaeological evidence is also useful for earlier periods, when studying food taboos.[111] The relative absence of pig bones in the highlands during the Iron Age is a classical discussion, which can be illustrated by a couple of examples. Brian Hesse and Paula Wapnish point out that pig avoidance was not unique for any one group in the ancient West Asia and argue that only in the Hellenistic period, with consumption of pigs in urban settings, could pig avoidance become a boundary marker. Against this, Israel Finkelstein claims that Hesse's and Wapnish's data are not updated and that pigs were not present in proto-Israelite Iron I sites in the highlands, while popular in proto-Ammonite and Philistine sites.[112] The question has generated more research through the years, and evidence suggests that the domestic pig was brought by the Sea Peoples and that pork was avoided in the Israelite areas during much of the Iron Age.[113] Zooarchaeology (fishbone analysis) may also bring some light on the pentateuchal prohibitions against certain fish.[114]

However, attempts to trace practices of physical impurity and ritual purification to the Iron Age through the study of domestic structures are less successful. For example, Avraham Faust and Hayah Katz argue that an empty room in a large house at Tel ʿEton could have been used for menstrual separation. They also try to reconstruct a water purification ritual, based on the archaeology of a particular house and biblical and other ancient West Asian evidence.[115] This requires an unwarranted amount of gap filling and speculation, including the assumption that the priestly rules about menstrual separation reflect practices from the First Temple period.[116] (For a discussion of preexilic purity practices in relation to the priestly rules and based on textual evidence, see ch. 4 in this volume.)

Jesus and the Gospels

My own research on purity was triggered by an interest in the historical Jesus.[117] Jesus's attitude to purity and impurity has been a sensitive area of

---

111. For an overview of the field of zooarchaeology, see Greer 2019.
112. Hesse and Wapnish 1997; Finkelstein 1997; cf. 1996.
113. Sapir-Hen et al. 2013; 2015.
114. Adler and Lernau 2021.
115. Faust and Katz 2016.
116. Cf. Katz 2012.
117. Kazen 2010a; see also 2013a.

research because of the long-standing tendency to portray Jesus in conflict with and overshadowing, if not abrogating, Jewish law. Typical examples of this tendency are Werner Kümmel's argument that the saying in Mark 7:15 probably goes back to Jesus himself and demonstrates his superiority over against the Torah, and Hans Hübner's statement that it must be understood either as explicit criticism of Lev 11 or at least as critique "im *bewußt* impliziten Sinn."[118] Purity rules were often understood as divisive, discriminatory, and excluding. Together with a christologically flavored tendency to portray Jesus as unique and superior,[119] this made purity a battleground for conflicting interests and sometimes made people tone-deaf for the finer nuances in the discussion.

Some have used purity as a lens through which they analyze overarching issues, such as political tension or eschatological visions. In 1984, Marcus Borg argued that at the time of Jesus a quest for holiness, understood as separation from that which is impure, was at the core of all Jewish renewal movements. Borg sees the Pharisaic holiness program for Israel as creating internal divisions and hostility to Rome, and he finds Jesus different in that regard.[120] Borg and others have been criticized in particular for the way they portray Jesus in contrast to Judaism. I have often tried to emphasize that Jesus must be interpreted in relation to the Jewish movements of his time, without lessening the stance of his adversaries. Cecilia Wassén claims that there is no evidence for Jesus being uninterested in purity laws but rather the opposite. She argues that Jesus did not transgress or challenge them, and she in fact goes so far as to deny that Jews in general actively avoided impurity at all.[121]

Others have understood purity as a dynamic quality, an expression of holiness, which is somehow contagious and can be transmitted somewhat like impurity but in reverse manner. Bruce Chilton suggests that Jesus possessed such a dynamic type of purity, capable of resisting various forms of impurity, and understands this as the basis for an eschatologi-

---

118. Kümmel 1973; Hübner 1986, 175.
119. Cf. Westerholm (1978, 91), who studies purity as one of several legal issues and concludes that Jesus displays an "an apparent indifference towards certain aspects of scriptural law," based on a fundamentally different conception of God's will.
120. Borg 1984. Similar arguments within a perhaps softer approach are found in Dunn 2003.
121. Wassén 2016a. See further discussion in chs. 11–12 of the present volume.

cal purity program.[122] Christian Grappe sees the dynamics of the coming kingdom as the framework for Jesus's relative indifference to impurity and understands this in terms of holiness invading the secular sphere.[123] Tom Holmén discusses Jesus's dealings with the ritually impure and suggests an inversion of the direction of contagion, based on a reading of Hag 2. According to Holmén, Jesus did not oppose or devaluate the purity paradigm but considered his own purity more contagious than others' impurity.[124] Simone Paganini and Boris Repschinski suggest something similar in a comparison between purity in Qumran and in the Jesus tradition. They suggest that Jesus shows a comparative lack of interest in purity issues and rather regards holiness as contagious. To some degree they see this as a discontinuity with Second Temple Judaism.[125]

Many of these arguments fall back on Klaus Berger's concept of *offensiver Reinheit/Heiligkeit*, from a 1988 article on Jesus as Pharisee.[126] The main problem with this line of interpretation, from my perspective, is that it tends to disregard the ordinary mechanisms of ritual purity and the halakic means for its purification, positing a ritual innovation that can at best be described as speculative, as it has little foothold in the sources and the historical context.

Just as I am finalizing this manuscript, Matthew Thiessen's *Jesus and the Forces of Death* is being published, in which he argues the thesis that the Synoptic Jesus is involved in a "broadscale purification mission." Jesus displays a strong concern for ritual purity, not by opposing the purity system but by systematically destroying the forces of death, including the *sources* of impurity.[127] I will have to save a thorough interaction with Thiessen for a later occasion, but for now I find it difficult to see how the destruction of impurity's sources could count as upholding the purity paradigm. Miraculous healings of skin disease or irregular discharges, the raising of the dead, and exorcism have no place or function within Jewish ritual purity

---

122. Chilton 1996. Chilton's overall construct is highly speculative and takes little account of historical and ritual aspects of purity conceptions.

123. Grappe 2004.

124. Holmén 2009. The same material also appears in Holmén 2011 (*Handbook for the Study of the Historical Jesus*).

125. Paganini and Repschinski 2012.

126. Berger 1988.

127. Thiessen 2020, 178. Thiessen's argument is *not* about the *historical* Jesus. His thesis and his claims refer to the Synoptic authors. However, I suspect that this qualification will often be forgotten or disregarded by readers.

conceptions, and I cannot believe that the Synoptic authors tell these stories to demonstrate Jesus's faithfulness to the purity laws. I rather tend to think that they use these traditions for quite different purposes and that hints about concerns for, or attitudes toward, ritual purity are mostly to be found in the history *behind* the Synoptic texts.[128] Thiessen has to tap into the paradigm that strongly associates impurity with death and sex to make his idea work, and the side effect is an idealism of sorts. Conditions of skin disease, irregular genital bleeding, and human death are reversed by the Synoptic Jesus, and impure spirits are exorcised. Thiessen sees this as the fulfillment of apocalyptic expectations: Jesus obliterates the sources of impurity, after which only the remaining state of impurity needs to be removed by ordinary purification rituals.[129] But for this construct to work, we would also need to include the other impurities of the priestly system: childbirth, normal menstruation, semen emission, and sexual intercourse, as well as contact with animal carcasses. If the Synoptic authors wish to portray Jesus as the destroyer of impurity's sources, this must then include the abolition of the whole cycle of procreation and death, with extremely encratitic consequences. We might possibly ascribe an ideal like this to Matthew, in view of the special Matthean material on castration and marriage (cf. Matt 19:12; 22:30), and some groups of early Christ-followers tended in that direction. But it seems unlikely that this is how all the Synoptics understood Jesus's mission, and it sounds incredible to me that this is envisaged as a way to uphold the priestly purity system. In any case, I cannot see how one could defend Jewish law and custom by destroying marriage, sex, and childbirth. Thiessen would, of course, never suggest anything like this, but my point is that one should not pick the theological raisins from the cake without eating the whole of it.[130] In the end, then, Thiessen's Synoptic Jesus is, as in the previous examples, the bearer of "a

---

128. This is how I often argue about Synoptic traditions in Kazen 2010a as well as in some of the chapters in the present volume; see, e.g., ch. 9.

129. Thiessen 2020, 19–20.

130. Thiessen (2020, 183) in fact briefly considers "a future when God will make redundant the legal requirements pertaining to ritual impurity by rewriting human DNA, so to speak," an immortal life in which human beings can no longer become impure by sex, disease, or death, and when this is realized, purity laws become immaterial rather than abolished. However, he does not draw out the consequences with regard to procreation (menstruation, semen emission, sex, and childbirth) but focuses on Jesus's healings.

force of holiness in the world that goes on the offense against impurity," achieving what the "temple apparatus" could not.¹³¹

Thiessen's interpretation has several affinities with a recent article by Elizabeth Shively, on purification and the reign of God in Mark. Shively suggests that Mark portrays Jesus as the embodiment of purity who inaugurates the reign of God by initiating the reparation of a damaged world through his healings and exorcisms. The strongest force disrupting divine-human relations is death, and the Markan Jesus achieves the ultimate rectification of impurity and death through his own resurrection.¹³²

John Meier discusses Jesus's attitude to purity halakah in the fourth volume of his still-not-completed multivolume work of the historical Jesus.¹³³ In an almost book-length chapter with sixty-two pages of endnotes, Meier focuses especially on Mark 7, which he basically regards as inauthentic. As a result of his criteria-based analysis of the Jesus tradition, Meier concludes that for Jesus the whole system of purity does not exist, because he has immediate access to the divine will. Jesus displays a "studied" indifference. I have criticized Meier's methods and results a decade ago in *Issues of Impurity* and will not repeat myself here.¹³⁴

The focus on the conflict narrative in Mark 7 for discussing purity issues in the early Jesus movement is understandable, although I have tried to point to other sources, too.¹³⁵ Opinions clash especially regarding the central saying (Mark 7:15). Does it represent Mark or Jesus? Should it be understood in a relative or in an absolute way? If understood absolutely, does "that which comes out" refer to wicked words, evil behavior, genital discharges, or excrement?¹³⁶ Other issues are whether "all foods" that the Markan Jesus declares clean (Mark 7:19c) refers to nonkosher food or to food purportedly defiled by hand impurity. These issues are usually discussed together. The difference between earlier interpretations, such as those of Kümmel and Hübner, and more recent ones is often striking.

---

131. Thiessen 2020, 180.
132. Shively 2020.
133. Meier 2009, 342–477.
134. Kazen 2010c, 151–67.
135. The approach in my dissertation (Kazen 2010a) was to analyze other Synoptic narratives within their historical context and against the background of the development of purity halakah.
136. For an interpretation of Mark 7:15 as a haggadic instruction, warning for the dangers of evil speech, see Svartvik 2000.

In a classical study from 1986, Roger Booth combines tradition- and redaction-critical analysis with legal criticism, as he interprets Mark 7:15 in a relative sense and suggests a very detailed reconstruction of the state of handwashing halakah at the time of Jesus.[137] James Dunn similarly argues for a relative reading in his redaction-critical analysis and suggests an earlier and less radical version of this saying, more in line with the versions we find in Matthew (15:11) and Thomas (Gos. Thom. 14).[138] In the original version of *Jesus and Purity*, I argued in line with the latter suggestion about Matthew's version being earlier, but later realized that this creates more problems than it solves.[139] However, I still think a relative reading (that which enters a human being defiles *less* than that which comes out of it) makes most sense in the context.

Others suggest an absolute reading. Peter Zaas argues that Jesus's view was similar to the Sadducees in that he considered biblical laws but not scribal laws. Discharge laws would have been considered biblical, while the chain of contagion from hands to food and eater was not; hence, what literally comes out of a person defiles.[140] Furstenberg suggests that handwashing finds its origins in Greco-Roman practice and was promoted by the Pharisees. Jesus, however, rejects an understanding of impurity as threatening a vulnerable body from without, via food, and defends a biblical understanding of the self as the source of impurity.[141] Friedrich Avemarie similarly suggests that Jesus reacted against a Pharisaic innovation, denying any defilement from the outside via defiled ordinary food (*ḥullîn*).[142] Thiessen seems to go along with the same line of thought.[143] John van Maaren agrees with the basics of Furstenberg's interpretation, that biblical impurities come from within rather than from the outside. He disagrees, however, with Furstenberg's understanding of the subsequent passage (Mark 7:16–23) as moralizing a halakic debate, suggesting that "moral impurity" is not separate from the concept of purity in verse 15. I have discussed some of these issues at length in *Scripture, Interpretation,*

---

137. Booth 1986.
138. Dunn 1990.
139. Compare Kazen 2002 with 2010a, 66–67.
140. Zaas 1996.
141. Furstenberg 2008.
142. Avemarie 2010.
143. Thiessen 2020, 187–95.

or Authority? (2013), and they surface in this volume, too, especially in chapter 9.

Another popular focus for purity discussions is Mark 5, in which the narratives of the hemorrhaging woman and the raising of Jairus's daughter are sandwiched. The intercalated narrative of the bleeding woman is frequently subject to feminist analyses.

In an early and often criticized study, Marla Selvidge suggests that the narrative of the woman with a blood flow portrays Jesus as discarding purity laws and liberating women from physical and social suffering. The assumption is that purity laws are restrictive and oppressive for women in general.[144] Charlotte Fonrobert, in contrast, is critical to many feminist interpretations of Mark 5, as she finds New Testament scholars often ignorant when they reconstruct the Jewish context of this story and condemn the oppression of women in Judaism. Fonrobert also sees this as an implicit condemnation of women today who observe menstruation laws.[145] Several scholars suggest that the purity laws are basically gender neutral, while some point to their role for male status and female subordination.[146]

Susan Haber suggests that the health of the woman, not the purity issue, is the focus of the Markan narrative.[147] Wassén analyzes the nar-

---

144. Selvidge 1990.
145. Fonrobert 1997.
146. See, e.g., Erbele-Küster 2008; cf. Ellens 2008. Goldstein (2015) points out that many impurities have nothing to do with gender, and when they have (as in Lev 15), they are consciously structured analogously. While P does not discriminate against women because of their blood, a development begins with H, which broadens the meaning of *niddah* to represent sin and moral impurity. Erbele-Küster (2011) discusses gender-neutral and gender-biased aspects of the purity laws, with special emphasis on *niddah* laws and the way in which the *niddah* concept is developed. She points out that in the ancient world, women were not impure most of the time due to the purity laws, but that *niddah* took on a pejorative and polemical meaning. Other feminist studies of the purity laws include Philip (2006), who suggests that in non-Priestly literature, female blood is mainly related to fertility, while P legislation relates it to impurity; Ruane (2007), who discusses the lack of an explicit demand in the priestly law for female genital dischargers to bathe—except that women are required to bathe after intercourse with a man—concluding that ritual bathing was a sign of male sexuality and privilege; and Ilan (2015), who, in relation to Ruane, discusses evidence for female immersion during the Second Temple period and argues that even if immersion initially began as a male-status mechanism, it became an all-female institution, used by men to subordinate women.
147. Haber 2003.

rative of the bleeding woman against the background of biblical and Qumran purity law. She suggests that Mark ignores the purity issue in the story because the woman would not transmit impurity if she had washed her hands, according to Wassén's interpretation of Qumran halakah.[148] I discuss this text particularly in chapter 9 and in relation to Haber's work.

Issues of moral impurity in the gospels are also studied. Regev points to social and religious implications of moral impurity as reflected in early Christian traditions as he analyzes Mark 7 and compares early Christian attitudes to moral impurity with those of ancient Greece and Qumran. He suggests that the priestly understanding that the temple needs protection from moral impurity is also found in early Christian discourse and that this is the background for Jesus cleansing the temple as a protest against the contaminating effects of money.

Early Christ-Followers

Purity and impurity continued as vital concepts in the early Jesus movement, especially in relation to questions of behavior and morals. A couple of textbook chapters, taking a social-scientific perspective, are often referred to. Jerome Neyrey's "Core Values" in 1996 lists Greek terms for purity and pollution and provides a short research history. Neyrey gives much attention to Douglas, whose approach he applies.[149] David deSilva's sociocultural and anthropological textbook for New Testament students from 2000 has two chapters on purity and taboo. Purity is understood as a way to structure maps of people, spaces, time, food, and body, resulting in a degree of segregation. The New Testament attitude is understood as rewriting Israel's maps and breaking boundaries.[150]

In many parts of the emerging movement of Christ-followers, various aspects of purity halakah were upheld, but exactly to what extent is subject to scholarly discussion and dissent. Poirier detects three distinctive views on purity laws in early Christian texts: (1) binding, since the law is authoritative; (2) binding as a religious reflex; and (3) not binding on Christians. The second position is often overlooked, but Poirier suggests it is the best explanation for Paul's attitude.[151]

---

148. Wassén 2008.
149. Neyrey 1996.
150. DeSilva 2000, chs. 7–8.
151. Poirier 2005.

The relationship of the Lukan writings to Jewish law is a much-discussed issue, and a number of studies explore Luke's attitude to purity. Clinton Wahlen discusses definitions of purity in the narrative of Peter's vision in Acts.[152] David Aune associates Luke's narrative of Paul's purification (Acts 21) with the numerous *miqwa'ot* discovered close to the temple and suggests that Paul's purification did not concern corpse impurity or the Nazirite vow as such but was an extra immersion before a temple visit.[153] Timothy Reardon, in a discussion of the translation of Acts 15:9, suggests that Luke thinks of moral cleansing in terms of almsgiving.[154] And Pamela Shellberg argues that Luke's portrayal of Jesus's cleansing of people with *lepra* is about boundaries (skin disease as breakdown of bodily boundaries and separation outside boundaries of communal life) and the permeating of boundaries (Jesus permeating boundaries between rich and poor, righteous and sinner, insider and outcast; Peter permeating boundaries between Jew and gentile).[155] The focus on boundaries relates to Douglas's continued influence also on studies of purity and impurity in the early Christ movement. (See, for example, Lockett's study of the letter of James, described earlier in this chapter.)

Others focus on the relationship between purity and the holiness of the temple. Michael Newton outlines the conception of purity in Qumran and compares it with the Pauline Letters. He compares views on the community as a temple, attitudes to sacrifice and the use of sacrificial language, purity and membership, and purity in practical life (food, sex, death, etc.). Newton thinks that Paul lacks the systematic temple/purity scheme found in Qumran texts.[156] Yulin Liu studies the temple metaphor and temple purity in the Corinthian letters against a background of concepts of temple purity in Jewish texts from the Second Temple period and temple purity in the Greco-Roman world, as exemplified in three temple cults. She suggests that the latter shed light on Paul's metaphorical use.[157] Lily Vuong analyses the Protevangelium of James and the narrative details that relate to Mary's purity status. She demonstrates how Mary is char-

---

152. Wahlen 2005.
153. Aune 2011.
154. Reardon 2016.
155. Shellberg 2015.
156. Newton 1985. The study is from the time before most of the Cave 4 fragments were published.
157. Liu 2013.

acterized primarily by her purity (ritual, menstrual, sexual/moral, and genealogical) and how her body transforms into a sacred temple.[158] In a recent study on purity and the sanctuary of the body in Second Temple Judaism, Harrington traces the development of the idea of the body as temple, from the Babylonian exile to Paul's Corinthian letters. Harrington discusses temple metaphor and purity symbolism through exilic, postexilic, and Second Temple–period literature, including the Dead Sea Scrolls and the New Testament. The result is a history of the concept of body as sanctuary, in which concerns for purity and holiness play a major role. Harrington explores this development in relation to four ideological currents: an understanding of the body as a sanctum that can be defiled and damaged, personal piety in light of the cult as a substitute for lacking access to the temple, the expansion of purity observance, and an understanding of holiness as a power or spirit.[159]

An Oxyrhynchus fragment from an unknown gospel (P.Oxy. 840) contains a Jesus tradition about purity that has attracted quite some interest.[160] Despite an initial skepticism against the purity conceptions assumed in this narrative, many scholars have affirmed their historicity. Daniel Schwartz reads the text as a critique against the priestly monopoly on access to holiness and interprets the phrase about looking at the holy utensils as evidence for the practice to exhibit temple utensils at festivals before pilgrims, to let the public share in the priests' prerogatives.[161] Michael Kruger examines the four categories of objection raised against this fragment and shows that the date fits a first-century Jewish context.[162] Ze'ev and Chana Safrai suggest that the author of Oxyrhynchus Papyri 840 was familiar with Second Temple–period halakah, that much earlier skepticism is unwarranted, and that we should not dismiss the role of historical memory.[163] And Niclas Förster understands the text to serve and

---

158. Vuong 2013.
159. Harrington 2019.
160. For an overview with references, see Kazen 2010a, 256–60; 2005b, 573–75; 2013a, 137–39.
161. Schwartz 1986.
162. Kruger 2005. The four categories refer to the Pharisaic chief priest, the *agneutērion*, the Pool of David, and immersion before temple visits. See the summary in Kruger 2005, 143–44.
163. Safrai and Safrai 2011.

strengthen the identity of a Jewish-Christian group, with memories of temple-related purity issues associated with Jesus.[164]

Among early Christ-believers, various conflicting views coexisted for a long period. This was true for food laws as well as for physical impurity. In his 2017 study, *Purity, Community, and Ritual in Early Christian Literature*, Blidstein provides one of the few existing comprehensive overviews. Blidstein traces the development of purity conceptions in early Christianity during the first three centuries. He examines how purity practices and purity language in early Christian texts develop in relation to Second Temple and rabbinic Judaism, as well as in relation to Greco-Roman society, and he discusses early Christian attitudes to food and corpse impurity, baptism as purification, and the purity of the community, including issues of sexual defilement. Blidstein suggests a development toward what he calls an "Origenist synthesis," an amalgam of Jewish, Greek, and Roman traditions, in which baptism is understood to purify from an inherent bodily defilement.[165]

Rabbinic Purity

Purity in rabbinic Judaism is a vast subject area in itself. Here we will only indicate a few relevant examples of research on purity in the Tannaitic period. The rabbinic reconfiguration, or perhaps reconceptualization, of purity practices and purity law is a fascinating topic. The scholarly discussion has centered on questions of both concrete development and dating. Early rabbinic (mainly Tannaitic) traditions have often been mined for hints about late Second Temple–period practices, but this requires conscious methodologies and critical discernment.[166] There are still many examples of New Testament scholars applying rabbinic traditions to construct anachronistic Strack-Billerbeckish backgrounds to gospel traditions. Others overreact and more or less dismiss rabbinic traditions as irrelevant for understanding earlier periods.[167]

Neusner was one of the first to discuss the concrete development and dating of rabbinic traditions with the help of historical- and form-critical

---

164. Förster 2015.
165. Blidstein 2017.
166. See my discussion in Kazen 2013a, 31–48.
167. Meier 2009 is an example of this.

methods. We have already mentioned his *The Idea of Purity*.[168] This was followed by *A History of the Mishnaic Law of Purities*, a twenty-two-volume work in which Neusner analyzes the sixth order of the Mishnah, discussing attribution, dating, logical argument, and interpretation of every Tannaitic purity regulation.[169] All subsequent critical research on Tannaitic purity halakah relates to Neusner in one way or another, even when his particular form-critical methodology is questioned. Subsequently, Neusner's approach to rabbinic halakah became more ahistorical, and in *Purity in Rabbinic Judaism* he reads rabbinic purity laws as a systemic discourse, an alternative to myth and theology for expressing a system and a worldview. He discusses sources, effects, and loci of impurity, followed by rites of purification, but since he thinks that the rituals were not supposed to be carried out, he argues that their purpose was to establish boundaries to sacred reality. Statements of law deal with metaphysical reality—the ritual is the myth.[170]

A different approach, and more convincing in my view, is taken by Mira Balberg in her study *Purity, Body, and Self in Early Rabbinic Literature*. Balberg suggests that the rabbis recomposed the Priestly Code's purity laws into a new form of halakah, reflecting a new understanding of the self. The emphasis on subjectivity profoundly changed the meaning of purity and impurity in rabbinic discourse. However, the Mishnah is not a work of philosophy or anthropology. The early rabbis did not ask questions about the self or think of their purity laws as (symbolic) self-reflection in disguise, but the development of these laws was guided by certain assumptions about, and created certain attitudes toward, the self. Impurity remains as real as before, but the self becomes a new focal point. These changes were triggered by Greco-Roman culture, inner-Jewish developments, and interaction with emerging and competing Christian communities.[171]

Research on purity in early rabbinic texts often relates to discussions about halakic practices in the Second Temple period, comparisons between the practices of various groups, and the development of purity halakah over time. These are usually debated issues, because of the diffi-

---

168. Neusner 1973.
169. Neusner 1974–1977.
170. Neusner 1994.
171. Balberg 2014. For a much more thorough description of Balberg, see Kazen 2015d.

culties in dating rabbinic traditions and questions of continuity and discontinuity between earlier practices and rabbinic traditions.

In a rare study, Rory Bóid analyzes discharge laws in Samaritan halakah. Bóid provides a critical edition and translation of the relevant halakic texts, as well as a detailed commentary. Details and principles are outlined and compared with Rabbanite and Karaite halakah. The results are relevant also for understanding the development of regulations regarding genital discharges during the Second Temple period.[172]

Much more often, however, rabbinic purity traditions are compared to Qumran, Pharisaic, or other Second Temple period practices. Topics often explored are food, outsiders, the corpse, and the connection between purity and the cult. Furstenberg argues that the early rabbis focused on the body rather than the temple and that they upheld their status by purity; that the Pharisees' view of purity was unique; that the tendency to blend moral and ritual purity was a broad phenomenon, not limited to the Qumran movement; and that the practice of handwashing originated with concern for ordinary food.[173] Furstenberg also traces the development of outsider impurity, from the Qumran view of all outsiders (Jews or non-Jews) as intrinsically impure, through rabbinic notions of three spheres (pure Jews, other Jews, intrinsically impure gentiles), to the evolution of a graded system.[174]

In his classical study on the Galilean *am-ha'areṣ*, now a century old, Adolf Büchler claims that during the time of the temple handwashing was practiced for sacrificial food but not for ordinary food except by a few, mainly Shammaites, and that further developments belong to the Ushan period.[175] We have already mentioned Alon's quite opposite view on this matter. (I discuss this issue further in chs. 8 and 11.) Büchler also suggests that the ritual (Levitical) impurity of gentiles was a rabbinic innovation around the turn of the era that did not substantially affect private relationships and general association between Jews and gentiles.[176] However, Günther Stemberger argues that at least prohibitions against gentile foods date back to the time before the Jewish revolt.[177] Aharon Oppenheimer analyzes how the rabbis viewed the *am-ha'areṣ* and argues that the concept

---

172. Bóid 1989a.
173. Furstenberg 2016a.
174. Furstenberg 2015a.
175. Büchler 1968.
176. Büchler 1926.
177. Stemberger 2012.

of "people of the land" traces its origin to the Hellenistic period, although the rabbis applied it to people who did not carefully observe certain purity and tithing rules or did not study the Torah.[178]

Rabbinic traditions about corpse impurity have received much attention. Emanuel Feldman interprets Israelite mourning rituals and corpse-impurity laws through a rabbinic theology of death as desacralization and estrangement. Life is seen as a key element in God's nature, and impurity halakah implies a specific worldview.[179] Hyam Maccoby's studies give much emphasis to skin disease and corpse impurity.[180] The most prolific writer on rabbinic understandings of corpse impurity is probably Noam, who often compares rabbinic traditions with earlier traditions from the Second Temple period, whether it is texts from Qumran or from Josephus or Philo. Noam explores the rabbinic understanding of corpse-blood as defiling, which is not mentioned in the Bible, and suggests that this idea is indicated also in the War Scroll and the Temple Scroll.[181] In a seminal article on two opposing perspectives on impurity in Tannaitic literature, Noam argues that impurity in Tannaitic halakah is based on a natural and realistic understanding, but mechanical and inorganic rather than demonic. Onto this is layered an opposite movement, which places emphasis on human awareness and intention. This "nominalistic" aspect, claims the author, has roots back in the first century BCE.[182] Noam's interpretations thus take on a slightly different nuance from the paradigm of Shemesh, already discussed above. Here we should again mention Furstenberg, who discusses the nature of impurity in the Pesiqta de Rab Kahana and in Mishnah Yadayim 4:6–7, arguing that Pharisees were not nonrealists but shared a realist conception of impurity.[183] Noam's comparisons between Josephus, Philo, the Temple Scroll, and rabbinic traditions, and her discussion of leniency towards the corpse-impure, has already been mentioned above.[184] Noam also explores what she calls a twofold or dual strategy of the rabbis, as they continued the Second Temple–period practice to

---

178. Oppenheimer 1977.
179. Feldman 1977.
180. Maccoby 1998; 1999.
181. Noam 2009.
182. Noam 2010a; cf. 2010b. For Amihay's suggestion to substitute the realism-nominalism nomenclature for legal essentialism and legal formalism, see above, n. 64.
183. Furstenberg 2015b.
184. Noam 2010c; 2012.

1. Introduction: Purity Research and Resources 37

observe purity conscientiously apart from the cult, but distinguished this from what they understood as biblical impurity, which in their view was limited to the sacred only.[185]

I have interacted with many of these discussion in previous publications. In the present study I discuss rabbinic traditions about purity, especially from chapter 8 onward, and I do it primarily as part of an attempt to understand halakic reasoning and purity practices during the Second Temple period. The question of purity practices apart from, or not particularly motivated by, the cult is the topic of chapter 11.

Keeping the Balance

Ten years ago, in the preface to *Issues of Impurity*, I compared research on purity to riding a unicycle and expressed my hope to keep the balance all right. Balancing the nuances is not always easy. A long history of prejudice and anti-Jewish sentiment looms large, especially in the West, over how issues of ritual and purity in early Judaism are analyzed and evaluated. Scholarly research is not immune to Christian supersessionist tendencies, or at least to a subtle—or not so subtle—and often confessionally induced bent to portray Second Temple and rabbinic Judaism in dark colors, for Jesus and his followers to shine the brighter.

At the same time, there is a reverse risk for Western ritual skeptics who may occasionally find themselves defending ancient religions from being associated with practices, values, and attitudes, which modern prejudice does not favor. I often suspect such tendencies at work when purity practices are downplayed, minimized, or trivialized, as is sometimes the case. I discuss some such examples in this study, particularly in chapters 8 and 10. The tendency to restrict the scope of purity to cult-related concerns, which I discuss in chapter 11, might also, in part, reflect a wish to make purity practices more understandable and portray them in a more palatable way for modern people.

Here is a difficult balance, and the field is full of misreading and misunderstanding. In my dissertation *Jesus and Purity Halakhah*, which was published almost two decades ago, I asked a question in the subtitle: *Was Jesus Indifferent to Impurity?* I have often been referenced as giving an affirmative reply to that question, which has caused me to reflect on the difficulties of communication, especially of communicating nuances. While

---

185. Noam 2007 in Hebrew; 2008 in English.

some scholars would be willing to follow Stephen Westerholm's or Meier's views of Jesus's stance as expressing "an apparent indifference," or a "lack of concern or studied indifference,"[186] I have always tried to talk about a *seemingly* indifferent attitude and occasionally about relative indifference. I have suggested that Jesus would probably have been understood as careless or indifferent to certain aspects of purity halakah by those I identify as expansionists, and I have tried to account for this by suggesting some contextual factors that could explain why certain groups would judge others, with different interpretations, practices, and priorities, in such a way. In one of the summaries in *Jesus and Purity* I wrote:

> To say that Jesus was indifferent to purity, however, is to take an interpretative leap which is not fully substantiated. Jesus' attitude was apparently understood as seemingly indifferent in his contemporary context. It is uncertain whether anyone who lived within a society imbued with such a purity paradigm could be genuinely so.[187]

I still find the idea of Jesus as indifferent to be "neither a satisfactory nor a sufficient interpretation."[188] This is not always noted. It has been suggested that Jesus's indifference is my principal thesis, and I still find scholars associating me with "fals[e ...] scholarly claims that Mark's Jesus was 'indifferent' to or intended to 'subvert' the laws pertaining to ritual impurity."[189] Thiessen, for example, says that I suggest "that Jesus repeatedly demonstrates laxity towards the Jewish ritual purity system."[190] And Shively states: "Like Dunn (and Neyrey), Kazen argues that the historical Jesus was indifferent to ritual purity."[191]

I think it should be quite clear that I never claimed that Jesus was truly indifferent but that he was probably understood so by some of his opponents. My case has been for Jesus's attitude as *seemingly* indifferent.[192] Shively also says that "unlike Dunn, he [Kazen] argues that Jesus was indifferent because he believed himself to be the authoritative agent of God's

---

186. Westerholm 1978, 91; Meier 2009, 411.
187. Kazen 2010a, 198.
188. Kazen 2010a, 344.
189. Dunn 2002, 461 n. 55; Thiessen 2020, 60, referencing me in n. 52. Thiessen talks of Mark's Jesus, while I discuss the *seeming* indifference of the historical Jesus.
190. Thiessen 2020, 179.
191. Shively 2020, 68.
192. Kazen 2010a, 197–98.

kingdom."[193] In the sixth chapter of *Jesus and Purity*, I discuss Jesus's exorcisms and the implications of his view of the kingdom for issues of impurity. I explore views of "dynamic" or "offensive" purity,[194] concluding that they assume an understanding "in which the holy status of the exorcist is understood as overcoming demonic impurity" and that the "prerequisite for such an understanding would be that Jesus regarded himself as the bearer of some intrinsic authority, signaling, or resulting from the coming reign of God." I do, however, question, whether this concept is warranted by the evidence,[195] even though it seems like the power of the kingdom was understood as strong enough to relativize needs for conventional purification.

In the concluding chapter of *Jesus and Purity*, I clarify my stance by saying that I find Jesus's kingdom eschatology compatible with the purity paradigm and that "I do not find it likely that this power perspective caused Jesus to disregard the purity paradigm in the sense that he should have totally scrapped the idea of bodily impurity." I also question the idea of a contagious holiness overtaking impurity as not sufficiently convincing, lacking enough evidence, and I qualify this by suggesting that

> it was not the inherent holiness of his own person, but the power of the coming reign of God, which Jesus believed overpowered demons and impurities. That power was certainly seen as residing with, or mediated by Jesus, but it should not be seen as a warrant for Jesus flouting the impurity concept altogether. It is more likely that this power made it possible for Jesus to relativize and to a certain extent disregard bodily impurity, but still within the framework of a basic purity paradigm.[196]

Today I would express myself even more cautiously and tentatively. In subsequent publications, including *Scripture, Interpretation, or Authority?*, which Shively also refers to, I have tried to clarify my position further: I do *not* think that the historical Jesus was genuinely indifferent to impurity, and I do *not* think of Jesus as overruling law by virtue of an inherent authority. I warn against crypto-christological constructs that refer to Jesus's unique authority but suggest that he took a pragmatic and prophetic

---

193. Shively 2020, 68.
194. For examples of such views, see above under "Jesus and the Gospels."
195. Kazen 2010a, 339.
196. Kazen 2010a, 346.

stance, again warning against merging Israelite prophecy with an anachronistic and individualistic understanding of a modern charismatic leader figure. Rather than special uniqueness, I suggest that Jesus's behavior represented "common custom and opinion, a traditional Israelite understanding of torah, and a prophetic critique of the elites," and that the authority ascribed to him was borne by collective and popular expectations.[197]

Another recent example of misreading is found in Myrick Shinall's article on the exclusion of people with skin disease, with which I interact in chapter 10.[198] Shinall says about Mark 1:40–45 that I see "in the mention of Jesus's touching a leper an emphasis intended to highlight Jesus's rejection of purity restrictions."[199] This is simply false. I suggest that the purity issue in this passage was not relevant to Mark, but that the details of the tradition might provide hints about the historical Jesus's attitude. I do not say that this was an attitude of rejection.[200] Once, in a different context, I suggested that Jesus "probably rejected the requirement for special immersion in order to enter the inner court,"[201] but I would not bet on such specifics, and I am not sure I would argue it today.

In view of various misreadings and misinterpretations, I ask myself whether my present stance is in fact somewhat removed from what I argued back then. To some extent, one's views always develop, and when I first embarked on the study of Jesus and purity, I probably expected a bit more indifference and inherent authority on the part of Jesus than I found—not unexpected, considering my confessional background. But I also suspected, from the very beginning, that what might on the surface look like halakic indifference could partly be a construct in others' eyes and partly be explained by contextual factors and differences between contemporary Jewish groups.

Today I would probably tread more carefully on mined land and try to use clearer language. In retrospect I can see that my attempts to offer a balanced discussion could be taken in directions I would not go, especially as expectations of results tend to skew their interpretation. But it is difficult to guard oneself against the future. I hope that the present volume will be read carefully, and I ask my readers to bear with slips and unclear details. I

---

197. Kazen 2013a, 293–302; quote from 299.
198. Shinall 2018.
199. Shinall 2018, 930 n. 46, referring to Kazen 2010a, 106.
200. Kazen 2010a, 106.
201. Kazen 2010a, 255.

would nevertheless not be surprised if, in the future, I am ascribed the view that only evolutionary and cognitive models are adequate for interpreting purity, that disgust explains everything, that the Israelite purity system was a Persian import, that everyone washed their hands before eating, that people with genital discharges and skin disease were always ostracized and disparaged, that purity had nothing to do with the cult, or that Jesus did not engage in halakic debates because he was a prophet. Be assured: it's all false. At least, this is not what I meant to say. And from those of my colleagues who find themselves misinterpreted by me I humbly ask for forgiveness and correction.

2
Purity and Impurity: A Short Summary

Ideas of purity/impurity are found globally. Impurity designates an array of physical conditions, food avoidances, and behaviors. Structuralist and symbolic explanations have been popular in the past, but the level of explanation is often unclear. The common divide between ritual and moral impurity turns out to vary from culture to culture. Linguistic expressions suggest a combination of aesthetic and affective origins. A basic concept of impurity can be accounted for through emotional disgust. Its extension can be explained through the use and spread of conceptual blends.

Although ideas of purity and impurity are found globally and play a role in most religions and regions of the world, this category of opposites is at least in part a modern construct. Under the conceptual umbrella of purity and impurity are gathered a number of conceptions, aversions, taboos, and apotropaic practices, which are neither of one piece, nor do all terms used for these phenomena belong to the same semantic domain. The once-popular view that impurity and holiness both evolved from an undifferentiated concept of taboo, as religion developed from primitive to more advanced stages, is no longer accepted.[1]

Semantics of Purity

A most cursory cross-linguistic examination of the semantics of purity illustrates the problematic nature of the concept. For example, Shinto

---

This chapter was first published as "Purity/Impurity," in *Vocabulary for the Study of Religion*, ed. Robert Segal and Kocku von Stuckrad (Leiden: Brill, 2015), 3:166–70. Used by permission. Only minor changes have been made.

1. Smith 1927, 152–64, 446–54.

impurity (*kegare*) is basically an amoral concept of aversion, associated with birth, death, disease, and menstruation,[2] while the ancient Egyptian word *bwt* characterizes a number of social, ethical, and cultic offenses. The Egyptian word for purity (*wab*) means their absence.[3]

The Akkadian terms for purity, *ellu*, *ebbu*, and *namru*, on the other hand, refer to the presence of a positive property: being clean, clear, or bright, in contrast to being dim, tainted, or sullied. The corresponding Hebrew term *ṭāhôr/ṭāhārâ*, like its Ugaritic cognate, can similarly mean "shining," or "radiance," although it is mostly used for purity as absence of contagion. There is also a conceptual overlap between purity and holiness, as the Semitic root *qdš* is sometimes used to denote purification.[4]

The Hittite word *papratar* often refers to pollution as a metaphysical threat, through gossiping, curses, sorcery, and bloodguilt.[5] The Hebrew word *ṭāmēʾ/ṭumʾâ* can similarly refer to pollution, either in the sense of culpability and moral transgression, or in legal contexts for impure physical conditions. The underlying meaning, however, is probably "dirt." The Syriac cognate verb can mean to be "soiled" or "sticky," in a concrete sense. The corresponding Egyptian Arabic root means "silt." The later Arabic word *ṭamā* means "be choked with mud." *Tammay* is "mud of the Nile."[6] The Semitic etymology thus suggests an association with physical dirt.

Sanskrit has terms for impurity related to dirt and decay (*mala*). It has other terms for purity and purification that carry connotations of radiance (*śauca*) or fitness for consumption or ritual use (*medhya*).[7] In Iranian religion purity (Avestan *yaozhdāh*) represents order, in contrast to chaos. Pollution (*âhitica*; cf. *irimant*) is a dynamic concept, associated with a female deceiver demon (*drug nasu*).[8] In Greek culture *miasma* similarly denotes a dynamic and dangerous kind of pollution,[9] the neutralization of which needs cultic manipulation. By contrast, *akatharsia* is the absence of purity and often refers to immoral behavior.

---

2. Abe 2003; Levine 2012.
3. Johnston 2004, 497–99.
4. Van der Toorn 1985, 27–37; Johnston 2004, 499–504; Feder 2014.
5. Feder 2014.
6. André and Ringgren 1986, 330; Paschen 1970, 27.
7. Malinar 2010.
8. Johnston 2004, 505–7; Choksy 1989, 1–22.
9. Parker 1983, 1–17.

Even this incomplete survey should warn us against making easy generalizations about purity and impurity. Impurity is used to designate a diversity of conditions and behaviors, including besmirched items, repelling substances, bodily fluids, certain physical states and diseases, corpses and carcasses, contagion by contact, food avoidances, disapproved sexual relations, breaches against moral and cultural codes, and various spiritual threats. At the same time this array of meanings does reveal certain common traits. An aesthetic aspect is present, as both human and divine beings are thought to enjoy that which is whole, clean, and radiant and to shun what is smelly, smeared, and smitten, especially when it threatens human life and order. As all linguistic expressions relate to human experience, lexical meaning is bound to contain an affective element, as becomes particularly obvious in the field of purity and impurity.[10]

Symbolism and Metaphor

In the following discussion, our main example will be that of early Judaism, which has one of the most elaborate purity systems and has been well studied.

The most common approach to Israelite purity laws has been to regard so-called ritual impurity (mainly caused by physical, bodily states) as primary and so-called moral impurity (the use of purity language for offensive behavior) as secondary. Yet the reverse view has also been argued.[11]

One of the most influential theories of purity and impurity has been that of anthropologist Mary Douglas in *Purity and Danger* (1966). She focuses on Israelite food taboos. She famously describes impurity as matter out of place—that is, as anomalous, as resulting from problems of classification. Concerns for the purity of the human body supposedly reflect concerns for the unity of the social group. The impurity of discharges from bodily orifices, which compromise the boundaries of the human body, are understood to symbolize or represent an experienced threat to the boundaries of the social body. Food taboos are similarly explained as anomalies in relation to zoological taxonomies. More broadly, purity concerns become structuralist allegories of the social and natural order.[12]

---

10. Feder 2014.
11. Hoffmann 1905–1906, 2:301–30, 340.
12. Douglas 2002, 141–59; 1978, 92–112.

Although Douglas later abandoned some of her views toward at least food taboos in favor of more theological interpretations,[13] *Purity and Danger* has remained influential. A major problem for structuralist and theological constructs alike concerns the level of explanation for which symbolic and systemic interpretations are claimed. It would be anachronistic, turning effect into cause, to understand purity conceptions as *originating* from symbolic construals or advanced allegorical interpretations.[14] These construals and interpretations are rather to be understood as ad hoc constructions and intellectual rationalizations for traditional rituals and behaviors. Modern scholarship argues for the primacy of ritual over belief in all religion and not just, as for Robertson Smith, in ancient religions, and also for the primacy of body over mind.[15]

Theological explanations at most reflect how practices of purity and impurity are integrated with a given worldview in a particular social situation. Although birth, death, discharge, and disease are often involved in various purity systems, claims that impurity is based on death, death and sex,[16] or even the human life cycle are unsatisfactory. The first is clearly insufficient to explain all data, the second can be suspected of Freudian anachronism, and the third is too broad since the human life cycle by definition encompasses all human behavior. Suggestions that purity concerns relate to those features that distinguish human from divine beings do not hold either, since concepts of impurity are found just as frequently in religions that conceive of their gods as sexual and mortal figures.[17]

Ritual and Morality

The distinction between ritual and moral impurity has given rise to much debate. In the study of Israelite purity laws, food taboos are usually placed in a category of their own, and the status of the use of impurity language in the conceptual domains of intermarriage and worship of foreign gods remains contested. The use of the concept of impurity to designate objectionable human behavior, both toward other humans—murder, prohibited sexual relations—and toward divinities—idol worship, child sacrifice—is

---

13. See Douglas 2002, xiii–xvi.
14. Cf. Smith (1927, 16–27) on myth and ritual.
15. Lemos 2013, 280–82, 292–94; Frevel and Nihan 2013, 3–10.
16. Death: cf. Milgrom 1991; death and sex: cf. Wright 1992.
17. Lemos 2013, 274.

incontestable. But this usage implies neither that impurity from contact with menstruation, seminal fluid, birth, or corpses is considered sinful nor that moral impurity can be removed by purificatory rituals.

Jonathan Klawans has argued that in the Hebrew Bible ritual and moral impurity are distinct categories. Ritual impurity is considered concrete or real, which for Klawans means literal. Moral impurity is understood either metaphorically or literally.[18] Klawans argues that the two categories were conflated in Qumran, but his claim has been challenged, and the association between impurity and sin in some of the Dead Sea texts can instead be understood as an evocative rhetorical device.[19]

Perhaps more importantly, no clear distinction between ritual and morality, not to speak of convention, holds cross-culturally, since these categories are culture specific and at least in part arbitrary.[20] In the words of Assyriologist Wilfred Lambert, "The god was just as angry with the eating of ritually impure food as with oppressing the widow and orphan."[21] Whether classified as ritualistic or moral from a modern perspective, an offensive act or state would in ancient times have been considered equally objectionable.

Disgust and Conceptual Blending

Much of the vocabulary of impurity and purity connotes dirt and decay versus cleanness and brightness. Other terms indicate aversion and threat. There is a combination of underlying aesthetic and affective experiences, with emotional disgust playing a key role.[22]

Disgust evolved as a survival mechanism to protect living organisms from contacting or incorporating dangerous, toxic, or unhealthy substances.[23] Human expressions of disgust are culturally shaped, and psychological research has identified a number of triggers of disgust.[24] All of them

---

18. Klawans 2000, 21–42, 158–62. Klawans suggests that certain serious moral impurities are to be considered literal because they are envisaged as real. I have elsewhere argued that this suggestion builds on a confusion of a linguistic designation (literal) with an ontological one (real); see Kazen 2010a, 204–7; 2014, 68.
19. Himmelfarb 2001. See Klawans 2000, 67–91, challenged in Holtz 2013.
20. Kazen 2011, 20–31.
21. Lambert 1959, 194.
22. Feder 2014; Kazen 2011, 33–36, 71–94.
23. Navarrete and Fessler 2006; Curtis 2013, 21–40.
24. Rozin, Haidt, and McCauley 2000.

find examples in Israelite conceptions of impurity. Disgust is present, to various degrees, in all three main areas of priestly purity legislation: food taboos, bodily contagion, and immoral behavior. The association of disgust and impurity is found cross-culturally.[25]

Emotional disgust cannot explain every case of impurity, and not all things disgusting are considered impure. The cognitive and affective mechanisms through which disgust extends conceptions of impurity are explained by both conceptual metaphor theory and blending theory. Metaphors are cross-domain mappings, carrying notions from one cognitive domain to another, providing the other domain with new impetus and meaning.[26] When different domains or conceptual spaces have certain elements in common, these spaces can easily be fused into a blended space in which other elements are combined into a new conceptual framework, influencing both thought and behavior.[27]

Conceptual metaphor theory explains how a primary notion of material dirt is mapped onto domains of disgusting creatures, unsavory human beings, and objectionable behavior, creating secondary notions of impurity. Blending theory explains the process through which two or more conceptual (input) spaces are blended into a new space. The theory makes it possible to bypass the artificial division between moral and ritual impurity by explaining both as conceptual blends. Both result from a blending of aversion to physical dirt and to decaying substances with another input space, whether revulsion to food or physical conditions (ritual) or disapproval of certain actions (moral).[28]

Regardless of whether the stimuli that evoke revulsion consist of animals, diseases, persons, or behaviors, all can be envisaged as metaphorically impure through a conceptual blending process, as if smeared with material dirt. Mold, skin disease, genital discharge, and corpse impurity can be thought of as dirt, which is transferred through contact and needs to be removed by washing or scraping (see Lev 12–15). Murder or sexual transgression can be likened to contact contamination as well as to laundry dirt, possible to wash away (see Ps 51), although physical water rites were generally not employed by ancient Israelites for these purposes. Disgust against vermin can be mapped onto quadrupeds that one is forbid-

---

25. Kazen 2011, 71–94.
26. Lakoff and Johnson 1980a.
27. Fauconnier and Turner 2002, 17–57; Coulson and Oakley 2000.
28. Kazen 2014.

den to eat (see Lev 11; Deut 14). Even the worship of foreign gods and intermarriage can be envisaged as impurity in conceptual blends through several steps (see Ezek 16; 23; Ezra 9; Neh 13). While biological evolution can account for a basic concept of impurity through emotional disgust, cultural evolution explains its extension through the use and spread of conceptual blends.

Purificatory rites employ various means of purification and typically involve water—bathing, washing, and sprinkling. In Islam, sand is allowed under special circumstances. Other rites employ particular materials or animals, including sacrifices. Some are carried out by the purifying person. Others must be performed by ritual specialists. One way to classify purificatory rites is by function—for example, into removal rites, apotropaic and magical protective rites, mitigating rites, and sanctifying rites.[29] These rites function to eliminate dirt, mitigate offense, turn away aversion, or protect against threats. The type of purification employed for a particular impurity is related to the specific conceptual blend from which that conception of impurity stems.

---

29. Such categories should be understood as heuristic and not always fully separable.

3
Levels of Explanation for Ideas of Impurity: Why Structuralist and Symbolic Models Often Fail While Evolutionary and Cognitive Models Succeed

> When trying to understand purity practices and conceptions of impurity, which often seem enigmatic, scholars construe "explanations" on very different levels and frequently do not distinguish clearly between cause and effect. In the present article, I seek to disentangle various levels or types of explanation, ranging from evolutionary and historical, through cognitive and social, to structuralist and symbolic. While many attempts to explain impurity look for origins, reasons, or at least backgrounds, others rather aim at the results, or functions, of various ideas and practices of purity. Some explanations focus on analogies and correspondences, even treating purity codes as object lessons or illustrations of beliefs. Several explanatory models are frequently used for claims at levels to which they do not belong. Special critique is directed against the misuse of functionalist, structuralist, and symbolic models beyond their validity at a certain level of reception, for arguing or implying more than they can actually accommodate. The usefulness and integration of biopsychological and cognitive-linguistic models for solving certain key questions without imposing ideological superstructures is argued.

> Many interpreters collapse the rituals' meaning with their religious and social function.
> —James Watts, *Ritual and Rhetoric in Leviticus*

Explanations of purity conceptions are numerous. Even if issues of ritual purity and purification were reduced to questions of history and phenomenology—historical behavior, perhaps—it would be difficult to approach

---

This chapter was first published in *JAJ* 9 (2018): 75–100. Used by permission.

a scholarly consensus. This is even more so the case when purity practices of various sorts are understood to carry *meaning* in their very fabric, so to speak, just awaiting our *interpretation*. We rarely think of such practices as neutral or nonmeaning behaviors. As we search for their meaning, we usually relate purity practices to particular historical, anthropological, social, political, economic, hierarchical, or religious contexts. In so doing, we inevitably draw on our innate and acquired frameworks and presuppositions, whether emotional, rationalist, symbolist, anachronistic, or simply fanciful.

As human beings, we have a cognitive urge to trace *reasons* for most phenomena. This is to a large extent due to our *narrativity*. As a result, we constantly attempt to identify connections between observable items and events, and we suggest, postulate, or invent such connections even when they are not evident. Many of these connections are understood by the human brain to be causative.[1]

Consequently, scholarly analysis is more often than not involved in tracing *cause* and *effect*. These are, however, slippery concepts. Cause can seemingly mean anything from concurrency to unique, contributing, necessary, or sufficient trigger. Likewise, with effect: an observable phenomenon is usually understood as the effect of some cause, even when no such cause can be identified. In spite of the two concepts being slippery and polysemous, they are not arbitrary; hence they can and should be distinguished from each other.

In the study of ritual purity and purification, scholars typically seek explanations for conceptions and behaviors that often seem irrational or enigmatic to modern people. To make them manageable for human cognition, we tend to "explain" them by constructing causal chains into which we draw our observations.

In the following I will attempt to analyze and sort claims and suggestions made by various explanatory endeavors. I suggest that these "explanations" function on very different levels and at times do not clearly distinguish between cause and effect. A particular practice may be explained with regard to its origin, based on historical circumstances and biological

---

1. For the thoroughgoing narrativity of the human mind and the human tendency to understand the world in terms of cause and effects, see Sperber, Premack, and Premack 1995; Danks 2009, 447–70; Newman 2012, 69–82; cf. essays on primate cognition in Heyes and Huber 2000. See also the Yale Perception & Cognition Laboratory Reference Guide: Causal Perception.

or psychological conditions; it may be explained by its social, political, or economic function or result; or it may be explained as an expression of a particular religious belief or as part of a religious system. Such explanations do not intend to answer the same question. They are all concerned with cause and effect, but move on different levels, and it is not always clear whether the phenomenon to be explained is supposed to take the position of cause or effect. Much confusion would be avoided if scholars were clearer about their underlying questions and at which level they attempt to answer them.[2]

Since my argument is mainly a methodological one, taking a broad range of explanations of purity conceptions into account, I cannot for practical reasons argue each specific underlying issue in any detail, but have to summarize and generalize. However, the discussion depends and draws on a number of previous studies, including extensive and in-depth analyses of primary texts and of historical developments. The reader is referred to these studies for the underpinnings of some of the interpretations and viewpoints that underlie this article's overall methodological argument.

"Explanations" of Impurity

In the literature on ritual impurity scholars tend to explain avoidance behaviors, conceptions of impurity, purity practices, and purity codes in a number of different ways. I suggest that we can identify at least seven types of explanations, or explanatory levels, on which various explanations lie. The typology I am here proposing could, of course, be construed differently, but I offer it in an attempt to clear up some of the confusion involved in the present situation. I suggest the following types of explanation:

1. Evolutionary, biological, and psychological reasons for/background to avoidance behaviors and general conceptions of impurity
2. Historical and contextual reasons for/background to the development of particular conceptions of impurity
3. Cognitive and linguistic reasons for/background to the development and extended use of impurity language

---

2. For a recent, principled discussion on explanation, see Jensen 2011, 44–47.

4. Social, political, and ideological reasons for/background to the shaping and systematization of avoidance behaviors into purity codes
5. Social, economic, and hierarchical results/consequences/functions of various purity practices and conceptions of impurity
6. Analogies/correspondences within a social system between structural patterns understood to be embedded in purity practices/purity codes and social practices/social organization
7. Symbolic interpretations of purity practices/purity codes as illustrations of philosophical ideas or theological beliefs

Because the concept of cause is in itself problematic, as already indicated, I prefer to talk of "reasons for/background to" ideas and practices for the first four explanatory levels. It is often unclear to what extent causal explanations define triggers that are unique, sufficient, or necessary for a particular effect, or rather describe contextual factors that contribute to certain developments and make them likely to take place—what cultural anthropologists call "thick description."[3]

For the fifth type of explanation I mention three interchangeable words: results, consequences, and functions. These are sometimes used as synonyms, but it may be argued that results/consequences, on the one hand, and functions, on the other, are not completely identical concepts. Claims that certain purity practices or conceptions of impurity have a particular function have frequently been (mis)understood to indicate an *intention* or a *purpose* behind, as if these practices or conceptions evolved or were shaped *in order to* have certain results, or at least were retained or reinforced because their results were desirable.[4] However, statements about the function of purity rules need not indicate much beyond their having an *observable effect* on, for example, social structures or individ-

---

3. For the concept of thick description, see Geertz 1973, 3–30.

4. Mary Douglas claims that although pollution beliefs *derive* from rational processes of classifying and ordering experience, they are not consciously *produced* by them but appear as spontaneous by-products. See Douglas 1975, 58. That distinction is, however, more often than not unclear in scholarly literature. Cf. Gane (2005, 12–18), who seems to collapse meaning, function, and purpose. Christophe Nihan suggests that the function of pollution and purification in Leviticus was to "consolidate the authority of the priesthood and the temple over the rest of society in Yehûd." See Nihan 2013, 362. This comes close to purpose or intention.

ual status.⁵ These differences are important to note; in all cases are there results or consequences, but only at times is intention or purpose involved. Function, in fact, does not by itself indicate any underlying intention. But since intention is often associated with function in general thought, we may get the false impression that the origins of certain purity practices are explained by their results. Explaining cause by effect is a teleological fallacy of sorts, but as we will see below, some functionalist/structuralist and symbolic interpretations come close to doing so.

The sixth level of explanation is often associated with an etic perspective, as it represents an outsider's observations and analysis of a social system. The analogies or correspondences we are talking of here are rarely articulated by insiders. They are usually suggested by outsiders trying to make sense of a system that they study but are not themselves part of. This is exemplified by the numerous functionalist and structuralist approaches to purity and impurity offered during the last half-century or so, beginning with and inspired by the early work of Mary Douglas.⁶

In contrast, the seventh level of explanation can be associated with an emic perspective, as it represents interpretations crafted by insiders trying to make sense of their religious tradition, negotiating ancient texts with more current concerns and convictions regarding the core and intent of "Judaism." Such explanations begin with Philo and the author of the Letter of Aristeas and are variously represented by scholars such as Jacob Milgrom, Douglas (in her later work), and Jonathan Klawans.⁷ Although basically emic, this type of explanation is employed by outsiders, too, who assume and search for past theological or ideological rationales underlying the formation or configuration of ancient purity codes. Despite certain clear differences between explanations 6 and 7, they are related and can sometimes be combined.

---

5. This is a more appropriate understanding of function. See further below.
6. See Douglas 1966; 1975.
7. Milgrom 1991; 1989; Douglas 1999; 2004; Klawans 2006. For examples from Philo, see *Special Laws* as well as *Quod Deus*. For further discussion of specific references from Philo and from the Letter of Aristeas, see the section on symbolic and allegorical explanations below.

Functionalist and Structuralist Explanations

Functionalism, or structural functionalism, is a theory of society focused on the social structures that shape it.[8] It finds its origins in the nineteenth century with the birth of sociology as a discipline. For Herbert Spencer, society could be compared to the human body. This analogy subsequently became extremely influential in anthropological research.[9] For Spencer, as well as for Émile Durkheim, the body analogy was largely about stability and cohesion. The system is primary and defines its parts. Durkheim understood social structures to influence the way in which people think.[10]

Structuralism is a twentieth-century movement, and the term serves as a label for similar developments in several areas: linguistics, philosophy, psychology, sociology, and anthropology, among others. It is related to, but also in certain tension with, functionalism. Structuralism assumes the existence of overarching and universal structures, whether in grammar, conceptualization, human behavior, or social organization. Details must be understood as parts of the whole and against the background of the larger structures in which they belong. In anthropology, structuralism has been employed analogously to grammar, in order to analyze rituals cross-culturally as parts of deep, universal structures. The frequent use of binary opposites is usually understood as a universal pattern.[11]

The most prominent structural anthropologist was Claude Lévi-Strauss. By applying linguistic concepts to anthropology, Lévi-Strauss analyzed rituals and myths as results of common human cognitive structures.[12] Just as elementary units of language, such as phonemes (or letters, according to Edmund Leach), have no meaning in themselves, ritual elementary units have no intrinsic meaning either, but it is their combination that produces meaning.[13]

The analogy between the human and the social body is crucial along this trajectory of thought. Structuralist interpretations of ritual assume strong links between social and cognitive structures. Thought is often

---

8. For a general discussion of structural functionalism, see Appelrouth and Desfor Edles 2011, 20–74.
9. Spencer 1906, 449–62.
10. Durkheim 1950, 8–10.
11. For a survey of structuralism, see Sturrock 1993; Baronov 2016, 85–110.
12. Lévi-Strauss 1963, esp. 18–21.
13. Meshel 2014, 11–13.

understood to precede and give rise to social patterns. This results in a priority of ideas and beliefs over practice, a notion that has been severely criticized in recent years, especially from the perspective of ritual studies.[14] In the words of Tracy Lemos, "the type of analysis that seeks ever to schematize almost always sees ritual as secondary to belief and the body as secondary to the mind."[15]

Durkheim, however, understood individual cognitive structures as part of collective and social structures, and thus as influenced by them. Although beliefs and practices go together, the former do not take precedence over the latter. Durkheim furthermore distinguished cause, effect, and function quite clearly, criticizing Spencer and Auguste Comte for explaining social facts by their usefulness, as if this could provide the reason for why such facts existed or even why they took the form they did.[16] In an occasionally cited passage Durkheim asserts:

> When … the explanation of a social phenomenon is undertaken, we must seek separately the efficient cause which produces it and the function it fulfills. We use the word "function," in preference to "end" or "purpose," precisely because social phenomena do not generally exist for the useful results they produce. We must determine whether there is a correspondence between the fact under consideration and the general needs of the social organism, and in what this correspondence consists, without occupying ourselves with whether it has been intentional or not.[17]

For Durkheim it was not enough to explain the historical cause of a social fact. Explanation also required an understanding of its function. Both were deemed necessary and important, but they were different things and should be kept apart. Most important, function was not to be confused with purpose in the sense of intention or motive. Questions of intention rather belonged to historical explanation and should not be confused with function. Function, on the other hand, determined the *consequences* of a particular social fact or ritual. Function for Durkheim, then, seems more related to result, or effect, than to cause or intention.[18]

---

14. Cf. Lemos 2013, 280–82.
15. Lemos 2013, 294.
16. Durkheim 1950, 90; cf. Rossides 1998, 157–58.
17. Durkheim 1950, 95.
18. Durkheim 1950, ch. 5 ("Rules for the Explanation of Social Facts"); cf. Coser 1977, 140–43.

Although some of the language could lend itself to teleological interpretation ("needs of the social organism"; "the function [the social organism] fulfills"), Durkheim does acknowledge the teleological fallacy inherent in arguments from usefulness and addresses the very problem discussed above, with regard to the fifth level of explanation. Unfortunately, Durkheim seems to have had little influence on the way in which *function* is being employed in contemporary discourse on ritual and purity. Hence, I think my caveat concerning the use of the term is valid. One could of course argue that a scholarly use of the concept based on proper definitions should be unproblematic. However, since *function* in practice is often taken to mean "intentional function," I think it would be wise to use the term sparingly and with caution, not least in discussions of conceptions of impurity and purity practices.

Functionalist and structuralist explanations of ritual purity belong to the sixth level in the above list. Such explanations have been and are still influential. Douglas's *Purity and Danger* (1966) has been hailed by scholars from Jacob Neusner to Klawans.[19] Douglas famously describes impurity as matter out of place.[20] Impurities result from problems of classification. Food taboos are explained as anomalies in relation to zoological taxonomies.[21] Early on, Douglas understood conceptions of impurity focused on the body, its emissions, and its borders to indicate a concern over social boundaries and the unity of the social group.[22] The impurity of discharges from bodily orifices compromises the boundaries of the human body and symbolizes an experienced threat to the boundaries of the social body. Purity concerns become structuralist allegories of the social and natural order. Purity laws express a human need to categorize. They are a function of an overarching social order, a worldview, and a cosmology.[23]

Critics have, through the years, pointed out a number of problems with this approach.[24] I will summarize them in five points. First, the

---

19. Neusner 1973; 1975, 15–26; Klawans 2006, 17–20.
20. Douglas 1966, 36. Douglas describes dirt as a by-product of systematic ordering.
21. See in particular Douglas 1966, ch. 3 ("The Abominations of Leviticus").
22. Douglas 1966, in particular ch. 7 ("External Boundaries").
23. For an analysis of Douglas's works and the development of her theories, especially with regard to ritual purity, see Lemos 2009.
24. The critique against functionalist and structuralist interpretations of purity laws and purity practices tends to go along the same lines as general criticism against structural functionalism as such.

approach assumes a universal structure of the human mind.[25] Second, it understands mind, theory, or idea to precede ritual behavior.[26] Third, it is acontextual, not paying enough attention to sociohistorical, political, and economic circumstances. Fourth, it is ahistorical, taking little account of the fact that the practices involved are older than the regulations in the texts.[27] Fifth, it is speculative and arbitrary, by importing interpretations from without with little foothold in texts or contexts, but more dependent on the imagination of the interpreter.[28]

Although Douglas did attempt to reply to some of the initial criticisms, "Deciphering a Meal" (1972) made little to remedy the main problems of her structuralist interpretations but only widened them by adding multiple factors that could similarly be understood as social analogies.[29]

Milgrom's approach also has strong structuralist features in taking a systemic approach to the priestly code. One of Milgrom's aims was to demonstrate the rationality and internal consistency of the Priestly source's worldview, and he embraced the anthropological belief that rituals reveal sociocultural values. Milgrom was to some extent open to historical change and development of ritual practices and valued comparative methods. Like Yehezkel Kaufmann, he both acknowledged a common ancient West Asian heritage, including "pagan vestiges," and argued for the systemic nature of the priestly project, including its monotheistic purge of the demonic.[30]

In one sense, then, Milgrom is not as vulnerable to critique for being ahistorical. In another sense, however, Milgrom's strong bent on symbolism tends to turn the comparative project and the prehistory of conceptions of impurity into prolegomena. For Milgrom, the universal cognitive

---

25. The assumption of common human structures of mind is not in itself a weakness; evolutionary theory seems to confirm that to a certain extent this is the case. Cf. Baert and Carreira da Silva 2010, 33. Problems appear when this is too readily "translated" into common patterns of thought and human behavior.

26. Cf. Lemos 2013, 280–82.

27. The ahistorical (and thereby acontextual) nature of structuralism is pointed out in almost every overview of sociological theory; cf. Watts's (2007, 27–32) emphasis on the difference between (the context of) texts and (the context of) rituals.

28. This I attempt to demonstrate below, in the next section, discussing Douglas and, especially, Ruane.

29. See for example the three reasons suggested to "explain" the impurity of the pig in "Deciphering a Meal" (Douglas 1975, 272).

30. Milgrom 1991, 42–51; cf. Watts 2007, 3–10.

structure that shapes purity practices is theological and concerns life and death. All types of impurity are understood to somehow carry connotations with or notions of death.[31]

Comparing Douglas and Milgrom, Lemos uses the pig as an example. While Douglas in her early work thinks the pig is impure because it is an anomaly, Milgrom explains its impurity by its association with chthonic deities.[32] But what about various contextual reasons for not raising pigs in the highlands of Israel, which may have a bearing on the fact that swine were not eaten and at a particular stage in Israelite history were judged unclean?[33] At this point, socioeconomic and historical perspectives as well as comparative ambitions recede into the background in favor of theological affirmations: purity laws taught Israel reverence for life.[34] The question is how much foothold in the text such an explanation has, or to what extent it is influenced by rabbinic interpretation, or modern liberal ideology.[35]

The problem can be exemplified with other impurities and other scholars. With Milgrom, however, we inevitably stand at the border to the world of symbolism and allegory, which we need to address before proceeding any further.

Symbolic and Allegorical Explanations

As already mentioned, symbolic and allegorical explanations of purity laws and conceptions of impurity (seventh level of explanation) can be traced back to the Letter of Aristeas and to Philo of Alexandria. The symbolism by which the author of the Letter of Aristeas explains the food laws is well known. The carnivorous nature of unclean birds illustrates a moral: those who follow the laws should be righteous and not tyrannize others, as the unclean birds do. Similarly, the division between clean and unclean animals acts as a moral lesson for Jews to practice virtue and separate themselves from the incestuous rest of humanity (Let. Aris. 139–169).

Philo, in particular, is known for his allegorizing virtually everything, including the law, in order to demonstrate that Israel's Scripture is fully compatible with, and even superior to, Greco-Roman philosophy and

---

31. Milgrom 1989.
32. Lemos 2013, 269–70.
33. Finkelstein 1997, 227–30; Hesse and Wapnish 1997.
34. Milgrom 1991, 735; Lemos 2013, 270.
35. Cf. Albert Schweitzer's emphasis on "reverence for life."

ethics. Philo expressly calls his interpretations "symbolic" (*symbolikōs*; see *Spec.* 1.206). A few examples from a vast sea of allegories: the ashes in the sprinkling water for purification from corpse impurity are explained as a reminder of the fact that human existence (*ousia*) is made up of earth and water, with the purpose to make people turn away from arrogance and pride (*Spec.* 1.261–266). Bodies partially or totally affected by skin disease represent ethical and philosophical truth about the soul, reason, and involuntary sin (*Deus* 127–130). Similarly, the rule that an affected house is only considered impure when the priest has entered to declare it unclean is explained as the soul being innocent as long as divine reason has not entered it (*Deus* 131–135). Such far-reaching allegorizing occasionally led people to abandon their literal adherence to purity laws, something that Philo himself vehemently denounces (*Migr.* 89).[36]

Symbolic and allegorical explanations became especially popular as the Christian church felt an increasing need to negotiate the tension between Jewish texts that belonged to its heritage with its actual theology and rejection of certain Jewish practices. Some Christians eventually came to use this interpretative method in the very manner that Philo opposed (cf. Barn. 10; Origen, *Homiliae in Leviticum*).

Although popular for centuries, allegory fell out of vogue with the entrance of modern biblical studies. Interestingly, it returns in ritual interpretation, piggybacking on structuralism. Or, if not allegory, at least symbolism does. The exact difference between the two is not always evident, although allegory, in contrast to symbolism, does not need to make claims about a text's or a ritual's intentional meaning. Both, however, treat their objects—practices, narratives, laws, and rituals—mainly as illustrations of philosophical ideas or theological beliefs.

In one sense, allegorical explanations are less problematic than symbolic ones. Of the five abovementioned problems applying to structural explanations, the first two (universal structure and priority of mind over ritual) need not be applicable to allegory, since allegory can do without universal claims. Not everyone can see and understand. Rather, it is only the wise who are able to explicate the true meaning hidden in stories and prescriptions alike. Although allegory in one sense is all about thought, it

---

36. For further examples and a discussion of Philo's allegorization of purity laws, see Neusner 1973, 44–50.

is not concerned with historical levels of the text and has no need to claim that it represents the cause or rationale for the rituals it interprets.

Theological symbolism, however, becomes more vulnerable to all of the criticisms that also apply to structuralism. If a ritual is to be understood as an object lesson, conveying an intrinsic theological message, we should expect the symbolism to be innate, or at least intended, from the time of the text's, or even the ritual's, origin. This presupposes that the meaning can be universally understood and requires theology to precede practice. To a certain degree, theological explanations need to be acontextual and ahistorical.[37]

To what extent is theological symbolism, just like philosophical allegory, speculative and arbitrary? The fact that different scholars come up with different versions of symbolic interpretations of purity and impurity must not be allowed to discredit symbolism. Conflicting interpretations are often just a sign of scholarly activity. The question to be asked is whether a symbolic explanation of a conception of impurity or a purity practice is indicated in the texts in question. Without textual indications, we need plausible arguments on other (contextual) grounds for this symbolic interpretation being assumed and taken for granted in a particular text. In their absence, symbolic explanations may very well be tantamount to arbitrary speculation.

This is precisely what makes the symbolism utilized by a number of modern scholars flawed. The priestly texts never or rarely provide a rationale for their rituals in general and purity laws in particular.[38] Milgrom's understanding of purity and impurity as always relating to life and death is not, it could be argued, confirmed by the texts but imposed on them. Although death can be associated with skin disease and pathological discharges, it is less than obvious that food avoidances, contact contagion, menstruation, semen emission, and childbirth all belong to the same grand schema. Others have tried to emend or supplement Milgrom's explanation, by adding controllability (Eilberg-Schwartz), or by giving sex a major role, either as part of the distinction between the human and the divine (Wright), or as characteristic of a major class of impurities (Feinstein).[39]

---

37. A divine author can of course be assumed to have injected further meaning into a text for the benefit of much later readers, but explanations based on such presuppositions move way beyond the domain of scholarly analysis.

38. See Lemos 2013 for an extended discussion of the following examples.

39. Eilberg-Schwartz 1990, 177–216, esp. 186–89; Wright 1992; Feinstein 2014.

The last example has the advantage of breaking up the neat divide between ritual and moral impurity suggested by Klawans, or the somewhat similar categories of pollution beliefs and danger beliefs (Frymer-Kensky), or tolerated and prohibited impurities (Wright).[40] Sex, however, cannot take the place of death as a global symbolic framework for purity practices and conceptions of impurity, and the combination of sex and death would seem anachronistically Freudian. Apart from that, universal explanations that need too many emendations to fit the evidence, or that are broad enough to embrace almost anything, eventually lose their explanatory value.

The later Douglas does not stay within general symbolic frameworks. Recanting from some of her earlier positions, at least with regard to Israelite religion, Douglas finds Leviticus occupied with implicit theology rather than with society.[41] Hence the purity rules indicate theological messages rather than social distinctions. They simply become object lessons about God and God's dealings with human beings and the world.[42] James Watts and Lemos have both delivered pointed critiques against Douglas's new explanations. Says Watts about *Leviticus as Literature* (1999): "Her analysis of Leviticus provides a rather extreme example of mixing textual meaning and ritual significance and folding both into a theological superstructure provided by the interpreter."[43]

Douglas's interpretations include a master analogy between Sinai and the tabernacle, and between both and the bodies of sacrifices and human Israelites. This is made possible through an arbitrary use of parallels, a random selection of elements, and an idiosyncratic structuring of Leviticus.[44] Watts also criticizes Douglas for her claim that the underlying concern of the food laws are animal protection, based on the impossibility (as she thinks) for a kind God to create abominable creatures.[45]

One of the results of Douglas's new theological reading is a blind eye toward the social effects of purity practices and purification rituals, especially in terms of power and hierarchy, which both Watts and Lemos

---

40. Klawans 2000; Frymer-Kensky 1983; Wright 1991.
41. Douglas 1999.
42. Douglas 1999, 39. Cf. impurity symbolizing humanity's exclusion from the divine presence in Trevaskis 2011.
43. Watts 2007, 17.
44. Watts 2007, 20–22.
45. Douglas 1999, 11; Watts 2007, 22–24.

have pointed out.[46] Lemos notes how Douglas's theological—and at times apologetic—perspective causes her to downplay and explain away inconvenient evidence, such as the attitude toward people with skin disease.[47] Douglas somehow turns these rules into something not so harsh for ordinary people that rather fell especially hard on the priests and prevented them from exploiting the laity: they are explained as "part of a system of control applied against them."[48]

A similar combination of theological and apologetic tendencies can be found in Klawans's work. Klawans mainly develops his symbolism in relation to sacrificial ritual, but in constant company with purity.[49] He thinks symbolic meaning can be argued from texts on a case-to-case basis.[50] Although he criticizes Douglas's "ubiquitous symbolism" for finding symbols everywhere, and Milgrom's "selective symbolism" for lacking criteria to do the selection, Klawans himself seems to argue for a merging of ritual and symbol of sorts, based on the symbolic actions of the prophets.[51] It is, however, altogether unclear how the mere fact that ancient Israelites were capable of symbolic thinking contributes to an interpretation of priestly ritual, such as sacrifice or purification.[52] Philo is an example of an extreme capacity in that regard, as William Gilders notes when he critiques Klawans for drawing a straight line between prophetic symbolic actions, for which interpretations are provided, and symbolic interpretations of priestly rituals, for which there are no clues in the texts.[53]

Gilders strongly criticizes Klawans's symbolic approach and argues with Dan Sperber that although the "attribution of sense is an essential aspect of symbolic development in *our* culture," this does not necessarily apply globally.[54] Gilders argues that symbolic meaning is contextual and conventional, not inherent.[55] In one sense only is symbolic meaning

---

46. Watts 2007, 26–27; Lemos 2009, 244–45.
47. Lemos 2009, 241–42.
48. Douglas 1996, 97–101, here 191.
49. Klawans 2006.
50. Klawans 2011, 106–22.
51. Klawans 2008, 85–90.
52. Cf. Gilders 2013, 10–11.
53. Gilders 2011, 102.
54. Gilders 2013, 7; Sperber 1975, 83.
55. Gilders 2013, 11–12. Gilders exemplifies with the Sukkot Festival, which is given a different interpretation in the text (Lev 23:42–43) from the one which scholars usually ascribe to it.

3. Levels of Explanation for Ideas of Impurity

inherent in ritual, says Gilders, in that ritual, just like all other cultural practices, is "the object of various types of meaning-making."[56] "The point, in short, is that we cannot assume that a ritual action will communicate some concept unless we first know what the concept is. The communication does not take place apart from the specific interpretation of the act."[57]

In spite of strong criticisms, the game is not over. Symbolic and theological explanations of purity practices continue to be popular. In a fairly recent article, Nicole Ruane argues that the pig is impure because it is multiparous. Leaning on Eilberg-Schwartz's claim that "rituals can be interpreted as acting out or living out the implications of those metaphors which dominate Israelite thought," Ruane suggests that pigs represent uncontrolled female fertility and offspring with multiple fathers.[58] Although "not stated clearly in the texts of Deut 14 or Lev 11," this makes them "inappropriate models for human reproduction."[59]

The presuppositions are clearly structuralist and symbolic: pigs are employed as object lessons to express social values by being prohibited to eat. Ruane furthermore argues that no clean animals are multiparous (although she later acknowledges that many do give birth to two) and that multiparous animals lack an identifiable firstborn to be offered. Borderline cases are said to have multiple but moderate offspring. (The camel, however, then becomes anomalous as an unclean animal by only giving birth to one.) Had the pig been clean, it would have been impossible to pick out the firstborn for sacrifice. This is argued with reference to discussions in the Babylonian Talmud about human twins. Hence pigs are "very poor animals with which to 'think' positively about lineage, social organization, and wealth management."[60]

Ruane boosts her speculations with Hittite evidence for associations between the fertility of pigs and the land, as well as Greek and Anatolian fertility rites, but from a historical point of view, the disparate pieces of evidence appealed to prove next to nothing. After further hypothesizing, she concludes that "the image of the pig challenges the form of controlled and restrained fertility imagined in the Bible."[61]

---

56. Gilders 2013, 18.
57. Gilders 2013, 18.
58. Eilberg-Schwartz 1990, 121; Ruane 2015.
59. Ruane 2015, 491.
60. Ruane 2015, 500.
61. Ruane 2015, 502.

Ruane's explanation of the ritual impurity of the pig is an outstanding example of structuralist, symbolist, and theological interpretation, and it displays nearly every conceivable problem in these approaches. The priority of thought over behavior is obvious.

> To eat pigs ... could be thought to invoke a principle of uncontrolled fertility or even the female power of fertility in contradiction to male power over it. It would simultaneously offend the biblical deity as well as the patrilineal system illustrated in the firstborn ritual. In that case, to shun the pig is to reject the construction of female-centered fertility as seen in multiparous animals and to embrace the biblical construction of fertility, which is controlled by males in both theology and social structure.[62]

To be fair to Ruane, in her conclusion she does allow for the pattern she discerns to be either "by design or by happenstance,"[63] thus opening for at least the possibility of no intent behind her construal. This does not, however, make her case more convincing. Although it would perhaps be *possible* to ascribe all of the named values and associations to pig eating, the key questions are who would do that, when, where, and why? Whether endeavors like Ruane's count as explanations for anything depends on how those four questions are answered.

Intention and Effect

It is not self-evident that ritual needs to have *meaning* in the conventional sense. While structuralism is often used to claim that rituals reflect and reveal particular meanings associated with, or even intended by, the cognitive structures from which they emanate, there is a different take. As we saw above, structuralists generally do not ascribe meaning to the elementary units, only to their combination. For Frits Staal, there is no semantic value in ritual at all—it has no meaning—only syntactical pattern. While rituals can be *invested* with meaning, this is not necessarily their *purpose*. The patterns, however, can function as signifiers or indices, to structure social roles, relationships, and hierarchies.[64]

---

62. Ruane 2015, 503–4.
63. Ruane 2015, 504.
64. Meshel 2014, 13–17; Watts 2007, 9; Staal 1979.

3. Levels of Explanation for Ideas of Impurity

The relationship between purpose, or intention, and result, or effect, is crucial in explaining ritual. A meal can have the effect of indicating a number of social relationships and hierarchies, but also the simple effect of providing a number of people with food. Both may be called functions, but the degree of purpose, or intention, might vary. Manners and circumstances might signify a number of details about status and organization, but whether such details have explanatory value depends largely on the questions being asked.

In the list of explanatory levels above, the fifth focuses on social, economic, and hierarchical consequences of purity practices. Impurity has frequently been understood to indicate social status. An impure person does not have full access to a number of social relationships. If we generalize the effects of the priestly laws and their further developments in the late Second Temple period, this becomes clear. People impure with long-term impurities cannot approach the temple. People with one-day impurities need at least an immersion before approaching holy space or touching sacred food. People with skin disease are barred from towns and from their own homes, including physical contact with others. People with genital discharges of various kinds are surrounded by restrictions, even though there is a debate about the extent and consequences of such restrictions. People following stricter norms of food purity are unable to share meals with those whose practices are less elaborate.[65] Such consequences of practicing purity can easily feed into existing social structures and value systems (ideologies, theologies) and probably also influence them. Noticing such *effects*, however, does not mean that these rules were crafted or shaped *in order to* have those effects. Even so, at a given point in time and in a specific context, particular people may exploit certain practices and rules precisely for those effects, with various degrees of conscious intention. This is just as complicated as we would expect any interaction between human behavior, social norms, and historical development to be.

Two categories stand out for which scholars have suggested that purity rules had negative and discriminatory effects: women and sinners.[66] Some have argued that the priestly purity system was especially disadvantageous

---

65. Discussions of the practice of priestly purity laws during the Second Temple period are numerous; see, e.g., Poirier 2003; Haber 2008; Kazen 2010c; 2016.

66. For sinners, see Blomberg 2005 and the criticisms of Crossley 2015, 96–133; For women, see discussion and references in Haber 2008, 125–41; Kazen 2010c, 91–111; 2010a, 127–64; Wassén 2008.

to women, because discharge impurity hit them harder than men. Women were impure for a long period after childbirth (Lev 12:1–5) and one week each month while menstruating (Lev 15:19–24). Moreover, childbirth impurity was longer at the birth of a girl (eighty days) than a boy (forty days). Men, on the other hand, were only impure one day after semen emission (Lev 15:16). Both men and women were continuously impure when having lasting (pathological) discharges (hemorrhage; gonorrhea) (Lev 15:2–3, 25), and both incurred a one-day impurity after intercourse (Lev 15:18).

The priestly legislation on genital discharges in Lev 15 incorporates several practices with diverse prehistories and systematizes them.[67] Some of these underlying practices may have carried misogynist connotations at an earlier stage, and others not. However, the general idea of genital discharges being impure seems quite gender neutral, and the priestly authors go to great pains to achieve a formal literary symmetry between male and female discharges in Lev 15.[68] The asymmetry between the length of impurity at ejaculation (one day) and menstruation (seven days) may possibly be accounted for by differences in duration, although this suggestion is somewhat speculative. The *effect*, however, is more severe for women than for men. Childbirth impurity (Lev 12) is another issue. It probably has different origins, but is integrated into the purity laws by the priestly authors.[69]

Biblical scholars are often accused of confounding ritual purity and morality to the extent that sin and disease are associated with impurity. Disease in general never seems to have been considered impure in Israel, and the simple identification of the sick and the sinner with the ritually impure is a misunderstanding. But although one must strongly resist the blurring of these concepts, one also has to admit the way in which purity language and concepts of impurity were extended and employed in relation to gentiles in general and certain moral behaviors in particular, which made purity a relevant factor for group identity and ingroup behavior

---

67. Kazen 2010c, 41–61.
68. Cf. Ellens 2008, 47–72; Hieke 2014, 526–47.
69. The parturient rules (Lev 12) are clearly dependent on and assume the general discharge laws (Lev 15), although they precede them in the literary structure. It is common to regard them as being added to the collection of purity laws somewhat later than the discharge laws. Some of their details indicate formation in the Persian period. See further Kazen 2015b, 453–54.

toward outgroup, exemplified in various types of segregation and ostracism.[70]

To point out the relationship between certain conceptions of impurity, or purity practices, and such effects (level 5) is not necessarily to suggest that these effects are intended. Certain purity practices at a given time and in a specific context may result in a particular type of discrimination, indication of status, economic stratification, or segregation and ostracism. These effects may be unintentional. But any effects will inevitably correlate with all other values and practices that operate in the social context in question. Purity practices may therefore function to reinforce certain behaviors, structures, and ideologies in a society without this being their *meaning*. This is true even when individuals or groups of people consciously employ or exploit purity practices for such purposes, or ascribe such meaning to them.

The question of purpose or intention turns out a bit differently when we turn our attention to the formative stage of the priestly purity rules. At some point in the Persian period when the Second Temple cult became established, the purity laws of Lev 11–15 were shaped and systematized, based on traditional avoidance behaviors and possibly also on some earlier written sources, although this is uncertain. In addition to customary practices and conceptions, the priestly authors may have added their own inventions, or at least practices and conceptions that had evolved or been influenced by contact with Babylonian and Persian culture and religion. All this material was shaped and systematized from a priestly perspective and ideology.[71] The main corpse impurity rules (Num 19) were added fairly late in the process and reflect further developments.[72]

Regardless of the previous history of the purity practices collected and systematized by the priests, we would expect their own values and interests to have influenced the texts. This is the issue at the fourth level of explanation above. Here, purpose or intention rightly comes into focus. What did the priestly authors wish to achieve, collecting and elaborating on earlier traditions, authoring and redacting these texts? Such questions need to be answered based on social, political, and economic considerations relevant to the fifth-century BCE vassal state Yehud within the context of impe-

---

70. Cf. Hayes 2002. The Ezra-Nehemiah narrative provides one particular example; cf. Olyan 2004.
71. Cf. Nihan 2007, 269–394, 608–19.
72. Nihan 2007, 554–55, 570–72; Achenbach 2009; Frevel 2013.

rial Persia. This context also and especially includes the need for (re)establishing an independent cult and asserting central religious and political authority in a fragmented region.[73] Aspects of social identity and postcolonial theory need to be taken into account for interpreting intention as well as function of the priestly purity laws. Some of the food laws, for example, can be explained as negotiating Persian and indigenous practices, while creating a distinctly national character. Some particulars of the contagion laws can be understood in view of the emerging temple and its holiness.[74]

However, we must not assume that every law was consciously shaped for explicit political or ideological purposes. At this stage, too, much of what these laws reflect could result from unconscious or subconscious processes. To be more precise, the particular social and political situation would inevitably influence the shape of these laws, and the social position of the priestly authors at the top of the temple state hierarchy would have significance for how the purity laws were presented.

Explanations at the fourth level would thus move along a scale between conscious purpose and contextual effect. They could also move along a scale between strong and weak causative links. We may suggest the shape of the priestly purity laws as *caused* by a number of contextual factors or, more weakly, as *reasonably understandable* against their particular social, political, and ideological background.

Evolutionary and Biopsychological Explanations

If we seek explanations for how and why conceptions of impurity have evolved in the first place, we need to turn our attention to evolutionary biology and psychology. One of the trickiest issues in research on purity is the variety of phenomena for which purity language is used. The Hebrew Bible employs the same or similar terminology for certain bodily conditions, for contact contagion, for food avoidances, for certain immoral behaviors, for idol worship, and for intermarriage.[75] The debate about how to solve this

---

73. Cf. Berquist 2006.
74. Cf. Kazen 2015b, 459–62.
75. Bodily conditions, cf. Lev 12–15; contact contagion, cf. Lev 11:8, 11, 24–40; 12:4; 13:1–46 (assumed from isolation, expulsion, and rituals of integration; cf. 13:45–46; 14:2–9); 14:36, 46; 15:4–12, 19–24, 26–27; 21:1–4, 11; Num 5:2–4 (assumed from expulsion); Num 19:13–16, 21–22; food avoidances, cf. Lev 11; immoral behavior, cf. Lev 18; 20; Num 35:33–34; Ps 106:34–41 (for further references, see Klawans 2000);

3. Levels of Explanation for Ideas of Impurity 71

conundrum is century-old and has mostly focused on attempts to separate "ritual" from "moral" impurity and how to understand impurity as a metaphor. Since I have discussed these issues extensively elsewhere I will not go into them further, except reminding of the unsatisfactory nature of most attempts to find a solution.[76]

The association of impurity with loathing has long been noticed.[77] It is conspicuous that disgust is expressed in relation to all the main areas in which purity language is being used. This indicates the possibility of emotional disgust as an underlying reason, not for each specific instance of impurity, but for general conceptions.[78]

Disgust as a primary emotion is a direct bodily response to repulsive stimuli, usually experienced through taste, smell, or touch. It is basically a survival mechanism that evolved to protect living beings from inhaling, digesting, or contacting unhealthy, toxic, or other dangerous substances. From this innate, ultimate base, a set of secondary emotions have evolved within a social framework and parallel with culture. As a result, there are levels of disgust that basically rest on cultural or proximate bases, although these can never be fully separated from their biological underpinnings. As a secondary emotion, disgust can be triggered by sight, memory, or thought, without direct engagement of other senses.[79]

Looking at conceptions of impurity in biblical legal texts, particularly the priestly purity laws and the Holiness Code (Lev 11–15; 17–26; Num 19), all main categories (food, bodily contagion, immorality) can be related to the nine disgust triggers identified and demonstrated in Paul Rozin's well-known empirical research.[80] These are food, body products, animals, sexual behaviors, contact with death or corpses, violations of the exterior body envelope (including gore and deformity), poor hygiene, interpersonal contamination (contact with unsavory human beings), and certain moral offenses. Particular reactions toward these triggers are of course learned through socialization, but they all depend on underlying biological conditions.

---

idol worship, cf. Ezek 16; 22–23; 36; intermarriage, cf. Ezra 9–10; Neh 9:2; 10:30; 13:23–30 (for further discussion, see Hayes 2002).
    76. Cf. Klawans 2000; Lemos 2013; Kazen 2014.
    77. Neusner 1973, 11–12.
    78. Kazen 2008; 2011, 33–36, 71–94; 2017.
    79. Preston and de Waal 2002; Haidt 2003; Curtis 2013, 21–40.
    80. Rozin, Haidt, and McCauley 2000.

Disgust language (*šeqeṣ*, "detestable") is used liberally in Lev 11 to characterize "swarmers": winged insect, crawly and slimy water animals, and vermin such as mice and the like. While the creation of this overarching category is a rhetorical move by the priestly authors, this is made possible because of the psychological and eventually biological substrata from which core disgust has evolved as a strategy for disease avoidance, by shunning the slimy, rotting, and decaying. The priestly authors build on the ultimate (biological) base for disgust on which archaic conceptions of impurity seem to rest, in order to create a category of unclean animals similar to the Zoroastrian evil Ahrimanian *khrafstra*.[81] However, the forbidden quadrupeds, although unclean, are not called disgusting by the priestly authors. Only in Deut 14:3 are they introduced as *tôʿēbâ*. Although there is little biological reason to feel more disgust for pigs or camels than for sheep and goats, culturally evolved or constructed food avoidances appeal to underlying associations between disgust and impurity.

The association of skin disease, genital discharges, and corpse impurity with disgust is quite easy to envisage, and there is an obvious fit with Rozin's disgust triggers. Skin disease (*ṣāraʿat*) involved scaliness, damage, and decay. Corpses and graves are associated with decaying matter. Genital discharges—especially in a world with different hygienic facilities—were both sticky and smelly. Reactions of aversion would easily be triggered by sight and smell, as well as fear, in all these cases. Cultural constraints and social constructions of impurity conceptions certainly influence what people feel, but an underlying emotional core disgust makes sense for all of the main types of bodily contagion.[82] Although disgust is rarely articulated in legal texts on contagious impurities, other texts clearly associate skin disease and genital discharges with emotional disgust, either expressly or by assumption (see Num 12:10–13; 2 Sam 3:29; Ezra 9:11; Lam 1:8–9, 17; Ezek 36:16–18). Compared to a symbolic explanation focused on death, disgust provides a more concrete, underlying explanation of why and how some basic conceptions of impurity evolved, and of the ultimate, biological foundation on which culturally construed conceptions of impurity rest. Death may still have a role to play in this game, but then in a concrete rather than symbolic sense, as the object of fear for which disgust—and

---

81. Kazen 2014, 70–72, 83–85; 2015b, 457–59.
82. Kazen 2008, 54–61; 2011, 71–94.

hence impurity—has evolved as a survival strategy.[83] This, however, is not what proponents of the seventh level of explanation argue for.

Just as in the case of the camel compared to the goat, emotional core disgust does not explain every culturally construed elaboration or extension of conceptions of impurity as bodily contagion. There is little biological reason for why anyone should regard marital sex as defiling, and nowhere in Israelite thought are mothers understood to be repulsive. Similarly, the branding of various types of norm-breaking sexual behavior and worship of foreign gods as impure and disgusting, particularly found in the Holiness Code and in prophetic literature, and often cited as examples of moral impurity, can only partially be explained on a biopsychological level.[84] On the one hand, disgust language is replete in both legal and prophetic denunciations of these behaviors and often juxtaposed to purity language. The capacity to feel aversion toward certain behaviors rests on evolutionary and biological underpinnings. On the other hand, impurity language is clearly used rhetorically to evoke aversion against a number of behaviors that hardly trigger primary disgust, but are rejected because of cultural constraints.

Evolutionary and biopsychological explanations, belonging to the first of our proposed levels, do not claim to explain the details of such cultural constructions, nor do they attempt to explain their social function or rhetorical purpose and effect. Such explanations must be sought on the second and third levels of explanation that we have outlined.

Historical and Contextual Explanations

As noted, every conception of impurity has a proximate, cultural base, which is to a certain extent inseparable from its evolutionary, biological underpinnings, but also to some degree possible to identify and analyze. Many food avoidances—the pig in particular—are contextual in origin. The impurity ascribed to the pig by the priestly authors (Lev 11:7) can be understood as resulting from a fusion of historical and ecological reasons for pig avoidance and biopsychological underlying aversions against certain other creatures, with the ultimate function to protect organisms against disease.

---

83. For an initial discussion about the relationship between fear and disgust in relation to purity conceptions, see Kazen 2010c, 24–25; 2011, 115–29.

84. Kazen 2014, 85–91.

The creation of a broad category of "swarmers" (Lev 11:9–12, 20–23, 29–38, 41–44) is plausible as a response to Persian (Zoroastrian) categorizations and practices, as already indicated. The diagnosis of some variants of skin disease (Lev 13:2–44) can be understood as the result of historical attempts to systematize and categorize disparate practices and conceptions. This probably applies to genital discharges as well, including an understanding of semen and sex in general as defiling (Lev 15).

The degree of detail that can be attested for the preexilic period is relatively basic, and the priestly purity laws contain numerous elaborations that represent various stages of historical development.[85] Some of these are probably impossible to trace, while others can to some extent be retrieved.

Purity practices concerning new mothers (Lev 12) present an interesting example of how conceptions of discharge impurity were extended and further elaborated under the influence of historical circumstances, again Persian (Zoroastrian) conceptions.[86] Various purificatory rites evolved through history and were shaped contextually. The development of various types of water rites presents another particularly interesting example. The issues include the evolution of sprinkling in contrast to ablution or immersion, the combination of the two rites, and the introduction and development of stepped pools for purification in water (in rabbinic terminology, *miqwā'ôt*) as an alternative to purification in running water.[87]

Historical explanations belonging to the second level in our schema neither try to provide a solution to the ultimate origins for conceptions of impurity nor claim to reveal the social effects of purity systems. They do, however, attempt to understand how and possibly why certain practices and conceptions developed in certain ways and in specific contexts during particular periods of history.

Cognitive-Linguistic Explanations

The final level of explanation to be discussed in this essay—the third—is rarely explored. Cognitive-linguistic explanations consider the relevance of conceptual metaphor and conceptual blending theories for understanding the rhetorical use and impact of purity language. While evolutionary

---

85. Kazen 2015b.
86. Kazen 2015b, 448, 453–54; 2014, 73, 85–87.
87. On the combination of the two rites, see Kazen 2010b. For recent discussions about the development of the *miqweh*, see Miller 2015; Adler 2016; 2018.

and biopsychological explanations explore the ultimate underpinnings of conceptions of impurity and their association with emotional core disgust, and contextual explanations attempt to reconstruct some of the historical lines of development along which purity practices and purification rites evolve and become more elaborate, detailed, and diversified, cognitive-linguistic explanations are useful for understanding the conceptual mechanisms that make purity and impurity into such an overarching and influential paradigm, especially in Second Temple Judaism.

While so-called moral impurity has usually been understood as a metaphorical extension, in contrast to ritual impurity, resulting in unconvincing categorizations, cognitive-linguistic explanations allow for more nuanced and sophisticated understandings of how and why purity language is extended to new categories and new areas. Since I have discussed this at greater length elsewhere,[88] I will only provide a brief outline here.

First, all conceptions of impurity and every use of purity language in ancient Israelite texts must be considered secondary or metaphorical to a certain extent. The Hebrew word for impure/impurity (*ṭāmēʾ*, *ṭumʾâ*) and its ancient West Asian cognates suggest a very concrete root meaning: dirt.[89] Only with gore, pus, or genital discharge do we come close to the concrete (literal) meaning. Any other use of impurity language is inevitably metaphorical. This means that most of what we usually call ritual impurity represents a metaphorical use of language.[90]

Second, such a use of purity language can be employed almost intuitively for items, animals, foods, persons, situations, or behaviors that easily evoke revulsion—culturally construed, to be sure, but biologically based.

Third, this metaphorical use of purity language can also be employed rhetorically, whether with studied purpose or rather innocently, in order/with the effect to extend the realm of impurity and the aversions associated with it to other items, animals, foods, persons, situations, or behaviors, which are disapproved of or rejected for various reasons.

Conceptual metaphor theory applied to the use of purity language suggests that impurity, which belongs to the concrete source domain of dirt, is used metaphorically in a variety of target domains. The effect of this cross-domain mapping is that the metaphor impurity carries with it notions from its source domain (dirt) to its various target domains,

---

88. Kazen 2014; 2017.
89. André and Ringgren 1986, 330; Feinstein 2010, 51.
90. Cf. Kazen 2014, 67–68.

which influences the ways in which we think about the target domains and relate to them. Three such target domains are the main categories for which impurity language is used in priestly texts: disgusting creatures (food avoidances), disgusting people (unsavory human diseases or situations), and disgusting acts (objectionable behavior). The manner in which purity language is being mapped onto these three target domains is quite similar, in spite of diversity in content. A notion of physical dirt and deep emotional revulsion against physical contamination is carried over from the source domain and influences the way in which the target domains are conceived of and experienced. This has effects on the attitudes and behavior of those involved in this mapping toward animals and people represented by the various target domains.[91]

Conceptual blending theory makes it possible to explain some of the more sophisticated mechanisms involved when purity language is used secondarily in new domains, and is particularly helpful for those instances in which impurity conceptions are expanded, or used in unusual or unexpected circumstances. Some details are better understood as blending rather than as one-way mapping processes. Blending theory works with conceptual spaces. These are frames within which images or mental representations function and form a network. In a blending process, input spaces with certain elements in common (a generic space) provide other elements that do not necessarily fit together to begin with into a blended space. The results may be something that is neither inherent in any of the input spaces, nor indicated by the generic space (common elements) that makes a blending of the two (or more) input spaces possible to begin with. This process results in new conceptual frameworks and new meaning, which also influences behavior.[92]

Contact with dirt and contact with certain unsavory people (cf. Lev 13–15) can be understood as two such input spaces that share avoidance and aversion, but little else. In a conceptual blend, such people are envisaged as "impure" and their impurity as contagious (it "sticks"!), to be removed by water. In a further step (cf. Ps 51), a blend between contact contamination, disapproved ("sinful") behavior, and dirty laundry (again sharing avoidance and aversion) envisages certain sexual behaviors as impure stains on one's inner being, in need of removal by water and

---

91. Kazen 2014, 77–80. Cf. Lakoff and Johnson 1980a; 1980b; 1999.
92. Fauconnier and Turner 2002, 17–57; Coulson and Oakley 2000.

hyssop. The impurity of the pig (cf. Lev 11), discussed above, may likewise be explained as the result of a conceptual blend in which input spaces related to food avoidances, but for quite different reasons, provide notions of impurity and disgust, originating with vermin, or with slimy and rotting creatures, to pork. Purity practices and rituals of purification relating to new mothers (cf. Lev 12), or to ordinary sexual intercourse (cf. Lev 15:17), may be understood as resulting from blends between spaces that have genital fluids in common, and therefore may be combined, although they concern phenomena that differ considerably in other regards.[93]

Conceptual blending is particularly useful to explain the processes through which some of the more complicated construals of behaviors and people as impure and repulsive take place, such as describing idolatry as bloodshed and menstrual blood (Ezek 36), child sacrifice as adultery and prostitution (Ezek 23), or non-Israelites as impure and intermarriage as illegitimate mixing of holy seed (Ezra 6:21; 9:2, 10–14). Conceptualizing—and hence labeling—a diversity of disapproved behaviors as impure definitely has a rhetorical function, whether or not this is a consciously deliberate strategy.[94]

There is no room to elaborate any further on the details, but these examples show that cognitive metaphor theories provide explanations for the growth of conceptions of impurity beyond their primary domains and for the extended, emotional, and rhetorical use of purity language. This level of explanation thus ties together the first two (evolutionary and biopsychological; historical and contextual) with the fourth and fifth levels (shaping and systematizing; results and functions).

What Explanations Do

We have discussed seven levels of explanation for conceptions of impurity and purity practices, found in scholarly discussions of purity in ancient Israel and early Judaism. The schema I have suggested may be construed and delimited differently. However, I hope that it has served as a helpful reminder that we often mean very different things when we try to explain.

---

93. Kazen 2014, 80–91.
94. Cf. Kazen 2014, 71, 80, 88–91; 2017, 109–14. Cf. Himmelfarb 2001. With regard to Qumran, Himmelfarb (37) concludes that "the association of sin and impurity in 1QS and 4Q512, and perhaps at Qumran altogether, was primarily evocative rather than halakhic."

Explanations help us understand, or at least envisage, how things are interrelated. All of the explanations outlined in this article have similar effects: they create pictures in which conceptions of impurity, purity practices, purification rites, and the use of purity language are connected and interrelated to biological, emotional, historical, social, political, ideological, or theological issues.

I have claimed that structuralist and symbolic models often fail. This is a strong claim, and to some degree false, since such explanations do establish connections. The question is to what extent those connections correspond with that which can be reasonably argued to take place in the world of the text, in the historical, social, and political world behind the text, in the ideological world of the ancient authors, or in the biopsychological world of human beings at large. Structuralist and symbolic explanations sometimes do establish meaningful connections on a *certain level of reception*. Some symbolic and theological models appear fairly early among ancient users of these texts. Others appear much later, in particular explanations of the structuralist type, and certain modern theological construals. Some of these explanations satisfy their inventors, but have little foothold in the past to be studied. Rather, they represent the interests of their originators and are pressed onto texts and social history as prefabricated models.

Evolutionary, contextual, and cognitive models, on the other hand, do not try to provide ideological superstructures. Their explanations focus on the necessary prerequisites for purity conceptions to evolve, on the historical and social circumstances that contribute to the development and shape of purity practices and purification rites, and on the conceptual conditions under which purity and impurity influence thought and behavior, including use of language and rhetorical function or effect. Such explanations are based on history, but their explanatory value is not limited to the historical. By integrating evolutionary, biological, psychological, historical, and linguistic perspectives, the first three levels of explanation (1–3) in our suggested schema lay the groundwork for the following two (4–5), and serve as a corrective for the structuralist and symbolic levels (6–7). In view of this, these last two explanatory models will need thoroughgoing revision and rethinking if they are going to be at all useful in the future for any wider explanatory purposes other than satisfying the imagination of their devotees.

4
Purity and Persia

> This chapter explores possible influences from Persian (Zoroastrian) practices on biblical purity laws (Leviticus and Numbers). The latter are compared on the one hand to traces of preexilic purity practices in the Deuteronomistic History, and on the other hand to Zoroastrian practices as reflected primarily in Vendidād. Special attention is given to those instances in which priestly purity regulations become detailed and specific. It is argued that some of these instances are pointers to recent developments and elaborations during the Achaemenid era, which go beyond previous practices in being influenced by Persian culture. Broad explanations for this process are indicated, including sociopolitical and religious factors, group-identity concerns, and postcolonial concepts, such as hybridity and mimicry.

In the introduction to his monumental commentary on Leviticus, Jacob Milgrom asserts that priestly theology negates the premises of "pagan religion," according to which deities are not supreme, but "dependent on and influenced by a metadivine realm," involving numerous entities subject to magical manipulation.[1] For this basic presupposition Milgrom refers to Yehezkel Kaufmann, and as part of what is sometimes called the Kaufmann school, he views Israelite religion and cult as thoroughly purged from the demonic; "the world of demons is abolished."[2] Although to some extent apologetic in its defense of the uniqueness of Israelite reli-

---

This chapter was first published in *Current Issues in Priestly and Related Literature: The Legacy of Jacob Milgrom and Beyond*, ed. Roy E. Gane and Ada Taggar-Cohen, RBS 82 (Atlanta: SBL Press, 2015), 435–62. Used by permission. Only minor corrections have been made.

1. Milgrom 1991, 42–43.

2. Milgrom 1991, 43. Compare Milgrom (42–51) on priestly theology with Kaufmann 1960, 21–121.

gion, this basic understanding does acknowledge the common ancient West Asian cultural and religious roots of a number of ritual practices and conceptions, including demonic beliefs behind ideas of impurity, and apotropaic purposes behind purificatory and sacrificial rites. The Priestly source is then seen to have removed all such traits, based on a thoroughly monotheistic outlook.

Hence Milgrom, following Kaufmann, endorses a comparative approach to Israelite religion and points to numerous ancient West Asian parallels as useful in analyzing and interpreting Israelite cult and purity rules. He goes further than Kaufmann in providing the reader with concrete comparative materials,[3] and although the interpretation of singular details could be discussed, there can be no serious doubt about the general tendency. Israel's conceptions of impurity and practices of purification bear many resemblances to those of its neighbors and have a similar conceptual background.

Dating the Texts

The question is which neighbors to blame most for the priestly purity "system"? Comparative material of a general character can be appealed to from Sumer to Rome, but the priestly conception and ritual maintenance of purity is a very specific one. To what extent does this purity system go back in time to Israel's early roots and common ancient practices and perceptions, and to what extent can we trace more specific influences at a particular point in time?

For such questions to be asked and answered, the dating of the priestly texts becomes crucial. Milgrom accepted and developed Israel Knohl's observations concerning the relationship between the Holiness source and the Priestly source.[4] Since then it has become quite common to follow Milgrom in understanding a Holiness source to have added the Holiness Code (Lev 17–26) to the first half of Leviticus and to have complemented priestly material, as well as other parts of the Pentateuch.[5] It has also become increasingly common, especially in Europe, to date the basic

---

3. Milgrom 1991, 763–68, 834–35, 948–53, 957–63, 976–79, 1067–84; cf. Kaufmann 1960, 101–21, 291–316.

4. Knohl 1995; Milgrom 1991, 3–42; 2000, 1319–64.

5. Milgrom (1991, 61–63; 2000, 1322–44; 2001, 2054–56) assigns the following parts of Leviticus to H: 3:16b–17; 6:12–18aα; 7:22–29a, 38b(?); 9:17b; 11:43–45; 12:8;

Priestly source narrative no earlier than the exile, and much of Priestly source law, as well as the Holiness source, to the Persian period, which is much later than Knohl and Milgrom maintain.[6] Knohl dates the Holiness source to the reign of Ahaz, with the Priestly source earlier than this, and Milgrom sees almost all of the Holiness source as preexilic, dating the Priestly source to the time of the Shiloh sanctuary.[7] For most scholars today, this is far too early, even for those who still regard the Holiness Code as the earliest part and origin of Leviticus.[8]

Recent research suggests that contacts and interactions in the ancient world caused transformations in the dynamics of purity conceptions from the Achaemenid period onward.[9] Considering a Persian-period dating for the priestly material on cult and purity, we would expect a comparison of detailed points to provide suggestive evidence. In this chapter, I will employ Milgrom's comparative approach, while considering a late dating of the relevant texts. I will not discuss dating issues in more detail, as there is no room for this; it has been aptly done by others. Although arguments for an earlier dating of parts of the Priestly source certainly can be made, a Persian-period dating for the final redaction of the Pentateuch, including much of the priestly legislation, has become a majority opinion in European research.[10]

Exploring the consequences of a fairly late dating of the relevant priestly material for interpreting ideas of impurity and their development, I will suggest that conceptions of purity and impurity in Leviticus and Numbers may owe more to Persian influence and a Persian-period

---

14:34–53(?), 54–57(?); 15:31; 16:2bβ, 29–34a; chs. 17–27. Knohl (1995) has minor variations. Cf. Nihan 2004; 2007, 395–575; Nihan and Römer 2004.

6. See, e.g., de Pury 2007; cf. Levine 2003, 15. For an overview of research history, see Nihan 2007, 4–11. Cf. Kazen 2011, 64–70. Dating P and H to the Persian period assumes H's dependence on D. For arguments, see already Cholewinski 1976, 334–44. Cf. Nihan 2004.

7. Milgrom 1991, 34; Knohl 1995, 204–24. Knohl (226), however, sees H as a continuous movement, redacting the Pentateuch into the Persian era.

8. E.g., Levine 2003; Kratz 2005, 110–11.

9. Frevel and Nihan 2013, 40–43.

10. Cf. Kratz 2005; Nihan 2007; Schmid 2012, esp. 25–30, 141–52, 176–81. An accessible overview can be found in Edelman et al. 2012, 11–50. The book presents itself as introducing studies on the Pentateuch "through a Persian lens" (quotation from the preface). For a somewhat "intermediate" position, see Wright 2012. Wright sees P and H as basically arising in the sixth century.

setting than some have previously believed. First, I will discuss the lack of firm preexilic evidence for many purity conceptions in Leviticus and Numbers, making some general suggestions as to how impurity could have been understood and handled during the royal period. Second, I will argue that certain particularities in priestly purity law could be plausibly explained as resulting from Persian influence, and that some discrepancies and developments within and between priestly texts could be explained by influence from, or adaptations to, Persian practices. Finally, I will briefly suggest how these developments could fit within the context of a Persian-period Jewish state, centered on Jerusalem.

Preexilic Purity

The lack of detailed evidence for purity practices in preexilic Israel creates a methodological problem. Conceptions of purity and impurity were part of the ancient world to such an extent that their presence in preexilic Israelite society must be assumed. The problem is exactly what to assume and on what grounds, because the relevant texts surrender so little information.

There are a few mentions of impure conditions in the Deuteronomistic History. In 1 Sam 20:26, Saul assumes that something with regard to purity has happened to David (מקרה הוא בלתי טהור הוא כי־לא טהור), since he does not turn up for the new moon feast. This could refer to an emission of semen, the impurity of which, according to Lev 15:16, lasts until evening. However, the impurity is not spelled out in 1 Sam 20. In fact, no particular term for "unclean" is used. The text assumes a condition in which it would be unsuitable or prohibited to attend a festival meal, and that condition is called "not clean" (לא טהור).[11] According to Num 10:10; 28:11–15, sacrifices were offered at the new moon festival. However, although a sacrificial meal, including some purity requirements, could have been ancient practice, the sacrificial protocol in Numbers is more likely to represent later developments.[12]

---

11. The idea of eating ordinary food in purity is found nowhere in the DtrH.

12. Achenbach 2003, 602–11. Cf. already Gray (1903, 410), who suggests that "though the sacred character of the days of new moon is ancient, the specific regulations of this law need not be." Gray reminds the reader of the fact that definite allusions to this protocol appear only in postexilic literature, and that the חטאת sacrifice required on new moons and other occasions is neither in Ezekiel's description,

4. Purity and Persia

In 2 Sam 3:29, David curses Joab for the murder of Abner: "may the house of Joab never be without one who has a discharge [זב], or who is leprous [מצרע], or who holds a spindle, or who falls by the sword, or who lacks food."[13] The זב and the מצרע are well known in the Second Temple period and represent the main categories of impurity in Lev 12–15.[14] Here in 2 Sam 3, however, they are not specified as impure, but are part of a derogatory list of possible punishments. This list is not associated with impurity, as victims of war and famine are not considered impure, and the much-contested reference to holding a spindle may possibly represent weakness or effeminate behavior.

In 2 Sam 11:4, after having been raped by David, Bathsheba is said to have been sanctifying herself from her impurity (טמאה). It is not entirely clear whether this refers to Bathsheba being in her menstrual period when David sent for her, or being envisaged as purifying herself before the intercourse, or whether this refers to her purifying after the intercourse but before returning home. The participial clause (והיא מתקדשת מטמאתה) is parenthetical and could perhaps be suspected of being a gloss with the intent of either worsening David's sin or portraying him and Bathsheba as at least respecting purity concerns. However, only the originality of the explicative "from her impurity" can be questioned textual grounds, as it is not found in 4QSam^a.[15] This text, then, does attest to an understanding of menstrual bleeding as impure and to some purification practice. If that purification is identical with the initial bathing scene on the roof (2 Sam 11:2), it would suggest purification in water, which is not explicitly demanded of the woman by Lev 15:19–24, nor does the manner of this purification correspond to later practice as we know it from the Second Temple period (in running water or a *miqweh*).[16]

---

nor part of the series of sacrifices prescribed for other festivals in Lev 23:37. On the possibility of a sacrificial meal being ancient practice, cf. Tsumura 2007, 515–16.

13. Unless otherwise noted, Scripture quotations in this chapter follow the NRSV.

14. The זב becomes paradigmatic for all dischargers. See Kazen 2010c, 41–61; 2013a, 156. Except for the formal heading תורת המצרע in Lev 14:2, Lev 13–14 does not employ מצרע to designate a person with skin disease but prefers to speak of the disease using the term צרעת.

15. Cf. McCarter 1984, 279, 286; Auld 2011, 451, 455–56. Chankin-Gould et al. (2008) argue against the participial clause referring to menstrual purification.

16. Although purification in water by the woman in Lev 15:19–24 is assumed in a systemic reading; see Kazen 2010c, 41–61. Running water as a means of purification is prescribed by Lev 15:13 for the זב and most probably assumed for the זבה. Since a

Naaman, the Syrian "leprous" commander, is healed by immersing seven times in the Jordan River. Although Naaman is repeatedly said to become clean (טהר) by washing (2 Kgs 5:10, 12, 14), the emphasis is on healing as restoration. Neither he nor Gehazi, who receives Naaman's "leprosy" (צרעת) in return for his greed, is explicitly called impure. As in David's curse, skin disease is mainly understood as a punishment or an unfortunate fate. Similarly, the four men with skin disease who discover the sudden flight of the Aramaean army (2 Kgs 7:3-20) are designated מצרעים, but they are never explicitly called unclean. Nevertheless, they are portrayed as excluded from the city, spending the night outside the gate, even under a siege. They contemplate entering the city, but instead choose the option of surrendering to the Aramaeans. In the narrative, their disease explains why they are outside the city gates, which makes possible their discovery of the Aramaean flight. Therefore, we should assume that the original audience would find it natural or necessary for מצרעים to stay out of the city, probably because of purity concerns, although the text does not specify this.

Separation or isolation is also presupposed in the narrative of King Azariah, who was struck "leprous" and had to live separately (2 Kgs 15:1-7). The Chronicler explains this by the fact that the king (here called Uzziah) was excluded from the temple (2 Chr 26:16-21), but with the Chronicler we are well into the Second Temple period and a context in which protecting the cult against impurity is crucial.

We have found that in the Deuteronomistic history, both "leprosy" and genital discharges are seen as divine punishments for misdeeds, mainly in their capacity as diseases. Separating out people with discharges and keeping those with skin disease out of settlements is well known from the ancient world, including at an early date, so the existence of such practices in preexilic Israel is not unlikely.[17]

---

spring or cistern was not considered to be defiled by a dead swarmer (Lev 11:36), a systemic reading led to the view that all immersions should take place either in spring water or in a pool of sufficient size (cf. the rabbinic requirement that such a pool should contain at least 40 *se'ah* of water; b. Eruv. 4b; b. Yoma 31a). Hence the frequent use of such pools, *miqwā'ôt*, during the Second Temple period, attested by numerous archaeological remains from all over Palestine. For references, see Kazen 2013a, 163 n. 180.

17. Milgrom (1991, 805) refers to a Babylonian *kudurru* inscription, a Mari letter (818, 911), and a Šurpu incantation (911); cf. Herodotus, *Hist.* 1.138 (Persian isolation of "lepers").

Leviticus 13–14 contains no *explicit* prohibitions against touch and no purification rituals after contact with a skin-diseased person, as in the case of discharge impurity. However, such rules are not needed because isolation and avoidance are taken for granted (13:45–46). Purification rules do apply to the reintegration of people with skin disease and are merged with sacrificial instructions. The fact that the focus lies on diagnosis and that avoidance of contact seems to be assumed, although not elaborated on, suggests that an earlier practice in which a number of things are taken for granted has been integrated into the cultic system of the Priestly source. If this reflects the situation during the early Persian period, we should expect isolation and avoidance to have been preexilic practices too. Only as צרעת rules are extended to houses and textiles (14:33–53) are such concerns for isolation and avoidance spelled out (14:46–47), indicating that extension of skin-disease categorization and rules to houses and textiles might be later, or at least secondary.[18]

In contrast to rules regarding skin disease, discharge rules (Lev 15) contain detailed instructions about contamination and washing, suggesting that all of these would not have been taken for granted at an earlier stage, but could represent later developments. A general concept of menstrual blood as impure is well attested throughout ancient history.[19] It is assumed not only in the story of Bathsheba, but also for the tongue-in-cheek polemic against idols by the author of the Jacob cycle, portraying Rachel as sitting on the household deities while menstruating (Gen 31:34–35). Furthermore, the metaphorical use of such נדה impurity to transfer the recipients' disgust against genital blood to moral and cultic misbehavior is found among the prophets (Ezek 36:17; Zech 13:1).[20] We can safely claim that נדה impurity was a preexilic concept. Pathological (continuous) bleeding would be subject to similar considerations, as Lev 15 suggests. Strangely enough, this text mentions washing in water neither for the menstruant nor for the זבה but only for those who touch their beds or clothes.[21] It is unlikely that ancient people would have envisaged purification from genital blood without washing it off, as the Bathsheba narrative suggests. In Samaritan tradition, the initial blood is considered to be

---

18. Cf. Nihan (2007, 270–77) for an overview of relevant source- and redaction-critical discussions.
19. Milgrom 1991, 763–65.
20. Cf. Kazen 2014, 62–92.
21. See further Kazen 2010c, 41–61.

the primary source of impurity.²² Also, ancient texts mention the stench associated with genital blood, which is quite likely in a premodern society lacking our hygienic facilities.²³ In Jewish tradition it was always assumed that the menstruant and the זבה had to wash as part of their purification.²⁴ This was probably taken for granted as part of general preexilic practice, with no need to mention it.²⁵

Corpse impurity is not part of the purity laws of Lev 11–15, but enters in the Holiness Code as a rule for priests (Lev 21:1–4; cf. 22:4).²⁶ Corpse-contaminated laity first appear in Num 5:2–4. They are supposed to be expelled from the "camp," together with people suffering from skin disease and those with genital discharges. Explanations of the nature and contamination of corpse impurity are only found as part of the instructions for the red-heifer rite, specifying circumstances for the use of purification water (Num 19:11–20; see also 31:19–24).

If a Persian-period dating of the Holiness Code is considered, and if the texts referred to from Numbers belong to the latest stages of pentateuchal formation, as many now suggest,²⁷ preexilic conceptions of corpse impurity cannot be based on these texts. Evidence from the Deuteronomistic History is ambiguous. In 2 Kgs 13:20–21, Elisha's bones cause miraculous resuscitation, with no indication of impurity, but in the narrative of Josiah's reform, human bones are used for defiling (טמא) the במות (23:13–14) and the altar at Bethel (23:15–16). This suggests that cultic defilement by human bones is part of Deuteronomistic theology.

Archaeological evidence is also ambiguous. Tombs may have been emptied to make room for additional dwelling space when Jerusalem expanded from the time of Hezekiah, and it seems likely that people were generally buried outside the city wall.²⁸ That does not, however, prove any particular concept of corpse impurity. Ezekiel complains about the corpses

---

22. For references, see Bóid 1989a, 141, 150–51, 154.

23. Cf. Pliny the Elder, *Nat.* 7.63–66.

24. Kazen 2010c, 41–61. This is assumed both in Qumran and rabbinic texts: 4Q274 1; m. Mikw. 8:1, 5.

25. Cf. Milgrom's (1991, 919) argument concerning the expression "unclean until evening" as always implying washing with water.

26. See Lev 10:1–7, where carrying dead priests by their tunics might possibly indicate corpse-impurity concerns. However, this passage is probably a late post-H insertion, anticipating the narrative in Num 16 (see Nihan 2007, 579–90).

27. Achenbach 2003; Frevel 2013.

28. Broshi 1974; Wright 1987, 115–28.

4. Purity and Persia

of the kings of Judah being buried close to the temple (Ezek 43:7–9), a practice repeatedly attested by Kings as well as by Chronicles.[29] Corpses and bones were thus understood to defile the cult when Ezekiel was written and the Deuteronomistic History was redacted, which takes us to exilic or postexilic times. As for the situation before that time, we have little evidence. Corpses were probably buried outside settlements, with rulers or important people as possible exceptions, but perhaps mainly for practical reasons. A basic preexilic notion of corpse impurity is not unlikely, but what it entailed and which purification rites it required, we do not know.

According to Hos 9:3–4, Israel "shall eat unclean food" (טמא יאכלו) in Assyria, and their sacrifices will not please God but be "like mourners' bread [לחם אונים]; all who eat of it shall be defiled [יטמאו]." This passage is (for other reasons) suspected of resulting from a late redaction,[30] but if the reference to mourners' bread is, in fact, preexilic, it could suggest ideas of contagion from the corpse to mourners and from them to a foodstuff, and again to others eating that foodstuff. The preceding reference to eating unclean food in Assyria would, however, rather suggest Israelite food taboos, which are different: not even in Lev 11 is defilement through contact with a source of impurity and the eating of forbidden meat merged, and the dating of the development of a concept of secondary contamination of food, based on Lev 11:32–38, is a bone of contention among scholars.[31] Hosea 9:3–4 could also imply a connection between impurity and foreign territory, which is more explicit in Amos 7:17. Here Amos speaks of the place of exile as unclean land (אדמה טמאה), but again and on different grounds, this verse is regarded as part of a redaction that is at least exilic.[32] The question, then, is how much weight these passages can bear and what they are evidence for when both the Deuteronomistic History and the preexilic prophets are understood to have been shaped and redacted during and after the exile.[33]

Food taboos are found across cultures. Samson's mother is told not to eat anything unclean (אל־תאכלי כל־טמא; Judg 13:4), although it is not exactly clear what this entails. Lists of unclean (טמא) animals are found

---

29. For a list of references and a fuller discussion, see Wright 1987, 117–19.
30. Yee 1987, 189, 198–207.
31. See Kazen 2013a, 162–76.
32. Nogalski 1993, 87–88 and n. 43.
33. On the redaction of the Book of the Twelve, see Schart 2000; Wöhrle 2006. On DtrH, see Römer 2005.

in Deut 14:3–21 and in Lev 11. If the final form of the purity laws (Lev 11–15) is later than that of Deuteronomy,[34] Deut 14 cannot be an abbreviation of Lev 11. In any case, this would be unlikely: How could one explain Deuteronomy's complete prohibition against eating a carcass and the near lack of rules for contact-contagion or Leviticus's elaboration of Deuteronomy's winged insects (שרץ העוף) into a whole category of "swarmers" (שרץ)? The reverse is not without problems, as the priestly authors would have expanded a simple and coherent list into an unclear and less coherent instruction, but this is fully possible.

Several scholars prefer to assume a common tradition behind both texts.[35] On the basis of the available texts, we can claim that a number of quadrupeds, water animals, and birds were considered unclean by the Deuteronomistic authors, which probably reflects exilic, and to some extent perhaps even earlier, food taboos. Archaeological evidence, consisting of the presence or absence of pig bones, suggests that pigs were not consumed in the hundreds of new villages that appeared in the hill country at the beginning of Iron Age I, although they were certainly eaten in the coastal plain, the lowland, and Transjordan.[36] Avoidance of pork can have a number of reasons, ranging from ecological to cultic, and if absence of pig bones were "diagnostic for the presence of ethnic Israelites, there were a lot more Israelites in the ancient world than we ever suspected."[37] Only in the Hellenistic period is there evidence for "extensive consumption of pig in urban settings" in Palestine,[38] and at this time avoidance of pork gained the status of a primary marker of Israelite identity. For our purpose, however, it is enough to conclude that widespread avoidance of pork was a preexilic practice, even if not exclusively Israelite.

Two references in Isaiah that denounce the eating of pigs' flesh (Isa 65:4; 66:17) can be understood as referring to particular cultic practices, rather than to general eating habits. Both do, however, associate the pig with other impurities: "foul things" (פגלים) in 65:4, defined as that which is detestable (שקץ), and mice or rodents (עכבר) in 66:17. This is reminiscent

---

34. *Pace* Milgrom; since H redacts P (see refs. to Milgrom in nn. 5–6) and rewrites D (Cholewinski 1976; Nihan 2004).

35. Cf. Nihan 2007, 283–90, *pace* Milgrom; Meshel 2008, 33.

36. Provan, Long, and Longman 2003, 187–89; Finkelstein 1997, 227–30; 1998, 18–20.

37. Hesse and Wapnish 1997, 238.

38. Hesse and Wapnish 1997, 263.

of Lev 11 more than of Deut 14, which would fit a Persian-period dating both of Trito-Isaiah and Leviticus, but these passages say little about food taboos in the preexilic period.

If the list of unclean foods in Deut 14 builds to some extent on preexilic practices, it is likely that aquatic creatures not considered as fish were not eaten, or at least were not supposed to be eaten according to Deuteronomist ideology. The categorization of edible fish in Deut 14:9–10 (fins and scales) is straightforward, and no species are specified. It is also likely that certain birds were deemed unacceptable for food (with no categorization), as well as flying insects. To what extent some of these possibly preexilic food taboos were associated with impurity, however, is a different question. Abstention from eating insects, slimy water animals, and carcasses can be explained on other grounds. On the other hand, it is a short step to use impurity language for that which seems repulsive to eat.[39] It is quite possible to envisage a process in which the Deuteronomist expanded a basic list of what to eat and not to eat, thus creating an incipient system of animals that were pure or impure for food.

For the preexilic period, then, we are left mainly with evidence for the pig as unclean food, possibly together with the camel and perhaps some rodents, since we would expect the Deuteronomic or pre-Deuteronomic categorization, although most likely an after-construction, to be based on a combination of ideology and actual practice. Such an after-construction may have resulted in more species becoming included among those that were considered unclean, but we should assume that something more than the pig was considered unclean to begin with. Similarly, we would expect certain birds to have been avoided, but whether they or slimy water animals, or insects, or carcasses would have been designated as impure in preexilic times, we cannot tell for sure.

Signs of Persian Influence

Can some of the developments for which there is little evidence in the preexilic period be better accounted for by exilic or postexilic factors, or more specifically, by Persian influence? I will suggest such influence in most areas: skin disease, discharge impurity, and, not least, corpse impurity and the development of a category of "swarmers" (שרץ).

---

39. Kazen 2008; 2011, 33–37, 71–94.

Persian influence on Israelite religion has long been discussed, often with a focus on the roots of Judeo-Christian theological ideas, such as angelology, eschatology, messianism, and the afterlife.[40] Comparative use of Zoroastrian texts is hazardous because of difficulties in dating the textual traditions. Generally, many parts of the younger Avesta, in particular the Yashts, are understood to go back to the Achaemenid era, thus reflecting Persian religious ideas during the fourth and fifth centuries BCE. For purity laws, the so-called Vidēvdāt or Vendidād is the most important text.[41] Although its history is contested and its language betrays a post-Achaemenid date, it is not uncommon to regard its contents as more ancient, perhaps even older than the Yashts.[42] Purity practices belong to those areas confirmed by classical Greco-Roman texts on Persian customs.[43]

Drawing on Vendidād, supplemented by other texts, both Mary Boyce and Jamsheed Choksy have outlined Zoroastrian purity laws.[44] The dualistic context places purity with goodness and impurity with evil that is placed within a demonic framework.[45] Thus impurity becomes the result of demonic influence, and purification rites take on a clearly apotropaic or exorcist character (cf. Vend. 10). The strongest impurities come from the human corpse and from all issues from the living body, whether it is sick or well. The more holy a person has been, the more impure the corpse becomes; most impure are corpses of priests. Corpse bearers are very impure and are required to keep themselves separate and eat from separate vessels. A special ritual diminishes the contagion of a corpse.

Even indirect contact with an impurity can defile. Purification rituals (*barashnum*) for the strongest impurities take nine days and assume degrees of impurity as well as graded purifications. Impure emissions include blood and semen, especially menstrual blood; menstruants withdraw and sleep alone. After childbirth, the mother is isolated for forty days. Other conspicuous details include the use of metal and stone for

---

40. Boyce 1982, 188–95; Shaked 1984; Grabbe 2004, 361–64; cf. Zaehner 1961, 33–61. Barr (1985) and Yamauchi (1990, 458–66) are skeptical.
41. All references to Vendidād are from Darmesteter 1895.
42. Malandra 2006; Gershevitch 1968; Boyce 1975, 17–21, 265–66.
43. De Jong 2013. These texts also confirm Zoroastrianism as the religion of the Persians.
44. Boyce 1975, 294–324; Choksy 1989; cf. de Jong 2013.
45. Cf. Colpe 2003, 316–26.

4. Purity and Persia 91

preventing the spread of impurity, the use of drawn water for purification, and the category of *khrafstra*: evil animals, such as insects, reptiles, and beasts of prey, the killing of which is meritorious.

One cannot avoid noting analogies with the development of Jewish purity law, beginning with the texts that were shaped and redacted during the Persian period. Colpe has argued for an analogous structure of Vendidād and Leviticus,[46] which is an exaggeration. By no means would I suggest that priestly purity laws develop from later Persian texts; for this there is no evidence. However, influence on Israelite religion and culture during the Achaemenid period from Persian ideas and practices similar to those reflected in Vendidād is reasonable.[47] Vendidād covers both discharges and corpse contamination. Instructions concern the separation or isolation of both categories, including details about contact contagion, distances between impurities and the pure, vessels for serving food or for purificatory sprinkling, and a list of body parts to be treated, which greatly exceeds the purification rite of the skin-diseased person in Lev 14.[48]

Although Vendidād never mentions skin disease, Herodotus (*Hist.* 1.138) claims that the Persians allow "leprous" people neither to enter a town nor to associate with others. Scholars often appeal to this as an example of skin-diseased persons being regarded as impure also among non-Israelites, and as an example of a Persian parallel to Israelite practices of isolation and expulsion.[49] However, the evidence for a preexilic concept of צרעת impurity that we have noted so far, including exclusion from settlements, and the relative absence of a discussion of contamination in Lev 13–14, suggest practices that were generally assumed and well established. For this we do not need specifically Persian influence, since similar ideas about skin disease were common in the ancient world. Milgrom refers to a Mari letter, a Šurpu incantation, and a Babylonian *kudurru* inscription.[50] Nougayrol identifies a number of such boundary stone inscriptions referring to *išrubu* (skin disease) covering the body of a person, who is driven out of a city and stays outside its walls so that others should not approach

---

46. Colpe 1995.
47. Cf. Achenbach 2003, 500–504.
48. Cf. esp. Vend. 3:15–21; 5:27–62; 8:23–25, 40–71; 16:1–18. Chs. 5–8 mostly deal with corpse impurity.
49. E.g., Gerstenberger 1996, 166–69.
50. Milgrom 1991, 805, 818, 911.

him.⁵¹ For explaining a basic concept of צרעת impurity in Israelite culture, we need no hypothesis of direct influence, whether from Babylonia or Persia.

It seems to be precisely in some of the details that go beyond a general conception that we detect possible Persian influence on the צרעת rules in Leviticus. I am not thinking of the very explicit instructions for diagnosis, which take up the main part of Lev 13. Their structure and details do suggest a context in which priestly control over the process of designating skin-diseased people clean or unclean is being prescribed, presumably against an earlier and less centralized practice that was based on more ambiguous criteria. We cannot tell, however, to what extent such a development was triggered by Persian practice. Nor do I think of the first part of the purification rite in Lev 14, involving two birds, which displays obvious apotropaic traits. Although Persian influence would be possible in theory, there is sufficient comparative ancient West Asian evidence from various contexts and involving birds to suggest a more general background to the bird rite.⁵² As for rules regarding textiles and houses in the latter portions of Lev 13–14, they are likely to have been shaped by analogy with skin-disease rules, but issues of contamination have been made explicit because they would not necessarily have been assumed for houses (14:46–47).

The details in the צרעת rules that may, in fact, betray Persian influence are those that regulate the purification of people healed from skin disease after the bird rite: they are now supposed to wash their clothes, shave off all hair, bathe, and sacrifice on the next day. The priest is then instructed to smear some of the sacrificial blood and some of the oil belonging to the sacrifice onto the right extremities of the ex-leper: the ear, the thumb, and the right big toe (Lev 14:8–17). What we find is a series of elaborate rituals, indicating a gradual process of purification.

There are two reasons for suggesting Persian influence here. The first is general: Zoroastrian purity practices as known partly from Vendidād and partly from other sources are very elaborate. Purification rituals (*barashnum*) for the strongest impurities can take up to nine days and assume degrees of impurity as well as graded purifications. An extended period of graded purification is exactly what the purification rites of Lev 14 suggest. The second reason is more specific: The application of blood and oil

---

51. Nougayrol 1948. Although the exact meaning is debated, the term seems to refer to some type of skin disease, corresponding to צרעת.

52. For further discussion with references, see Kazen 2011, 130–34; cf. 156–57.

onto outer extremities has a clear parallel in Zoroastrian purification rites, including the nine-day *barashnum* rite, although the latter are much more elaborate and involve sprinkling (with *gomez*, i.e., cow's urine) of many more body parts.[53] In Vendidād, this procedure is not associated with skin disease, as the text does not deal with that issue, but with purification by driving away the *drug nasu*, the corpse demoness. It is, however, quite reasonable to assume that such or similar elaborate rites may have inspired the priestly elaboration of Israelite purification rites for צרעת, also in view of the fact that skin disease is frequently associated with death (cf. Num 12:12; Job 18:13; Josephus, *Ant.* 3.264; m. Kelim 1:4; m. Neg. 13:7, 11; b. Ned. 64b).

In the case of discharge impurity, Persian influence could be suspected of triggering an expanded understanding of contamination. Leviticus 15 spells out a number of details concerning the ways in which impurity from a זב, a זבה, or a נדה is transmitted. These are basically by direct touch or via the bed, seat, saddle, or anything underneath the impure person. Vessels are also contaminated by contact. Descriptions of contact contamination are elaborate.[54] These details may have been needed because they were not obvious or commonly agreed on but of fairly recent date, probably as part of priestly elaboration and systematization. We have no preexilic evidence for such details.

Comparisons with discharge impurity rules found in Vendidād are interesting, and here we must also note what is presupposed by the text. First, male and female discharge (Vend. 5:59) as well as menstruation and irregular genital bleeding (16:1) are discussed together, as in Lev 15.

Second, both menstruants and women with irregular bleedings must purify after the cessation of symptoms by washing twice with *gomez* and once with water (Vend. 16:1, 12). Although washing with water is not explicitly required of women according to Lev 15, but only of male dischargers (v. 13), it is probably assumed, as I have argued above. Such washing is, as we have seen, implied in the Deuteronomistic History (Bathsheba); it is explicitly mentioned in rabbinic texts, not as an innovation, but in passing

---

53. Hands, between brows, back of skull, jaws, right ear, left ear, right shoulder, left shoulder, right armpit, left armpit, chest, back, right nipple, left nipple, right rib, left rib, right hip, left hip, sexual parts, right thigh, left thigh, right knee, left knee, right leg, left leg, right ankle, left ankle, right instep, left instep, right sole, left sole, right toe, left toe (Vend. 8:35–72; 9:15–26).

54. For details and discrepancies, see Kazen 2010c.

as taken for granted; and it is likely understood from the juxtaposition of rules in Lev 15, as I have argued elsewhere.[55]

Third, according to Vendidād, bedding and clothes become contaminated and are then subsequently purified by being washed in *gomez* and water. Although this is explicitly articulated in cases of corpse contamination, the textiles are then assigned to dischargers during their waiting period (Vend. 7:10–19), as they cannot be used by other people. This can be compared to the repeated mention in Lev 15 of bedding and clothes transmitting impurity.

Fourth, we learn that contamination by the touch of female as well as male dischargers is assumed (Vend. 5:59; 7:19). In Lev 15:11, the man with a discharge is said to transmit impurity unless he has washed his hands.

Fifth, we find instructions regarding the contamination and purification of vessels, although again, the issue is corpse impurity, which is the overarching concern in Vendidād. Vessels for eating that are made of metal and stone can be cleansed, while vessels of earth, wood, or clay cannot (Vend. 7:73–75).[56] This must be considered together with a passage about vessels used for bringing food to women with blood discharges, which must be made "of brass, or of lead, or of any common metal" (16:6). According to Lev 15:12, wooden vessels can be purified by water, while earthen vessels must be broken.

Sixth, even involuntary semen emission is punished (Vend. 8:26),[57] and the death penalty applies to anyone who has sex with a bleeding menstruant (16:17–18). This is stricter than the corresponding rules in Lev 15:16–17, 24, but more in line with the Holiness Code, which prescribes the כרת penalty for intercourse during menstruation (18:19, 29; 20:18).

Closely related to the discharge laws of Lev 15 are the rules concerning a woman who gives birth in Lev 12. This chapter is probably somewhat later than the rules of Lev 15, or at least depending on and assuming the formulation of the general discharge laws.[58] In their present form, the

---

55. Kazen 2010c.
56. Stone only in Vendidād Sādah (Darmesteter 1895, 92–93).
57. The circumstances are unclear. In the first edition (1880) Darmesteter translates "if a man involuntary emits his seed [*vifyeiti vifyeitica*]," which must refer to ejaculation. In the second edition (1895) this expression is interpreted to mean male same-sex activity ("if a man, by force, commits the unnatural sin"), but since this is explicitly condemned later in quite different terms (8:32), the reasons for reading such an interpretation into 8:26 are not compelling.
58. See Elliger 1966, 157–58; Nihan 2007, 281–82.

fairly short rules of Lev 12 serve the purpose of integrating purification rituals for new mothers with other cultic practices, suggesting the need for a mitigating sacrifice in such a case.[59] In Vendidād, the impurity of new mothers is not addressed as a general issue, nor as a result of their discharge of blood, but only in cases of a stillborn child, which causes corpse impurity (5:45–56; 7:60–69). In Zoroastrian practice, however, childbirth in general is associated with impurity and purification. The question, then, is whether this is assumed in Vendidād or represents a later development. In the Ṣad dar e-naṣr,[60] understood to represent old traditions, a new mother is regarded as impure for forty days, of which the first twenty-one days are set out as a period when she is especially restricted. After twenty-one days, she is allowed to wash her head, which she does again when the forty days have passed, after which she can again touch wooden and earthen utensils, and resume cooking and similar activities. For another forty days, her husband is not allowed to have sex with her.[61] A similar period of time is mentioned by the Persian Rivayats, collected between the fifteenth and eighteenth centuries CE but preserving and representing much older materials. A parturient should "sit apart" for forty-one nights.[62] In the Rivayats, the content of Ṣad dar 76:1, 5 is rendered almost verbatim.[63] The uncertainties concerning the history and development of late Zoroastrian texts make it precarious to draw safe conclusions, but in many instances the Rivayats merely interpret issues found in Vendidād without adding much more than what is implicit in the earlier text. Menstruants, for example, are suggested to take their meals with two gloves and a metal spoon from a metal dish, without touching their clothes, and warnings for contamination via clothes, gloves, or dish are issued. This certainly contains further developments, but Vendidād assumes severe hand impurity for dischargers and implies that hands are covered (5:59; 7:19).

Some details in Vendidād correspond to developments of Israelite practices further into the Persian and Hellenistic periods. While the detailed contamination rules of Lev 15 presuppose that dischargers live at home, the stricter tradition in Num 5:2–4 orders that they be excluded from the

---

59. For the mitigating function of the חטאת sacrifice, see Kazen 2011, 152–62.
60. Later than the Pahlavi works but earlier than the Persian Rivayats (de Jong 2013, 320–21).
61. Ṣad dar 76, West 1885, 339–40; also in the Qissa-i Sanjan.
62. Persian Rivayats, in Dhabhar 1932, 224 (MU. 1.223, ll. 2–5 = H.F. f. 382).
63. Persian Rivayats, in Dhabhar 1932, 224–25 (MU. 1.223, ll. 7–12 = H.F. f. 129).

"camp," and certain texts from Qumran suggest special places and minimum distances for such people (11Q19 XLV, 15–18; XLVI, 16–18; XLVIII, 14–17; 4QMMT B 64–72; 4Q274 1 I). Following those who consider this and certain other sections in Numbers as part of a later redactional phase, we are able to suggest a development of Israelite practices under continuous influence from Persian practices. According to Vendidād, menstruants and women with irregular bleedings should be isolated in a special building[64] and kept away from that which is holy, as well as from pure people, at a certain distance (16:1–6). We also hear about such practices among later Israelite groups (Samaritans, Karaites, and Falashas).[65]

In Num 5:2–4, the stricter practice of quarantine or isolation also applies to people with skin disease and those who are impure from corpses. As already mentioned, general rules for corpse impurity are only found in Numbers, in late compositional layers. It is perhaps in the area of corpse impurity that the strongest case can be made for Persian influence on Israelite purity rules.[66] This does not mean that such conceptions were absent previously; we have also noted the presence in Lev 21:1–4 of prohibitions against corpse contamination for priests. Considering the Holiness Code as somewhat later than the first half of Leviticus, but earlier than the latest sections of Numbers, we can detect an evolving process by which popular ideas of corpse impurity, including an apotropaic rite of burning a red cow and employing its ashes for purification by sprinkling, were domesticated by the priestly authors and barely squeezed into their cultic system (Num 19).[67]

A comparison with Persian ideas and practices supports such a hypothesis of Persian influence. First we should emphasize the dynamic character of corpse impurity in Zoroastrianism. Corpses are entered by the *drug nasu*, the corpse demoness, immediately after death.[68] Regarded as the most contagious of all sources of impurity, corpses necessitate numerous precautions and apotropaic purification rites, including the peculiarities

---

64. Later called *dashtānistān*. The Rivayats add that menstruants may not contact each other; cf. 4Q274 1 I, prohibiting different categories of (purifying?) individuals from touching each other.
65. Milgrom 1991, 765; Kazen 2010a, 72.
66. Cf. Achenbach 2009.
67. For further discussion with references, see Kazen 2011, 133–34, 137.
68. Except in cases of murder or sudden death, when the corpse demoness is unprepared (Vend. 7:4–5).

of Zoroastrian burials (Vend. 6:44–51; 7:1–3; 12). In Second Temple Judaism, the corpse became the most contagious of all sources of impurity, at least in theory, and to the rabbis it was the "father of fathers of impurity," in spite of the fact that it plays a minor role in Leviticus and is not expressly singled out as the principal or most severe impurity in Numbers. The red-cow rite, with its similarities to the bird rite in Lev 14:1–7, clearly has an apotropaic background and character.[69]

Second, according to the Vendidād, the purification of a corpse-impure person does not seem to require a priest; it can be carried out by anyone (8:35–71, 97–103).[70] This is also the case with the Israelite rite. Although the priest is assigned the role of throwing ingredients into the fire, the text of Numbers assumes that ordinary people burn the cow, gather the ashes, mix them with water, and sprinkle the mixture on the unclean (Num 19:2–10, 17–19).

Third, a higher degree of holiness makes a person more vulnerable to impurity. In Vendidād, the defiling radius of a deceased priest is wider than that of a warrior, which in turn is wider than that of a commoner (5:27–28; 7:6–7).[71] It is conspicuous that, as Israelite purity laws evolved, corpse impurity was at first only perceived as a problem for priests (Lev 21:1–4). The long-standing and fruitless scholarly debate as to whether impurity was avoided for its own sake or mainly because of its threat against sancta and the cult would benefit from considering Zoroastrian purity practices. The fact that impurity poses a greater threat to that which is holy does not make it unproblematic for ordinary people.

Fourth, corpse impurity in Zoroastrianism, at least of the more serious kind, requires the longer and more elaborate *barashnum* rite, including the digging of nine holes in the ground, the purifier washing in *gomez*

---

69. In both cases, hyssop, cedarwood, and crimson material are employed, and a mixture of the blood or the ashes of an animal and water is sprinkled onto the person to be purified. An understanding of impurity as the result of demonic activity, in need of exorcist rituals, was common in ancient West Asia, as was the use of red wool and sprinkling for warding off demonic threat. The rabbis were aware of the red-cow rite's exorcist character (Pesiq. Rab Kah. 4.7). For further discussions, see Kazen 2011, 130–34. The special emphasis on the demonic danger of the corpse is conspicuous in Zoroastrianism.

70. At least not according to the text. The purifying person washes in *gomez* and in water, but others are needed for bringing the dog, digging the holes of the *barashnum* rite, and sprinkling the purifier.

71. Followed by different types of dogs.

(in six holes) and water (in three holes), after which there is an elaborate sprinkling of body parts (Vend. 8:37-71).[72] Except for the sprinkling or smearing of some of the right extremities of the person healed from skin disease with blood and oil (Lev 14:14-17), purification in Lev 12-15 is mainly effected by washing oneself in water. The corpse-impurity rules, however, involve both washing (oneself) and being sprinkled (by others), in combination (Num 19:17-19), while secondary contact only renders a one-day impurity, requiring bathing.[73] The introduction of special sprinkling in addition to traditional ablution or bathing in Israelite purification practices is conspicuous.

Fifth, examples of the effect of (corpse) impurity on vessels and their cleansing (cf. Vend. 7:73-75) are first found in Leviticus in the context of swarming creatures (Lev 11:32-35) and discharge impurity (15:12), then as part of corpse impurity rules (Num 19:15).

Sixth, according to Vendidād (8:11-13), corpse bearers immediately perform a preliminary purification rite after having left the corpse at the *dakhma* building,[74] not as a substitute to the subsequent *barashnum* rite, but presumably to lessen their contamination in the meantime. Ideas of graded impurity and gradual purification enter Israelite purification rules first through the purification rituals of the person who had previously suffered from skin disease (Lev 14:8-9), then through the combination of sprinkling and washing or bathing for corpse impurity (Num 19:17-19), and subsequently (after the final redaction of the pentateuchal text) they come to full expression in the later Second Temple period practice of a first-day ablution.[75] Other issues that become more prominent during the

---

72. Cf. the even more elaborate nine nights' *barashnum* (Vend. 9). If the *sag-did* ceremony (the gaze of a particular dog on the corpse) had been performed and the *drug nasu* driven away, contact with a corpse rendered a lighter type of impurity for which a simple *ghosel* purification ritual was sufficient (Vend. 8:36), involving washing with *gomez* and water. If the ceremony had not been performed, contact caused an impurity requiring the much more elaborate *barashnum* rite.

73. Not explicit but implied in Num 19:22 and assumed throughout the Second Temple period.

74. A tall building on which corpses are exposed to the sun and consumed by dogs and birds.

75. Definitely for corpse impurity and possibly in certain cases of genital discharges. See Kazen 2010c, 81-87, 91-106; 2013a, 146-48. Cf. Ezek 44:25-26; Tob 2:9; 4Q414; 4Q514; 11Q19 XLIX, 16-21; L, 13-16; 4Q274 1; Philo, *Spec.* 1.261; 3.205-206; Milgrom 1995, 67.

latter part of the Second Temple period are the preoccupation with impurity from graves and the reburial of bones, both of which could, perhaps, be compared to Zoroastrian concern for the ground, not burying corpses in it, searching it for corpse material, and depositing corpses on *dakhmas* (Vend. 6:1–9, 44–51).

All these points are not equally strong arguments for Persian influence on the development of Israelite conceptions of corpse impurity, but several are conspicuous enough to suggest some influence, particularly when we consider that they evolved, or at least were shaped and included in the literary corpus being formed, precisely at a time when such influence would most likely have taken place.

In addition to the similarities described above regarding discharge laws and an evolving concept of corpse impurity, the food and contagion laws of Lev 11 focus on animals similar to those belonging to the Zoroastrian *khrafstra* category. Leviticus's category of swarmers (שרץ), which, together with birds of prey and certain quadruped carnivores, are not allowed for food, covers approximately the same ground as the Ahrimanian or "demonic" animals in Zoroastrianism, the killing of which is considered meritorious.[76] The category of *khrafstra* is already assumed in Vendidād,[77] although there are no complete lists of animals involved. Snakes, cats (?), tortoises, frogs, ants, earthworms, and certain flies are explicitly mentioned, and wolves also belong to those animals that should be killed (Vend. 14:5; 18:65). Elsewhere in later texts, we learn that the *khrafstra* category includes a number of crawling creatures, reptiles, and vermin, such as mice and rats and similar rodents, as well as a number of carnivores. These are good to kill, cannot be eaten, and defile food.[78] Considering the possibility of Lev 11 building and elaborating on a tradition close to Deut 14,[79] we could suggest that the priestly authors expanded on a list of animals not allowed for food, including a prohibition to touch their carcasses. In doing this, they would have created a bridge between food rules and subsequent instructions concerning contact contagion in Lev 12–15 by transferring the focus from eating to touching. In expanding on earlier tradition, they also would have created a separate and

---

76. Choksy 1989, 14–15.

77. E.g., Vend. 7:2–5; 8:16–18, 71; 9:26; 16:12; 17:3; 18:2. The term already appears in the Yashna, but not necessarily as a category of animals.

78. See Dhabhar 1932, 268–70.

79. See above and my discussion of the structure of Lev 11 in Kazen 2011, 72–80.

superordinate category of swarmers (שׁרץ), which were branded as detestable (שׁקץ). In Deuteronomy, שׁרץ is only used for winged insects or "bird swarmers," but in Lev 11, prohibited water animals are also labeled שׁרץ המים (11:10), and the list of eight "ground swarmers" (11:29–30) completes the picture, so that we are presented with three types of swarmers. The introduction to the instructions concerning their contamination states that "these are unclean to you among all swarmers" (11:31), and should thus be read as referring to the contaminating power of the carcasses of all three types of שׁרץ.

The similarities between the category thus created by the priestly authors and the *khrafstra* are conspicuous, both with regard to the kinds of animals and the emphasis on their contamination. In no way is this to suggest that Israelite food taboos in general would have originated from contact with the Persians. However, the particular way in which food rules were shaped and categorized by the priestly authors makes it likely that extended contact with Persian concepts and practices would have been of some import.

In some of the cases discussed in this section, one could perhaps argue the reverse direction of influence, from Israelite purity conceptions to Persian (Zoroastrian) practices, at least as a theoretical possibility. However, I find such an idea highly unlikely. One important reason is the nature of the influence I have been suggesting, which is less a matter of taking over singular rules than about a global influence on one "purity system" from another more impressive and elaborate one, and in this particular case from a dominant majority culture onto a vulnerable immigrant minority, or a subservient vassal community. The social, political, and economic situation of Achaemenid Yehud thus supports our interpretation.

Conclusion: The Role of Purity in Persian Yehud

Without denying that some of the basics of Israelite purity conceptions have other ancient parallels and a preexilic history, I have suggested that many of the explicit details in the purity rules of Leviticus and Numbers represent relatively recent developments during the Persian period. So far, the results fit with what we can find (or not find) in our sources about purity before the exile, and also with the kinds of topics and special interests that reasonably could have been evoked or triggered by contact with Persian practices. A final question is whether these issues make sense as recent developments within the context of Persian Yehud, with Jerusalem and its newly rebuilt temple at its center, during the fifth and early fourth centuries BCE.

With little space for discussing the political and economic development of Judea during the Achaemenid period, this final section must be brief. Although a debated issue, it has become clear that Jerusalem was much smaller, and inhabitants of Persian Yehud (even into the Hellenistic period) were much fewer than the population of the region of Samaria.[80] Returning migrants had varying motives, but they included elite groups, such as people of priestly descent, who struggled to establish themselves while the divide between returnees and already-resident Judahites became apparent.[81] The once popular idea of the formation and canonization of Jewish law through Persian imperial promotion and authorization is seriously questioned today.[82] The colonized nature of Yehud must be fully acknowledged, and priests would, as part of a larger group of returnees, have been given certain privileges, such as land rights, but this does not necessarily make their interests identical with those of imperial administration and control, even if these interests partially coincide.[83] Postcolonial concepts, such as mimicry and hybridity, suggest a more nuanced and productive understanding of priestly activity in Achaemenid Yehud, including the formation of purity laws.

We would thus assume a small vassal temple state, with returnee elites struggling with the relative insignificance of their context and anxious about their identity.[84] Among them would be ritual specialists intent on consolidating the cult and exerting control over it, seeking general acceptance while asserting their status and power, in a process that also involved the incorporation of diverse popular practices.

A match between our results and such a context will be indicated in four concluding points. All of these need further corroboration, for which there is no room here; they are only offered as suggestions that deserve to be pursued in the future.

First, a number of recent developments in purity practices lend themselves to promoting priestly status and enhancing priestly control, which

---

80. Lipschits 2006; Knoppers 2006; Lipschits and Tal 2007.
81. Berquist 1995; Kessler 2006.
82. Frei and Koch 1984; Blum 1990, 333–60; Watts 2001; LeFebvre 2006; Ska 2006, 218–26.
83. Berquist 1995; 2007; Hoglund 1992, 207–47; Eskenazi 2006.
84. Berquist 2006.

is particularly important for an elite group competing for influence and leadership.⁸⁵ Both the bird rite and the red-cow rite may have earlier and popular origins, but they are brought under priestly authority. The red-cow rite is even loosely attached to the sacrificial cult by being designated a חטאת, in spite of the fact that so many of its activities are performed by laymen. The diagnosis of צרעת is completely assigned to the priest, conferring status and control to him. The purification of new mothers is entirely placed under priestly authority and brokerage, as the priests "effect removal" by sacrificing.

The last instance also exemplifies the second main point, that many of the developments function to protect the cult, preventing impurity from defiling the newly (re-)built temple, hence emphasizing its status and the significance of Jerusalem.⁸⁶ During her prolonged period of impurity, the parturient "must not touch anything holy, or enter the sanctuary" (Lev 12:4), and the motive not to defile the sanctuary concludes the elaborate details regarding defilement by contact with menstruants and זבים (15:31). Preventive measures, such as the extension of practices of exclusion or isolation of people with skin disease to other categories of impure people (Num 5:2–4), can plausibly be seen along the same lines, and although the explicit motive in Num 5:3 is only to prevent defilement of the "camp," 19:13, 20 explicitly specify defilement of the tabernacle or sanctuary as the rationale for general purification from corpse impurity.⁸⁷

Third, some developments reflect a concern for holiness and a need for identity that fits the context of a struggling community seeking to overcome disparity and to create a common narrative and ethos. Although general purification from corpse impurity is motivated by concern for the temple, the Holiness Code's explicit rationale for requiring priests to avoid corpse impurity altogether is holiness; priests must be holy, like God (Lev 21:6). An ideal of holiness, not only for priests but for Israelites in gen-

---

85. Cf. Nihan 2013, 351–63. I basically agree, except on "the partial transfer of priestly competencies to non-priests" (357). Rather, I see signs of the opposite process.

86. Cf. Frevel 2013, 405–8. However, pointing out the cult-protecting *function* of some of these developments is not to argue that they were primarily *shaped* or *motivated* by such concerns. Cf. ch. 3 in this volume. For a thorough discussion of the role of purity practices in relation to the cult and to daily life, see ch. 11 in this volume.

87. An understanding of impurity and purification as graded, exemplified by the handwashing of the זב (Lev 15:11) and the first-day ablution of the person purifying from skin disease (Lev 14:8), was later applied to other cases of impurity as well, mitigating stricter practices of exclusion. See further Kazen 2010c, 63–111; 2013a, 150–74.

eral, is often acknowledged as characteristic of the period we are discussing. Such aspirations should not be confused with laity wishing to imitate priests, but express a reasonable concern to live according to high divine standards, compatible with an ideal group identity, in order to consolidate the success and future of a restoration community. This is a plausible context for the extension of concerns for corpse impurity from priests to the general population, which we find in Num 19. Also, the further developments of food prohibitions, including the creation of a special category of swarmers, are explicitly motivated by holiness concerns (Lev 11:44–45), and while this particular motivation is likely to result from a Holiness source redaction, this very fact underscores the role that these developments came to play for holiness and identity concerns.

My final point is that all or most of the developments and innovations that may result from Persian influence on Israelite purity conceptions can be understood from a postcolonial perspective as examples of hybridity and/or mimicry, as appropriation of, or assimilation to, cultural practices of the colonial masters. Such processes can be quite unconscious and need not be sensed to compromise integrity or identity, but can rather effect the opposite, especially when imperial influence is refracted through indigenous conceptions. Note that in the process of Zoroastrian influence on the formation of Israelite purity rules, the most conspicuous characteristic of Persian practices is curtailed: the demonic. In Milgrom's words, by their "thoroughgoing evisceration of the demonic," the priestly authors "also transformed the concept of impurity."[88]

---

88. Milgrom 1991, 43.

5
The Role of Disgust in Priestly Purity Law: Insights from Conceptual Metaphor and Blending Theories

Common anthropological and structuralist approaches to Israelite purity law are often problematic. Disgust is a more promising explanation for the diverse impurities reflected in priestly texts. But not all impurities fit into a pattern of disgust equally well. Disgust language also characterizes impurities that ought not to evoke revulsion easily. I have previously suggested a transfer of emotional disgust from obvious triggers to objects that are clearly culture specific by means of a secondary use of disgust language as value judgment. In the present article I explore this further with the help of cognitive linguistics. Conceptual metaphor theories as well as more elaborate blending models help clarify how disgust intrinsic to certain conceptions of impurity can be extended and transferred to others, which at times bear only slight resemblances. As a result, I suggest that disgust is the most comprehensive explanation for the wide variety of conceptions of impurity found in priestly legislation.

In the present essay I revisit and elaborate on my previous work on impurity and disgust, in which I explored the basic emotion of disgust as a common denominator underlying the various Israelite understandings of impurity for which we have evidence in the Hebrew Bible in general, and particularly in the priestly purity laws of Leviticus and Numbers.[1]

I developed my hypothesis partly because I found several common structuralist and anthropological explanations for the biblical purity

---

This chapter was first published in *JLRS* 3 (2014): 62–92. Used by permission. Only minor changes have been made.

1. See Kazen 2011; 2008.

conceptions unconvincing and unable to account for the varied use of purity language and the diverse conceptions of impurity that appear in the texts. These unconvincing explanations include: (1) The understanding of impurities as primarily resulting from problems of classification, that is, as matter out of place, or as anomalies, falling between clear categories.[2] (2) The understanding that concerns for unity and purity of the human body mirror social concerns for the social body. Discharges from bodily orifices are thought to compromise the boundaries of the human body and reflect an experienced threat to the boundaries of the social body.[3] These two views are usually associated with Mary Douglas and her seminal work, *Purity and Danger*. They have been immensely influential among biblical scholars, and the second is an example of advanced symbolism, implying that purity practices and purity rituals depend on social structures and are shaped by them.[4] (3) Similar symbolic systems construed with a theological rather than a social emphasis. A prominent example is the idea that explains biblical purity conceptions as focused on life and death. Jacob Milgrom understands all types of impurity to somehow carry associations with death or notions thereof.[5]

Problematic Explanations

All these explanations assume that ideas go before behavior. In her recent insightful article, "Where There Is Dirt, Is There System?," Tracy Lemos points out that "the type of analysis that seeks ever to schematize almost always sees ritual as secondary to belief and the body as secondary to the mind."[6] She thus criticizes the bent for symbolism that supposes that rituals somehow emanate from theology or social structures, which goes against the present trend in ritual studies. This is valid criticism both of Douglas's earlier social anthropological views and of her more recent theologi-

---

2. Douglas 2002.
3. Douglas 2002, esp. 141–59 (ch. 7: "External Boundaries"); 1978, esp. 92–112 (ch. 5: "The Two Bodies").
4. Klawans 2000, 7–10. Exactly on what level of explanation such analogies are envisaged by theorists has never become completely clear to me. (Now, see Kazen 2018a = ch. 3 in this volume.)
5. Milgrom 1991, 766–68, 816–20, 1000–1004.
6. Lemos 2013, 294; cf. 274, 280. See also Lemos's earlier critique of Douglas in Lemos 2009.

cal ones.⁷ Lemos also points to inconsistencies in Milgrom's explanations. Whereas in her early work Douglas regards the pig as anomalous, Milgrom associates it with chthonic deities, and therefore with death.⁸ Thus, theological considerations lie behind the revulsion for the pig and the classification of animals not chewing the cud as unclean. Although death can be associated with skin disease and perhaps also with some pathological discharges, it is less obvious to explain menstruation as loss of life, or semen emission as loss of life force. It becomes even more artificial to explain childbirth as an example of death. Feces do not fit at all into Milgrom's scheme, which needs some fairly strained arguments to hold water.⁹

The notion of death needs to be at least complemented. Lemos mentions several such attempts. Howard Eilberg-Schwartz suggests complementing the focus on death by controllability. Controllable discharges are considered less defiling than uncontrollable ones; therefore, semen is less impure than menstrual blood, and saliva and urine are not impure at all.¹⁰ But this does not explain discharges such as sweat or blood from a wound, which are not considered unclean although they are uncontrollable. Lemos points out that all defiling discharges are genital.¹¹ Some attempts to revise Milgrom's scheme focus on sexuality. David Wright suggests that impurity is associated with death, disease, and sexuality as distinctly human features, contrary to divine nature.¹² This, however, does not explain several differences between various impurities,¹³ and would almost require that

---

7. As is well known, Douglas (1999; 2001; 2004) changed her mind about biblical purity conceptions in favor of a decidedly theological and, some would argue, apologetic one. As an example, Douglas (2002, xiii–xvi) came to regard the food laws as having nothing to do with abhorrence against certain animals, and suggested that it would have been inconsistent on the part of a compassionate God to create abominable animals and that the priestly authors would have found it abominable to harm the animals not used for sacrifice. Cf. the criticism in Lemos 2013.

8. Douglas 2002, 51–71; Milgrom 1991, 650–52.

9. For Milgrom's view, see n. 5 above. Cf. Kazen 2011, 81–84, 93; Lemos 2013, 270–72. It is often claimed that feces do not figure in Israelite conceptions of impurity. Although this is true of priestly law, it is not consistent with the broader evidence. For a discussion, see Lemos 2013, 270–72, 286–87.

10. Eilberg-Schwartz 1990, 177–216, esp. 186–89.

11. Lemos 2013, 273.

12. Wright 1992.

13. Lemos 2013, 274. For further discussion of such discrepancies, see Kazen 2007, 41–61.

conceptions of impurity from genital discharges were completely absent from preexilic Israelite religion, to evolve only with monotheism, as the Israelite God became completely asexual in postexilic times. It is now generally acknowledged that divine beings were hardly without sexual characteristics in early Israelite religion, and ideas of Yahweh having a consort survived in some quarters for very long. Lemos points out that Robert Parker implausibly makes a similar argument for Greece, although Greek gods were known to engage in sexual activity, and that similar purity conceptions are found in Mesopotamia, where gods could even be killed.[14] Lemos asks why Israelite theological ideas should be understood to produce conceptions of purity found also in surrounding cultures with different theologies.

Although an understanding of human impurity in opposition to God's immortal and asexual nature could have been part of priestly theology, this does not suffice to explain the origin or development of conceptions of genital discharge impurity in general. Nor does a combination of death and sex provide a satisfactory and comprehensive explanation for the way in which Israelite texts use impurity language in several contexts for various bodily states or afflictions, as well as for particular human behaviors. At best, explanations become strained and interpretations arbitrary.

To be persuasive, an explanatory model must embrace varying conceptions and somehow keep them together, without overlooking their diversity. In Israelite texts, impurity language is being used in several contexts for various bodily states or afflictions, as well as for particular human behaviors. There is no fixed or self-evident way of organizing or categorizing these. The priestly laws in Lev 12–15 deal with "leprosy" (ṣāraʿat; scale disease) and with genital discharges, natural as well as pathological, including postpartum bleedings. The Holiness Code in Lev 17–26 introduces a concept of corpse impurity for priests (Lev 21), which is extended to laypeople in some late sections of the book of Numbers (5; 19; 31). All of these impurities are envisaged as contagions for which purification rites exist. The Holiness Code also uses impurity language for sexual offenses and idolatry, complemented by bloodshed in Numbers (35; cf. Deut 19; 21). A similar use of impurity language is found also in the Psalms and in some of the prophets, often in a more sweeping manner, referring not only to sexual offenses, idolatry, and bloodshed, as in the Torah. We also

---

14. Parker 1983; Lemos 2013, 274.

find impurity language in Ezra-Nehemiah for denouncing intermarriage. Moreover, the food laws in Lev 11 and Deut 14 classify certain animals as impure for consumption, without prescribing purification, except that in Lev 11 the carcasses of some of these animals are associated with impurity by contagion, similar to the impurities of Lev 12–15, which demand purification.[15]

There is no simple or self-evident way of categorizing the different types of impurities. The most common solution is to distinguish physical impurities transmitted by contact and purified through various rites from those associated with sinful behavior. Already by the early twentieth century, David Hoffmann and Adolph Büchler distinguished between Levitical impurity and defiling sin.[16] Jonathan Klawans has recently argued that ritual and moral impurity are "two distinct conceptions of defilement articulated in the Hebrew Bible."[17]

Lemos reviews several other attempts. Tikva Frymer-Kensky distinguishes between pollution beliefs and danger beliefs. Danger beliefs are associated with wrongdoing and incur divine sanctions, whereas ritual pollutions can be removed through purification rites.[18] Wright prefers a division between prohibited and tolerated impurities, which partly overlap those of Frymer-Kensky.[19] Eve Levavi Feinstein suggests that we should rather think of a category of sexual pollution than speak of moral impurity.[20] None of these suggestions, however, accounts neatly for all the purity conceptions in the Hebrew Bible.[21]

A compelling categorization must fit all, or at least most, of these conceptions. Some have attempted to solve the problem by making one category primary and the others somehow secondary. Büchler regarded Levitical impurity as primary, and moral impurity as a metaphorical use of impurity language.[22] Hoffmann did the opposite: he considered impurity as an ethical category, which is concrete, and understood Levitical

---

15. For extended discussions of the Israelite purity laws, see Kazen 2010a; 2010c; 2011, 24–28; 71–94; 2013a, 140–76.
16. Hoffmann 1905–1906, 2:301–8, 340; Büchler 1928, 212–74.
17. Klawans 2000, 158.
18. Frymer-Kensky 1983.
19. Wright 1991; 1992.
20. Feinstein 2010; 2014.
21. Lemos 2013, 275–77, 279–80.
22. Büchler 1928, 212–74.

impurity as symbolical. It is the food laws, as usual, that do not quite fit. Hoffmann regarded them as concrete, together with the moral rules.[23] This is logical from one point of view, because in neither case is ritual purification prescribed for these impurities. From another perspective, however, food laws have often been interpreted allegorically, as symbols for moral issues, somewhat similarly to Levitical impurities or bodily contagion, although an even greater effort is required to make sense of the latter in this way.[24] An additional problem is presented by certain sexual laws that are viewed both from a ritual and from a moral perspective, and it is difficult to place the so-called genealogical impurity.[25]

If one set of purity conceptions is considered primary and the others secondary or metaphorical, an overall explanation of impurity needs to account only for the primary conception; the secondary ones could be explained as arising out of analogy, metaphor, or allegory. Hoffmann's understanding of moral impurity as concrete, symbolized by ritual impurity, cannot withstand the criticism of prioritizing theology over ritual or behavior.[26] If, however, ritual impurity is understood as the primary category, it would be sufficient to find an underlying common denominator for impurity as contagion, to explain the other categories as extensions. None of the suggestions can accomplish even this limited result.

Klawans assumes that contact with natural processes, such as birth, death, and sex, accounts for ritual impurity, but insists that moral impurity is an independent category.[27] Klawans's book *Impurity and Sin in Ancient*

---

23. Hoffmann 1905–1906, 2:301–8.

24. Purity rules were explained allegorically, for example, by the Letter of Aristeas and by Philo. Note that Philo, at some distance from the temple, provided an allegorical explanation for the purity laws, while still applying them literally. After the destruction of the temple, we find allegorical interpretations both by the church fathers and by rabbinic commentators.

25. Christine Hayes's (2002) term "genealogical impurity" is in itself problematic, as is John Meier's (2009, 347) wholesale acceptance of it as a separate category; cf. Kazen 2010c, 5–6, 154. The most conspicuous example of a sexual law that is viewed both from a ritual and from a moral perspective is perhaps the law against sexual intercourse during menstruation: Lev 15:24; 18:19; 20:18. The discrepancies have been variously explained and cannot be further discussed here.

26. See the general criticism of Lemos (2013, 280), referring to the increasing realization that the dichotomy of belief and ritual is false, following the growth of ritual studies. Cf., among others, Bell 1992.

27. Klawans 2000, 21–42.

Judaism has been highly influential, but in my opinion it contains several basic mistakes.[28] My theory about disgust as an underlying common denominator for impurity was prompted most likely by my dissatisfaction with Klawans's particular way of distinguishing between ritual and moral impurity, and his understanding of when impurity should be regarded as a metaphor and when not.[29]

Klawans tries to solve the problem of classification by on one hand agreeing with Büchler that Levitical or ritual purity is concrete, and admitting that this purity language can at times be used metaphorically for moral issues, but on the other hand claiming that moral impurity, particularly when relating to the "three heinous sins" (certain sexual sins, idolatry, and murder), represents a distinct conception of defilement, which is not metaphorical but just as literal as ritual impurity. One of Klawans's points is that moral impurity in these cases is just as "real" as ritual impurity.[30] My critique was that he confuses *real* and *literal*, mistaking a linguistic designation for an ontological one. It is still not clear to me why some of Klawans's examples are considered metaphorical and others literal. I also suggested that the so-called ritual impurity is often just as metaphorical as moral impurity, because the terminology itself suggests the besmirching of an item with physical dirt, while in both cases it is used to ascribe an item (whether a state or a behavior) a negative value, regardless of whether any physical substance has been transferred.[31] Here I stopped short and did not pursue the issue of metaphor further. I attempt to do this in the present study.

My Previous Attempt at a Solution

The solution I suggested, first in a 2008 article, then in my 2011 *Emotions in Biblical Law*, attempted to find an underlying common denominator for all types of purity conceptions. I noticed that expressions of emotional disgust, aversion, or loathing were frequent wherever impurity was discussed.

The idea that concepts of impurity originated in disgust is not new. Jacob Neusner enunciated it in his classical work on purity (1973),[32] but neither he nor anyone else made much of it. In psychological research,

---

28. Kazen 2010a, 200–222; 2011, 25–28.
29. Kazen 2008; 2011, 20–31, 71–94.
30. Klawans 2000, 32–36.
31. Kazen 2010a, 204–7.
32. Neusner 1973, 11–12.

disgust is often regarded as a moral emotion, belonging to the other-condemning family, according to some taxonomies.[33] Core disgust should be seen as a primary emotion, a direct bodily response to repulsive stimuli, which has evolved to protect living beings from inhaling, digesting, or contacting unhealthy, toxic, or otherwise dangerous substances.[34] Disgust is basically a survival mechanism, but as in all emotional fields, a set of secondary emotions has evolved from an innate or ultimate base; these emotions are also important for survival, but within a social framework, as they have evolved in parallel with culture.[35] Hence there are levels of disgust that have predominantly cultural or proximate bases, although the biological and cultural underpinnings are not fully separable, as the final wiring of the human brain takes place through interaction with social and cultural experiences during periods of plasticity in childhood and adolescence.[36] As a secondary emotion, disgust may be triggered by sight or even by memory or thought, without smell, touch, or taste being present.[37]

I have reviewed various studies on disgust elsewhere.[38] Paul Rozin's psychological research on disgust is well known, and I have related my analysis of various Israelite purity conceptions to his nine empirically demonstrated triggers for disgust: food, body products, animals, sexual behaviors, contact with death or corpses, violations of the exterior envelope of the body (including gore and deformity), poor hygiene, interpersonal contamination (contact with unsavory human beings), and certain moral offenses.[39] Most of these are, to varying degrees, learned through socialization, but they also have biological bases, which causes a problem when disgust is used to express moral values and appealed to or relied on as a normative pointer.[40] Although the relevance of disgust in a particular situation can be questioned, the emotion does not necessarily disappear for that reason.

---

33. Haidt 2003; Kazen 2011, 32–36.
34. Rozin, Haidt, and McCauley 2000; Curtis 2013, 21–40; cf. Miller 1997, 60–88.
35. Damasio 1994, 129–39; Looy 2004, 219–35; Rozin, Haidt, and McCauley 2000, 647–48. Cf. Kazen 2011, 9–19.
36. Haidt 2001. Cf. Preston and de Waal 2002.
37. Miller 1997, 60–88.
38. Important studies include Darwin 1989; Angyal 1941; Kolnai 2004; Miller 1997; Menninghaus 1999; Miller 2004; Curtis 2013. For further discussion, see Kazen 2011, 33–36.
39. Rozin, Haidt, and McCauley 2000, 637.
40. See the criticism of Nussbaum 2004, 13–15, 72–171; cf. Curtis 2013, 103–7.

In my previous study I pointed to the presence of disgust in descriptions and in motivations for conceptions of impurity in the three main areas of priestly legislation: food laws, bodily contagion, and immoral behavior.[41] Food is one of Rozin's disgust triggers, but the list of unclean animals in Deut 14 is comparably neutral in this regard. Only the introduction (Deut 14:3) defines the subsequent animals listed as tôʿēbâ, "abominable." There is every reason to regard this as a rubric by the Deuteronomistic authors or redactors, by which they subsume dietary restrictions under a larger umbrella, covering various behaviors considered unacceptable for Israelites to engage in, and of which God strongly disapproves.[42] But in the traditional lists of animals, even in their redacted and expanded form, we find no further elaboration on the disgust motif.

By contrast, the corresponding tradition in Lev 11 uses disgust language more liberally, as all types of "swarmers" are branded "detestable" (šeqeṣ). The priestly authors have created an overarching category of swarmers from the traditional winged insects ("bird swarmers;" šereṣ hāʿôp), underlying Deuteronomy's list, extending it to include both water and ground swarmers.[43] With this move they managed to include several animals that in Persian religion were considered as evil Ahrimanian creatures, called khrafstra.[44] The likelihood of Persian (Zoroastrian) influence on Israelite priestly purity laws during the postexilic period is a topic on its own, which I discuss elsewhere.[45] My point here is that disgust is being used rhetorically by the priestly authors to attribute or extend impurity to a large number of creatures that would appear as naturally disgusting to people in a variety of contexts. There is, of course, a cultural component involved in what human beings regard as naturally disgusting, but it is reasonable to assume a biological base for human disgust against vermin and various slimy and crawling creatures in rotting environments.[46] The combination of decayed life and exagger-

---

41. Kazen 2008; 2011, 72–94.
42. Tigay 1996, 138; Nihan 2007, 284–88, 293.
43. Cf. Kazen 2011, 78–79.
44. Choksy 1989, 14–15. The category of khrafstra is assumed already in Vendidād (cf. 7:2–5; 8:16–18, 71; 9:26; 16:12; 17:3; 18:2). See also the Persian Rivayats (Dhabhar 1932, 268–70).
45. Kazen 2015b = ch. 4 in this volume.
46. For the argument that disease avoidance is a main function of disgust, see Navarrete and Fessler 2006; Curtis 2013, 21–40.

ated fertility has been shown to trigger human disgust.[47] The swarmers may also illustrate Rozin's category of "animal-nature disgust."[48] Note, however, that the priestly writers do not call the forbidden quadrupeds disgusting. And there is little biological reason for finding pigs or camels more disgusting to eat than cows and goats. There are different reasonable social and ecological explanations for avoiding pigs in the Israelite heartlands that originally have little or nothing to do with Yahwism or with particular Israelite ethnicity.[49] We have already seen that death does not provide a sufficient explanation for this avoidance. What about disgust? I have suggested a transfer of emotional disgust from more obvious triggers to others that are clearly culture specific, a disgust-by-association through the secondary use of disgust language as value judgment.[50]

It is fairly easy to associate skin disease, genital discharges, and corpse impurity with emotional disgust. The skin conditions defined as ṣāraʿat probably had to do with scaliness, damage, and decay of the body envelope, which is one of Rozin's basic disgust triggers. The association of a corpse or a grave with decaying matter is an obvious example of another of Rozin's triggers. Genital discharges would involve several of these triggers, in particular when considering the difference in facilities for personal hygiene between the ancient and the modern world. Discharges and corpses would naturally have caused foul smells, as probably did to lesser extent certain pathological skin conditions. In the latter case, revulsion could be triggered not only by fear of death and unsavory appearance, but by mere odor—something that is corroborated by theories and research

---

47. Miller 2004, 47–58; Kolnai 2004, 52–62; Miller 1997, 38–59.

48. Rozin, Haidt, and McCauley 2000, 641–42. Rozin's category of animal-nature disgust has been questioned by Feinstein (2010, 27), who argues that "if the primary function of disgust were to conceal our similarity to animals, we would surely be more disgusted by relatively human-like creatures, such as primates and other 'higher mammals,' than by insects and worms."

49. Archaeological evidence (the presence or absence of pig bones) suggests that pigs were not consumed in the many new villages that appeared in the hill country at the beginning of Iron Age I, although they were eaten in the coastal plain, the lowland, and the Transjordan. Pork was avoided or not eaten for several reasons and in several places that were not within the sphere of ancient Israelite culture. Cf. Provan, Long, and Longman 2003, 187–89; Finkelstein 1997, 227–30; 1998, 18–20; Hesse and Wapnish 1997.

50. Kazen 2011, 81–89, 93–94; cf. Neusner 1973, 11.

on disgust.[51] The contempt with which dischargers and people with skin disease are spoken of in some contexts (cf. 2 Sam 3:29), and the disparaging remarks about menstrual blood found not only in biblical literature but globally,[52] also attest to disgust as an important underlying explanation for these conceptions of impurity.

Death and decay could, in a broad sense, fit in some of these instances as a possible underlying explanation, but disgust does as well or better. Admittedly, disgust language is rarely used in legal texts on contagious impurities, but descriptions of individuals with skin disease, comments about them and about dischargers, and the use of menstrual-discharge language to enhance emotional indignation against idolatry are evidence of appeals to emotional disgust, or that disgust is at least assumed. Disgust fits less well, however, in explaining the postpartum impurity of new mothers, lasting forty or eighty days (Lev 12). Although genital bleeding is involved, what is the meaning of the long periods of impurity? It is unlikely that new mothers would be perceived as being more disgusting than some of the pathological dischargers, and nowhere in Israelite thought are mothers understood to be repulsive. Here again, we must assume that conceptions of impurity, initially based on aversion against people with pathological genital discharges, were transferred by analogy to new mothers because of their genital bleeding.

The Holiness Code (Lev 17–26) is replete with disgust terminology when referring to inappropriate or immoral behavior, branded as impure. This is particularly apparent in Lev 18 and 20 with regard to behaviors that are perceived as sexual offenses of various kinds: incest, as well as sexual relations between men, during menstruation, with animals, and so on. Certain moral offenses and sexual behaviors in particular belong to Rozin's already-mentioned disgust triggers. One of the most conspicuous terms in the varied disgust vocabulary of Lev 18 and 20 is *tôʿēbâ*, "abomination," specifically used in Lev 18:24–30 to summarize prohibited behaviors. Elsewhere (Deuteronomy, 1–2 Kings, Isaiah, Jeremiah, Ezekiel), this

---

51. Kazen 2011, 34–35, 82.

52. Milgrom (1991, 763–65) provides several examples from ancient Egypt, Babylonia, Persia, pre-Islamic Arabia, the Hittites, Greece, etc. Pliny's disdain of menstrual blood is often noted (*Nat.* 7:64): "Contact with it turns new wine sour, crops touched by it become barren, grafts die, seeds in gardens are dried up, the fruit of trees falls off … even bronze and iron are at once seized by rust, and a horrible smell fills the air" (Rackham 1961). Cf. the strong feelings expressed by Ezek 36:17.

term relates to idolatry, and in Proverbs it refers to serious sins in general. Throughout Deuteronomy it is also used to denote defective sacrifice, invalid offerers, false weights, and certain remarriages, as well as unclean food, as we have already seen.[53] Although capable of expressing a primary disgust reaction, *tôʿēbâ* has often been used secondarily to characterize unacceptable acts to such an extent that it has lost its embodied emotional base and has become primarily a value judgment. In the Holiness Code, however, it seems to retain some of its primary force. In Lev 20, other terms are also used to describe divine disgust with Israel's sexual sins and eating of unclean foods. In some of the prophets, especially in Ezekiel and Lamentations, idolatry is frequently denounced by the use of menstrual imagery, implying divine revulsion.[54] The coarse and raw language employed by some of the texts is clearly intended to evoke disgust. As Klawans has pointed out, at times murder is also associated with impurity, at least excessive bloodshed, murder of the innocent (Ps 106:34–41), and bloodshed in which the perpetrator is unknown and cannot be punished.[55] In the latter case the land in particular is considered defiled (Num 35:33–34), but disgust language is not used explicitly here, as it is in the case of the land being defiled by sexual sins and idolatry, according to the Holiness Code. Although certain immoral behaviors that are thought to defile the land are also understood as disgusting, the question arises whether disgust is capable of explaining the full range of immoral behaviors associated with impurity.

I have mentioned above some of the issues that my hypothesis can raise. I never claimed, however, that disgust could explain every detail in the priestly purity laws. I only suggest that disgust presents a plausible common denominator for at least the three main *types* of impurity outlined in the legal texts: food laws, bodily contagion, and immoral behavior. I also suggest that several details and some specific impurities can be explained as extensions and analogies, and that the language of impurity and disgust is used at times secondarily, having lost its immediate emotional and embodied grounding, often in order to transfer indignation to items that would not by themselves necessarily evoke disgust.[56] As an underlying explanation for the wide and varied use of impurity language

---

53. Cf. Preuss 2006, 591–604.
54. Cf. Lemos 2013, 290–92.
55. Klawans 2000, 26–29.
56. See n. 50 above.

in the Hebrew Bible, I find disgust more plausible and coherent than any combination of birth, death, sex, and disease that has been suggested to date, even when such combinations are subsumed under an abstract heading such as "the cycle of mortality."

Despite using cognitive tools for understanding the *emotional* side of impurity in my previous studies, I did not use the potential of cognitive linguistics to explain the *use* of emotional impurity *language*. This is, however, precisely what is needed for bridging the gap between the obvious examples of immediate emotional disgust involved in some conceptions of impurity and those features that I have described as extensions or analogies. Martha Himmelfarb has argued that the association of sin and impurity in Qumran texts is primarily evocative rather than halakic.[57] Himmelfarb's context is related to Klawans's understanding of the Qumranites as conflating ritual with moral impurity, which he regards as separate categories.[58] I have previously criticized Klawans's categorization for being arbitrary and not considering ritual impurity as a metaphor in itself, as well as for assuming that purity ceases to be a ritual category when applied to moral matters.[59] I now suggest that conceptual metaphor theory, and conceptual blending in particular, can help explain how purity language is used to evoke emotions of disgust originally associated with particular items and substances in new contexts.

Conceptual Metaphor and Blending

Conceptual metaphor theory understands metaphor to be more than a comparison or analogy by figure of speech.[60] According to this theory, popularized primarily by George Lakoff and Mark Johnson, metaphors carry notions from one cognitive or conceptual domain to another, providing the latter with new impetus, different understanding, and change of meaning. Metaphors are cross-domain mappings from a source to a target domain, and as such relate not only to language but to our way of thinking, and eventually influence our actions or behavior (see fig. 5.1). According to Lakoff and Johnson, metaphors highlight and organize certain aspects

---

57. Himmelfarb 2001, 37.
58. Klawans 2000, 67–91.
59. Kazen 2010a, 204–7.
60. Lakoff and Johnson 1980a; 1980b; 1999.

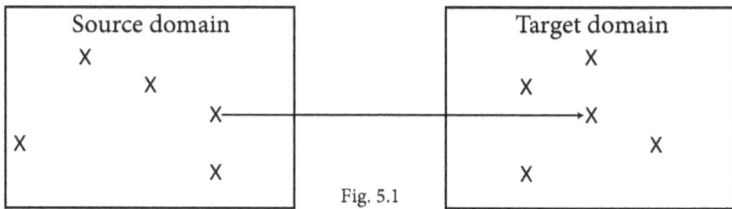

Fig. 5.1

of our experience, and their entailments guide our future actions, reinforcing the metaphor and turning it almost into a self-fulfilling prophecy.[61]

Conceptual blending, as defined by Gilles Fauconnier and John Turner, further explains the kind of influence that metaphors have on our actions or behavior, which goes beyond mere analogical projection.[62] According to mental space theory, meaning is located in the mental representations of the speaker and the addressee. Mental spaces are frames within which images or mental representations function, and these spaces form a network (see fig. 5.2). Various spaces relate to different cognitive domains. We can then consider an underlying, or as spatially represented in the following figures, an overarching generic space (GS) that maps (upper dashed lines) those particular elements (x) that are common to several input spaces (IS), and makes it possible to relate those spaces to each other (solid lines) at a first level. But several other elements (x) in the input spaces may not seem to fit into the same category, and when some of these are combined in a blend (lower dashed lines), the result is something that is not inherent in any of the input spaces. The blended space (BS) is facilitated by the generic space, but becomes a new type of conceptual framework, which creates new meaning and leads to novel integrated action. Blends are a natural part of human language and conceptual integration; indeed, children may accept and make some blends more readily than adults because they lack certain domain-specific knowledge.[63]

Similarly to Fauconnier and Turner, Seanna Coulson and Todd Oakley distinguish three blending processes: composition, completion, and elaboration. The blended frame can be completed or complemented with inferences from a source domain, and elaborated by mental or physical simulations, which can be coupled with activity. In action blends, activity from

---

61. Lakoff and Johnson 1980a, 156.
62. Fauconnier and Turner 2002.
63. Fauconnier and Turner 2002, 17–57; Coulson and Oakley 2000.

5. The Role of Disgust in Priestly Purity Law

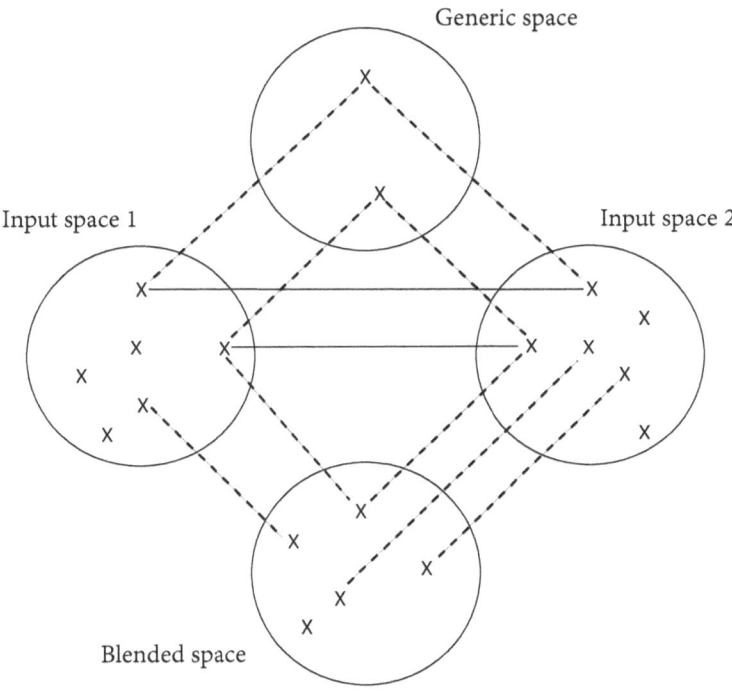

Fig. 5.2

one domain can be applied to elements from another. Blending can help us better understand the relationship between language, thought, and activity in general.[64] Eve Sweetser describes a causal relationship between two mental spaces, one for representation and one for the represented. She suggests that depictive representations (e.g., language, art) are attempts to adapt representations (words, pictures, etc.) to the world, while performative representations (through words, pictures, or rituals, etc.) attempt to reverse the relation, making the world fit one's representations. Thus, two types of causal relationship are possible between the representation and the represented space, and in the second type the real world is understood to be affected and changed by its representations.[65]

---

64. Coulson and Oakley 2000, 142–43.
65. Sweetser 2000, 305–33.

Impurity as a Conceptual Metaphor

Our first step is to consider various conceptions of impurity as conceptual metaphors within a simple framework of cognitive or conceptual domains, where the direction is from a source to a target domain. The origin and meaning of the most common Hebrew word for impure and impurity, *ṭāmēʾ*, *tumʾâ*, has been much discussed. The Syriac cognate verb can also mean to be "soiled" or "sticky," and the corresponding Egyptian Arabic root means "silt." Later Arabic *ṭamā* means "be choked with mud," and *ṭammay* is "mud of the Nile."[66] Wilfried Paschen suggests "feuchter Schmutz," moist dirt, as the original meaning of *ṭāmēʾ*.[67]

Etymology is not necessarily an indication of meaning, and in this case the etymology is uncertain. But the suggestion that the notion of literal dirt lies at the root of the term used for a variety of conceptions of impurity makes good sense and makes it possible to explain the variety of usages with the help of conceptual metaphor theory. The original source domain for *ṭāmēʾ* can be construed as the experience of being sullied by some dirty substance, an experience associated with feelings of discomfort and disgust and with a wish to have the dirt removed, which in the case of literal dirt would be effected by scraping or washing.

One target domain consists of experiences of unsavory human beings, who evoke similar feelings of discomfort and disgust (see fig. 5.3). Mapping the notion of dirt onto this domain, classifying such people and their state as *ṭāmēʾ*, dirty, makes contact with them or their fluid or scaly issues into a kind of defilement that can be purified by water. The people involved would naturally have to be subjected to various degrees of restriction, isolation, or expulsion, and in certain cases their impurity may require more than washing with water in order to be removed. This

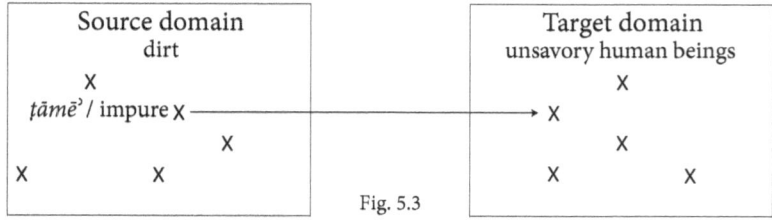

Fig. 5.3

---

66. André and Ringgren 1986, 330. Cf. Feinstein 2010, 51.
67. Paschen 1970, 27.

5. The Role of Disgust in Priestly Purity Law 121

Source domain dirt		Target domain objectionable behavior
X		X
ṭāmēʾ / impure X ——————————→		X
X		X
X X		X X

Fig. 5.4

Source domain dirt		Target domain disgusting creatures
X		X
ṭāmēʾ / impure X ——————————→		X
X		X
X X		X X

Fig. 5.5

corresponds to what we find in Lev 13–15 about impurity from skin disease, mold, and genital discharges.[68]

Another target domain consists of experiences of objectionable behavior, such as sexual offense or bloodshed, that also evoke feelings of disgust or at least discomfort (see fig. 5.4). Mapping the notion of dirt onto this domain classifies such acts as impure and thus in need of being "removed." Unlike contact with unsavory humans, this is not merely a case of personal contamination but rather a sense that social structures are being defiled. Because such dirt cannot be washed or scraped away, the feeling of contamination must be addressed by the removal of the perpetrator. This corresponds to the moral impurities found in the Holiness Code (Lev 17–26) as well as in other texts, resulting in the death or *kārēt* penalty, or in expulsion from the land. Conceptions of blood revenge also fit in here (Num 35:9–34; Deut 19:1–13; 21:1–9).[69]

A third target domain consists of experiences of "yucky" creatures, creepy and slimy things associated with rotting, as well as carcasses (see fig. 5.5). By mapping the notion of *ṭāmēʾ* onto these, they are classified as

---

68. In the case of skin disease, shaving is required in addition to washing, (Lev 13:33; 14:8, 9), and scraping and the removal of stones is required in the analogous extension of *ṣāraʿat* laws for mold in houses (Lev 14:33–53).

69. Note the provisions for unintended manslaughter (cities of refuge), and the magical/apotropaic rite of breaking a heifer's neck to effect removal for the people and free them from bloodguilt in case the murderer could not be found and removed by blood revenge or refuge. Cf. Kazen 2011, 135–37.

unfit to eat or to have contact with, as stated in Lev 11. It is difficult to envisage how such "dirt" could be removed if eaten, short of a rite for rinsing the digestive system; therefore, we find no purification rites for having eaten these unclean foods. But touching carcasses of such disgusting things (*šeqeṣ*) results in contact contamination, as in the case of coming in contact with impure human beings, which can be removed by purification in water.

Some of the discrepancies between these three domains with regard to contamination and purification turn out to be natural variations, when we consider that they result from the mapping of a source domain with the notion of *ṭāmēʾ*, as discomforting or disgusting dirt in need of being removed, onto target domains that similarly focus on discomforting or disgusting issues. Consider what the reasonable results would be of mapping "yucky dirt" onto worship of other gods, murder, foreign women, divorced women, same-sex intercourse, or foreign lands. Not all of these would intrinsically trigger feelings of discomfort or disgust, but biblical texts describe all these issues using impurity language and associate them with disgust.[70]

How are we to understand such metaphorical transfer? Is idol worship, for example, condemned and branded impure because it evokes disgust? Or is the use of purity and disgust language a rhetorical means by which worship of other divinities is condemned? Is a divorcée experienced as repulsive to her former husband (perhaps because someone else has subsequently had sex with her)[71] and hence regarded impure and forbidden to him? Or is her return to her former husband called *tôʿēbâ* to underline the prohibition and evoke feelings of repulsion, and thus prevent him from taking her back? Are unclean animals forbidden because they are experienced as yucky, or are they called disgusting to emphasize the taboo and persuade people not to eat them? We can sense a power play under the surface of the text, as a worldview is constructed and formulated through particular applications of impurity language, but simple conceptual metaphor theory goes only so far in explaining how this happens; it moves only in one direction, from source to target domain, which is enough to support an understanding of disgust as an underlying *general* explanation for

---

70. A few examples: worship of foreign gods, child sacrifice, and murder: 2 Kgs 21; Jer 44; Ezek 16; 23; 36; foreign women: Ezra 9–10; divorced women: Deut 24:1–4; same-sex intercourse: Lev 18:22; 20:13; foreign lands: Amos 7:17; Hos 9:3–4.

71. Pressler 1993, 60–61.

5. The Role of Disgust in Priestly Purity Law 123

different conceptions of impurity, but not enough to explain all the *details* and *nuances*. At this point, blending theory can complement the picture.

Disgust in Conceptual Blends

Conceptual spaces are similar to domains, but they are often understood to be more limited, drawing on wider domains. For our present purpose, however, a clear differentiation between spaces and domains is not crucial. Usually four-space models are used. Our first example of mapping the source domain of being sullied by dirt onto the target domain of unsavory people (fig. 5.3) is illustrated in figure 5.6.

Avoidance of repulsive experiences can be construed as a generic space that the two input spaces have in common. Input space 1 is contact with dirt, which is experienced as repulsive, to be avoided, and defined as impure (*ṭāmēʾ*). Dirt usually sticks and can be removed by washing. Input space 2 is contact with certain people (in this case, people with skin disease or dischargers), who are likewise felt to be repulsive and thus avoided. Such people

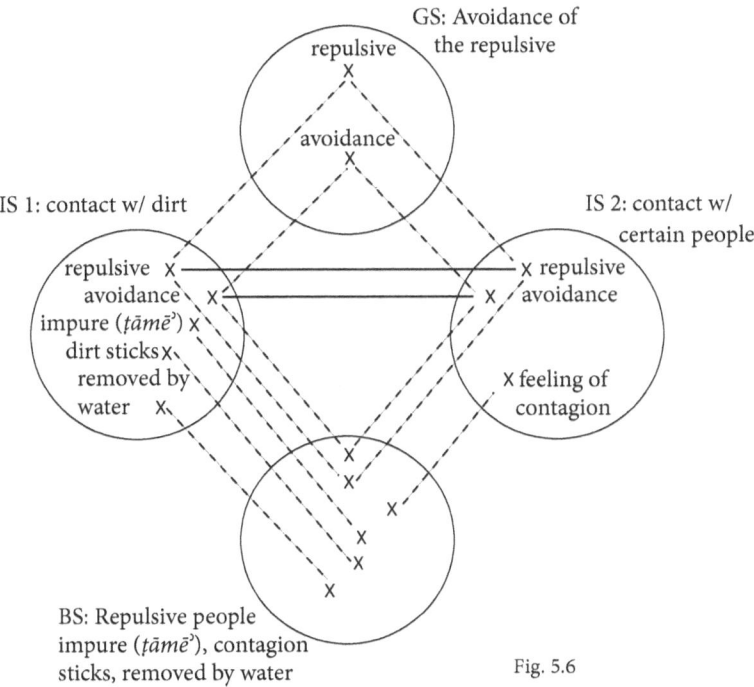

Fig. 5.6

often trigger uneasy feelings of contagion. It is not clear, however, what this something is or how it could be removed. In the blended space, some of the particulars from input space 1 are combined with those of input space 2, so that the repulsive categories of people are understood as impure (dirty, *ṭāmē'*) and contact with them as causing impurity and requiring removal. Such impurity can then be envisaged as possibly removable by water, as in the case of ordinary dirt, or in certain instances by other means.[72]

This is an example of how a fairly simple blend is composed and completed using inferences from two input spaces, and it can be further elaborated in several steps. Certain details, common to the two spaces, facilitate the blend. Others are specific to one of the spaces and produce innovations in the blend. The blend can function as a kind of simulation, a mental experiment of sorts (what happens if we think this way about that or that way about this?), and bring about action (in this case, water rituals or other types of ritual).

To apply blending theory to the discussion of moral and ritual impurity, we resort to one of Klawans's examples of metaphorical use of ritual language, Ps 51:4, 9 (ET 51:2, 7).[73]

> Wash me thoroughly from my iniquity,
> and cleanse me from my sin....
> Purge me with hyssop, and I shall be clean;
> wash me, and I shall be whiter than snow.[74]

The blending process is illustrated in figure 5.7. I am assuming a similar generic space as before, but with a focus on the need for removal of whatever is perceived as repulsive. Input space 1 is contamination by contact with impure (*ṭāmē'*) and repulsive categories of people (cf. the previous blend), which is understood to be removable through various purification rites, mainly by washing, but also by certain magical rites using special materials, including hyssop.[75] Input space 2 is sinful behavior, in this case rape or murder or both, similarly repulsive and normally "removed" by

---

72. Such as shaving and scraping, n. 68 above.
73. See Klawans 2000, 35–36. Klawans regards this example of moral impurity as a metaphor, in contrast to other instances where he calls it "literal."
74. All scriptural quotations in this chapter follow the NRSV.
75. Cf. the purification rites for *ṣāra'at* (Lev 14) and the production of purification water for sprinkling the corpse impure (Num 19).

5. The Role of Disgust in Priestly Purity Law

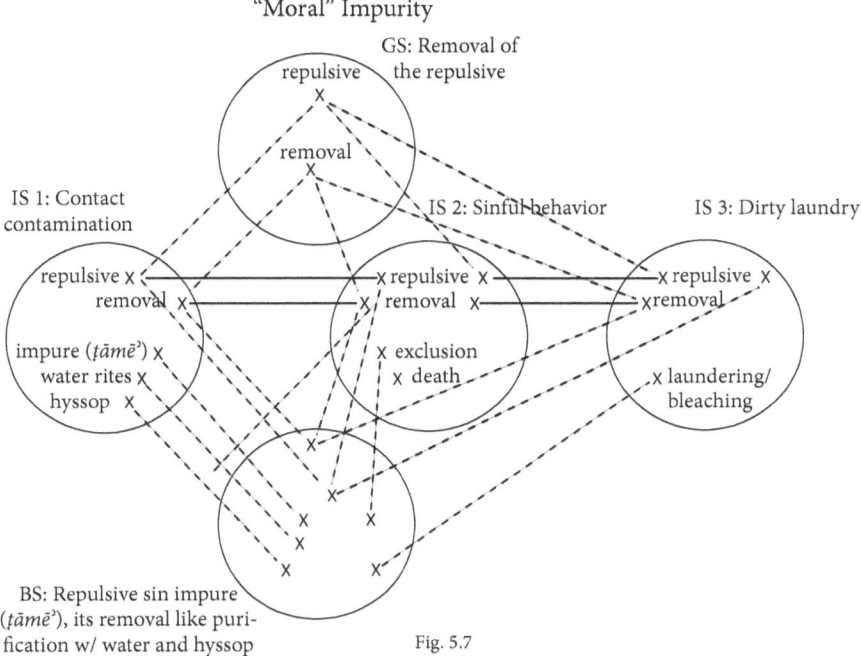

Fig. 5.7

death (blood revenge) or some form of exclusion. Input space 3 refers to dirty clothes (stained laundry), supposedly repulsive, with the dirt being removed by laundering and bleaching.

The outcome in the blended space, as expressed in Ps 51, is that David's sinful and repulsive behavior is understood as impure (*ṭāmēʾ*), and that this impurity is envisaged as removable both by laundering and by special purification rites, using water and special ritual materials (hyssop). In one sense, the use of impurity language for moral sin is evidently metaphorical, but in another sense it is not secondary in relation to so-called ritual impurity because both depend equally on a blend with the notion of physical dirt.

Although the reference to washing away sin is often seen as a secondary or metaphorical appeal to a more literal rite of purification from contact contamination or from bodily discharges, from the perspective of blending theory, what matters are the *effects* to which the blend leads. All three input spaces share notions of repulsion and the need for removal. In addition, input space 1 brings in washing and hyssop as ritual means of purification; input space 2 implies exclusion, rejection, blood revenge, and death penalty; input space 3 contributes notions of physical dirt, laundering, and bleaching. The resulting blend is a piece of innovative poetry in which iniquity is envisaged as washable away, the guilt of rape and murder removable by purification with water and hyssop, and the person, the inner being represented by the heart, as capable of being laundered and bleached. All this involves several layers of metaphor, which might be further disentangled. One could perhaps argue that the focus is on the rape/murder issue and that the metaphorical process can be better understood as a simple one-way movement in which both contact contamination and dirty laundry are mapped onto a moral failing. Blending theory, however, helps us see the details and nuances of the metaphorical process much better.

As noted before, there are several details within the main conceptions of impurity that do not immediately seem to fit the suggested disgust paradigm. One of these is the impure pig, for which there is little reason to feel disgust. I have already suggested that this is an example of an extension. Blending theory can provide a fuller explanation, as we can see in figure 5.8 (Lev 11; Deut 14).

The generic space is again understood as avoidance, but in this case it is specified as food avoidance. Both pigs (input space 1) and swarmers (input space 2) are to be avoided, based on the lists of unclean animals in Deut 14 and Lev 11. The problematic nature of the precise relationship between these two texts complicates this case somewhat; therefore, the following argument does not depend on intertextual relationships but is based on the development of underlying conceptions.[76] As noted, a traditional list of forbidden quadrupeds behind either of these versions is likely not to have referred to disgust, although the list in Deut 14, in its redacted setting, is prefaced by the command not to eat anything abominable (*tôʿēbâ*).[77] Disgust is primarily associated with the small creeping or crawling animals called "swarmers" (*šereṣ*), a term that refers only to insects in Deut 14, but is elaborated in Lev 11, where all such animals are explicitly said to be repulsive or disgusting (*šeqeṣ*), and their carcasses must not be touched.

---

76. For further discussion of the relationship between Lev 11 and Deut 14, see Kazen 2011, 72–81; for a discussion of food avoidances in preexilic Israel, see Kazen 2015b = ch. 4 in this volume.

77. See n. 42 above.

5. The Role of Disgust in Priestly Purity Law

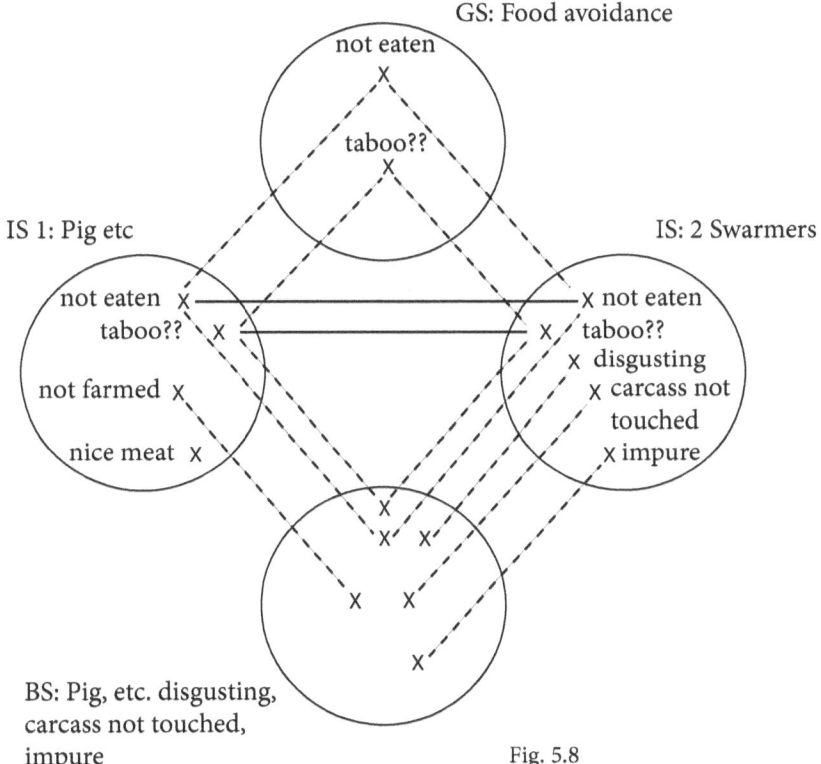

Fig. 5.8

Whether or not pigs were completely taboo in preexilic Israel is open to discussion, but they were not raised in the Israelite heartlands.[78] They do not taste bad, however, and together with several of the other larger quadrupeds branded as unclean they would have been excellent sources of protein. The broad category of repulsive swarmers is specifically created by the priestly authors of Lev 11, although "bird swarmers" (insects) are mentioned in Deut 14, as noted. This can be understood intuitively as a result of primary feelings of disgust toward creatures of this kind. But it is difficult to use these explanations to account for considering pigs and some other quadrupeds as unclean and repulsive to consume or to come in contact with when they are dead. This outcome may be explained as a result of conceptual blending whereby the pig and some other land animals not gen-

---

78. See n. 49.

erally eaten by Israelites acquired characteristics (repulsive, unclean, and forbidden to consume or touch) typical of small, crawling creatures such as insects and vermin, which were subsequently categorized as swarmers in Lev 11. Whether these swarmers were initially designated as impure (*ṭāmēʾ*) only to touch or also to eat is a moot point, which I do not discuss here.[79] The net result, however, is that the pig is perceived as unclean, therefore implicitly disgusting, and at times even explicitly *declared* to be repulsive, as in the introductory use of *tôʿēbâ* in Deut 14:3. By the use of such rhetorical means, emotional disgust is extended to animals that would ordinarily not evoke disgust for any intrinsic reasons. Feinstein explains that

> biblical authors are not, by and large, interested in promoting an attitude of disgust toward ritual pollutants and do not mandate total rejection of them.... The description of an entity as disgusting and the demand that people revile it are rhetorically useful only when total rejection of the entity is desired, and when disgust at the entity is reasonably possible but cannot be assumed.[80]

It is possible that the pig belongs to the earliest traditional food avoidances, and that these were complemented and transformed by influences of Persian practices (swarmers, cf. *khrafstra*). The result is similar, however, in that emotional disgust associated with one input space is applied to animals from another input space in the blend, creating a new or refined system.

A similar example is that of new mothers, illustrated in figure 5.9 (Lev 12). This looks like a straightforward case but elicits many questions. The similarity between menstruating women and new mothers is clear: both bleed, which is a natural part of life. One case, however, is a regularly recurring event associated with impurity and disgust in Israelite thought. The other case is less regular, and associated with the birth of new beings, which for every other reason is a cause of joy. Although similar, in many respects the two types of bleeding are opposites. In the blend, the impurity of menstrual blood is mapped onto childbirth. Although menstrual impurity seems to follow from feelings of disgust, this does not necessarily mean that new mothers are perceived as disgusting. Not everything impure

---

79. This, for example, is suggested by Milgrom (1991, 656–59, 671), but it is debatable. Cf. Nihan 2007, 284–88, 291; Kazen 2011, 72–81.

80. Feinstein 2010, 78.

5. The Role of Disgust in Priestly Purity Law

The *Yôledet*

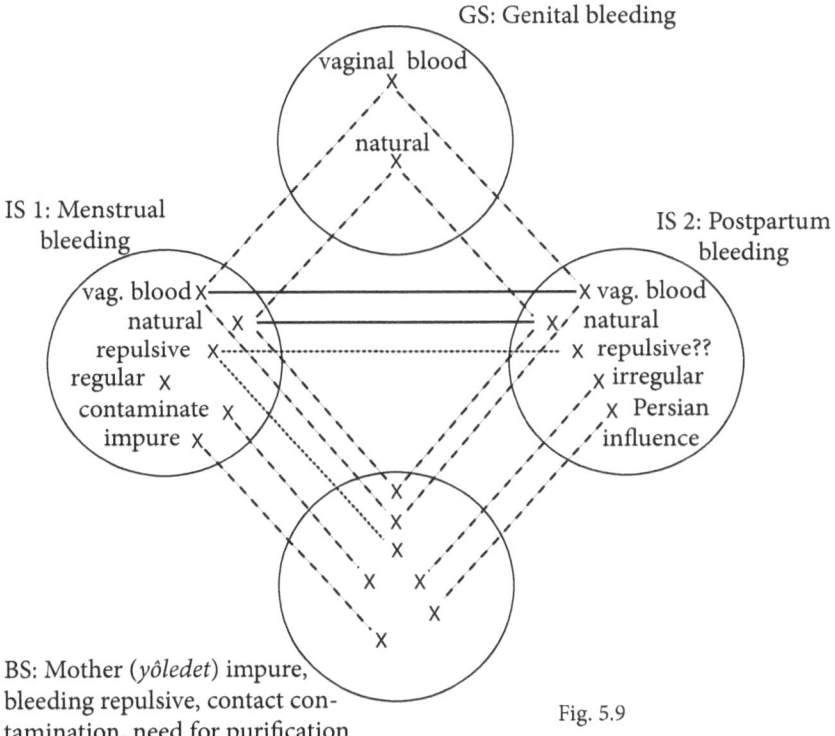

Fig. 5.9

(*ṭāmēʾ*) acquires the quality of disgust, and not everything disgusting is thought of as impure. Did women with postnatal bleeding smell like menstruating women probably did in premodern ancient West Asian societies because of lack of modern hygienic facilities? And did they do so for forty or eighty days, as indicated by the time frames in Lev 12? Probably not, and even if they did, this would not necessarily have categorized them as impure. What makes them *ṭāmēʾ* is the cognitive blend, which in this case results from systemic reasoning. Elaboration of this blend naturally leads to an understanding of new mothers being somehow restricted or isolated during an extended purification period and having to undergo elaborate rites, similar to those performed in the case of other genital dischargers, but not identical. All this fits with the common view of Lev 12 as having been inserted into the purity laws (11–15) at a late stage in the development or redaction of the material. In addition to some possibly magical

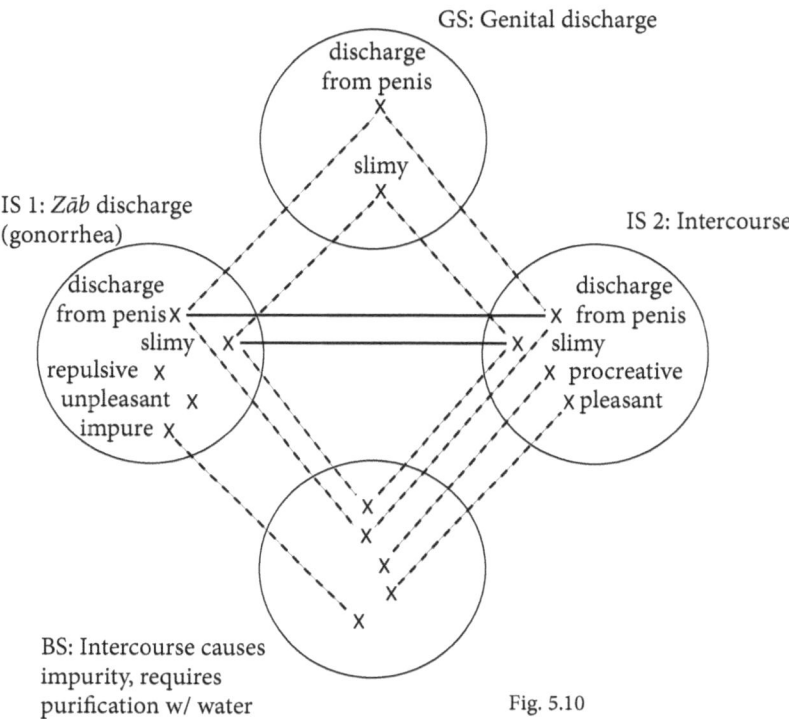

Fig. 5.10

underlying conceptions, we can also suspect Persian influence on certain tendencies in Lev 12.[81]

Sexual intercourse is another example (Lev 15) for which blending can provide some explanation of conceptions that would otherwise be difficult to understand. It is unlikely that Israelites would feel aversion to marital sex in general, and there is no reason to assume disgust behind the impurity and purification rituals associated with sexual intercourse as such. Nevertheless, disgust could easily enter the picture through a simple blending process. This is illustrated in figure 5.10.

Although we can use a simple conceptual metaphor model to map impurity onto intercourse, this does not provide as complete an explanation as blending theory does. The decisive link is probably provided by the fact that intercourse involves a discharge of semen, which, how-

---

81. See Kazen 2015b = ch. 4 in this volume.

ever dissimilar it may be from pathological discharge caused by diseases such as gonorrhea, may have been experienced as sufficiently close in many respects. A man with a pathological genital discharge (*zāb*) was considered *ṭāmēʾ*, probably because of feelings of disgust toward the fluid, the emission of which could not be controlled. (The disgust toward the male fluids may have been reinforced by disgust toward female discharges, for which we have more evidence.) The crucial issue for *zāb* impurity seems to have been contact with the fluid. A mind bent on systemic thinking can easily find reasons to extend such impurity to contact with semen in general. There is no mechanism forcing the notion of disgust onto such extensions of impurity, and no reason to assume an underlying feeling of disgust toward sexual intercourse. The blend is an innovation based on common as well as dissimilar traits. As a result, sex becomes associated with impurity, an association that has long-term effects.

A conceptual blending perspective has the potential to shed new light on several conceptions of impurity and their development. Such analyses can be carried out at various levels of detail and refinement. One obvious candidate for an extended analysis is the Ezra-Nehemiah tradition that denounces intermarriages because of the impurities and abominations of the people of the land, and speaks of "pure seed."[82] But suffice it for now to close with a few examples from the book of Ezekiel. Although it is a prophetic text, it is closely related to priestly theology and law. These texts denounce idolatry using the language of disgust in a cognitive blend, appealing to revulsion against both menstrual blood and female sexuality in general (Ezek 36; 16; 23).[83] The first of two examples is taken from Ezek 36:16–18 (see fig. 5.11).

> The word of the LORD came to me:
> Mortal, when the house of Israel lived on their own soil, they defiled it with their ways and their deeds; their conduct in my sight was like the uncleanness of a woman in her menstrual period. So I poured out my wrath upon them for the blood that they had shed upon the land, and for the idols with which they had defiled it.

---

82. See especially Ezra 9–10, and in particular Ezra 9:1–2, 11–14. Cf. Hayes 2002; Harrington 2004, 112–28.

83. I am indebted to Tracy Lemos for bringing to my attention the relevance of the Ezekiel texts for this discussion.

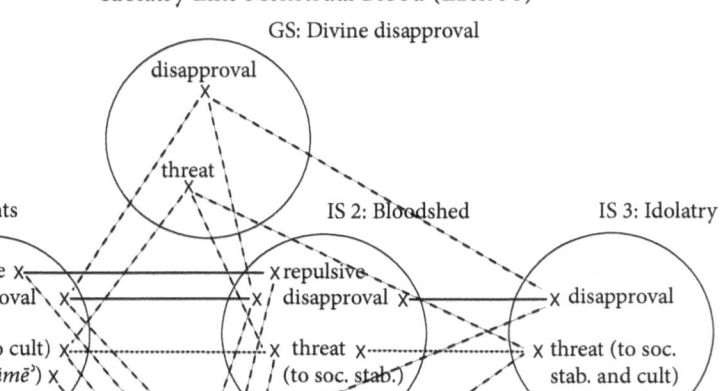

Fig. 5.11

In this text, disgust toward genital discharges, menstrual blood in particular, which is considered to be impure, is mapped onto bloodshed and idolatrous practices. The general space concerns divine disapproval, and it corresponds in a sense to the threat against the people of Israel that is envisaged by the author(s). Input space 1 provides the connection between impurity and disgust. The menstruating woman and menstrual blood are assumed to be disgusting and therefore impure. Input space 2 is in itself somewhat of a blend. It shares bleeding with input space 1. Bloodshed can be thought of as immediately emotionally disgusting in itself, but the association with genital bleeding makes it more susceptible to notions of impurity. Input space 3, worship of other divinities, is not intrinsically emotionally repulsive, but it is strictly forbidden in the world of Ezekiel (as in that of the Deuteronomist). Both input space 2 (bloodshed) and input space 3 (idolatry) are understood to be socially destabilizing and threatening, just as menstrual impurity in input space 1 threatens the cult. Therefore, the two are associated with each other, and through the blend, with menstrual blood, thus acquiring notions of impurity and disgust.

5. The Role of Disgust in Priestly Purity Law   133

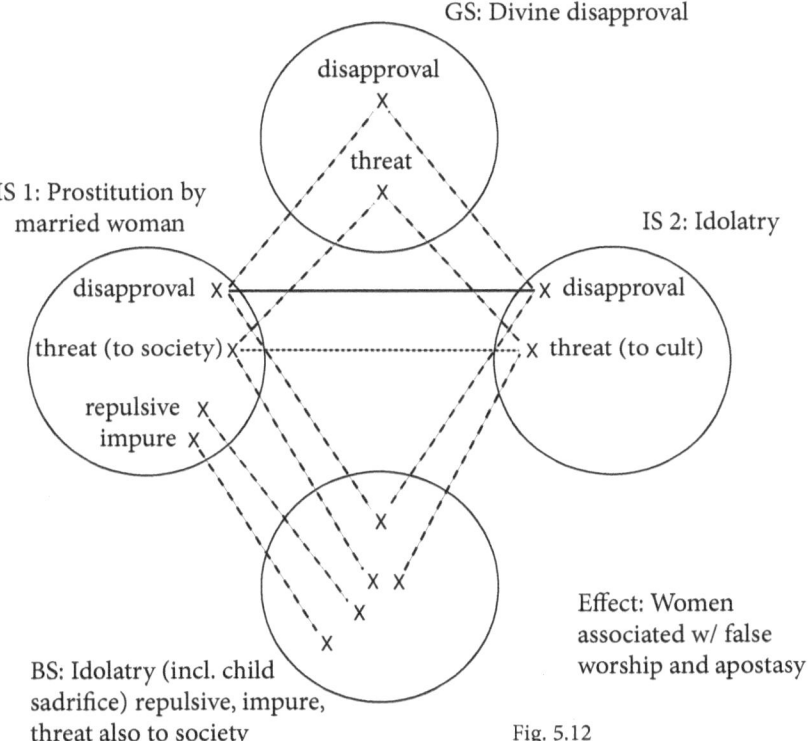

Fig. 5.12

Something similar takes place in the highly misogynist parables that compare Samaria and Jerusalem with adulterous women (wives) playing the whore (see fig. 5.12).

> You also took your beautiful jewels of my gold and my silver that I had given you, and made for yourself male images, and with them played the whore; and you took your embroidered garments to cover them, and set my oil and my incense before them. Also my bread that I gave you—I fed you with choice flour and oil and honey—you set it before them as a pleasing odor; and so it was, says the Lord GOD. You took your sons and your daughters, whom you had borne to me, and these you sacrificed to them to be devoured. As if your whorings were not enough! You slaughtered my children and delivered them up as an offering to them. And in all your abominations and your whorings you did not remember the days of your youth, when you were naked and bare, flailing about in your blood. (Ezek 16:17–22)

> Samaria has not committed half your sins; you have committed more abominations than they, and have made your sisters appear righteous by all the abominations that you have committed. (Ezek 16:51)

> When she saw them she lusted after them, and sent messengers to them in Chaldea. And the Babylonians came to her into the bed of love, and they defiled her with their lust; and after she defiled herself with them, she turned from them in disgust. (Ezek 23:16–17)

> Your lewdness and whorings have brought this upon you, because you played the whore with the nations, and polluted yourself with their idols. (Ezek 23:29–30)

> For they have committed adultery, and blood is on their hands; with their idols they have committed adultery; and they have even offered up to them for food the children whom they had borne to me. Moreover this they have done to me: they have defiled my sanctuary on the same day and profaned my sabbaths. For when they had slaughtered their children for their idols, on the same day they came into my sanctuary to profane it. This is what they did in my house. (Ezek 23:37–39)

In these texts, disgust at prostitution is mapped onto idolatry in general and child sacrifice in particular. The generic space is divine disapproval, and as in the previous example, it includes the particular threat against Israelite society and cult, which prostitution (input space 1) and idolatry (input space 2) were understood to pose. It is the combination of disapproval and fear that makes the blend possible, where emotional disgust and conceptions of impurity are associated with idolatry through metaphors of prostitution. The result is that worship of other gods is thoroughly despised and shunned. An additional result, however, is that women are intrinsically associated with false worship and apostasy. The disgust expressed at prostitution in input space 1 results from a general perception of patriarchy, women, and sexuality, itself a blend of the more general kind that we have already noted. The view of women behind input space 1 is further reinforced by the blend that results from mapping input space 1 onto input space 2. This of course does not appear for the first time in Ezekiel, but it is expressed with exceeding clarity in these texts. The manner in which the blend is further elaborated consolidates not only the links between impurity and disgust but also some of the underlying value systems.

Summary

I do not claim that emotional disgust is intrinsic to *all* conceptions of impurity in priestly law, nor that it explains every use of impurity language in biblical texts. Not everything disgusting is impure, and not everything impure is disgusting. I have suggested, however, that disgust is a common denominator underlying the three main categories in priestly law for which disgust language is used. Some expressions of impurity, both in legal texts and elsewhere, are extensions of conceptions with which they share only slight resemblances. Applying conceptual metaphor and blending theory, I have shown that there are reasonable explanations for the association of such expressions with conceptions of impurity that are more immediate expressions of emotional disgust. In my opinion, disgust is the most comprehensive and plausible explanation for the range of conceptions of impurity found in the biblical material. Biological evolution (emotional disgust) accounts for the basic mechanisms. Cultural evolution (the use and spread of conceptual metaphors) explains the further extension of conceptions of impurity to an expanding array of spaces or domains.

6
Disgust in Body, Mind, and Language: The Case of Impurity in the Hebrew Bible

> Disgust has evolved as a survival strategy to protect living beings from incorporating toxic substances and pathogens. But disgust in human beings is also a conceptual and cultural construction. Impurity language in the Bible is based on emotional disgust but operates on several levels. This chapter discusses the interaction between experiences or concepts of impurity and feelings of disgust in the human body, mind, and language. The tools employed are psycho-biological and cognitive-conceptual. Psychological and biological research supply insights into the mechanisms of disgust and its basic association with impurity. Conceptual metaphor and blending theories provide models for the extended use of impurity and disgust language in a variety of contexts and for various purposes. These tools are applied on a selection of texts representing the broad spectrum of use for impurity language in the Hebrew Bible.

This chapter explores the multileveled function of disgust in biblical purity discourse as an embodied emotion, a conceptual framework, and a rhetorical strategy. The methodological approach is broadly evolutionary (biopsychological) and cognitive-conceptual, including insights from neuroscience and linguistics (metaphor and blending theories). The texts referred to and analyzed represent a variety of genres (legal, narrative, prophetic) and are selected to illustrate different aspects and functions of disgust, ranging from ritual indexing and taboos, to moral indignation and general value judgments, to ostracism and ethnocentrism. The aim is to demonstrate how biological underpinnings and cultural constructions

---

This chapter was first published in *Mixed Feelings and Vexed Passions: Exploring Emotions in Biblical Literature*, ed. F. Scott Spencer, RBS 90 (Atlanta: SBL Press, 2017), 97–115. Used by permission.

of disgust interact and thereby provide resources for a better understanding of impurity and disgust reflected in biblical texts. The argument builds on my previous studies on impurity and disgust and incorporates some of their analyses and conclusions.[1]

Evolved Survival Strategy and Cultural Construction

From an evolutionary perspective, emotional disgust has evolved as a survival strategy, in order to protect living creatures from poison and pathogens in air, water, and potential food, as well as from contact with contaminated matter and individuals.[2] The extent to which various species of animals display signs of disgust is a much-discussed issue,[3] but for our purposes we can stay content with results from research on human beings.

Core disgust is usually understood as a primary emotion, a direct bodily response to repulsive stimuli. From this innate, ultimate base, a set of secondary emotions has evolved, which are also important for survival—but within a social framework, as they have evolved in parallel with culture.[4] Hence certain levels of disgust have predominantly cultural or proximate bases, although the biological and cultural underpinnings are not fully separable, as the final wiring of the human brain occurs through interaction with social and cultural experiences during periods of plasticity in childhood and adolescence.[5]

The psychological research of Paul Rozin and his colleagues is now well known. Rozin identifies nine empirically demonstrated triggers for disgust: food, body products, animals, sexual behaviors, contact with death or corpses, violations of the exterior envelope of the body (including gore and deformity), poor hygiene, interpersonal contamination (contact with unsavory human beings), and certain moral offenses.[6] It is interesting to

---

1. Kazen 2008; 2011, 9–94; 2014 = ch. 5 in this volume; 2018a = ch. 3 in this volume. For more detailed and overarching discussions of impurity, see also Kazen 2010a; 2010c; 2013a, 113–94.

2. Cf. Rozin, Haidt, and McCauley 2000, 639–40. For the argument that disease avoidance is a main function of disgust, see Navarrete and Fessler 2006; Curtis 2013, 1–40.

3. Cf. Darwin 1989; Curtis 2013, 38–40.

4. Damasio 1994, 129–39; Looy 2004; Rozin, Haidt, and McCauley 2000, 647–48. Cf. Kazen 2011, 9–19.

5. Haidt 2001. Cf. Preston and de Waal 2002.

6. Rozin, Haidt, and McCauley 2000, 637.

note the degree to which all of these triggers combine biologically evolved (ultimate) underpinnings with culturally construed (proximate) responses. Emotional disgust as we know it is always a mixture of innate and acquired capacities that have coevolved with culture, a combination of biological and psychological reactions blended and shaped within social contexts.

This complex emotional matrix is important to keep in mind as we take a closer look at a number of texts that explicitly or implicitly associate disgust with impurity. Although certain things that are labeled impure may be near universally experienced as disgusting, others do not commend themselves as particularly repulsive unless so learned through socialization in a particular context. Since culture pervades all human life, some measure of cultural construction is always present in disgust reactions, but the degree of visceral immediacy sometimes becomes quite acute. As we will see, such gut reaction may be transferred to and invested in new fields through culture, particularly through language and cognition.

Conceptualisation and Experience

Although many understand disgust as primarily triggered by taste and centered on the mouth (in line with the etymology of the term), others have rather emphasized the role of smell and touch.[7] A number of studies, from Charles Darwin's *The Expression of the Emotions in Man and Animals* and onward, have pointed out the ambiguous character of disgust as based on something "actually perceived or vividly imagined."[8] As a secondary emotion, disgust can be triggered by sight, memory, or thought, without direct engagement of other senses.[9]

The fact that disgust can be associated with a number of senses and can be not only imagined, but actually felt without any physical catalyst, is important to notice. An emotion is no less an emotion—and resides just as much in the body—when caused by nonphysical stimuli.[10] Dis-

---

7. See some of the classical studies of disgust. For an emphasis on taste and the mouth, Darwin 1989, 195; Angyal 1941, 395, 402, 411; for inclusion of smell and touch, cf. Kolnai 2004; Miller 1997, 6, 12, 60–79.

8. Darwin 1989, 195.

9. Miller 1997, 60–88; Haidt 2003, 857; Curtis 2013, 1–40.

10. This applies to all sense perceptions. The brain processes them in basically the same way, regardless of where the input comes from. See, e.g., Damasio 1994, 83–164, esp. 129–39.

gust can erupt from remembering or conceptualizing various objectionable items, situations, people, or behaviors, which normally evoke disgust in one's social and cultural context. This capacity makes disgust useful also for rhetorical purposes, since merely associating something with another typically disgusting item is quite efficient—a kind of disgust by association. Disgust thus becomes a ready way of expressing and transmitting values.

Morality, as increasingly acknowledged in recent thought, is not a matter of human rationality fighting against animalistic and selfish natural propensities, but a complex interaction of emotion and cognition, in which most of our "moral" behaviors derive from evolutionary adaptations and develop further through cultural and contextual coevolution. According to John Teehan, morality results from "our emotions, our cognitive processes, and the complex relationship between the two."[11] Hence we can talk of "moral emotions," with disgust usually counting among them. In Jonathan Haidt's view, moral emotions *"are linked to the interests or welfare either of society as a whole or at least of persons other than the judge or agent."*[12] These include emotions that motivate prosocial action, but also other-condemning emotions, such as contempt, anger, and disgust. The latter put constraints on people in social contexts by responding to injustice and protecting human integrity.

That disgust plays a prominent role in this game is clear from the way it often signifies moral dislike. As many have pointed out, however, the involvement of disgust in moral evaluation does not mean that moral rules should be based on universally felt disgust.[13] Socially conditioned emotions can hardly be trusted for moral guidance, since they are precisely that—socially conditioned. To use disgust as a normative yardstick is risky, not to say dangerous.[14] Such caveats notwithstanding, disgust remains a rhetorically powerful tool, a bodily emotional reaction, that can be evoked not only by exposure to physical experiences, but also by mere conceptualization. In the following, we will examine some expressions of disgust in biblical texts to see how they resonate with bodily experiences, mental conceptualizations, and rhetorical use of language.

---

11. Teehan 2003, 58.
12. Haidt 2003, 853, emphasis original.
13. Kekes 1992, 438, 441.
14. Nussbaum 2004, 13–15, 72–171.

Disgust and Impurity in the Law, Prophets, and Writings

The concept of impurity is especially suited as a topos for exploring disgust emotions, since it frequently uses disgust terminology, and even when not explicitly employing expressions of revulsion, the context usually implies aversive feelings. Although priestly legal discourse on impurity and purification is often phrased in fairly "neutral" language,[15] the underlying visceral aspects of impurity are not far below the surface.

The food laws patently associate impurity and disgust. Deuteronomy 14:3 introduces its list of clean and unclean animals with the injunction not to eat anything abominable (*tôʿēbâ*). The complex text of Lev 11 brands all three categories of "swarmers" (*šereṣ*)—water, winged, and ground swarmers—as detestable (*šeqeṣ*), just like birds of prey.[16]

The subsequent ritual purity laws concerning impure conditions (skin diseases, molds, genital discharges) and their purification through ablutions, shaving, scraping, and certain apotropaic practices (Lev 12–15) do not explicitly employ disgust language. This does not mean, however, that these conditions were not regarded as repulsive, only that the technical instructions for removing the impurity did not require emotional motivation. The culturally conditioned attitude to such conditions is evident from other texts. Though no disgust terminology is used, Aaron's description of the "leprous" Miriam (Num 12:10–13) clearly appeals to the disgust felt at the sight of particular types of skin disease (*ṣāraʿat*). The contempt with which people with skin diseases and discharges are mentioned in 2 Sam 3:29 also strongly suggests an underlying emotional attitude of disgust toward their physical conditions.

The clearest example of emotional disgust associated with genital bleeding may be found in Ezekiel's use of menstrual imagery (*niddâ*) for defiling behavior (36:17), which in the larger context (36:31) is characterized as abominations (*tôʿēbôt*) and associated with loathing (*qûṭ*). Similarly, the impurity of menstruants (*ṭəmēʾat hanniddâ*) in Ezek 22:10 is juxtaposed to abomination (*tôʿēbâ*) and pollution (*ṭimmēʾ*) in verse 11. In certain contexts, as in Lev 20:21 (and probably also in 2 Chr 29:5), the term *niddâ* takes on a broader meaning, denoting something indecent and objectionable or aversive in general. In Ezra 9:11, the land to which the

---

15. As in the discharge laws of Lev 15. Cf. Wright 1991.
16. For a discussion of "swarmers" in Lev 11 and the relationship between Lev 11 and Deut 14, see Kazen 2011, 72–80; 2015b, 445–47, 457–59 = ch. 4 in this volume.

exiles return is described as a *niddâ* land, defiled by the *niddâ* of the people of the land and by their abominations (*tôʿēbôt*); here *niddâ* is juxtaposed to, and more or less synonymous with, the disgust term *tôʿēbâ*. Isaiah's reference (30:22) to idols and ephods being thrown out like a bleeding woman (*kəmô dāwâ*) also breathes disgust, although no such terminology explicitly appears.[17]

When impurity language characterizes disapproved behavior, such as various sexual acts, worship of other gods, or bloodshed, a common term is *tôʿēbâ*. The term is especially prominent in the Holiness Code, Deuteronomy, Proverbs, and Ezekiel, at times seemingly *without* its affective character, simply meaning "disapproved."[18] However, in contexts of impurity, it tends to retain its aversive character. For example, the sexual behaviors denounced in Leviticus 18 are summarized (vv. 24–30) as abominations (*tôʿēbôt*) and characterized as defiling both the people and the land, to the point that the land will vomit (*qiʾ*) the people out. The argument recurs in 20:22–24, this time with even more overt disgust terminology—God is said to loathe (*qûṣ*) people with such behavior—and juxtaposed to an injunction not to become detestable (*šāqaṣ*) by eating unclean animals (vv. 25–26).[19]

All of this serves to emphasize that emotional disgust frequently associates with impurity language, whether the issue is prohibited foods, various conditions involving genital discharges or skin ailments (pathological or not, but technically understood as unclean and possible to purify), or disapproved behaviors.[20] The point is not to claim that every use of impurity language must involve emotional disgust, but to show that disgust attends very different types of impurity. There has been a tendency to classify impurity into various categories, which are then easily multiplied. A basic differentiation between "ritual" and "moral" impurity has long been suggested—a differentiation frequently referred to in the form it has received through the work of Jonathan Klawans.[21] Others have suggested different categories, and some have added genealogical impurity, sin-

---

17. Cf. Goldstein 2015, but with slightly different interpretations.
18. Kazen 2011, 86–87; Humbert 1960.
19. Cf. Kazen 2011, 87–88.
20. For the sake of space, I have not included molds on houses or clothing, or corpse impurity, in this brief summary.
21. Klawans 2000.

impurity, sexual pollution, gentile impurity, and the like.[22] In our human urge for categorization, we run the risk of an essentialism of sorts. We are probably seduced into endless categorization because of the one area in which purity discourse is very precisely employed and technically treated: the priestly ritual "system." This is the only purity discourse in the Bible to which a set of purification rites are attached.

So how do we understand other purity discourses? To some, the simplest solution categorizes ritual impurity as literal and other uses of purity language as metaphorical. To others, this distinction has proved unsatisfactory, since some usages of purity language appear difficult to classify. Deficient theories of metaphor have confused the issue further, resulting in discussions whether "moral" or "genealogical" impurity should be taken literally or metaphorically.[23]

My view is that taxonomies of purity issues—which could theoretically be multiplied even further—are largely futile and misguided. Although we might want to continue using some of these labels for convenience's sake, they need to be seriously questioned. I want to suggest that by carefully exploring the relationship between emotional disgust and impurity in terms of human cognition and language, we will find more satisfying explanations for the ways in which purity discourse develops and mutates in biblical texts.

Disgust in Body: Literal Impurity

We must of course beware the etymological fallacy, by which *present-day meaning* is falsely deduced from lexical history; nevertheless, terminology may reveal something about the *conceptualization* of experiences and the *evolution* of word *usage* in various contexts. Purity terminology suggests a concrete, literal understanding at the roots. The underlying meaning for Hebrew *ṭāmēʾ/ṭûmʾâ* is probably "dirt." The Syriac cognate verb can mean to be "soiled" or "sticky," and the corresponding Egyptian Arabic root means "silt." Later Arabic *ṭamā* means "be choked with mud," and *ṭammay*

---

22. For genealogical impurity, see, e.g., Hayes 2002. For sin-impurity, see, e.g., Ginsburskaya 2009. For sexual pollution, see, e.g., Feinstein 2014. For gentile impurity, see, e.g., Hayes 2002, including her discussion of the views of Schürer, Alon, and Büchler; Klawans 2000; Harrington 2008; Balberg 2014.

23. See my discussions of this problem elsewhere, e.g., Kazen 2008; 2014 = ch. 5 in this volume; 2018a = ch. 3 in this volume.

is "mud of the Nile."[24] Paschen suggests "feuchter Schmutz" ("moist dirt"), as the original meaning of *ṭāmēʾ*.[25] Hebrew *ṭāhôr/ṭohŏrâ*, like its Ugaritic cognate, can mean "shining" or "radiance." This can be compared to Akkadian terms for purity (*ellu*, *ebbu*, and *namru*), which refer to being clean, clear, or bright, in contrast to being dim, tainted, or sullied.[26]

When this linguistic data is taken seriously, we see that much of the literal-metaphorical debate is misguided. "Ritual" impurity is taken to be literal by default due to its concrete effects, and to some, even certain "moral" issues are presumed to be more literal than metaphorical because of their "real" consequences.[27] Yet metaphor is not an ontological, but a *linguistic*, category. How one conceptualizes the effects of various types of impurity has little to do with whether the language is used figuratively. From a linguistic point of view, much of what is generally called ritual impurity reflects a metaphorical use of purity language. The contagion that ritual impurity incurs via contact has no physical substance, even in the case of contact with corpses. Skin-disease impurity does manifest material signs, but the scales and rashes involved are not precisely dirt; rather, they represent a secondary use of impurity language.[28] Only genital fluids with their capacity to become smeary and smelly might earn their place as literal impurities, except that in the priestly legislation it is no longer the substance per se that defiles, but the impure state of the discharger, regardless of the amount of fluid. Excrement constitutes the prototypical literal impurity, but although it figures as unclean in certain biblical contexts, it is conspicuously excluded from the priestly system (cf. Deut 23:12–14; 2 Kgs 10:27; Zech 3; Ezek 4:12–15).[29]

Thus, impurity and disgust have a complex, equivocal relationship. Not everything disgusting is called impure, and not everything called impure is disgusting from a biopsychological point of view. While some "disgusting" impurities lack emotional and ultimate evolutionary under-

---

24. André and Ringgren 1986, 330. Cf. Feinstein 2010, 51.
25. Paschen 1970, 27.
26. See van der Toorn 1985, 27–37; 2004; Feder 2014.
27. Especially so by Klawans 2000.
28. See also Kazen 2018a = ch. 3 in this volume.
29. For a discussion of the biblical evidence, see Lemos 2013, 285–87. Cf. discussions of the impurity of excrement in Qumran (including comparisons with biblical and rabbinic evidence); see Harrington 2004, 19, 64–65, 106–8; Magness 2011, 130–44.

pinnings, associations between disgust and impurity in biblical texts are ultimately based on experiences of visceral, bodily, emotional disgust toward literal impurities of dirt, contaminated matter, and other physical entities understood as harmful to ingest, breathe, or contact. The feeling of disgust antipathetic to "dirt" is, however, easily transposed to other experiences, and with it often follows their conceptualization as impure. This is a process that takes place in the *body*, through the *mind*, and by figurative use of *language*.

Disgust in Mind: Impurity as Conceptual Metaphor

What are the conceptual mechanisms that make it possible for purity issues to develop into such an overarching and influential paradigm, especially in Second Temple Judaism? How do we explain the transfer of dirt properties and disgust feelings from the literal level to other domains? I suggest that conceptual metaphor and blending theories can help us understand this process.[30] I employ these theories here in an eclectic and simplified manner. Conceptual metaphor theory in Mark Johnson and George Lakoff's popularized version contends that metaphors carry notions from one cognitive or conceptual domain to another, providing the latter with new impetus, different understanding, and change of meaning. Metaphors are cross-domain mappings from a source to a target domain that relate to the way we conceptualize and influence actions and behaviors (see fig. 6.1).[31]

Applied to purity discourse, such cross-domain mapping suggests that impurity carries notions from its source domain (dirt) to various target domains, thus influencing the ways we think about those target domains and relate to them. The most conspicuous of those notions is disgust, and hence avoidance, but others may also follow, such as washing away the (now metaphorical) dirt. This process clearly plays out when the concept of disgusting impurity is mapped onto target domains of unsavory human beings, objectionable behavior, and repulsive creatures (dietary taboos). By mapping the notion of dirt onto detestable people, their state is classified as *ṭāmēʾ* (dirty), and contact with them or their fluids or scaly residues becomes a kind of defilement that can be purified by water. By mapping dirt

---

30. See further Kazen 2014 = ch. 5 in this volume.
31. Lakoff and Johnson 1980a; 1980b, 453–86; 1999.

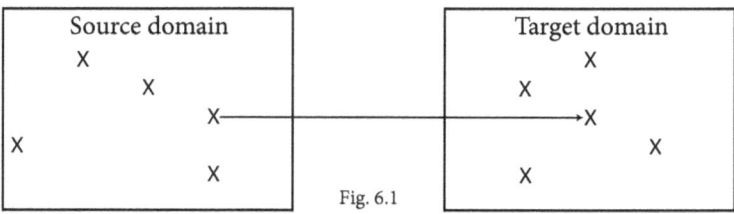

Fig. 6.1

onto objectionable behavior, certain acts are understood as impure and disgusting, in need of being removed, whether by atonement, the *kārēt* penalty, expulsion from the land, or blood revenge.[32] By mapping dirt onto certain animal species, they are tainted with disgust and classified as unfit to eat.

This model partly explains what happens when we "think with" (or experience with) literal dirt in other domains. But why does disgust get involved in certain domains and not in others? Why do certain dirt-related conceptualizations, such as washing, scraping, or other types of removal, emerge here but not there? Blending theory offers a somewhat different way of construing mental (and experiential) processes. It explains some of the more sophisticated mechanisms involving secondary uses of purity language in new domains, and proves particularly helpful in cases where conceptions of impurity are expanded or used in unusual or unexpected circumstances. Blending theory focuses on conceptual spaces or frames within which images or mental representations function as a network. Rather than conceptualizing figurative expressions as one-way mapping processes, blending suggests that input spaces, which already have certain common elements (generic space), provide a blended space with other elements, which are not common and do not necessarily or entirely fit together. The resulting blend is not really inherent in any of the input spaces, nor indicated by the generic space (common elements) that makes blending possible in the first place. The outcome of the process is thus in a sense unanticipated, which is precisely why it results in new conceptual frameworks, new meanings, and new behaviors (see fig. 6.2).[33]

---

32. This example (mapping dirt onto objectionable behavior) partly corresponds to the "moral impurities" of the Holiness Code (Lev 17–26). Note also the provisions for unintended manslaughter (cities of refuge), and the magical/apotropaic rite of breaking a heifer's neck to effect removal for the people and free them from bloodguilt in case the murderer could not be found and removed by blood revenge or refuge (Num 35:9–34; Deut 19:1–13; 21:1–9). Cf. Kazen 2011, 135–37.

33. Fauconnier and Turner 2002, 17–57; Coulson and Oakley 2000.

Conceptual Blending

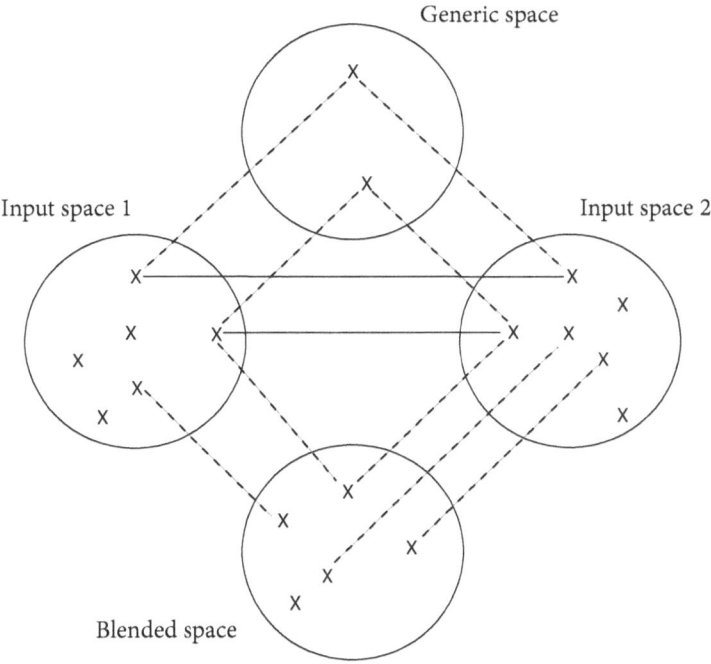

Fig. 6.2

Blending theory can be effectively applied to the three domains just discussed. Contact with dirt and contact with unsavory people can be understood as two input spaces that share avoidance and aversion (disgust) but little else. These shared items, however, make possible the evolution of a blended space, which conceives of such people as impure and their impurity as contagious ("sticky"), requiring removal by water. In a further step (cf. Ps 51), a blend between contact contamination, disapproved ("sinful") behavior, and dirty laundry (again sharing avoidance and aversion) envisages certain sexual behaviors as impure stains on one's inner being, necessitating cleansing by water and hyssop. The first blend results in ritual impurity being purified by literal water; in the second blend, however, the water and hyssop function as symbolic elements for removing evil rather than as literal components of a purification ritual. But this makes little difference to the fact that the *impurity* imagined in both cases represents a metaphorical mapping on physical dirt. This point becomes even clearer concerning the impurity of the pig (see Lev 11), which may be explained as a blending of traditional avoidances of certain meats and aversions against slimy and rotting vermin.[34] The resulting blended space becomes imbued with notions of impurity and disgust, even though pork seems no more intrinsically disgusting or dirty than any other animal flesh.[35]

While in the first two cases (unsavory people and disapproved behavior), disgust seems to belong to the generic space, which makes blending possible and sometimes even likely, it operates differently in the third example. What is shared here is avoidance: neither "swarmers" nor pigs are eaten (for whatever reasons), but the visceral disgust felt for small, creepy animals (vermin, slimy water creatures, and the like) is imported into the category of non-cud-chewing and non-cleft-footed quadrupeds. This creative blend constitutes a rhetorical move as much as a conceptual one, resulting in a kind of disgust by association. This point leads into the next section, focusing more fully on the role of language and social construction in developing conceptions of impurity and purity discourse.

Disgust in Language: Impurity as Rhetoric

As the grounds for viewing the pig (or camel or hare) as both impure and disgusting are scarcely obvious, the same problem applies to several other phenomena. Why, for example, are new mothers severely restricted and regarded as impure for a long time according to priestly law? Although never explicitly labeled disgusting, does their impurity evoke notions of aversion by virtue of being associated with—mapped onto the domain of—genital dischargers in general? On what grounds do the authors of the Holiness Code, Isaiah, Ezekiel, and Ezra-Nehemiah associate foreign practices and worship of other gods, implicitly or explicitly, with emotional disgust (e.g., Lev 12; 18; 20; 26; Isa 30; Ezek 22; 36; Ezra 9)?[36] There is little ultimate, biopsychological basis for visceral aversive reactions to culturally proximate religious practices and worship. How is Ezra-Nehemiah able to muster such aversive feelings against other ethnic groups (or

---

34. Figures illustrating these and other examples of blends are found in Kazen 2014 = ch. 5 in this volume.

35. Although the dirty character and scavenger status of the pig is sometimes referenced, anyone who owned a he-goat will have a hard time finding reasons why one should evoke disgust but not the other.

36. See further the discussion above.

perhaps against people of the same ethnic group as well), separated by circumstances and differing fates and experiences (Ezra 9–10; Neh 13)?

The conceptual processes by which such mutations take place can be profitably described and understood with the help of blending theory. The genital bleeding of a woman with pathological (long-term) discharge impurity (*zābâ*) and a new mother are similar enough to constitute grounds (generic space) for blending. Whether the ensuing blend at some point actually resulted in viewing a parturient with disgust is not, however, certain. The possibility would, in any case, lie close at hand.

Aversion against certain practices and worship rites can be interpreted as part of a general tendency to shun that which is different and foreign. A large body of literature discusses the evolutionary basis and adaptive function of ethnocentrism and xenophobia.[37] From this starting point, a long step extends to the cultural construction of "the other" and the rhetorical creation of an ethnic and national identity, as evidenced in texts such as the Holiness Code, Ezra-Nehemiah, and many prophetic writings. Although the differences between the groups are relatively minor, mechanisms of group dynamics and social identity formation make it easy to exploit them.

My argument is that feelings of disgust, associated with experiences of impurity (dirt), are sufficiently grounded in human bodies and minds for human language to exploit rhetorically. Such rhetorical effects (and affects) happen when purity discourse breaks away from its physical-literal anchoring and invades domains or blends with spaces where it has little foothold, often including disgust as a secondary emotion. To some degree, purity and disgust rhetoric always reflects general conceptual developments, so that texts express what people feel and think.[38] But these evolutionary and cultural conditions provide a ready playground, or a resonating sounding board, for exploitative and rhetorical innovations, whether fortuitous or studied, to associate emotional disgust with actions, items, or peoples through the use of impurity language.

---

37. E.g., Navarrete and Fessler 2006; Curtis 2013; Faulkner et al. 2004; McEvoy 2002; Freedman 1961; Dunbar 1987; Fishbein 2012.

38. I.e., texts express what at least *some* people feel and think. Texts are, of course, biased: most texts reflect a patriarchal bias, some have priestly bias, and all texts have been more or less processed by a scribal elite. Still, socially and culturally conditioned expressions ultimately rest on general conceptual developments.

A few examples indicated in the list of questions above may suffice to illustrate this point. Let us first look at two fairly late Isaianic texts.[39] In Isa 64:5 (Isa 64:6 in English), the anonymous prophet confesses: "Everyone of us has become like impurity [*ṭāmēʾ*], and like a menstrual cloth [*beged ʿiddîm*] all our righteous acts."[40] Although the rendering "menstrual cloth" is partly conjectural, it is a likely option.[41] The sentence is an obvious parallelism in which impurity or a thing classified as *ṭāmēʾ* is synonymous with a menstrual cloth. Human beings and their (purportedly righteous) actions are likened to dirt, impurity, and genital blood. These expressions, based on emotional revulsion against dirt and genital discharges, tell us something about cultural and contextual conceptions of menstrual blood. The blend of dirt and discharge is common enough, and the setting is not particularly legal or ritual. The rhetorical dynamics depend on an inseparable mixture of evolutionary (ultimate, emotional, visceral) conditions and culturally constructed conceptions. The resulting blend, however, evokes and invokes disgust reactions against behaviors of quite a different character. The rhetoric enlists visceral and emotional elements in the service of a value-laden and programmatic agenda: to blame the present disasters on the actions of the people.

Another late Isaianic example is found in Isa 30:22: "You will defile [*watimmēʾtem*] the plating of your silver idols [or: your silver-plated idols] and the gold covering of your ephods [or: your gold-covered images]. You will throw them out like a bleeding [woman] [*dāwâ*] 'Get out!' you will say to it/him." Certain translation issues complicate the interpretation of this passage. Concerning the referent in the last suffix (*lô*), it cannot refer to the *dāwâ* as such, but rather to that which is thrown out and for which the *dāwâ* serves as a simile. For the sentence to be grammatically correct, this can refer either to the first masculine noun in the phrase, plating (*ṣippû*), or possibly to the silver (*kesep*) and gold (*zāhāb*), respectively,

---

39. The lament in Isa 63:7–64:11 is usually understood to be either exilic or early postexilic. Cf. Smith 1995, 44–47; For a postexilic dating, see Hanson 1979, 79–100; for a date during the second half of the sixth century BCE, see Tiemeyer 2014; cf. Goldingay 2014, 382. Isaiah 30:19–26 "is nowadays widely agreed to be post-exilic" (Williamson 2015, 24). Cf. Wildberger 2002, 170–72.

40. All translations are my own. Cf. Lam 2016, 194.

41. Translations like "stained clothes" are common, but imprecise. Although the exact meaning of *ʿēd* is unclear, it is used in rabbinic texts for the test rag with which Jewish women checked for signs of menstruation. See further Lam 2016, 194–95.

which cover the idols. In any case, the ultimate reference must be to the *idols*, comparing the defilement (in the sense of desecration) of silver and gold images to a menstruating woman. But again, to what precisely does this comparison refer? One suggestion envisions the people disposing of their idols in the same manner as a woman disposes her menstrual *cloth*.[42] However, I consider this an overinterpretation, especially as the cloth is not in the text, but must be supplied.[43] More probably, the passage likens the disparaging, expulsive treatment of former idols (throwing them out) with the disparaging treatment of a menstruating woman expected by the text's male recipients: "Get out of here!" Once more we sense a combination of ultimate-emotional and proximate-cultural reactions against dirty, sticky, or smelly substances in general, and genital discharge in particular, rhetorically exploited for religious propaganda against unacceptable types of worship.

Ezekiel 36 affords a similar rhetorical use of impurity language. Here Israel is accused of having defiled (*wayṭamməʾû*) the land by their ways and deeds, like the impurity of menstruation (*kəṭumʾat hanniddāh*). The defiling ways and deeds are identified as bloodshed and idol worship (Ezek 36:17–18). For this reason, God scattered Israel among the nations, but since they profaned his name there, he will now gather them from these countries in order to defend his honor (name). The logic of this argument may be faltering, but the argument continues: "I will sprinkle pure waters on you and you will be pure from all your impurities [*ṭumʾôtêkem*] and from all your idols I will purify you" (36:25). Further: "I will rescue you from all your impurities [*ṭumʾôtêkem*]" (36:29). When this salvation happens, the Israelites will remember their former evil deeds and loathe (*nəqōṭōtem*) themselves because of their sins and abominations (*tôʿăbôtēkem*; 36:31).

Here we observe the full register of disgust and impurity language at work. The imagery is partly inconsistent, but the author's ultimate purpose is evocative and rhetorical, not declarative and logical. Feelings of disgust, based on various causes ranging from evolutionary adaptive avoidances of dirt and pathogens to patriarchal aversions of female blood, blend with notions of murder and misguided divine worship. The rhetoric produces an implicit value statement of unequaled strength: the people need cleansing from their disgusting state. The fact that the defiled land recedes into

---

42. Lam 2016, 197–98.

43. Also, rags were likely to have been washed and reused, even as cloth diapers are in modern times.

the background does not seem to trouble the author and probably not the recipients either. The intended effect is that they feel disgust for themselves because of their (or their ancestors') past behavior, which makes purification necessary. As the purity metaphors evoke: God will sprinkle them with pure water to purify them from the idols (36:25). These rhetorical effects depend on the previous blend of idol worship with impurity and disgust and thus should not be taken literally, just as the next verse's language about replacing the heart of stone with a heart of flesh is obviously figurative (36:26).

Our last example comes from Ezra 9:11. An overly literal interpretation reads: "The land you are coming to possess is a *niddâ* land by the *niddâ* of the people of the land by their abominations [*tôʿēbôt*] by which they have filled it from mouth to mouth by their impurities [*ṭumʾātām*]." It is a moot point to what extent *niddâ* retains its visceral character and reference to genital bleeding.[44] It is not used as a simile but rather seems to designate impurity in a strong sense. In any case, it complements and reinforces two very general terms for impurity (*ṭumʾâ*) and disgust (*tôʿēbâ*). The Ezra author exploits *niddâ* in order to evoke strong emotional disgust toward groups of people designated by "the people of the land," from which the audience must separate themselves, and toward their practices, stereotyped as "abominations" and "impurities." Again, rhetorical use builds on underlying metaphorical and literal levels. Disgust is evoked by language, through the mind, in the body.

Conclusion

In this essay, I have tried to demonstrate the multileveled character of disgust, ranging from visceral emotional *body* reactions toward physical substances, animals, and human beings who evoke aversive feelings because of their characteristics; through various types of metaphorical conceptualizations in the *mind*; to conscious rhetorical *language* strategies for influencing moral values, behaviors, and actions against disapproved individuals or groups. This chapter has focused on the case study of the concept of purity/impurity in biblical literature, which interacts and intersects with emotional disgust at all levels, albeit in various ways and degrees.

---

44. For various views on the use of *niddâ* in this text and others, such as Zech 13:1 and those discussed above, see, e.g., Maccoby 1999; Goldstein 2015; Philip 2006, 19–42.

We have found that the rhetorical effects and uses of the disgust-impurity paradigm rest on a diversified metaphorical framework, which can be profitably interpreted with the help of conceptual metaphor and blending theories. We have also found that at all levels, rhetorical and/or metaphorical expressions of disgust in relation to various types of impurity build on and presuppose visceral core disgust reactions as their emotional underpinnings. Although disgust and impurity language may occasionally become fairly conventionalized, it always presupposes aversive feelings as an underlying and innate capacity. Biblical-textual expressions of disgust rest on and receive their power from an inseparable blend of ultimate and proximate emotional triggers: reactions due to evolutionary adaptation and to contextual cultural construction.

7
Purification

Ritual purity was a major goal of cultic activities in the Mediterranean world, but in a number of contexts, purity was also considered a desirable condition regardless of cultic participation. This chapter discusses the concept of purity and purification from phenomenological, linguistic, and ritual perspectives. Attention is given to the variegated use of purity terminology and to the use of cognitive metaphor and conceptual blending theories to understand and explain the broad and common usage of purity-related language in various domains. The chapter surveys and analyzes a limited selection of purification rites from Egypt, Mesopotamia, Persia, Israel, Greece, and Rome. This is done both with a view to historical development, influence, and interaction, and with the help of theorizing on ritual efficacy and social effects of purity codes. Particular attention is given to purifications with water, especially in Second Temple Judaism, as these are crucial to the further development of water rites in emerging Christianity.

Rituals of purification are found virtually everywhere in the ancient world. This chapter will discuss purification rites in Mesopotamia, Egypt, Greece, and Rome, with special emphasis on purification in Second Temple Judaism, since early Christian rituals largely evolve from Jewish practices.

Conceptually, purification primarily suggests the removal of dirt, pollution, or contaminating matter. Contextually, purification at times partially overlaps with other concepts, such as sanctification and healing. Some purificatory rituals are self-administered, while others are performed by ritual specialists. Not only persons and objects, but also places, buildings, and in some instances foodstuff and drink can be puri-

---

This chapter was first published as "Purification," in *The Oxford Handbook of Early Christian Rituals*, ed. Risto Uro, Juliette J. Day, Rikard Roitto, and Richard E. DeMaris (Oxford: Oxford University Press, 2018), 220–44.

fied. Since impurity is usually understood as an acquired state that can be entered and exited, purification rituals are repeatable. However, some exceptional impurities for which there are no purification rituals prescribed are regarded as permanent and can only be handled by removal or destruction.

Purification may be necessitated by anything that evokes divine displeasure or wrath, such as murder, incest, war, or lack of attention to and respect for the gods, including breaches of cultic prescriptions or codes of conduct. But purification may also be necessary in a number of situations that do not involve any type of willful transgression but rather belong to the course of normal life, such as birth, death, marriage, and disease. In addition, purification is a natural preparation for situations of heightened religious experience, when people encounter divine powers, whether in the mysteries or during ordinary feasts, and when they visit sanctuaries to perform regular sacrifices. Purification thus becomes of utmost importance for maintaining emotional stability, human dignity, and social order.

Means and modes of purification vary a great deal. Purificants can be poured, sprinkled, daubed, rubbed, burned, eaten, or killed. Impurities can be removed, buried, sent away, or destroyed. Water is the most common purificant and can be used in numerous ways: immersion, ablution, sprinkling, laundering. Fire at times appears as a radical method for purification. Other purifiers are smoke and incense, salt, and various vegetable and animal products, including garlic, eggs, and animal carcasses. Some of these are mostly locally attested, while others, such as sacrifice and blood, appear universally. In some contexts, oil can be used, but more often for sanctification than for purification.

Impurity and Purification in the Ancient World

Concepts of Purity and Impurity

Ideas and practices of purification presume and correspond to specific ancient understandings of purity and impurity. Concepts of impurity include a diversity of conditions and behaviors, including besmirched items, repellent substances, bodily fluids, certain physical states and diseases, corpses and carcasses, contagion by contact, food avoidances, disapproved sexual relations, breaches against moral and cultural codes, and various spiritual threats. At the same time, this array of meanings does reveal certain common traits. Aesthetic and emotional aspects are present, as both human and divine beings are thought to enjoy what is whole, clean, and radiant and to shun what is smelly, smeared, and smitten, especially when it threatens human life and order. An affective element is also detectable in the linguistic expressions, which all relate to human experience one way or another.[1]

In Egypt, *bwt* originally characterized a wide range of social, ethical, and cultic offenses, but mainly came to designate various types of taboos. Purity (*wab*) basically meant the absence of pollution (*abw*) and could be achieved by ritual washings.[2]

In Mesopotamia, purity rather characterized a positive quality, a state of perfection. The Akkadian terms *ellu*, *ebbu*, and *namru* carry meanings of being clean, clear, or bright, in contrast to being dim, tainted, or sullied. Impurity can be expressed by negations of purity or by terms for soiled or muddy (*luʾû*, *dalḫu*, *waršu*), or dull (*ešû*).[3]

Similarly, Hebrew *ṭāhôr/ṭohŏrâ*, like its Ugaritic cognate, can mean "shining" or "radiance," although it is mostly used for purity as absence of contagion. Impurity (*ṭāmēʾ/ṭumʾâ*) refers to pollution in the form of impure physical conditions, often in legal contexts, but can also be used in the sense of culpability and moral transgression. The underlying meaning is probably dirt. The Syriac cognate verb can mean to be "soiled" or "sticky," in a concrete sense. The corresponding Egyptian Arabic root means "silt." The later Arabic word *ṭamā* means "be choked with mud." *Tammay* is "mud of the Nile."[4] The Semitic etymology suggests an association with physical dirt, and to purify (*ṭihēr*) can thus be understood in its root meaning as cleansing from dirt. Because of the conceptual overlap between purity and holiness, as well as between impurity and sin, *qiddēš* (sanctify) and *ḥiṭṭēʾ* ("de-sin") are sometimes also used to denote purification.[5]

The Hittite word *papratar* often refers to pollution as a spiritual threat, through gossiping, curses, sorcery, and bloodguilt.[6] In Iranian religions, purity (Avestan *yaozhdāh*) represents order, in contrast to chaos, while

---

1. Feder 2014.
2. Meeks 1979; Frandsen 2004.
3. Van der Toorn 2004; Guichard and Marti 2013, 51–52.
4. André and Ringgren 1986, 330; Paschen 1970, 27.
5. Van der Toorn 1985, 27–37; Feder 2014.
6. Feder 2014.

pollution (*âhitica*; cf. *irimant*) is a dynamic concept, associated with a female deceiver demon (*drug nasu*). Hence purification takes on exorcistic traits, requiring priestly purifiers.[7]

In Greece, *miasma* similarly denotes a dynamic and dangerous kind of pollution, the neutralization of which requires cultic manipulation. The partially overlapping *agos* seems to be more particularly tied to the sacred. By contrast, *akatharsia* is the absence of purity and often refers to immoral behavior. All of these terms, however, can designate an impurity caused by human behavior regarded as objectionable to the gods, including bloodshed, sacrilege, and faulty ritual practice. To be pure (*katharos*) meant basically to be free of anything offending the gods, which included adherence to local (sanctuary) rules. An overlap with *hagnos*, similar to the overlap between Hebrew *ṭm'* and *qdš*, can be observed, although in Hellenistic Greek *hagios* is usually employed for the latter meaning, and both *katharos* and *hagnos* came to be used for purity of character and moral behavior. Purification could be achieved by sacrifice, water rites, and "medicines" (*pharmakoi*, such as ritual expulsion of human scapegoats).[8]

Although there are those who claim that except for death, the Romans were "relatively free of the sense that there exists a class of naturally occurring things that pollute in and of themselves," such a view cannot be corroborated by evidence.[9] It is true that there is no Latin noun corresponding to the Greek *miasma*; It is also true that serious crime, such as bloodshed, was increasingly handled by the judicial system.[10] Blood nevertheless remained a pollutant, together with sexual activity, especially of an impropriate kind, childbirth, and the corpse. Ordinary life events, laxity, and ritual negligence caused divine anger and needed expiation, sometimes in the form of the purification of cities.[11] And both Greek and Roman mystery cults required various purificatory rites in preparation for initiation.[12]

---

7. Choksy 1989, 1–22; 2004.
8. Parker 1983, 1–17; 2004; Blidstein 2017, 19–38.
9. Quotation from Beck 2004, 509; on the lack of evidence, see Lennon 2014, 19–20.
10. Beck 2004; Fantham 2012, 60; Lennon 2012, 43, 54.
11. Lennon 2012; 2014.
12. Blidstein 2017, 28–31.

Impurity, Sin, and Evil

The equation of impurity and sin, especially in earlier scholarship on Judaism, has been severely criticized for reflecting Christian or Western anti-Jewish and/or supersessionist bias.[13] The discussion frequently becomes heated and is often not only troubled by conflicting interests but also obscured by confused categories. It is true that a number of physical conditions or ritual states, experienced as intimidating, threatening, and in particular as objectionable to other people and to the supernatural powers, and thus identified as impure, are not necessarily to be understood as sinful, in the sense of incurring moral guilt. Purity language is nevertheless employed in moral discourse, and the same or similar purification rituals are employed for a variety of purposes.[14]

According to the Israelite priestly system, *ḥaṭṭāʾt* and *ʾāšām* sacrifices are employed in order to atone or effect removal (*kipper*), as part of the process of purification from childbirth impurity, skin disease, and genital discharges (Lev 12–15). (The law for purification from corpse impurity in Num 19 is somewhat later and identifies the burning of the red heifer as a *ḥaṭṭāʾt* sacrifice, without ascribing to it a *kipper* function.) The same sacrifices are, however, used to effect removal in cases of inadvertent sin (Lev 4–5); the *ḥaṭṭāʾt* is also employed in the Day of Atonement rituals (Lev 16) and the *ʾāšām* in certain cases of sexual sin (Lev 19:20–22). Although it could be argued that the *kipper* function of these two sacrifices has more to do with negotiating the offense against the divinity caused by impurity and sin respectively than with purification per se, this does not become overly clear even in the priestly system.[15]

A comparison with Greek evidence rather suggests a situation in which such distinctions are difficult to uphold.[16] In ancient Greece, pollution (*miasma*) was understood to result from such diverse things as liminal states (childbirth, death), bloodshed, sex, sacrilege (including minor violations), and even disease.[17] Related concepts and the same type of reasoning are used for pollution as offense against the gods, as a dynamic and demonic force, as resulting from indecency and lack of decorum, and as a

---

13. Cf. Klawans 2000; 2006.
14. Kazen 2011, 23–28.
15. Kazen 2011, 152–64.
16. Parker 1983, 10.
17. Parker 1983, 32–73, 74–103, 104–43, 144–90, 207–34.

consequence of murder. Similar considerations apply to Rome, where *polluere*, although not so frequently used, can refer to pollution by illicit sex, immoral action, sacrilege, and murder,[18] but also to the impurity caused by death (*funestus*). As for childbirth and licit sex, evidence is not so clear as in Greece, but abstinence is associated with being pure (*purus*), and newborn children are purified (*lustrare*).[19] Public and communal cleansing of the whole city is described not only in exceptional situations, but as part of regularly recurring calendrical rites.[20]

In the east, too, offenses against the gods and against fellow humans were often understood to be defiling in a sense close to the defilement of impurity caused by disease, by natural processes, and liminal experiences.[21] The Egyptian category *bwt* indicates a large admixture of moral, social, and cultic offenses, including the breaking of purity rules. Purity is the absence of *bwt*. There is a conspicuous blend of impurities and "sins"; two examples are the negative confessions, as in chapter 125 of the Book of the Dead, and the so-called cult monographs, for example, Papyrus Jumilhac XII, 16–21.[22] Even though sin and pollution were not identical concepts in ancient Mesopotamia, both could be envisaged as stains and in need of purification,[23] and purification was at times achieved by magic and exorcism.[24] For some impurities only superficial purifications were necessary, as when diviners prepared themselves to question the gods. Other pollutions went deeper and required elaborate rituals, whether resulting from conscious transgression, unconscious lawbreaking, or even being subject to sorcery.[25]

The demonic character of impurity is perhaps most accentuated in Persian religion (Zoroastrianism), in which pollution is associated with the corpse demoness (*drug nasu*). Although most Zoroastrian texts are late, Vendidād probably dates at least from the Achaemenid period.[26] Here the corpse is the paramount source of impurity, occasioning a much

---

18. Fantham 2012, 60–61.
19. Lennon 2014, 58–64.
20. Graf 2010, 422–23; Lennon 2012, 55–56.
21. Kazen 2011, 28–31.
22. Meyer 1999; Frandsen 2004; 2007, 89.
23. Van der Toorn 2004.
24. Guichard and Marti 2013, 57–59.
25. Guichard and Marti 2013, 80–90.
26. No later than 300 BCE; de Jong 1999, 304.

more elaborate purification rite (*barashnum*) than polluting body fluids.[27] Corpse impurity takes on metaphysical proportions. Purification from it becomes part of a cosmic struggle between good and evil.

Motives for Purification

It is commonplace to state that purification is necessary in order to approach the sacred, sacrifice to the gods, and visit temple areas. While this is certainly true, it is not the whole truth. Studies of purity in early Judaism sometimes claim that except for extremists and sectarians, purity practices were restricted to, or at least heavily focused on, the Jerusalem temple. Impurities from menstruation, sex, or burial would not have concerned anyone except in view of a temple visit. This is hardly tenable.[28]

At first sight, however, such views seem to go well together with the focus on purity regarding the cult that we find in many studies of other ancient religions, too. From Egypt, we have door inscriptions warning priests and visitors about the food taboos and body purity required for entrance. Purity seems to be primarily a matter for priest and rulers and other members of the elite. Herodotus (*Hist.* 2.37, 41) suggests reservations against contact with foreigners and claims that priests shaved their body daily, immersed twice daily and twice a night, and also observed certain food restrictions. As for ordinary people, the evidence is ambiguous. But the fact that visitors and workers in temples were required to observe special purity regulations does not by itself indicate that they were without purity rules under ordinary circumstances. Evidence that the scribal elite considered certain professions dirty suggests that a minimal level of purity was normally expected. Local purity rules for each district (*nome*) are quite common and include taboos on certain foods, certain sexual acts, and certain behaviors, which do not seem to be restricted to cultic officials but apply to the population at large.[29]

When purity in ancient Greece is discussed, it is often done in view of the "sacred laws."[30] We must, however, consider that religion and everyday life were in no way separated, and temples and cult sites were everywhere present in the ancient world. The idea that purity would only be an issue

---

27. De Jong 1999, 308–19; 2013, 187–90.
28. Kazen 2016 = ch. 12 in this volume. See now also ch. 11 in this volume.
29. Meyer 1999; Quack 2013.
30. Bendlin 2007; Günther 2013; Robertson 2013.

in relation to the sacred and, therefore, would not be of much interest to the majority of people for most of their time, assumes anachronistically a society in which the sacred was much more limited and circumscribed than was actually the case in the ancient world. True, sacred areas were delimited, and purity was crucial in those contexts, which motivates purifications in view of temple visits. However, purifications relating to birth, death, sex, bodily fluids, and sometimes disease, or for that matter to the land, seem to have covered the broader scope of human civilization and society in general.[31] In this regard, the role of purity in everyday life in Zoroastrianism is conspicuous.[32]

A special feature of Second Temple Judaism is its lack of temples; even considering the few existent diaspora examples, Jerusalem occupied a unique place. The priestly rules regarding purification rites were to a large extent shaped during the Persian period, with Yehud as a limited vassal state gathered around the rebuilding of the temple and the reconstitution of a renewed cult. The political and religious situation explains some of the focus on purity for the sake of the sanctuary in the priestly laws, such as purification after childbirth (Lev 12:4), the summary at the end of the discharge laws (Lev 15:31), and the corpse-impurity rules (Num 19:13, 20). However, this does not restrict the demand for purity to the sacred sphere, which is not the focus of these rules. The rules for contact contagion assume any contact with skin-diseased persons to be by all means avoided, and the prescribed purifications are necessary for access to one's house and reintegration in society at large (Lev 13–14). The details of the discharge rules are aimed at avoiding every contamination (Lev 15). Both archaeology and textual evidence suggest extensive observance of purity rules and purification rituals, including frequent, perhaps daily, immersions in stepped pools (*miqwā'ôt*) far from the temple as part of "household religion." No decrease in these practices can be shown until after the Bar Kokhba revolt.[33]

It should be noted that materials used in various purification rituals were usually taken outside the city, buried in the wilderness, or thrown into the sea.[34] Also, both the Greek *pharmakos* and the Jewish scapegoat, as well as the live bird used for purifying the scale-diseased person ("leper"),

---

31. Cf. Parker 1983, 322–27.
32. Choksy 1989, 78–110.
33. Adler 2011; 2014a; 2016; Miller 2015; Kazen 2016 = ch. 12 in this volume.
34. Graf 2010, 422; Hutter 2013, 166–68; cf. HL 44b; Lev 16:27.

were driven out from inhabited areas and sent into the wilderness (Lev 14:2–7; 16:20–22).[35] Building materials affected with ṣāraʿat ("leprosy") were supposed to be deposited outside the city (Lev 14:29–45). This suggests an understanding of impurity as something to keep away from human habitations in general, not just from sanctuary space. Although the role of everyday purity and frequent purifications for the general population might have differed between, for example, Egypt and Judea,[36] purifying rites in the ancient Mediterranean world were neither reserved for the elite nor restricted to sacred precincts.

Contexts for Purification

It is often asserted that impurity is a function of the human condition. Human beings may be expected to purify themselves or to be purified in a number of situations belonging to the general life cycle, such as menstruation, marriage, sex, childbirth, and death. While this is part of the truth, the conclusion that pollution concerns everything that is particularly human in contrast to the divine sphere does not follow. Even if such a distinction could be argued for Judaism, it fits poorly with some other religious systems, in which gods in fact can be born, give birth, and die, as well as engage in sexual activities.[37] People may be considered impure for other reasons than sex and death. And impurity also affects vessels, artifacts, foods, fabrics, buildings, cities, and lands. Divine images and temples nevertheless seem to be especially vulnerable to pollution from human sources. Impurity turns out to be part of human life—and so does purification.

Actual practices often have to be gathered from scattered passages and remarks in a wide variety of texts, together with some material evidence, such as paintings and reliefs, in which purificatory rituals occasionally figure. A coherent and systematic picture is difficult to find, except for Second Temple Judaism, for which we have priestly purity codes, and to some extent Zoroastrianism, based on Vendidād. In the following, the most important types of impurity and purifications will be reviewed.

---

35. For Hittite and Babylonian parallels, see Wright 1987, 15–91.
36. Cf. Quack 2013, 140–43.
37. Lemos 2013, 274.

Body Fluids

Not all body fluids are commonly treated as impure. Feces and saliva occur occasionally, but are not considered unclean in most traditions. It is genital discharge in particular—semen and vaginal blood—that are generally understood to pollute.

The impurity of vaginal blood in the ancient world is, however, an ambiguous issue. There is Egyptian evidence for purity concerns: the Egyptian word for menstruation (*ḥsmn*) is related to the term for purification, and certain demotic contracts (third century BCE) indicate that buildings could have special rooms where menstruating women could stay. Some evidence for menstrual separation in Egypt can be found even in Byzantine-era texts. Impurity from menstruation and miscarriage belong to the abominations prohibited for specific cities or districts in the so-called cult monographs. Moreover, absentee lists for workers from Deir el-Medina indicate that men stayed home from work when their wives and daughters menstruated. Menstruation was definitely understood as something negative, but to what extent and how it polluted except in temple contexts is somewhat unclear.[38]

Mesopotamian evidence covers a long time period and in addition several different cultures. The Sumerian poem Enki and Ninhursaga describes the pure land of Dilmun as a place without destructions, without death, without disease, and perhaps, depending on the translation, without menstruation.[39] This piece of evidence is uncertain. However, a number of terms for which the exact range is uncertain, but referring to women bleeding from the womb for one reason or another, do occur in ancient West Asian texts. Although their interpretation is contested, some Akkadian texts and fragments can be taken to indicate the impurity of bleeding women and even their isolation, or at least as prohibitions against contact or sex.[40] Childbirth seems to have incurred impurity, too, according to both Babylonian and Hittite[41] texts.

Greek and Roman evidence is similarly ambiguous. We have no clear evidence from the classical period that menstruation was regarded as polluting. Aristotle (*Somn.* 459b–460a) says a menstruant dims the mirror,

---

38. Frandsen 2007; Quack 2013, 142.
39. Guichard and Marti 2013, 60–65.
40. Van der Toorn 1994, 51–55; Philip 2006, 5–7.
41. Stol 2000, 205–6; Beckman 1983, 251–52.

and Roman writers, such as Pliny (*Nat.* 7.63–64; 28.70–82), later add more details. Menstrual blood is clearly regarded as powerful and most likely seen as negative, but the question is whether and to what extent it was understood to pollute. Except for medical texts, there is little or no mention of menstruation in classical times, not even in comedy, which made Robert Parker ask whether it perhaps was regarded as too shameful to speak about.[42] Roman writers are not as reticent, and menstruation is clearly viewed as polluting, although prohibitions relating to the sacred are missing.[43]

Express prohibitions against menstruants entering sacred precincts are few and late but do exist in the sacred laws, usually referring to temples of Eastern gods. They are required to wait for seven to nine days. The waiting time after childbirth varies between seven and forty days; a period of forty days is confirmed by third-century CE Roman writer Censorinus (*Die nat.* 11.7).[44] Birth pollution was sometimes considered extremely serious, as in the case of Delos, the sacred island of Apollo, where both burial and childbirth were banned in 426/5 BCE, after a Delphic oracle; women had to give birth on the adjacent Rheneia (Herodotus, *Hist.* 1.64; Thucydides, *Hist.* 3.104).[45]

Although its focus lies on corpse impurity, the Zoroastrian Vendidād reveals a clear stance on vaginal blood and also touches on male discharges. All or most issues from the human body, whether sick or well, are considered to pollute, including blood and semen. This necessitates that menstruants withdraw and sleep alone. Parturients must be isolated for forty days. Menstruants and women with irregular bleedings must purify by washing twice with *gomez* (cow's urine) and once with water (Vend. 16:1, 12). Textiles that have once been polluted by corpse impurity can after purification only be used by purifying dischargers during their waiting period (7:10–19). Contamination by touch from male as well as female dischargers is assumed (5:59; 7:19). Vessels used for bringing food to impure women must be made of metal (16:6), since stone and metal vessels can be purified after contamination (7:73–75). Even involuntary semen emission is punished (8:26), and the death penalty applies to anyone who has sex with a bleeding menstruant (16:17–18). Childbirth

---

42. Parker 1983, 102.
43. Lennon 2010; 2014, 81–89.
44. Blidstein 2017, 23.
45. Günther 2013, 250.

as such is not addressed by the Vendidād, but only stillbirth; in Zoroastrian practice, however, childbirth is always associated with impurity and purification. Purity has little to do with temple visits or sacrifice, but rather with the Zoroastrian view of the sacredness of the fire and the ground. There is no distinction between everyday matters and the sacred sphere.

The priestly rules about genital discharges that lay at the bottom of the practices of Second Temple Judaism may well have been shaped under influence of Persian religion.[46] Leviticus 15 is shaped symmetrically, with rules regarding male and female discharges (natural and pathological) balancing each other.[47] The priestly authors have managed to create an at least superficially coherent system from material of fairly disparate origins. Semen emission incurs impurity until evening. Menstrual impurity lasts for seven days, like the waiting period for pathological male and female dischargers after the cessation of their symptoms. The latter are required to bring sacrifices of removal on the eighth day. All are expected to bathe their bodies and probably launder their clothes, too; although this is not explicitly stated about the menstruant, it is probably assumed.[48] Consequently, sexual intercourse also incurs impurity until evening. The point of the rules is to avoid contact, which incurs impurity until evening.

Childbirth rules (Lev 12) are short and were probably added somewhat later; they assume the discharge rules. Pollution of the parturient lasts for a first stage of seven days and a second stage of thirty-three, in the case of a boy; for a girl, the numbers are doubled. The difference has puzzled many, but as we have seen, periods of approximately forty days are found elsewhere and differences in length, too. The purification period is concluded with a sacrifice, and immersion is most probably assumed although not explicitly mentioned.[49]

Disease

Disease in the ancient world was often seen as divine punishment, and in contexts where divine disapproval was understood in terms of pollution, disease could be subject to purification. One example is the Hippo-

---

46. Kazen 2015b = ch. 4 in this volume.
47. Ellens 2003; Hieke 2014, 526–47.
48. Wright 1987, 181–96; Milgrom 1991, 919; Kazen 2007.
49. Kazen 2007.

cratic text On the Sacred Disease (ca. 400 BCE), which accuses purifiers of trying to purify epileptics just like any polluted person. This does not mean that any disease was understood as pollution and subject to purification. In addition to pathological discharges, skin diseases seem to have been regarded as particularly polluting, at least in the East. Often translated as "leprosy" (but not referring to Hansen's disease), skin diseases both prevent access to temples and are subject to strict rules of isolation and quarantine, and demand purification after their healing.

One example from Egypt prohibits access to the temple of Esna.[50] Babylonian evidence includes, for example, a Mari letter, a Šurpu incantation, and a Babylonian *kudurru* inscription.[51] One such boundary-stone inscription refers to the *išrubu* (skin disease) covering the whole person, who is driven out of the city and has to stay outside the walls so that no one should approach him.[52] Although the Vendidād does not mention it, Herodotus (*Hist.* 1.138) says that the Persians do not allow "leprous" people to enter a town or to associate with others.

This fits with the priestly laws in Leviticus and Numbers (Lev 13–14; Num 5:2–3), which place skin-diseased persons outside settlements with the express purpose to prevent contact with others, which accords with what we know from some of the Dead Sea Scrolls, as well as from Jewish practice according to first-century CE texts.

The priestly purification rites (Lev 14:1–32) were elaborate and were not aimed at healing the disease, but at keeping it away once the symptoms had abated. The formerly skin-diseased person who had recovered had to undergo a bird rite outside the settlement, then launder, shave, and wash, before being readmitted into the settlement. However, before being allowed into their home, healed "lepers" had to wait for seven days and then do another round of laundering, shaving, and washing. In addition to this there were three types of sacrifices on the eighth day, one of which included the daubing of blood from one of the sacrificial victims onto the outer extremities of the body.[53] All of this together effected purification and removal (*kipper*).

---

50. Quack 2013, 120.
51. Milgrom 1991, 805, 818, 911.
52. Nougayrol 1948.
53. Cf. the even more elaborate purification of various body parts in Zoroastrian rites (Vend. 8:35–72; 9:15–26).

Corpse Impurity

Purification from "death impurity" or corpse contamination was a common idea in the ancient world. "Everything that died a natural death is impure" (*sua morte extincta omnia funesta sunt*; Festus, *Verb.* 161.1).[54] In practice, however, Roman attitudes to death and pollution were more ambiguous and more pragmatic.[55]

As part of the already mentioned purification of Delos, graves were moved from the island. Such views were not global, however. In Egypt, with its particular views on death and the afterlife, tombs and corpses were certainly susceptible to pollution and could need purification, but they themselves did not pollute, even though mourning behavior did.[56] Neither Mesopotamian nor Hittite evidence suggests an understanding of the corpse as contagious.[57] In Greece, tombs of heroes seem not to have been considered polluting and could actually be housed within cities.[58] Generally, however, the Greeks regarded death as polluting, incurring a ten- to forty-day waiting period for the household or after contact with a corpse.[59] In Athens, a container with water was placed outside the house of a deceased person in order for people to wash themselves (Euripides, *Alc.* 98–100).[60]

Zoroastrianism presents the most dynamic concept of corpse pollution. As soon as a person dies, the corpse is entered by the corpse demoness (*drug nasu*). Interestingly, the more holy a person has been, the more impure the corpse becomes. Its contagious power quickly has to be diminished with the *sag-did* rite, including the gaze of a dog. Burial includes exposure of the corpse to flesh-eating birds on a burial tower (*dakhma*), in order to protect both fire and ground. Corpse bearers are highly polluted, are required to keep separate and eat from special vessels, and have to undergo a preliminary purification as soon as possible. Purification of polluted people requires washing in *gomez* and water, as well as the *barashnum* rite.[61]

---

54. Graf 2010, 421.
55. Bodel 2000; Lindsay 2000.
56. Quack 2013, 143–52.
57. Feinstein 2014, 26–27.
58. Ekroth 2002.
59. Blidstein 2017, 22.
60. Graf 2010, 422.
61. Choksy 1989.

In Second Temple Judaism, corpse impurity and associated purification rites were subject to continuous development. From being a concern mainly for priests (Lev 21:1–4), it became an issue for everyone (Num 19). Pollution from contact with a corpse or presence within the same space rendered a seven-day impurity, and purification was effected by both immersion and sprinkling. Although regarded as the strongest form of impurity, its contaminating force was mitigated through the employment of an extra first-day ablution, not attested in the biblical laws but in later sources. Contact with a corpse-impure person resulted in defilement until evening.[62] Stepped pools for purification adjacent to burial grounds, which have recently been excavated, attest to the attention given to death pollution in practical life and the urgent need to diminish its force immediately.[63]

Bloodshed

Homicide (war or legal execution sometimes excepted) was generally thought to cause impurity, but exactly how that pollution is envisaged differs. According to Mesopotamian texts, bloodshed pollutes, and even gods had to purify after killing.[64] But it has been claimed that blood was only thought to pollute individuals, not societies or territories. Only the murderer would thus be affected.[65] Others question this restriction when other than legal texts are considered.[66]

In any case, there is a difference compared to the Israelite legislation regarding undetected murder and the pollution of bloodshed (Deut 21:1–9). The law assumes that premeditated murder should be punished and not included under the provisions made by cities of refuge for unintended homicide (Deut 19:1–13; Num 35:10–34). Unavenged intentional bloodshed pollutes (*ḥnp*) and defiles (*ṭmʾ*) the land (*'ereṣ*; Num 35:33, 34) or people (*'am*; Deut 21:8), and if the pollution cannot be removed (*kpr*) by the death of the murderer (Num 35:33), it must be done by breaking the neck of a heifer by throwing her down an uninhabited ravine.

---

62. Kazen 2010b.
63. Adler 2008b; 2009.
64. Attridge 2004, 73.
65. Barmash 2005, 94–115.
66. Dietrich 2010, 191–96.

If looked at in isolation, it is questionable whether this counts as a purification rite. Although it is barely integrated into the priestly system and formally neither a sacrifice nor a purification, the rite does remove (*kpr*) the bloodguilt (*dām*; Deut 21:8), which in later texts is spoken of in terms of pollution and impurity (Num 35:33–34). Such an understanding seems quite reasonable and hardly anomalous when compared to Greek and Roman evidence. In Greece, the pollution of murder, its disastrous effects on the land and on the people, and its purification by an array of rites, including exile and sacrifices, was a well-known topos in myth, tragedy, and history.[67] Here we also find the concept of purifying blood with blood, for example, the blood of a piglet, which is then washed off. This is also one of the contexts in which the use of *pharmaka* as purificant was in force.[68] In Rome, pollution and purification from bloodshed were still an issue, but less of a threat to society at large, as the Roman legal system turned this more into a question of individual rights.[69]

Objects, Buildings, and Grounds

The purification of cult images, cultic instruments and vessels, altars, and temples, as well as both sacred and secular precincts, is widely attested in ancient Mediterranean and West Asian texts. Since everything surrounding the cult required as high a state of purity as possible, the purification of cultic attire does not necessarily indicate previous defilement, as in Egyptian rituals of consecration and "decoration."[70] Other temple purification rites, such as the Israelite Day of Atonement ritual, specifically aimed to remove pollutions that had accumulated over time (Lev 16). Greek purifications of temples and cities were likewise elaborate arrangements. Fumigation was used to purify objects and spaces. In Rome, fields were purified with the *circumambulatio* rite, and in both Greece and Rome the annual cycle was introduced by a purification period—in Rome, this took place during February. Some of these rituals contained regular *pharmakos* rites and the cleansing of cult images in the sea.[71] Although pollution of the land is an issue in the Israelite priestly Holiness Code (Lev 18:24–30;

---

67. Parker 1983, 104–43.
68. Burkert 1985, 80–81; Parker 2004, 507–8; Graf 2010, 421–22.
69. Lennon 2014, 92–100.
70. Quack 2013, 116–18.
71. Graf 2010, 422–23.

19:22–26), there are no purification rituals for that purpose (except in the above case of pollution by bloodguilt), but rather instances of rhetoric by means of evocative metaphor.

Explanations of Impurity and Purification

The broad range for which purity language is used has been puzzling to many scholars. In the Israelite priestly texts, purification rituals are only prescribed for those "technical" types of bodily contagion that are included in the purity laws (Lev [11]12–15; Num 19). These are often called "ritual," while various behaviors understood to cause impurity, for which no purificatory rituals are prescribed, have been designated as "moral." Within such a framework, food taboos find themselves sitting on the fence. There is a lively discussion about to what extent moral impurities are to be understood metaphorically or literally.

Some of the distinctions based on these priestly texts are difficult to claim, based on what we know of purification practices elsewhere in the Mediterranean and ancient West Asia. Even within the priestly system, sacrifices of removal function similarly, whether in contexts of impurity or in relation to other types of moral or cultic offense, although purificatory water rites are only prescribed for impurities caused by corpses, carcasses, and bodily contagion. In many neighboring cultures, there is little difference in the removal of various kinds of pollution and offense, which makes clear and fast distinctions difficult.

Language and Metaphor

Taking semantic considerations into account, we may suggest that most conceptions of impurity and most usages of purificatory language are in fact metaphorical, unless the removal or washing away of literal substances is envisaged. This use of language is profitably explained by conceptual metaphor theory, which sees metaphors as cross-domain mappings that carry notions from one cognitive domain to another and provide the other domain with new impetus and meaning.[72] A primary notion of material dirt (impurity, pollution) is mapped onto domains of disgusting creatures, unsavory human beings, or objectionable behavior, thus creating

---

72. Lakoff and Johnson 1980a.

secondary notions of pollution. These are all to some degree metaphorical, whether or not they are integrated into a system that involves their removal by concrete purifying rituals.

A more nuanced understanding can be gained by applying conceptual blending theory: domains or mental spaces (input spaces) that have certain elements in common (generic space) can easily be fused into a blended space in which certain other elements from the input spaces are combined into new conceptual frameworks. The effect is not restricted to language only, but new blends will influence both thought and behavior.[73]

Such explanations assume that beneath the surface, conceptions of pollution and impurity depend on basic notions of revulsion and offense, which are variously extended, elaborated, and culturally construed.[74] They also explain why many cultures lack distinct categories for different types of impurity and use similar purification rites for very diverse offenses.

Psychobiological and Sociocultural Explanations

To suggest that disgust or revulsion lies at the very bottom of purity concerns is not the same as claiming this to explain every purification ritual. Core disgust evolved as an adaptive trait to protect living organisms against danger. As a survival mechanism, aversion has an ultimate biological base, but most or all levels of disgust of which we are aware are more or less shaped by cultural evolution.[75] Simply put, pollution and its purification in various human societies have sometimes traveled far from their innate origins. In spite of this, some degree of ground-level aversion is usually present in all contexts in which pollution is handled by various purifying and removal rites, however culturally construed.

Evolutionary and psychobiological explanations do not claim to explain the details of such cultural constructions, but focus mainly on the necessary prerequisites for purity conceptions to evolve. Historical and sociocultural explanations are needed to understand how and why general aversions developed into more specific conceptions of impurity in particular contexts. For example, the general use of water rites for purification is quite intuitive, while the particular evolution of various types of ablution,

---

73. Coulson and Oakley 2000; Fauconnier and Turner 2002, 17–57.
74. Kazen 2011, 33–36, 71–94; 2014 = ch. 5 in this volume
75. Kazen 2014 = ch. 5 in this volume.

immersion, and sprinkling, and the precise combination of these for various purposes, requires historical and contextual explanations.

Historical and sociocultural factors are also important for understanding how avoidance behaviors and purificatory strategies are shaped and systematized into fixed practices, customs, and, at times, elaborate purity codes. Depending on the context, such customs and codes are integrated and interact with dominating social, cultural, economic, and hierarchical patterns. To that extent we may speak of their function, remembering that the meaning has little to do with intention or purpose, but is more in the Durkheimian sense of correspondence, or perhaps effect. Such effects will naturally correlate with all other values and practices that operate in the social context in question. Purity practices may therefore function to reinforce certain behaviors, structures, and ideologies in a society without this being their meaning. This is true even when individuals or groups of people consciously employ or exploit purity practices for such purposes, or ascribe such meaning to them.[76]

Functionalist and Symbolic Interpretations

Unfortunately, function is often understood in quite a different manner. In the past, it has been quite popular to explain concepts of pollution and practices of purification as reflections of social structures, or theological teachings, at times to the point of allegory.[77] Functionalist or structuralist understandings of impurity associate impurity with classification and boundaries of the social body, and sometimes read purity codes as cosmological ciphers.

This priority of mind and theory over behavior and ritual is problematic; it is not only unlikely on cognitive grounds but more often than not reveals acontextual and ahistorical traits. In addition, it turns the interpretation of purity concerns and purification rites into an arbitrary and speculative enterprise that at times has little foothold in the text.[78] This is true also of theological versions of functionalist-structuralist interpretations.

Closely related to these perspectives but with ancient roots are symbolic and allegorical understandings, the difference perhaps being that allegory does not need to make any claims about a ritual's intended

---

76. Kazen 2017 = ch. 6 in this volume.
77. Cf. Douglas 1978; 2002.
78. Watts 2007, 15–27; Lemos 2009; 2013.

meaning, while symbolism tries to explicate it. Neither needs to bother much about historical levels, and in the end both often turn out to be as speculative as functionalist-structuralist readings, depending more on the interpreter's leanings than on textual or contextual clues. Purificatory rites, just like sacrificial rituals, especially those found in the Bible, are particularly vulnerable to symbolic overinterpretation, when interpreters struggle to find relevant meaning in texts and rites from the past.

Purification as Ritual Activity

The study of ritual has flourished during the latest decades, and the depreciative Protestant attitude of previous times is all but gone. In its place, and replacing older ideas of primitive religion, a number of new theories have appeared. Some of these may shed light on purificatory rites.

Frequency, Agency, and Efficacy

According to the ritual frequency hypothesis,[79] rituals typically tend toward one of two attractor positions: low-frequency rituals usually go together with high-sensory stimulation, while high-frequency rituals are normally low in sensory pageantry and cause less excitement. To some degree this is common sense and perhaps even slightly tautological, since that which is repeated regularly effects habituation and thus cannot excite or enthuse in the long run. Even the most spectacular scenery becomes commonplace to the person who constantly lives with it. To a certain extent, then, what counts as sensory pageantry is contextual and subjective.

The basic observation of the ritual frequency hypothesis nevertheless makes sense. Rituals repeated daily or even several times a day are usually much less elaborate and spectacular than those that occur once in a lifetime. For example, the infrequent purification of a Greek city, through the expulsion (probably not killing!) of a *pharmakos* or *katharma*[80] or the purification of homicide with the blood of piglets or dogs (*LIMC* 7, Orestes 48; Plutarch, *Quaest. rom.* 280b–c) were more spectacular events than the simple washing with water from a container placed outside the

---

79. McCauley and Lawson 2002; Whitehouse 2002.
80. Parker 1983, 257–80; Hughes 1991, 139–65.

house of a deceased person (Euripides, *Alc.* 98–100).[81] Similarly, in ancient Mesopotamia, *šurpu* and *namburbû* rituals, aimed at particular and occasional evils, seem to evoke a "medium level" of sensory excitement.[82] In Zoroastrian religion, the simple *padyab* ritual, sprinkling cow's urine (*gomez*) over affected body parts, could be repeated several times a day, while the nine-night *barashnum* for direct corpse contamination was so elaborate that it eventually came to be performed vicariously.[83] In Second Temple Judaism, the conglomerate of rites ascribed for the annual Day of Atonement (Lev 16) involve much more sensory pageantry than the daily handwashing before meals that came to be increasingly practiced toward the end of the Second Temple period.

According to Thomas Lawson and Robert McCauley's theory of ritual form, rituals, just like all other actions, involve agents, instruments, and "patients." Within this "action representation system," divine (superhuman) agents, or gods, can be particularly involved at any level, either through the ritual agent or through the ritual instrument or patient. In the first case, the ritual is called a "special agent ritual," and in the second and third cases, it is called a "special instrument" or "special patient ritual." Whether divine agency is transmitted and manifested first and foremost through the person performing a particular ritual, through the means of the ritual, or through the instrument or recipient of the ritual is not always self-evident, but Lawson and McCauley suggest that it is possible to discern where the supernatural agent enters the ritual structure initially and with as few enabling rituals as possible. Be that as it may, the point is that special agent rituals are supposed to go together with high-sensory pageantry and low frequency, while special instrument and patient rituals are thought to be less exciting but often repeated. When highly exciting special agent rituals are too frequently repeated, there is sensory overload. In contrast, the loss of sensory pageantry in rarely repeated special agent rituals creates a deflated system that becomes boring and encourages splinter groups.

This multitheory has been criticized, both for being overly complicated and for not fitting Judaism very well. In fact, neither Second Temple Judaism nor rabbinic Judaism seems to make use of special agent rituals![84]

---

81. Graf 2010, 422.
82. Cf. Guichard and Marti 2013.
83. Choksy 1989, 23–52; de Jong 1999.
84. Ketola 2007; Biró 2013.

Sacrifices are by definition understood to be special patient rituals (they are repeated), although their sensory pageantry, especially during feasts when thousands of animals were slaughtered, must have been enormous. Nor is circumcision, in spite of being a once-in-the-lifetime event, a special agent ritual, since, at least in theory, anyone is in fact allowed to perform the rite. In that regard, it is similar to Christian baptism, which does not require a priest to become valid, but water and, in due time, the Trinitarian formula.

Returning to purification rites, some fit the theories discussed above fairly well. The just-mentioned nine-night *barashnum* rite requires a professional purifier to perform it, whether or not it was undertaken vicariously. It could be classified as a special agent ritual, relatively infrequent, and with high sensory impact. Similar considerations might apply to the Greek purification of cities, such as that of Athens by the legendary Epimenides. Professional purifiers (*kathartai*) seem to have found a traditional place in Greek society.[85] In the already-mentioned On the Sacred Disease, however, purifiers are grouped together with charlatans and quacks (*agyrtai kai alazones*; Morb. sacr. 1.3-4). Describing their misguided methods, the author accuses them of treating epileptics just like they would deal with any polluted person: "for they purify those having the disease with blood and the like, as if they had some pollution, or curse, or were bewitched by a human being, or had done some profane act" (*kathairousi gar tous echomenous tēi nousōi haimati te kai alloisi toioutois hōsper miasma ti echontas, ē alastoras, ē pepharmakeumenous hypo anthrōpōn, ē ti ergon anosion eirgasmenous*; Morb. sacr. 4.36–40). We see here an interesting list of categories supposed to be in need of blood purification: those variously polluted (*miasma ti echontas*); those under a curse or haunted by bloodguilt (*alastoras*); those bewitched, or possibly scapegoated, by other human beings (*pepharmakeumenous/ pepharmagmenous*); and those who had done something sacrilegious (*ti ergon anosion eirgasmenous*). Whether the efficacy of such rites depended on the purifiers' special status must, however, be questioned; these are repeatable rites that might be better classified as special instrument rituals, depending on blood as purificant. The category of special instrument ritual probably fits the *barashnum* better, too, in view of the emphasis placed on the exact performance of every detail in order for the rite to be valid.

---

85. Borgeaud 1999; Ronen 1999.

Whether the supernatural agent primarily works through the purifier or through the rites or through the purificants used in the rites is sometimes a moot question, and there is a risk of classifying rituals so as to confirm the theory of ritual form.

Jewish purification rituals present special challenges, as they often do not need a priest. Ablutions and immersions are usually self-administered: the agent and the patient are identical. The closest entry for the supernatural agent in such cases is the water, and most water purifications are probably best understood as special instrument rituals not only in Judaism, but also in other religious systems in the ancient world.[86] Similarly, purificatory practices such as laundering, shaving, and the removal of polluted materials are best described as special instrument rituals. Even the concomitant sacrifices, which normally would be understood as special patient rituals, could be reconsidered as instrument rituals, because of the uncertainty of the recipient of the sacrifices and their intended effects. The sacrifices of removal (*ḥaṭṭāʾt* and *ʿāšām*) are indeed brought before Yahweh (e.g., Lev 4:3; 5:15), and like the main sacrifices of Lev 1–3 are also designated as sacrificial gifts (*qorbān*), but some ambiguity remains even within the priestly sacrificial system as to how the removal is envisaged—hence the uncertainty regarding their classification as special patient or special instrument rituals.

One could in fact argue that most or all purifying rituals are special instrument rituals, since their purpose is to remove pollution from the patient with the help of concrete and specific purificants. This focus on method and means is a trait shared with magic. With or without the involvement of specific divine beings, supernatural power is ascribed to the rites performed and the instruments used. From such a point of view, the transformation of purificatory immersion in water into baptism by John and by the early Jesus movement must be regarded as a mutation of sorts; there is now a ritual agent, and the rite is understood as a more or less singular event. This makes baptism susceptible to being understood as a special agent ritual, although Paul argues against the significance of the baptismal agent (1 Cor 1:10–17). According to the gospel tradition, baptism is closely associated with the gift of the spirit and could from that perspective be thought of as a special patient ritual—only that this does not fit the theory. In any case, the efficacy of purifying rites in gen-

---

86. Uro 2016, 86.

eral does not seem to depend on the purifying agent, but on the purificant, or instrument.

Purification as Commitment Signaling

Another avenue for studying ancient purification rites is the theory of commitment or costly signaling, which explains personally disadvantageous behavior and elaborate rituals by the long-term advantage of confidence and goodwill one receives from the larger community by performing them. The focus here is not on the efficacy of the rituals in themselves, but on evolutionary and psychological explanations for their adherence. Faithful observance proves that one is not a cheater or free rider, but a trustworthy person, prepared to invest in common concerns.[87] Complex purification rituals may be seen as hard-to-fake signals.

By strict adherence to purity codes and frequent purifications, one demonstrates faithfulness to vital group values and confirms group identity. Conversely, a lax attitude and lack of observance signal unreliability and a lack of loyalty. Such considerations override arguments from common sense that have frequently been presented against historical adherence to complicated rules. Well-known examples are the isolation or quarantine of menstruants in Second Temple Judaism, and the increasing observance of handwashing before ordinary (profane) meals. Claims that even priests, some of whom were poor and unable to afford the cost of strict adherence, might wink at the rules[88] carry little weight in light of the power of commitment signaling. The already-mentioned Zoroastrian nine-night *barashnum* rite is costly, and going down the steps into a roofed, dark, and sometimes muddy immersion pool is probably unpleasant, but people did such things out of commitment.

Several purity systems in the ancient world evolved from disparate practices into organized systems, with increasingly elaborate detail and new rites. Purificatory practices were well suited to express commitment and foster group cohesion and cooperation. The formation of the two most coherent systems we know of, Jewish and Zoroastrian purifying practices, seem to go together with the rise of cultural and/or national

---

87. Irons 2001; Bulbulia 2010.
88. Sanders 1990, 135, 233.

identity. Commitment signaling provides at least a partial explanation for this phenomenon.[89]

Purification and Emotional Impact

The role of emotions in rituals, which range from anxiety relief to satiety feelings, is debated.[90] It is a highly controversial issue whether ritual should be understood as an evolutionary by-product or as an adaptation for social interaction and communication.[91] Purification can be cheap or costly, simple or strenuous, high or low arousal, but in one way or another, purification rites appeal to the senses: sight, hearing, smell, and touch, some also to taste. The immediate meanings of rites are those experienced by the people who take part in them, regardless of what official and theological interpretations are attached. Since human experience is embodied, the emotional impact of a ritual will play a decisive role, and in the case of purification rites, this relates to the means and modes that are used.

The most common means of purification is water, whether by washing, sprinkling, or immersing. Water can be experienced as refreshing and life giving, but also as threatening, and water rites are bound to have emotional impact. First, to wash items, images, or clothes as part of purifying rites comes close to, and at times even coincides with, the literal cleaning from dirt that ritual purification is mapped on. Emotionally, such rites will thus effect a sense of real change in status and quality. Similar considerations would apply to other rites that involve manual cleaning, such as wiping, scraping, or decorating. There is a decisively tactile aspect to such purifications.

Second, to submit one's own person to water rites is more dramatic than the washing of inanimate objects. This applies in particular to immersion, which is an emotionally salient rite, experienced in and through the entire body. The embodied experience of contact with water supports a feeling of change and removal that compensates for the fact that the pollution from which the person is purified is often neither visible nor material. The movement in space, down the steps into a basin, into the water, crouching or bending, inscribes an embodied memory that reinforces the sense of validity and efficacy. This feeling is further

---

89. Uro 2016, 128–53.
90. Cf. Michaels and Wulf 2011.
91. Cf. Boyer and Liénard 2006, with open peer commentary.

enhanced in rites that involve the smearing of mud or blood onto the purifying person, thus materializing impurity, before washing it off. Purification rites thus generate an embodied and extended knowledge that is experiential rather than theoretical.[92]

Third, water rites can elicit collective emotions that enhance solidarity, a sense of belonging, and group identity. While sprinkling is performed by a ritual agent and can be applied to many people simultaneously, immersion is usually self-administered (except for the innovation of John and the subsequent Jesus movement) and individual. This does not, however, necessarily result in an individualistic attitude. It has often been mistakenly assumed that for rituals to evoke collective emotions, those involved must share collective experiences and a common identity. What is needed, however, is shared appraisals of (representational and motivational) contents in relation to individual needs, goals, and values, which will elicit similar emotions. The very character of the rite can trigger similar appraisals, especially within the context of preexisting groups.[93]

Other types of purification are emotional, too. The use of blood is dramatic; although animal blood, it reminds of human vulnerability and mortality. As a condition for life, it represents power. The sight and feel of blood can evoke fear. Similar considerations apply to the use of animal carcasses for purifying sacred buildings. While incense has a pleasant side, smoke and fire are dramatic and ambiguous, with threatening characteristics. Scapegoat and *pharmakon* rituals evoke feelings of exposure and victimization, reinforcing group loyalty and belonging. Many of these rituals have traits that typically instill a sense of awe, which is still a little-studied emotion, but seems to lie at the roots of human religiosity. Awe has been shown to lessen the need for cognitive closure and to increase prosocial tendencies and cooperation.[94] Purification rites can thus be understood to be functional from both an evolutionary and a psychological perspective.

---

92. Uro 2016, 154–77.
93. Von Scheve 2011.
94. Keltner and Haidt 2003; Shiota, Keltner, and Mossman 2007; Piff et al. 2015.

8

Concern, Custom, and Common Sense: Discharge, Handwashing, and Graded Purification

This chapter interacts with Ed P. Sanders's work on purity, building on some of his insights while disagreeing on other points. Sanders's appeal to historical imagination and common sense is discussed and problematized. The essay deals at length with issues such as the expulsion, isolation, and integration of various impurity bearers, and the emergence of additional water rites to mitigate impurities and prevent unnecessary contamination. The evidence under discussion includes the Hebrew Bible, Dead Sea texts, Philo, Josephus, New Testament, and rabbinic literature.

For many students of the historical Jesus and Second Temple Judaism, Ed P. Sanders's writings have provided a major route into an otherwise incomprehensible area: the complex subject of Jewish purity laws. Sanders's detailed discussions, first in *Jewish Law from Jesus to the Mishnah*, then in *Judaism: Practice and Belief*, are in no way simple to follow, but nevertheless have generously opened a door into a fascinating world for many students of the New Testament previously inexperienced in rabbinic studies.[1] Sanders's picture of Second Temple purity practices is one of general custom, shared by the majority, with a heightened degree of concern among certain groups, yet modified by a good portion of common sense. Some of the details in this picture will be spelled out below.

This essay was first written in 2008 for a publication that never materialized. Much of the contents were incorporated in Kazen 2010c, chs. 5–6. I apologize for some substantial repetitions, but I think it is in this form, as an explicit discussion with Ed P. Sanders, that the material is most interesting. The essay was revised and updated in 2015 and published in *JSHJ* 13 (2015): 150–87. Used by permission.

1. Sanders 1990; 1992.

In this chapter I build on Sanders's insights and discuss further two of his major topics: the question of whether the Pharisees tried to emulate priestly practice by eating ordinary food (*ḥullîn*) in purity and the question of the extent to which female dischargers were isolated or expelled. Although these questions have received much attention[2]—there is little new under the sun—I hope to contribute a few details and perspectives. Both relate to purificatory practices, such as handwashing and immersion, and both are relevant when discussing Jesus's attitude and practice, although the latter is not in focus in this chapter. As will become clear, both questions are profitably associated with ideas about levels of (im-) purity and graded purifications that were current at the end of the Second Temple period.

Sanders on Jesus and Purity

In spite of his profuse writing on the topic, purity laws play little role in Sanders's reconstruction of the historical Jesus. In *Jesus and Judaism*, Sanders states that Jesus's temple action had nothing to do with "purification."[3] Purity was not the issue between Jesus and his opponents. Jesus had "no substantial dispute about the law, nor ... any substantial conflict with the Pharisees."[4] Jesus's eating with "sinners" was not criticized as a transgression of the purity code.[5] "Making *purity* and *table-fellowship* the focal points of debate trivializes the charge against Jesus."[6]

The picture found in *The Historical Figure of Jesus* is basically similar, although here Sanders notes that legal disputes "were part and parcel of Jewish life" and that "it is plausible that Jesus had major conflicts about what

---

2. I attempt nothing like a *Forschungsbericht* or a full bibliography, but for a few more or less representative examples, old and new, relating to various aspects of these issues, see Büchler 1968; Alon 1977 (collection of articles from the 1930s and onward, originally in Hebrew); Neusner 1971; 1979; Westerholm 1978; Hübner 1986; Booth 1986; Tomson 1988; Milgrom 1991; Harrington 1993; Deines 1993; Zaas 1996; Maccoby 1999; Baumgarten 1999a; Regev 2000a; Kazen 2010a; Poirier 2003; Haber 2003; Crossley 2004; Wassén 2008; Furstenberg 2008; Avemarie 2010; Amit and Adler 2010; Kazen 2010b; 2010c; 2013a, 113–94; Miller 2015, 210–48; Adler 2016.
3. Sanders 1985, 61–76.
4. Sanders 1985, 292.
5. Sanders 1985, 209–10.
6. Sanders 1985, 187, emphasis original.

seem to most people today to be minor matters."[7] However, Sanders emphasizes the high degree of tolerance that we find in Second Temple Judaism. Everyone was used to differences in, and disputes about, legal interpretation.

In *Jewish Law from Jesus to the Mishnah*, Sanders stresses that Jesus did not challenge the purity laws, but rather accepted them. There is no mention of Jesus going to Tiberias, which was built on burial ground, and "had Jesus wanted seriously to challenge the purity laws he could have gone there and told them [i.e., the inhabitants] that they were fine just as they were."[8] To neglect handwashing was not a serious issue, and even if the tradition in Mark 7 were historical the events portrayed would not have infringed any biblical law.[9] In the case of the man with skin disease ("leper"), Jesus accepted biblical laws, including the purificatory sacrifice.[10] Similar arguments, sometimes based on silence and often with references to Sanders, have also been repeated or developed by others.[11] Paula Fredriksen, for example, suggests that Jesus's instructions to the leper not only presuppose purification rituals on the part of the leper but on Jesus's part, too, and although an argument from silence, "the loudness of this silence … gives the measure of our own *un*familiarity with and distance from the ancient world."[12] John Meier, on the other hand, interprets Jesus's silence in the gospels to mean that he "was simply not interested in the purity rules." Meier also strangely claims that neither *zābâ* impurity, nor "leprosy" impurity, was communicated by contact (touch) and goes out of his way to explain away Josephus's statements (*Ag. Ap.* 1.281–282; *Ant.* 3.261–268).[13] More recently, Cecilia Wassén has argued that impurity was mostly an issue for certain groups, whose "lifestyle was quite extreme," while Jews in general did not actively avoid impurity, since intercourse, childbirth, and tending the dead were good and necessary activities.[14]

Sanders has been extremely influential in dealing with misconceptions about Judaism among New Testament scholars. This is a process that was

---

7. Sanders 1993, 205.
8. Sanders 1990, 40.
9. Sanders 1990, 30–31, 40, 90–91; cf. 131–254.
10. Sanders 1990, 41, 91.
11. Cf. Fredriksen 2000; Avemarie 2010; Wassén 2008.
12. Fredriksen 2000, 206.
13. Meier 2009, 409–13. For further discussion, see Kazen 2010c, 164–66.
14. Wassén 2016a.

begun already with *Paul and Palestinian Judaism*.[15] Sanders's portrayal of Jesus has the important aim of correcting a number of misunderstandings that are based on Christian prejudice against Second Temple Judaism in general and against Pharisees in particular. These include the supposition that Jesus was killed because of legal conflicts and the idea that conflicts between Jesus and his opponents were basically conflicts between Jewish externalism and Christian emphasis on internal values and love. But Jewish Pharisees were nothing like their Christian caricatures. Jesus was not *killed* because of legal conflicts, and he was not killed by the *Pharisees*.

It is not difficult to imagine how such ideas came about. On one hand, the Pharisees are portrayed in the Synoptics as Jesus's main opponents during his Galilean ministry.[16] On the other hand, the leaders of the Jewish nation were increasingly blamed for Jesus's execution, although historically they were not solely or even mainly responsible for it.[17] In the light of subsequent early Christian conflicts with rabbinic Judaism, it was easy to conflate these two more or less historical remembrances, although even in the redacted text of Mark we can easily see that this does not hold water, since the Pharisees more or less disappear before the passion. Jesus died rather at the hands of the political authorities and not because of legal disputes about Sabbath and purity.

Once this is agreed on—and today many scholars are convinced—a number of questions remain, however. Exactly what type of Jew was Jesus, and how do we relate him to the various factions that we know of? I would not say that the misunderstandings above are all straw men today, but perhaps the ongoing debate about the character of the historical Jesus is better served by simply leaving some of the most flagrant non-Jewish interpretations aside, rather than combating them. It is still fairly common for proponents of a "Jewish Jesus" to address interpretations and issues that are similar to those championed by the majority of exegetes a number of decades ago. This was necessary at the end of the last century, but today such an approach is risky: this kind of polemic may obscure finer nuances, not least when it comes to purity issues.

---

15. Sanders 1977.

16. The historical accuracy of such a picture may be questioned. I have elsewhere argued that the Pharisees were gaining influence, although not necessarily dominance, in first-century Galilee, and that Jesus and his adherents were seen as competitors. See Kazen (2010a, 263–99) for a discussion and further references to this debate.

17. Cf. Sanders 1985, 294–318.

Common Sense and Historical Imagination

One of the marked characteristics of Sanders's scholarly work is his repeated emphasis on the need for historical imagination and common sense, not least in dealing with purity rules. Discussing how priests managed both to have sex and eat, Sanders suggests the possibility "that they winked at the rules."[18] For common people to apply priestly rules to ordinary food "would make ordinary life impossible."[19] Dealing with the possible separation of genital dischargers, he reminds the reader that "houses were on the whole not that large, and furniture not that plentiful."[20] Seclusion is deemed possible only for the rich, and many priests were poor; they would have found it difficult to keep these laws, and their wives had to eat something.[21] Sanders agrees that a high level of purity was generally aspired to and that purity was sought also outside cultic contexts,[22] but he emphasizes practical aspects in reconstructing the way in which purity laws were actually applied.

The problem with common sense is that, while absolutely necessary, it is also treacherous, since it rests in the eye of the beholder and is extremely context sensitive, constantly at risk of becoming anachronistic, by ruling out what *could* at times have been common sense to the ancients. One example is the assumption that menstrual laws would generally upset every household once a month. In antiquity, however, most women were either pregnant or breastfeeding through much of their fertile period.[23] Menstruation was surely common enough to be understood as a natural and recurring discharge, and purity rules for menstruants were thus more lenient than for a *zābâ*, but the situation was nevertheless quite different from modern experience. We might, like Sanders, ask ourselves

---

18. Sanders 1990, 135.
19. Sanders 1990, 149.
20. Sanders 1990, 145.
21. Sanders 1990, 223, 160, with a reference to Josephus, *Ant.* 3.261–262.
22. A general tendency during the Second Temple period to maintain a high degree of purity for its own sake is supported by other scholars, too. See, e.g., Regev 2000a; 2000b; Poirier 2003. Cf. Kazen 2010a; 2010c; 2013a; Miller 2015; Adler 2016. Poirier (2003, 248) points out that although Sanders "demonstrates that the purity halakah went beyond the temple, he continues to regard the sanctity of the temple as the motivating principle behind purity in general."
23. This has been pointed out by a number of scholars, e.g., Milgrom 1991, 953; Wenham 1979, 223–24.

about food preparation during the woman's period, in case she was subject to seclusion or restrictions: Would the men cook every fourth week?[24] In addition to the comparative infrequency of menstruation, such a commonsense question disregards ancient family structure. In an extended family there would normally be some woman not menstruating for one or another reason.[25] An argument from poverty is similarly flawed, because strict practices, including separation and seclusion of menstruants, are attested among a number of groups, such as the Qumranites, Samaritans, Karaites, and Falashas. Evidence for this ranges from literary prescriptions to actual real-life examples.[26]

While common sense is important for sifting and interpreting evidence, it cannot produce it. When common sense seemingly goes against evidence, there is reason to examine both the common sense and the evidence once more.

Within or Outside?

One key issue in discussing halakic practice at the end of the Second Temple period concerns the way in which genital dischargers were dealt with. The priestly rules (Lev 15) presuppose that dischargers lived within society, since the text outlines in great detail a number of ways in which their impurity can be transmitted and what purificatory measures are required as a result of such contagious contacts. This is very different from the skin-disease rules (Lev 13–14), which presuppose that a person with skin disease (a *maṣorāʿ*) is kept outside society and thus never comes into contact with others. Nothing is said about impurity or purification due to

---

24. Cf. Sanders 1990, 150. Sanders rhetorically asks whether the men had one week a month off.

25. I thank Teresa Callewaert for reminding me of this quite obvious fact. Sanders (1990, 351 n. 20) does acknowledge this type of argument but dismisses it with the arguments that women who live together often menstruate at the same time, and that there is no evidence for extended families in Jewish society during this period. I do not find these arguments conclusive, however.

26. For references, see Kazen 2010a, 72 n. 187. Here, too, Sanders (1990, 350–51 n. 17) does mention contemporary societies separating menstruants, but argues that such practices would have left signs in legal texts. This supposition may, however, be questioned. The use of stone vessels is not much elaborated on in rabbinic texts, yet their abundance during the first century, evidenced by archaeological remains, suggests a significance that cannot be deduced merely from texts.

contact with a *məṣorāʿ*, although at the end of the Second Temple period contamination through touch and overhang (similar to corpse impurity) was assumed to be biblical.[27]

The two sets of rules probably have different origins. I have elsewhere discussed discrepancies *within* the discharge laws from a number of possible angles.[28] It seems clear that they have to some extent been systemically shaped by priestly redaction and were increasingly homogenized by halakic interpretation and practice toward the end of the Second Temple period. This is further accentuated when discrepancies *between* various sets of purity laws are noted.[29] When the required purificatory rites are compared, we see that dischargers (*zābîm* and *zābôt*) offer pigeons as *ḥaṭṭāʾt* and *ʿōlâ* sacrifices on the eighth day (Lev 15:14–15, 29–30),[30] while the corresponding sacrifices for the purifying *məṣorāʿ* should consist of lambs, or pigeons if the offerer is poor, and also include an *ʾāšām* sacrifice, which in any case must be a lamb, as well as food offerings (Lev 14:10–31). Such differences could possibly be understood to reflect the relative seriousness of these two types of impure conditions, and associated with the expulsion of lepers but not of dischargers. This does not provide sufficient explanation, however. While these rules have clearly been redacted and adapted to fit into a priestly system, they still carry a number of disparate traits.[31] The obviously apotropaic bird rite initiating the purification of a *məṣorāʿ* (Lev 14:1–7) has no equivalent when we look at other impurity

---

27. The gap was soon filled in by analogy with other types of impurity and by deduction from rules about contamination from leprous houses (Lev 14:36, 46–47), combined with the statement (14:8) that a purifying *məṣorāʿ* can enter the "camp" but not his house until the seven-day period is finished. Cf. Kazen 2010a, 112–16; 2013a, 150–55.

28. Kazen 2007.

29. Cf. Kazen 2010c, 91–135.

30. Just like the corpse-impure (Num 19:11–22; see below), the semen emitter and the menstruant (*niddâ*) are not required to offer any sacrifices according to biblical law (Lev 15:16–24). This is often explained by the frequency and normality of these conditions. The parturient (*yôledet*), however, is required to offer a lamb as *ʿōlâ* and a pigeon as *ḥaṭṭāʾt* sacrifice (two pigeons if she is poor) after the purification period of forty (boy) or eighty (girl) days (Lev 12). While birth is as frequent as death and as normal as menstruation, the childbirth law represents yet another variant, which at least in the biblical text is only partially harmonized with the discharge laws.

31. For a discussion of some of these traits and possible Persian influence, see Kazen 2015b = ch. 4 in this volume.

bearers, except that it resembles the red-heifer rite (Num 19:2–10) that provides the purification water necessary for removing corpse impurity. Both these rites are carried out "outside the camp." Those involved have to bathe and wash their clothes before they can enter the settlement again (Lev 14:8; Num 19:7, 10, 19, 21).[32]

Corpse-impure people are naturally envisaged within settlements, since death occurs at home; people are thus expected to become contaminated, and appropriate measures for purification are prescribed. The removal of the corpse itself from the settlement is, however, presupposed. Mere contact with a grave was considered to transmit corpse impurity, according to Num 19:16, and the phrasing suggests that graves were located outside settlements (אֶל־פְּנֵי הַשָּׂדֶה). Although kings are regularly said to have been buried "in the city of Jerusalem,"[33] archaeological evidence before the exile is somewhat ambiguous. In general, graves seem to have been kept outside the city wall.[34] Some uncertainties remain regarding earlier practice, since complaints against the burial of kings inside the city as well as the corpse-impurity rules of Num 19 are probably late.[35] In any case, it is clear that corpses were removed from settlements during the Second Temple period, while corpse-impure people were generally not.[36]

Numbers 5 and Possible Criteria for Expulsion

"Lepers" and corpses are thus assumed to be excluded from settlements, while dischargers and the corpse-impure are not, at least according to the biblical text of Lev 12–15 and Num 19. Varying origins and contexts

---

32. As an explicit requirement for entering the camp, this is stated only of the priest, but the priest in this passage (Num 19:1–10) is clearly inserted by the priestly redactors in their attempt to integrate this rite into the official sacrificial system, bringing it in under the category of *ḥaṭṭāʾt* sacrifices, in spite of it having little to do with a normal *ḥaṭṭāʾt*. The role of the priest is marginal, but his participation associates the rite with the sanctuary. Cf. Milgrom 1981. The requirement to bathe before entering the camp may lie behind the first-day ablution for the corpse-impure that had apparently become standard practice at the end of the Second Temple period.

33. See Ezekiel's protest against such a practice in Ezek 43:7–9. The rabbis discussed possible exceptions for kings and prophets from the general rule (a minimum distance of 50 cubits from the city limit). See t. B. Bat. 1:11; cf. m. B. Bat. 2:9.

34. Cf. Broshi 1974; Wright 1987, 120–22 and notes for further references.

35. Kazen 2015b, 441–42 = ch. 4 in this volume.

36. Cf. Kazen 2015b, 177–79 = ch. 4 in this volume.

of these laws may account for such discrepancies. I have elsewhere suggested that some of the details and developments of discharge and corpse-impurity practices reflect influences from Israelite contact with Persian (Zoroastrian) culture.[37] As rules were increasingly harmonized and read systemically, however, one might expect less diversity. Such considerations may perhaps lie behind Num 5:2–4, which requires expulsion of all corpse-impure people, lepers, and dischargers (apparently *zābîm* and *zābôt*, but not lesser impurities). This stricter tradition could be associated with the war laws in Num 31:19, 24, requiring soldiers who had touched corpses to stay outside the camp until the end of the seven-day purification period. The strict legislation of Num 5 is motivated by the divine presence in the camp (אֶת־מַחֲנֵיהֶם אֲשֶׁר אֲנִי שֹׁכֵן בְּתוֹכָם) and is phrased as an additional commandment, adjusting or correcting an earlier, more lenient practice. Some scholars have discussed whether the stricter practice in fact has more ancient roots than the lenient one, or perhaps represents an alternative contemporaneous tradition.[38] Although expulsion practices in some cultures are certainly ancient, I am today much more inclined to understand the strictures in Numbers to reflect late developments within a limited temple state run by a priestly elite in Persian-period Yehud.[39]

Jacob Milgrom points to the ancient West Asian roots of expulsion practices, but associates strict rules with the idea of airborne impurity threatening the sanctuary from afar and the requirement to bring a *ḥaṭṭāʾt* sacrifice.[40] I am not convinced by the idea of airborne impurity, however. There is little evidence for it elsewhere, and it depends on an instrumental interpretation of Lev 15:31 ("by their contamination"). Hyam Maccoby has suggested that the preposition can just as well be interpreted as temporal or conditional ("when/if they contaminate").[41] Also, the *yôledet* is required to bring a *ḥaṭṭāʾt* sacrifice but is not expelled even according to the stricter tradition. The corpse-impure person, on the other hand, is expelled but not required to bring a sacrifice.

If the requirement to bring *sacrifices* were to be taken as indicating in some fashion how serious the impurity was considered to be, we might not

---

37. Kazen 2015b = ch. 4 in this volume.
38. Cf. Kazen 2010a, 147–50.
39. Kazen 2015b, 441 = ch. 4 in this volume; cf. Achenbach 2003, 499–528, 598–628; Nihan 2007, 554–55, 570–72; Frevel 2013.
40. Milgrom 1976, 390–99; 1991, 999.
41. Maccoby 1999, 172–73.

only expect the *zāb* and the *zābâ* to be expelled, together with the *maṣorāʿ*, but *also* the *yôledet* and *not* the corpse-impure. So is there any logic to be found beyond that of disparate historical origins and contexts? Is it worth exploring this issue also from a systemic point of view, asking for a certain logic, if not *behind* the strict traditions,[42] at least in the *reception* and *application* of practices of inclusion, seclusion, and expulsion, during the Second Temple period? Are there any consistent *criteria* by which some impurity bearers would be expelled and others not? In the following, a number of such criteria will be tried out, in addition to the requirement to sacrifice, which has already been dismissed.

If the *length* of various impurities is considered, the *maṣorāʿ* together with the *zāb* and the *zābâ* ought to be expelled, since they will be impure for an indefinite period of time until their symptoms cease. From this perspective, the burial of corpses outside settlements is only logical. Again, however, the *yôledet* should be a more serious case than the corpse-impure, since her impurity lasts forty or eighty days, while corpse impurity only lasts for seven days, and from this perspective must be considered analogous to the impurity of a menstruant.

If we instead apply criteria of *normality* as against permanent status or chronic disease, the *maṣorāʿ* would again have to be expelled, but *not* the corpse-impure person. From this perspective, however, the *zāb* and the *zābâ* constitute a trickier case. In theory their impurity could be of indefinite length, just like that of the *maṣorāʿ*, but in actual practice we would expect most cases of unnatural discharges to be *temporary* conditions.[43] This at least seems reasonable from the type of cases and questions that are discussed in rabbinic literature; much concerns how to define these discharges and distinguish them from normal semen or menstrual blood,

---

42. The requirement to bring sacrifices is sometimes associated with impure diseases ("leprosy," pathological genital discharges) while "natural" impurities would not require sacrifices. However, the parturient then forms the exception. From a historical-origins point of view, sacrifices may well have been related to disease, but if so, the relationship has been overruled already in the harmonized priestly texts of Lev 11–15, in which the parturient in Lev 12 is aligned with the genital dischargers of Lev 15.

43. Sanders (1992, 219) suggests that most irregular bleedings were caused by miscarriages. To some extent, leprosy (today often translated by "skin/scale disease") might also be regarded as a temporary condition, since it had nothing to do with Hansen's disease, and legislation deals at length with procedures of reintegration. Possible causes would, however, suggest that symptoms of leprosy were generally of longer duration than irregular discharges.

and how to count days when defining which discharges should be seen as normal or as causing *zāb/zābâ* impurity.[44] We do not get the impression that these conditions are necessarily permanent, but that they are due to discharges outside normal semen emission or menstruation. Reasoning from normality thus yields ambiguous results: either we could expect a lenient stance that only requires the expulsion of lepers, or we might suppose a stricter or at least ambivalent stance toward irregular dischargers. Neither variant of a criterion of normality ought, however, to require the expulsion of the corpse-impure.

If, however, we consider the *contamination potency* of various impurities, the picture changes somewhat. The corpse-impure, lepers, and dischargers all transmit a one-day impurity to persons, items,[45] food, and drink. When later rabbinic systematization is taken into account, we see that this transmitted impurity is understood to be at the first remove, namely, all of the abovementioned impurity bearers transmit (mainly by contact) a first-degree impurity to others, which may be transferred[46] to profane food (*ḥullîn*) and liquid at one further (i.e., a second) remove, to priestly rations (*tərûmâ*) at a third, and to sacrificial food (*qodāšîm*) at a fourth remove. It would be only logical to treat all these impurity bearers alike. This comes close to the strict ruling in Num 5, but does not account for the excepting of the *yôledet* and the menstruant.

So far, this exercise has been entirely theoretical, and readers may perhaps doubt its value. It will, however, be useful when we attempt to reconstruct actual first-century practice. As we have just seen, most perspectives or criteria that we have attempted to apply would not require the expulsion of corpse-impure people, except for the last one, and *all* attempts to find a logical principle leave us with anomalies or ambiguities when it comes to the category of genital dischargers. While this should count as strong evidence for diverse historical and contextual origins of different parts of the

---

44. This becomes immediately evident from a quick glance at the tractates Niddah and Zavim in the Mishnah as well as in the Tosefta.

45. In rabbinic discussion, susceptible items are mostly limited to rinseable utensils formed as receptacles; see m. Kelim. Cf. Wright 1987, 94.

46. This is never stated or implied in the biblical text. Wright (1987, 220) states that "*a person or object that receives impurity which lasts only one day cannot pollute other persons or objects in the profane sphere*" (italics original); cf. 179–219. Rabbinic texts, however, take for granted that persons with a one-day impurity may contaminate ordinary food, liquid, and hands at one further remove (cf. Harrington 1993, 141–260).

purity legislation, our main interest here concerns first-century practice. There is an ongoing harmonization and systematization, which begins already in the biblical text and ought to reach its fulfillment in rabbinic literature, but is simultaneously undermined by rabbinic tendencies toward an increasing leniency and a restriction of many purity practices to the cultic sphere, which turned them into voluntary undertakings since the temple was no longer in place.[47] We thus find several principles guiding rabbinic systematization of impurity: the contamination potency of various contaminants, the degree of susceptibility (i.e., differences in capacity to receive contamination corresponding to various degrees of holiness), and a system of removes in which contamination is envisaged as a chain of contacts. These are neither clear-cut nor clearly differentiated, but interact, and other types of systematizations are used, too.

Temple Scroll, Criteria, and Custom

As we inquire into actual customs with regard to genital dischargers at the end of the Second Temple period and try to interpret textual as well as material evidence, we may benefit from the theoretical discussion above to make sense of what we see.[48] The Temple Scroll requires very strict rules for the temple city. After intercourse a man must not enter it for three days (XLV, 11). All three categories of purifying impurity bearers (dischargers, the corpse-impure, and lepers) must stay out until the seven days of purification are over (XLV, 15–18). Three places are to be made east of the city for lepers, dischargers, and semen emitters (XLVI, 16–18). This rule is even stricter than that of Num 5.[49]

---

47. See Kazen 2010a, 54, 155–56; Poirier 2003, esp. 259–65. Whether purity was observed mainly for the sake of the temple or for its own sake, as part of household religion, is a contested issue, but the evidence increasingly points to the latter. See, e.g., Adler 2016; Kazen 2016 = ch. 12 in this volume. Now see also ch. 11 in this volume.

48. Some of the evidence that follows is also discussed by Wassén 2008, but with somewhat different conclusions.

49. Several interpreters, following Yadin, suggest that the Temple Scroll with its strong utopian traits gives no room whatsoever for women living within the temple city, since entrance after sexual intercourse is prohibited (XLV, 11; cf. Haber 2003, 177), but strictly speaking the restrictions would apply to women of fertile age and married couples (cf. Wassén 2008, 649–50). The extent of the "temple city" (עיר המקדש) is crucial for interpretation: Does it refer to the temple proper (Schiffman, following Levine) or to the city in its entirety (Milgrom, following Yadin)? Sidnie White Crawford (2000,

8. Concern, Custom, and Common Sense

The following column (XLVII) makes it clear that the purity of the temple city is higher than that of ordinary cities. Further on, ordinary cities are discussed: special burial grounds are prescribed for every four cities, apparently to limit the areas defiled by graves (XLVIII, 10–14). Then comes an ambiguous passage, dealing with lepers and dischargers (XLVIII, 14–17).⁵⁰ At first sight the preposition ב seems to indicate the presence of these two categories within cities (ובכול עיר ועיר), but this cannot be the case, since the purpose of making places for lepers (תעשו מקומות למנוגעים בצרעת ובנגע ובנתק) is explicitly stated to be to prevent them from *entering* the cities and defiling them (אשר לוא יבואו לעריכמה וטמאום). "In every city" must thus be taken to include the surrounding country. While a similar treatment (וגם ל-) is indicated for male and female dischargers, menstruants and parturients (לזבים ולנשים בהיותמה בנדת טמאתמה ובלדתמה), the purpose in their case is expressed as preventing them from "defiling in their midst" (אשר לוא יטמאו בתוכם).⁵¹ This *could* possibly be read as if dischargers were supposed to be *secluded within* settlements rather than expelled, like lepers. The most *natural* reading, however, is that both categories were supposed to *stay outside*. This rule comes close to that of Num 5 but is stricter since it explicitly expels menstruants and parturients, too. In the next column (XLIX), however, we find the rule more lenient, since the corpse-impure are not supposed to be expelled.

How are we to account for such discrepancies? When we compare them with the theoretical discussion above, we find all those who are required to offer a sacrifice expelled from the ordinary city—but also the menstruant. We find all seven-day impurity bearers expelled—except for the corpse-impure. A distinction between normality and chronic disease provides no rationale. Contamination potential seems not to account for the omission of the corpse-impure.

---

49) attempts a compromise, suggesting that the temple city "is not envisioned by the author/redactor of the Temple Scroll as having permanent residents, but as a place of *temporary* residents." The whole city would thus be looked on as a temple area for visiting pilgrims and cultic personnel, with God as the only permanent resident.

50. This text is quoted and discussed in detail in Kazen 2010a, 157–59.

51. The concluding נדת טמאתם in the full phrase בנדת טמאתם בתוכם יטמאו לוא אשר טמאתם should probably be understood generally as "defilement of their impurity" rather than as referring specifically to menstruation.

But in fact it does. The secret lies in the postbiblical requirement of an initial first-day ablution (and washing of clothes):

> he shall wash his clothes and bathe on the first day; and on the third day he shall sprinkle and wash his clothes and bathe; and on the seventh day he shall sprinkle a second time and he shall wash his clothes and he shall bathe and by sunset he will become pure. (L, 13–16)[52]

This extra rite was somehow thought to peel away the most aggressive layer of corpse impurity, although it did not shorten its duration, and provides some explanation for the position of the Temple Scroll.[53]

We cannot know to what extent, if at all, the detailed requirements of the Temple Scroll were practiced in actual societies at the end of the Second Temple period. The exclusion of dischargers cannot be dismissed by arguments from common sense; as we have already mentioned above, a number of groups through history, known from texts but also from living examples, did adhere to strict rules of isolation and/or expulsion of such people. Poverty or practical considerations (from our perspective) seem not to have caused any obstruction to strict practices.[54]

The Temple Scroll must, of course, be at least in part idealist or utopian. Although not sectarian, but representing one type of a more general expansionist stance,[55] its many rules on sacrificial matters could not have been realized unless its adherents were in power. This does not, however, exclude the possibility that the purity rules regarding the ordinary city might have been applied in societies or settlements of people who held these views or that some of their presuppositions of these rules reflect more general practices of the Second Temple period.

---

52. Translation from García Martínez and Tigchelaar 1998, 2:1269.
53. Milgrom 1978; 1992; cf. Baumgarten 1992, 205–6; Eshel 1999, 138; Regev 2000a, 177–81. Regev calls this "gradual purification." For further discussion, see Kazen 2010b.
54. Cf. Poirier's (2003, 258–59) discussion.
55. The date of the Temple Scroll before the founding of the Qumran community and its affinity with other pseudepigraphic literature point to a general expansionist or maximalist stance. See Crawford 2008, 88, 92–93.

Corpse Impurity and a First-Day Ablution

A first-day ablution after corpse impurity must be counted among these; it seems to have been generally practiced during Second Temple times.[56] In a section about those who offer sacrifices, Philo discusses necessary purifications.

> Regarding the body, it [the law] purifies it by washings and sprinklings [λουτροῖς καὶ περιρραντερίοις], and does not allow the one who sprinkled or bathed himself one time [περιρρανάμενον εἰς ἅπαξ ἢ ἀπολουσάμενον] to enter immediately [εὐθὺς] into the sacred areas, but orders him to stay out for seven days and be sprinkled twice [δὶς περιρραίνεσθαι] on the third and seventh day, and after that, when he has bathed [λουσαμένῳ], allows him both to enter and do his service without fear. (Philo, *Spec.* 1.261)[57]

In another context, discussing injury to the point of possible murder, Philo touches on the same issue:

> Also those having touched a dead body, which had died naturally, cannot immediately [εὐθὺς] become clean until they are purified by sprinkling and bathing themselves [περιρρανάμενοι καὶ ἀπολουσάμενοι καθαρθῶσιν]. He did not allow the very clean to even enter the temple within seven days, having ordered them to sanctify on the third and the seventh. Further, he ordered even those entering a house in which anyone has died to touch nothing until they have bathed themselves [ἀπολούσωνται] and washed the clothes they were wearing. (Philo, *Spec.* 3.205–206)

Sanders deals with these passages at length, pointing to the difference in terminology for sprinkling/washing and bathing. It may be questioned whether λούειν and ἀπολούειν refer to immersion and not just washing, but Sanders notes that Philo uses these terms for ritual bathing elsewhere. He argues, however, that by λουτροῖς καὶ περιρραντερίοις Philo is describing a domestic diaspora ritual of sprinkling, which developed from pagan influence and was used independently of any temple visit. According to Sanders's interpretation, those having undergone such a ritual were con-

---

56. Kazen 2010a, 185–89; 2010c, 81–89, 98–101, cf. 101–4; 2013a, 146–48, cf. 157–61.

57. Unless otherwise noted, all translations are mine.

sidered "really pure," although not allowed into the temple. Still, such a rite was practiced, because Jews in general saw purity as "part of godliness."[58]

I have no problem with the idea that Jewish purity practices were shaped and developed by influences from surrounding cultures, and I agree that the rite in question was not reserved for temple visits. I think, however, that Philo gives evidence for more than a domestic diaspora rite. It rather seems to me that Philo attests to the widespread practice of an extra first-day ablution.[59] To what extent such a first-day ablution might have been practiced independently of subsequent purifications on the third and seventh day in Alexandria may remain an open question. I cannot see, however, that this first-day ablution is being separated from the rest of the rite in the two passages above.

What the terminology does suggest is that both sprinkling and bathing were involved, and at least the first passage indicates that *neither* sprinkling *nor* bathing on the first day were considered sufficient for entering the temple *immediately*; a full seven-day period was required.

The alternatives suggested by *Spec.* 1.261 for an extra first-day ablution—sprinkling or bathing—are highly interesting, not least in view of the fact that rabbis, Karaites, and Samaritans at times disagree on whether immersion is required or mere washing suffices.[60] While we may expect varying practices at the end of the Second Temple period, some sort of first-day ablution must be assumed. Such a practice may be implied already in Ezek 44:25-26, and in Tob 2:5, 9 it is definitely presupposed.[61] The Temple Scroll mentions it explicitly, as does the fragmentary 4Q414. The idea is implied by 1QM XIV, 2-3, too.[62] Samaritan texts take it for granted.[63] Together with Philo, these texts represent a broad variety of traditions. In addition to textual evidence, recent material finds of stepped pools adjacent to burial places are suggestive.[64] We should consider a first-

---

58. Sanders 1990, 263-71.
59. Cf. Regev 2000a, 177-81.
60. Bóid 1989a, 332-36.
61. A discussion of differences between various Hebrew, Aramaic, and Greek versions, suggesting that they are due to differences in opinion concerning sunset and bathing, is found in Bóid 1989a, 321-22.
62. Here the context is that of battle. The idea of a first-day washing is probably present in 4Q514 as well, this time with reference to dischargers. See below for further discussion of this text.
63. Kitâb al-Kâfi III [43]; XIII [11-13]; Bóid 1989a, 153-54, 242-43, 324.
64. Adler 2009, 55-73. Stepped pools have been found both as part of burial com-

day water rite neither particularly sectarian nor only a diaspora invention. It could have evolved through outside influences, and it may have been applied in various ways. It fits with evidence for people coming to Jerusalem one week in advance of Passover (Josephus, *J.W.* 6.290; John 11:55).[65]

For our present purpose we need not decide whether the ashes of the red heifer were available outside Jerusalem[66] and to what extent the full seven-day rite could have been employed in Galilee or in the diaspora. The point is to show that a first-day ablution was generally practiced (whether in view of temple visits or not) and considered somehow to mitigate or lessen corpse impurity. Such a practice makes it possible to explain how a relatively strict stance, close to that of Num 5, could have been interpreted and applied by expansionist groups at the end of the Second Temple period. Because of a first-day ablution, the people behind the Temple Scroll—probably not only Qumranites or Essenes—envisaged the possibility of keeping the corpse-impure within ordinary settlements, while requiring both lepers and dischargers to stay out.

Genital Dischargers in the First Century

After this detour, arguing for a first-day ablution for the corpse-impure as common practice, we now return to the question of genital dischargers. Resuming our theoretical reasoning above, a focus on contamination potency would result in the exclusion of all genital dischargers, as the Temple Scroll seems to demand, according to the most probable interpretation. This is far from Sanders's view of actual practice. As we have seen above, Sanders doubts that menstruants were even secluded within society. The discussion is focused on the interpretation of Josephus. In *Ant.* 3.261 Josephus states that

---

plexes and close to tombs. Adler suggests that these pools were used for purification from lesser one-day impurities by onlookers. While this may be so, a much more likely immediate reason for constructing such pools in the immediate vicinity of burial places would be instant gradual purification from a seven-day corpse impurity, which would make such people less contagious. A one-day impurity would not be as virile and could easily be taken care of once back home. It is the seven-day impurity that would cause most problems and hence would need particular attention and immediate mitigation.

65. Sanders (1992, 132–35 and notes) explains how Josephus's counting is evidence for the same waiting period.

66. Baumgarten 1995b.

[Moses] expelled [ἀπήλασε] from the city both those who were sick with *lepra* and those with genital discharges; also the women who the natural flux came over, he set aside [μετέστησε] until the seventh day, after which he allowed [them] to live in their place [ἐνδημεῖν] as already pure. Similarly also for those attending a dead [person], after so many days [he allowed them] legitimately to live in their place [ἐνδημεῖν].

It is quite clear that Josephus makes a difference between lepers and *zābîm* on the one hand (expulsion), and menstruants and the corpse-impure on the other (seclusion, isolation). Sanders points to this distinction when discussing this and other passages from Josephus, but in the end he concludes that "Josephus here probably reflects the rules which he and his kind—the aristocratic priesthood—followed" while "people who occupied small houses could not have lived in the same way."[67] The argument is mainly practical. Other arguments against Josephus describing contemporary practice claim that he is only commenting on the text, thinking of the time of Moses, or talking of an ideal.[68] Of this, however, I am not easily convinced.

While a certain amount of idealization must be expected from Josephus, I find his statement here fully in line with other passages where he deals with this issue, such as *J.W.* 5.227: "to dischargers and 'lepers' the whole city on one hand [μὲν] and to menstruating women the temple on the other hand [τὸ δ' ἱερὸν] was closed [ἀπεκέκλειστο]." This evidently means that menstruating women were not allowed into any of the temple courts, which fits with the statement in *Ag. Ap.* 2.103 (only preserved in Latin) that the outer court was open to everybody, including foreigners, but excepting menstruants.

All of these references from Josephus, including *Ant.* 3.261, should be understood as referring to Jerusalem.[69] Menstruants and the corpse-impure are envisaged within the city, but subject to restrictions. Lepers and *zābîm* are kept out. This comes close to the rules of the Temple Scroll for the *ordinary* city, although in the Temple Scroll the same rule applies to *all* dischargers, whether we understand them as supposed to be expelled from or secluded within cities (the ambiguous phrasing is discussed above). Deviating opinions probably depend on how different spheres of

---

67. Sanders 1992, 157–60.
68. Sanders 1992, 157; Maccoby 1999, 36; cf. Kazen 2010a, 113–14, 156.
69. In *Ant.* 3.261 this is not explicitly stated, but Josephus talks of the "city" in the singular.

holiness are understood and how the temple city is defined; the later m. Kelim 1:6–9, outlining ten degrees of holiness, is evidence for such ideas. In this rabbinic text, the first degree is the land of Israel (1:6). The second degree consists of cities surrounded by a wall; they are considered more holy than the land, because lepers are not allowed inside (1:7). While the wall of Jerusalem demarcates a third degree, it is not associated with any further exclusion of impurity bearers. The fourth degree, however, is defined by the Temple Mount, where no discharger, whether *zāb*, *zābâ*, menstruant, or parturient, is allowed (1:8).

We cannot trust the schematized and systematic lists introducing the Seder Tohorot to provide an accurate picture of first-century practice. They do, however, give clues to the kind of logic that might have been involved. It should be noted that all extant texts discussed so far suggest *stricter* practices of exclusion and/or seclusion than those implied by m. Kelim 1. The Temple Scroll assumes ascending degrees of holiness, too, but seems to have moved holiness one step forward or impurity one step back, depending on the stance we prefer to take.

Coming back to Josephus, we noted that he seemingly placed the corpse-impure and menstruants on the same level, within Jerusalem, but subject to restrictions. The Temple Scroll thinks of both outside Jerusalem, but when it comes to the ordinary city the corpse-impure person is allowed within, while the menstruant is probably placed outside, together with other dischargers. The rabbis seemingly think of the corpse-impure person as even allowed within the court of gentiles (m. Kelim 1:8)! In the latter case we must, however, reckon with a first-day ablution, lessening the power of corpse impurity, as taken for granted; just as such a rite explains the presence of the corpse-impure person within the ordinary city of the stricter Temple Scroll, it is needed to explain his presence in the court of gentiles, according to later and much more lenient rabbinic views. We must ask, however, whether Josephus's *equal* treatment of the corpse-impure and menstruants may also be explained by a similar logic.

Two of the criteria discussed earlier, length and normality, would equate corpse impurity with menstruation. Both last for seven days from their inception, and both are natural, being part of the life cycle. If contamination potency is taken into account, however, we might ask whether a mitigating rite for menstruants, similar to that of a first-day ablution for corpse-impure, may have existed.

The suggestion has been raised before by Milgrom and Baumgarten, who suggest the presence in Qumran of a first-day purificatory rite not only for corpse impurity but for other cases, too.[70] Milgrom refers to 4Q514, which I quote in full:

> [...] a woman [...] he must not eat [...] for all the im[pu]re [...] to count for [him seven days of ablu]tions; and he shall bathe and wash [his clothes] on the d[a]y of [his] purification [ו]‏[בי]‏ום טהרת[ו] [... And] who[ever] has not begun to purify himself of "his spri[ng]" [החל לטהור ממק]ר[ו] is not to eat, [nor shall he eat] in his original impurity [בטמאתו הרישונה]. And all the temporarily impure [טמאי הימים], on the day of their [pur]ification [ביום ט]הרתם], shall bathe and wash [their clothes] in water and they will be pure. [*Blank*] Afterwards, they shall eat their bread in conformity with the regulation of [pu]rity. He is not to eat insolently in his original impurity [בטמאתו הרישונ{ה}ים], whoever has not started to cleanse himself from "his spring" [החל לטהור ממקרו], nor shall he eat any more during his original impurity [בטמאתו הרישונה]. All the temporarily [im]pure [ט[מאי הימים]], on the day of their pu[rification,] [ביום ט]הרת[ם] shall bathe and wash [their clothes] in water and they will be pure and afterwards they shall eat their bread in conformity with the reg[ulation. No-]one is to [e]at or drink with anyo[ne] who prepares [...] ... in the [ser]vice [...][71]

Milgrom argues that "the first-day ablution allows the person to eat from the common food of the community."[72] The text is not entirely clear, however. While the temporarily impure (טמאי הימים) refers to purifying impurity bearers during their seven-day purification period (here including dischargers), and the original impurity (בטמאתו הרישונה) of which a person must begin to purify himself (החל לטהור) before eating must refer to the beginning of the seven-day purification period, bathing takes place on "the day of his/their purification" (ביום טהרתו/ם), the meaning of which is uncertain. Whether the text is evidence for a first-day ablution for dischargers or not depends on how this expression is interpreted: as the first or final day of the purificatory process. However, in view of the linking of washing with eating in many Qumran texts, and the emphasis on begin-

---

70. Milgrom 1995, 67; Baumgarten 2000 (more or less identical with Baumgarten 1999a, 83–87).

71. Translation from García Martínez and Tigchelaar 1998, 1043. The fragment is quoted in full. The 2000 paperback edition translates הרישונה with "primary" instead of "original," but the replacement is not consistent.

72. Milgrom 1995, 67. Cf. Milgrom 1991, 969–76, 991–1000, for further discussion about first-day ablutions and intermediate levels of impurity.

ning purification, "the day of purification" is most reasonably understood as the first day of the seven-day period.

Baumgarten argues from other texts for a general use of purification water (מי נדה) in Qumran, not only for removing corpse impurity but also for all sorts of impurities, not least those caused by discharges.[73] He refers to 4Q277 1 II, 8–9, where purification water is said to effect purification from corpse impurity and "any other impurity" [ומכל טמאה] אחרת, which is followed by a discussion of the *zāb* (ll. 10–12). The translation is uncertain, however, due to the fragmentary state of the text, and an alternative reading would be that every other impurity must be removed by immersion before sprinkling. Another piece of evidence is found in 4Q512, fragments 1–3, where the sprinkling of purification water is envisaged for the temporarily impure, which would include all sorts of purifying impurity bearers. Baumgarten also refers to 4Q284, fragment 1, where מֹי נדה להת[קד]שׁ is followed directly by "seminal discharge."[74] Less decisive is 4Q274 2 I, where a first sprinkling is juxtaposed to the seventh day, followed by a discussion of semen emission.[75] Baumgarten finally suggests that the list of various forms of ablution found in 1QS III, 4–5 indicates that sprinkling was not used only for corpse impurity.

While the evidence is far from conclusive, Baumgarten also provides a few non-Qumran references supporting an extended use of sprinkling for general purification.[76] I would suggest that, although some of the evidence just mentioned is capable of varying interpretations and may be disputed, the "expansion of ritual washing to new uses not known in the Hebrew Bible"[77] was a general expansionist phenomenon during the Second Temple period, not at all restricted to Qumran, and that this development served the purpose of mitigating impurity through graded purification. Several texts from Qumran reflect a broader expansionist

---

73. Baumgarten 2000.
74. García Martínez and Tigchelaar (1998, 638) reconstruct מי נדה להזו[ת אי]ש. In fact, in this phrase only five letters are clearly visible in the fragment (נדה לה), but מי is a likely conjecture, although the remains are minimal.
75. Cf. Baumgarten 1999, 104.
76. I.e., from Sifre Zuta; Philo, *Spec.* 3.63 (Philo uses the same terminology that he does when he discusses corpse impurity); Baraita de Maseket Niddah. In addition, Baumgarten mentions 4Q272, 4Q277, and 4Q278 (where *zāb* impurity and corpse impurity are juxtaposed).
77. Cf. Lawrence 2006, 189.

movement, and even sectarian texts often reveal presuppositions that were more generally held.

In 4Q274 1 I, 1–9, various *purifying* impurity bearers are warned during their seven-day purification period not to touch other impure people who are not at the same stage of purification. I cannot go into details, since I discuss this text more extensively elsewhere.[78] Lines 7–8 in particular have been subject to varying interpretations and misunderstandings.[79] The point is that "one who counts" must not touch a menstruant in her initial *niddâ* impurity (בדוה בנדתה), unless she has purified from it (כי אם טהרה מֹ[נד]תֹה), "for behold, *niddâ* blood is considered like a discharge [to] the one touching it [לֹ[נוגע בו] יחשב כזוב הנדה דם הנה כי]."[80] This reconstruction and interpretation makes sense of the whole fragment and is further evidence for ideas of graded or intermediate impurity being present throughout the Second Temple period. In Samaritan halakah a clear difference is being made between *niddå* blood and *dåbå* blood. The former refers to the initial bleeding, which is considered more virulent and has to be washed off before the counting of days can start. It contaminates with a seven-day impurity and continues to do so if the woman does not wash. The latter refers to continued bleeding after washing and contaminates with a one-day impurity.[81] While Samaritan texts as we have them are relatively late, the halakah is often shown to have ancient roots. In this

---

78. Kazen 2010b.

79. Milgrom 1995; Baumgarten 1995a; Harrington 1993, 85–89; cf. Werrett 2007, 244–48, 280–81, and Wassén 2008, 652–53, who are puzzled by impure people being within reach of each other and also close to pure people. But the text rather discusses the seven-day intermediate status of *purifying* people (including menstruants and semen emitters), which necessitates special instruction. Wassén (2008, 658) adds 4Q274 as further evidence to 4QD (4Q272 1 II, 3–18; 4Q266 6 I, 14–6 II, 13) claiming that "it is because they are around other people that it becomes necessary to provide laws so that they can function in the society." But the latter texts mainly refer to unexpected discharges or childbirth, which are likened to the standard types. They say nothing of whether *zābîm* and *zābôt* normally were supposed to be around.

80. This is my reconstruction and translation. Cf. García Martínez and Tigchelaar (1998, 628), who also have יחשב instead of Baumgarten's ואשׁרֹ in the *editio princeps*. For further discussion, see Kazen 2010b.

81. Kitâb aṭ Ṭubâkh [2–15]; Kitâb al-Kâfi XI [48–60, 84–87], XIII [13–18], in Bóid 1989a, 141, 149–51, 154. Cf. Bóid's (1989a, 198–205, 231, 235–36) comments. Note also the Samaritan special case of the more severe impurity of the left hand (used for washing away the *niddå* blood). Could a similar idea possibly explain the mention of "her hand" (ידֹה) in the fragmentary 4Q272 1 II, 17?

case we have a first-day ablution for a female discharger, which is similar to what is suggested by 4Q274 and equivalent to the first-day rite for the corpse-impure that was practiced during Second Temple times. This is evidence for practices of graded purification, which would have made it possible to equate menstruation and corpse impurity from a first-century perspective focused on contamination potency.

Getting Practical

What conclusions are we to draw so far? What practice was adhered to at the end of the Second Temple period? To what extent were dischargers expelled or restricted?

The answer partly depends on who ran what, and we should bear Sanders's answer to his own question in mind. "It varied."[82] Those behind the Temple Scroll were hardly in power in Jerusalem, so we should not expect their views to have been in force there. It is entirely possible, however, that all dischargers were required to stay out of some other towns or villages where such strict views were dominant. It is also quite probable that groups of people adhering to such rules tried themselves to implement them even if others did not. Such diversity would, of course, cause problems that had to be met by extra precautions, but this is exactly the kind of situation we find at the end of the Second Temple period. Practices such as immersion before meals, handwashing, and voluntary associations may be partly explained by the fact that people lived by different standards or according to differing degrees of consistency within one and the same society. While agreeing on basic facts and rules, diversity in interpretation and application necessitated special arrangements by those most concerned.

There is no reason to regard Josephus as more utopian or idealist than the Mishnah, especially in view of a notable tendency toward increasing leniency on the part of the rabbis, including their limitation of purity observance to the cultic sphere. Menstruants would in any case have been allowed inside Jerusalem, although according to Josephus they were somehow quarantined, and we have suggested a first-day ablution as one possible explanation that could have made this acceptable even for those taking

---

82. "Who Ran What" is Sanders's (1992, 490) heading of the last chapter in *Judaism: Practice and Belief*.

a strict stance.⁸³ Concerning the *zāb* and the *zābâ* I am more inclined to trust Josephus for first-century practice than m. Kelim 1, but this also depends on which area of Jerusalem the city was thought to embrace. If they nevertheless were allowed within the city walls, they were probably subject to severe restrictions, in view of the stance reflected by Josephus that they should not really have been there.

In other places the *zāb* and the *zābâ* probably lived inside the town or village, but subject to restrictions; in places where expansionists such as those behind the Temple Scroll dominated, they may have been expelled, or their presence would at least have been questioned. The rabbinic evidence of m. Nid. 7:4, suggesting the existence of a special place for seclusion, should not be too easily disregarded, especially in view of evidence from Num 5 and from the Dead Sea texts; there is no room to discuss it here, but I have dealt with the manuscript evidence and Tosefta's misinterpretation elsewhere.⁸⁴ As I have indicated above, evidence for seclusion or restriction should not be dismissed by arguments from poverty, especially not since analogies can be found.

Where dischargers receive a fuller differentiation, the *zābâ* appears near the top of the list, above the *zāb* and next to the leper, bone, and corpse (m. Kelim 1:4). The *zāb* seems to have one advantage: according to Lev 15:11, he contaminates others by touching them with unwashed hands. This implies that he might touch others without contaminating them if his hands have been washed. While nothing is said explicitly about the touch of a *zābâ*, systemic reading and equalization at the end of the Second Temple period meant that touching and being touched by any discharger was considered all the same in principle.⁸⁵ In practice the *zāb* who had washed his hands may have been the exception; although heavily damaged, 4Q277 seems to confirm Lev 15:11.⁸⁶ This leaves the *zābâ* as

---

83. The *yôledet* (parturient) should be included with the menstruant, although not mentioned by Josephus. She is in most respects likened to the menstruant: in Lev 12 her case is modeled on that of the menstruant, her discharge is natural, and, like the menstruant, her contamination potency lasts for seven days (after the birth of a boy), although this is followed by a further period of lesser potency (and doubled in the case of a girl).

84. Kazen 2002, 160, esp. n. 371. Cf. Sanders 1990, 155–56.

85. For further discussion and references, see Kazen 2007. This is different from Wassén (2008), who argues for harmonization but claims a distinction between touching and being touched by an impurity bearer.

86. 4Q277 1 II, 10–11: "And anyone touched by [a man who has] a flux [ ] [and

the most vulnerable among all dischargers. As long as irregular bleeding continued, her contamination potency could probably not be lessened by any first-day rite, as in the case of the menstruant.[87]

I am not arguing that the *zābâ* was normally expelled from ordinary towns, only that she must have been subject to restrictions and that she was worse off than other impurity bearers, except for the leper. It is a reasonable speculation that stone vessels, which were in general use during the first century and considered by most people, possibly except for the Essenes, not to transmit impurity, were of great help in making everyday life more practical, not least for female dischargers.[88]

Handwashing for Secondary Impurities

It seems that first-century Jews were able to combine a high degree of concern for purity with commonsense practical solutions, by mitigating or lessening the contamination potency of primary *impurity bearers* in a number of ways. In addition to restrictions, we have so far noted first-day ablutions, handwashing, and the employment of stone vessels.

Similar arrangements are found when we look at *secondary impurities*, that is, one-day impurities acquired by *contact with the impurity bearers* discussed so far. The most conspicuous of these devices is probably the custom to wash or immerse as soon as possible after contracting a one-day impurity, even though full purity would not be attained before evening. This practice was understood to mitigate light impurities similar to how first-day ablutions were understood to mitigate severe impurities.

The practice of early immersion is often understood as a Pharisaic innovation and equated with the rabbinic concept of *ṭəbûl yôm*.[89] Early

---

whose] hand[s were not] r[in]sed in water becomes [unclean]" (trans. Baumgarten 1999a, 116).

87. We could, of course, speculate that the handwashing of the *zāb* might have been applied to the *zābâ* as well. However, while there is evidence that touching and being touched came to be regarded as equal (see Kazen 2010c, 42–45), there is no evidence that a *zābâ* could mitigate her impurity like the *zāb*, by washing her hands.

88. Deines 1993; Magen 1994, 255–57. Cf. Kazen 2010a, 81–85. For an updated and problematizing discussion about stone vessels, their use and function, see several of the chapters in Miller 2015. On the Essenes, see Harrington 2004, 21, 76–77; cf. Eshel 2000.

89. The concept is assumed all through the Mishnah's Seder Tohorot; see especially the tractate Tevul Yom.

purification is assumed in rabbinic literature as Pharisaic custom, which was not accepted by the Sadducees (m. Parah 3:7). Since the discovery of 4QMMT, it has been generally argued that early purification was commonly practiced during the Second Temple period, since those behind the halakic letter protest against it.[90] Today many scholars are realizing the anachronism in reading the full rabbinic concept of *ṭəbûl yôm* back into the Second Temple period.[91] In contrast to many other issues, the rabbis hardly defend the concept of *ṭəbûl yôm* by advanced exegesis, and the idea that immersion rather than sunset removes impurity represents a fairly simple, realist understanding.[92] This is in fact the case with the major impurities in Lev 11–15, as purity at sunset is only decreed for minor, one-day impurities. The exception is corpse impurity, where all people involved are unclean until evening (Num 19). This text in Numbers probably belongs to the latest additions to the Torah and seems to be triggered by the priestly instructions about corpse impurity in the Holiness Code (Lev 21:1–4, 10–12), which in turn is later than the purity laws in Lev 11–15. In the Holiness Code's summary of purity concerns for priests (22:4–9), purity at sunset after the mention of contact with minor impurities can be understood to concern *all* impurities. This makes it likely that the idea of *every* impurity lasting until evening, regardless of when immersion took place, resulted from close reading and interpretation of Scripture, in contrast to common understanding and previous custom. Dissensions about this seem to be rooted and reflected already in the redaction of the Pentateuch. Although the developed *ṭəbûl yôm* is a rabbinic concept, the understanding of (at least partial) purity after washing, without waiting for evening, is hardly a Pharisaic innovation, but rather represents popular custom and common sense.[93]

The custom of immersing for secondary impurities must then be regarded as to some extent functionally equivalent to first-day ablutions for primary impurity bearers, since it removes (one layer of) impurity immediately, in advance of full purification. Two other methods, hand-

---

90. The concept of *ṭəbûl yôm* and its practice and function is a much discussed issue; see, e.g., Baumgarten 1980; Sanders 1992, 36–37; Schiffman 1994; Kazen 2010a, 72–85; Crossley 2004, 197–200.

91. Himmelfarb 2010.

92. For the methodological principles behind this kind of argument, see Shemesh 2009. Cf. Schwartz 1992.

93. Kazen 2013a, 164–74; cf. Himmelfarb 2010.

washing and stone vessels, seem to have been used for lessening the contamination potency of one-day impurities, too.

While the use of chalk-stone vessels is largely deduced from interpreting material evidence,[94] handwashing before common meals is well evidenced in rabbinic texts. It is taken for granted (e.g., m. Ber. 8:2), and its purpose is evidently to prevent food from becoming impure at the second remove. For handwashing before common meals to be meaningful at all, at least in subsequent rabbinic theory, it is necessary to presuppose that hands are separately susceptible to impurity, and that liquids always become impure at the first remove and interpose between the eater and the food.[95] As we will see below, actual practice during the Second Temple period held ideas about hand impurity and of the eater becoming impure at the same level as the food, long before the elaborate Tannaitic understanding of chains of contamination and an advanced system of removes had evolved.

Not Living like Priests

The discussion about when, and to what extent, the practice of eating ordinary food (ḥullîn) in purity was adhered to is vast, and Sanders (e.g., 1990) has been one of the most prominent participants in this debate.[96] Sanders's

---

94. Seminal studies on chalk-stone vessels are Magen 2002; Cahill 1992; Deines 1993. For more recent discussions, see Miller 2015; Adler 2014a; 2016.

95. The clearest statement on liquids always reverting to the first remove and of hands contaminating ordinary food is perhaps found in t. T. Yom 1:3, 6. For further discussion, see Kazen 2010a, 81–84; 2013a, 165–68.

96. The supposition that the Mishnah reflects first-century custom was questioned already by Büchler, who suggested that handwashing for ordinary food was practiced only by a few at the time of the temple. Alon, on the other hand, claimed that handwashing was fairly common before the destruction of the temple, although the eating of defiled ḥullîn was not forbidden. The necessary presuppositions concerning hands and liquids are included in the list of ten items making tərûmâ unfit, which we find in m. Zavim 5:12. The Talmuds count these ten among the eighteen decrees that were passed in the upper room of Hanina/Hananiah, when the Shammaites outnumbered the Hillelites (y. Shabb. 1, 3c–d [V. 1, 7]; b. Shabb. 13b–17b; cf. m. Shabb. 1:4; t. Shabb. 1:16–21). In a detailed and speculative reconstruction Roger Booth (1986, 162–73) has suggested that this event, including the decree on the separate impurity of hands, took place in 51 CE. Others have dated it to a Zealot synod in 66/67 CE that passed a number of antigentile decrees (see Tomson 1988). Peter Tomson (1988) has argued that although the ten items from m. Zavim 5:12 might have been formulated

arguments concerning handwashing have been principally aimed at refuting Jacob Neusner's claim that the Pharisees were a pure food association emulating priestly practice. In this Sanders is absolutely right. Pharisees, or other nonpriestly expansionists for that matter, did not attempt to live like priests. Neusner, partly following Gedalyahu Alon, suggests that the Pharisees tried to keep priestly purity laws outside the temple, applying them to their own meals.[97] Sanders objects, pointing among other things to the fact that (1) a number of rabbinic post-70 sayings do *not* require the eating of *ḥullîn* in purity, (2) the "houses" distinguished between priests' food and their own, (3) prohibitions against impurity bearers touching pure food are absent in the Mishnah, (4) we find no discussions about eating other types of food prohibited to priests, (5) biblical purity laws did not apply to priests and the temple only, and (6) Neusner's full analogy between the altar and the table "is neither implied in Leviticus nor specified in pharisaic material."[98]

Trying to live like priests would entail much more than eating *ḥullîn* with washed hands. Priests would have to avoid corpse impurity for all but next of kin (Lev 21:1–3).[99] Neither Pharisees nor other nonpriestly expansionists seem to have followed this. Pharisees did not even *eat* like priests, since priests could *not* eat after immersion, but only after sunset, which is later reflected in the rabbinic rule that a *ṭəbûl yôm* contaminated *tərûmâ* (priestly food; m. Zavim 5:12).[100] Qumranites followed this practice for their ordinary food, but Pharisees did not. Furthermore, Sanders points repeatedly to the crucial significance of Lev 11:32–38 for the idea of eating *ḥullîn* in purity,[101] which is not particularly aimed at priests, but as a general law. Yet Sanders concedes that the Pharisees made minor symbolic gestures toward living like priests. This concession seems to me quite unnecessary. It is sufficient to note, as does Sanders on numerous occasions, that many people at the end of the Second Temple period, Phari-

---

at some tumultuous gathering toward the very end of the Second Temple period, they cannot possibly have belonged to the eighteen decrees. Rather, the core of m. Zavim 5:12 was formulated by R. Joshua, it belongs to the oldest layer of the Mishnah, and had already existed for some time in Pharisaic tradition.

97. Neusner 1974–1977, 22:106, 108; 1971, 3:288; 1979, 14.
98. Sanders 1990, 173–76.
99. Sanders 1990, 187.
100. Cf. Maccoby 1999, 209–10; Booth 1986, 201.
101. Sanders 1990, 148, 163–66, 200–205.

sees included, aspired to a higher degree of holiness and purity than was required by Scripture—although I would hasten to add that many such practices were triggered by close reading of Scripture and probably understood as scriptural. The results of such behavior could at times look similar to priestly custom, especially in hindsight, but this was neither its *rationale*, nor does this provide an explanation of the origin of such customs. In my opinion the idea of living or eating like priests could just as well be completely abandoned.

The key for Sanders's admission that the Pharisees made minor gestures towards living like priests is his interpretation of m. Hag. 2:7.[102] If we take *midrās* literally here, as referring to impurity transmitted by pressure from any of the main dischargers, this passage can easily be misunderstood.[103] It does not, however, describe various degrees of scrupulousness among different groups of people. It rather provides one among several outlines for contamination potency or susceptibility. The Hebrew is indeed condensed in comparison with various paraphrasing translations; even the following translation is wordy: "Clothes of an ʿam hā-āreṣ are *midrās* to *pərûšîn*; clothes of *pərûšîn* are *midrās* to those eating *tərûmâ*; clothes of those eating *tərûmâ* are *midrās* to [those eating] *qôdeš*; clothes of [those eating] *qôdeš* are *midrās* to [those handling] *ḥaṭṭā'ṭ* [water]." The point is *not* that ordinary people were less scrupulous than Pharisees, who were less scrupulous than priests, and so on. This is clear from the two examples immediately following, which prove that even the most scrupulous person makes no difference in this chain of ascending degrees. The preceding section similarly emphasizes that purification with regard to one level is never valid for higher levels, only for lower. Sanders seems to affirm such a perspective when he states that m. Hag. 2:7 provides "a sequence of ascending purity,"[104]

---

102. Sanders 1990, 205–6, 232, 234, 258.

103. Neusner (1974–1977, 22:55, 71) argues for an early origin of the concept of *midrās*, and even of the corresponding *maddāp*, but the references to the houses of Shammai and Hillel (m. Kelim 20:2; 26:6) are introduced into rabbinic discussions of a type that are definitely late, judged from the character of the arguments. Although an *incipient* concept of *midrās* can be understood to be early, as outlined in the biblical text (Lev 15), the development from a realist understanding of contamination by sitting or lying to an abstract concept of contamination by pressure and weight, based on nominalist arguments (cf. m. Zavim 3:1), is late. Cf. Kazen 2013a, 161–62. As *midrās* became a Tannaitic category, however, the concept could then be used to designate an intermediate type of impurity in principle.

104. Sanders 1990, 205.

but if this is true it cannot mean that Pharisees were necessarily less careful than priests in avoiding impurity from dischargers via pressure. *Midrās* is here used representatively to *exemplify* an *intermediate impurity* and how its contamination potency depends on the susceptibility of various categories. Our neat charts with four levels or removes of secondary impurities were not available even to the Tannaim;[105] hence their need to express ideas and relationships like this in a number of ways. What this mishnah suggests is that *pǝrûšîn*—whether understood as Pharisees, a sectarian fringe group, or expansionists in general—reckoned with weak or intermediate levels of impurity acquired from ordinary people impure with a secondary, one-day impurity. Priestly rations (*tǝrûmâ*), however, could be defiled at one further (third) remove, sacrificial meat (*qodāšîm*) at a fourth, and, according to this passage, (the one handling) the water mixed with ashes used for purifying the corpse-impure could be defiled at a fifth remove.[106]

The preceding m. Hag. 2:5–6 suggests that purification before eating could always be achieved by immersion, but only *qodāšîm* required it; for eating *ḥullîn*, tithe and *tǝrûmâ* handwashing was sufficient. While priests could wash their hands, too, they specifically had to immerse before eating sacrificial food. There is nothing particularly priestly in handwashing, however. It is rather to be understood as an evolving purificatory practice, based on close reading of the purity laws[107] and systemic harmonization, aimed at mitigating or lessening contamination potency. With regard to impurity bearers, it was practiced by the *zāb* and had analogies in various types of first-day ablutions. It apparently became instrumental with regard to secondary impurities, as well.

Concerned First-Century Practice

This discussion, of course, does not tell us to what extent handwashing was practiced at the time of Jesus. The Tannaitic portrayal of the *ʿammê hā-āreṣ* in the Mishnah is a contested issue, as is the identity of the rabbinic

---

105. For examples of such charts, see Wright 1987; Milgrom 1991; Harrington 1993; Kazen 2010a, 79, 82; 2013a, 169.

106. A fifth remove is not generally acknowledged in the various scholarly reconstructions. As I have repeatedly pointed out, rabbinic texts do not have their origin in a fully systematized scheme but reflect a number of perspectives.

107. Lev 15:11 on hand washing for the *zāb* and Lev 11 on the impurity and susceptibility of liquids.

pərûšîn,[108] and the use of these expressions indicates a second-century shaping of the sayings in m. Hag. 2:5–7. This, however, does not tell against the antiquity of the handwashing practice. The separate impurity of hands as well as the susceptibility of liquids are found to be pre-70 Pharisaic or rather general expansionist customs, based on realism and harmonization, and a number of scholars today would accept or argue for handwashing being practiced fairly widely at the end of the Second Temple period.[109] This fits the picture of widespread concern for everyday purity being part of household religion in Judea and Galilee during the late Second Temple period and up to the Bar Kokhba revolt.[110]

While direct contact with primary impurity bearers resulted in a first-degree impurity and required immersion, contact with secondary impurities (i.e., persons or items, such as food or vessels, including clothes) caused an intermediate impurity. Mark's picture (Mark 7) of Pharisees and "all" (a fair number of?) other people immersing after visiting the market and washing their hands before meals makes perfect sense at the end of the Second Temple period. Although Mark may be suspected of exaggerating the number of committed people, it is entirely unlikely to think that he grasped a recently invented rabbinic decree and presented it to his readers as ancient practice, nothing of which they understood anyway, judging from his elaborate explanations, and only in order to let Jesus make a point about purity of food that had nothing to do with the original handwashing issue, but was relevant to his gentile recipients.

The rabbinic claims that impurity of hands originated as a rabbinic decree to protect *tərûmâ* are definitely late. The rabbis of both the Mishnah and the Talmud explain away the relevance of hand impurity for food by strained exegesis and nominalist arguments, claiming that defilement of vessels by liquid, food impurity from liquid defiled by hands, and contamination of people via food were only safety measures, decreed by the rabbis, in order to prevent contamination of *tərûmâ*, and hence not binding in the same way as biblical rules.[111] This downplaying strategy, which facilitates the observance of purity by limiting it to the cult and turning it

---

108. Kazen 2010a, 44–48, 269–73.
109. Tomson 1988; Regev 2000a; 2000b; Poirier 2003; Crossley 2004, 183–205.
110. Cf. Miller 2015; Adler 2016.
111. See m. Shabb. 1:4; m. Zavim 5:12; m. Tehar. 10:4; b. Shabb. 13b–14b; b. Pesah. 14b. Cf. b. Pesah. 17b–20b; Sifra Parashat Shemini Parashah 8, for rabbinic claims that the capacity of liquids to defile food was only a rabbinic decree.

into a voluntary undertaking in ordinary life, is much more of an innovation than the early and probably simple form of handwashing custom, which evolved organically from close reading and systemic understanding of the scriptural purity laws. The motives behind such a practice would not have been limited to a wish to protect *tərûmâ*, but should be understood as part of an increasing aspiration for a high level of purity among the general population.

The Rabbis on Graded Purifications

The two main issues discussed in this chapter—discharge impurity and handwashing—both attest to an early understanding of graded impurity and graded purifications. This concept, although in a much more elaborate and advanced form, is presupposed in a number of rabbinic texts. Concerning the purification of the leper, m. Neg. 14:2–3 states that after the bird rite and an initial immersion he is clean of the impurity applying to entry (into a town) but defiles like a "swarmer" (שרץ); after immersion on the seventh day he is clean from swarmer impurity, but defiles like a *ṭəbûl yôm*.[112] At sundown he could eat *tərûmâ*, and after the eighth-day sacrifice he could eat *qodāšîm*. This, of course, neither suggests that the rule applies only to priests (who eat *qodāšîm*) nor that a dead swarmer would be involved, but the phrasing is schematic, outlining levels of purification apparently corresponding to levels of secondary impurity.[113] The text (m. Neg. 14:3) concludes by stating that three (levels of) purity can be found in the (purification of the) leper, similar to the three stages for the parturient (*yôledet*).

The latter is discussed in m. Nid. 10:6–7, but with other categories. Sanders returns to this text on several occasions. A *yôledet* "sitting out the purification blood" (i.e., waiting for the final thirty-three or sixty-six days to pass) was considered as one who had touched a corpse-impure according to the school of Hillel. This is another way of defining a second-

---

112. Here, the reference to a "swarmer" and a *ṭəbûl yôm* may be understood representatively, indicating a certain level of impurity, similarly to the reference to *midrās* impurity in m. Hag. 2:7, discussed above. At the same time, the reference to specific sources or types of impurity suggests a context in which neat four- (or possibly five-) level schemes were not spelled out.

113. Cf. the near technical language: טמא בביאה; טמא כשרץ; טבול יום.

ary impurity that can be further transmitted to food.[114] According to the standard chart,[115] she would then be impure at the first remove, but the saying is further defined: she is like one who had touched a corpse-impure person with regard to *qodāšîm* (כמגע טמא מת לקדשים). One possible way to interpret this is that she is understood to defile sacrificial food only, but neither *ḥullîn* nor *tərûmâ*. The school of Shammai disagreed: she is considered as unclean as a corpse-impure person. The style and *genre* of the Mishnah require, however, that we supply "with regard to *qodāšîm*" from the preceding statement. Using another terminology, a *yôledet* in her second-stage impurity would make *qodāšîm* unfit according to Hillelites, but unclean according to Shammaites, that is, she contaminates at two further removes. This fits with their disagreement on immersion: only Shammaites claim that this is necessary at the end of the period. So how is it that they agree that she might separate *tərûmâ*? Here we must presuppose handwashing. Passages such as m. Tehar. 10:4 show, as Sanders has argued,[116] that while the schools disagreed about the point at which handwashing should be done, they agreed that it should at least be done before separating *tərûmâ*. This would have made the task possible for a second-stage *yôledet* even according to the stricter Shammaite view.

In the previous example above (m. Neg. 14:2–3), a leper after immersion on the seventh day is likened to a *ṭəbûl yôm*. According to the Shammaite view, the second-stage impurity of a *yôledet* (m. Nid. 10:6–7) could also be considered somehow equivalent to that of a *ṭəbûl yôm*. If we try to align these statements with the standard chart, we could perhaps talk of the second remove, but all of this becomes forced, as the standard chart is too simple and too systematized. Moreover, the second remove in rabbinic discussion is ordinarily applied to food, liquid, and hands only. What texts such as these show is that the basic idea of graded impurity and graded purification is developed in many directions and variants. In m. Zavim 5:10 the idea that anything that has been in contact with a "father of impurity" contaminates at two further removes is expressed as a general principle. This is not, however, related to varying degrees of susceptibility. When these are taken into account, qualifications such as those of m. Nid. 10:6

---

114. The reference to touching a corpse-impure person must likewise be understood representatively; see n. 111.

115. I.e., the system that can be construed, based on a systemic reading and harmonization of biblical and rabbinic texts; see n. 104 above and Kazen 2010c, 169.

116. Sanders 1990, 197.

above ("with regard to *qodāšîm*") are needed. This is visible in the Tosefta, too (t. Tehar. 1:4–6): a *ṭəbûl yôm* as well as (unclean) hands are said to be *the beginning* with regard to *qôdeš* (תחלה לקדש), namely, both are secondary impurities contaminating *qodāšîm* in two further removes. This is explicitly spelled out, together with the concomitant result that *tərûmâ* is defiled (made unfit). This is a different terminology and a slightly different logic as compared to the rest of the discussion in the same context, where the first to the fourth removes are numbered with regard to various items. In this case, however, the end result for the *ṭəbûl yôm* and (unclean) hands becomes the same.

The idea of unclean hands and the *ṭəbûl yôm* at the same or a similar level is expressed in several texts. We have already discussed m. Zavim 5:12, where hands and the *ṭəbûl yôm* are both included in the list of ten items that contaminate *tərûmâ*. In m. T. Yom 2:2, however, a *ṭəbûl yôm* who touches a pot with liquids contaminates them if they are *tərûmâ*, although the pot remains clean.[117] If the liquids are *ḥullîn* all is clean. Then it is added that if (his?) hands were unclean all becomes unclean. It is not clear whether the last statement refers to *ḥullîn* only or to *tərûmâ* liquid as well, and the passage is difficult to interpret. Possibly, "hands" refer to the hands of the *ṭəbûl yôm*, which are *presupposed* to be separately washed, indicating that at least for some purposes a *ṭəbûl yôm* could lessen his impurity even further by washing his hands to the point of becoming all but fully clean. He would then be able to touch ordinary liquid and *tərûmâ* food, but not *tərûmâ* liquid. However, I find this unnecessarily speculative. A simpler alternative is to understand the passage as a principled comparison between the contamination potency of a *ṭəbûl yôm* and that of unwashed hands in general, claiming a slight difference. In spite of the two *generally* being equated, m. Parah 8:7 makes an exception for the *ṭəbûl yôm*: whatever makes *tərûmâ* unfit also makes ordinary liquid unfit—except for a *ṭəbûl yôm*.[118] This fits with m. T. Yom 2:2, which ends in a

---

117. It is a difficult point whether the *ṭəbûl yôm* is thought to touch the liquid while the pot itself is not susceptible to impurity at the third remove, or whether he is thought to touch the pot, which is not itself susceptible, but nevertheless transfers impurity via moisture to the liquid. While it could be argued that the exception (if hands are dirty) only refers to recontamination (a *ṭəbûl yôm* would normally be supposed to be clean by virtue of immersion), it is more likely that a difference between a *ṭəbûl yôm* and hands in general (not *his* hands) is intended. See below.

118. This, of course, cannot mean that a *ṭəbûl yôm* could touch *tərûmâ*, but that,

comparison between a *ṭəbûl yôm* and hands: both are judged more leniently *and* more stringently as compared to each other, suggesting that they are basically at the same level, yet subject to different rules in certain cases. This explains the need for the very detailed halakot concerning the touch of a *ṭəbûl yôm*, which follows immediately; his category is an extremely complicated intermediate one, similar to hands, but yet not quite. As a result, immersion for secondary impurities lasting until evening would make separate handwashing redundant for the purpose of preserving the purity of ordinary food, while in situations where no secondary impurity called for immersion, but hands had become separately impure by contact with such impurities, handwashing would be crucial to prevent the contamination not only of *tərûmâ*, but also of ordinary food (*ḥullîn*). This indicates that both immersion and handwashing—depending on the type of impurity contracted—were originally nonpriestly measures to safeguard the purity of ordinary food, despite the tendency in rabbinic texts to limit purity to the cult and hence purity of food to protection of *tərûmâ*.[119]

Coming to a Close

Although these detailed discussions represent rabbinic developments in the second century CE, our observations indicate that extra immersions and handwashing were part of a multileveled and elaborate web of graded impurities and graded purifications with roots stretching deep back into the Second Temple period. A number of impurities could be lessened or mitigated by various purificatory practices, through which a high level of concern could be combined with practical aspects.

Just as various first-day ablutions and early purifications were increasingly made available for impurity bearers, secondary impurities were handled by similar means. We cannot explain all such custom from a systematic standard chart with fathers of impurity and four levels or removes of secondary impurities, however we elaborate the details; that would be anachronistic, since such a system is a harmonized abstraction in hindsight. The rabbinic material discussed in this chapter rather suggests a web of purity conceptions that even in the Tannaitic period were only superficially homogenized. At the end of the Second Temple period we need

---

in spite of being basically at the same level as unwashed hands, defiling *tərûmâ*, he does *not* (like unclean hands) contaminate ordinary liquid.
119. See further Kazen 2010c, 119–23; 2013a, 171–72.

to allow even more for a much less developed level of abstraction and harmonization. The issues of eating *ḥullîn* in purity and of how to deal with female dischargers during the first century CE need to be seen in the light of a great deal of diversity, a growing expansionist concern for purity, and an evolving system of graded purifications, which lacked many of the details that were later supplied. Most, perhaps all, of the rites or customs we encounter have precedents in the biblical text; it is only that they are applied in new situations.

A high concern for purity for its own sake was embraced by more than a small fringe group, although interpretation and levels of consistency varied. The focus was not only on the temple but also on daily life, not least on meals, although this had nothing to do with a desire to "play priests." In such an environment, dischargers were circumscribed, and the *zābâ* in particular would be seen as problematic, probably even in ordinary towns. In such an environment, various types of ablutions and handwashings, as well as the use of stone vessels, served to mitigate or lessen the contamination, both of impurity bearers and a number of secondary impurities. In such an environment, neglect in matters of handwashing could be understood by the careful and consistent as a serious matter, indicating a lax attitude.

Although this chapter has not at all focused on Jesus, it has discussed the historical situation in which we need to envisage him. To do this is crucial, which is exactly what Sanders's work shows. As we continue in this tradition, we find it reasonable that historically, purity *was* an issue between Jesus and his opponents. We should even imagine that such conflicts could become very heated, if some of his opponents thought he behaved in a negligent or indifferent manner. We also find it reasonable for historical remembrances to lie behind Markan traditions about handwashing as well the bleeding woman. We may, with Sanders, think that Jesus's "followers … carr[ied] through the logic of his own position in a transformed situation."[120] This does not, however, mean that Jesus attempted to abolish *torah* or dismiss halakah—that would go against common sense, if we see Jesus as a historical figure and a Galilean Jew of the Second Temple period.

---

120. Sanders 1985, 340.

9
Jesus and the *Zābâ*: Implications for Interpreting Mark

This chapter is a conversation in retrospect with Susan Haber, whose untimely death in 2006 broke off our incipient discussion. I use Haber's analysis of the Markan tradition of the hemorrhaging woman (Mark 5:25–34) as a springboard for disentangling historical, literary, and theological aspects in the narrative. I then employ some of the insights to shed light on the Markan tradition of ritual handwashing before meals (Mark 7:1–23). In conclusion, I emphasize the importance of distinguishing between levels and audiences, and of keeping Mark's theological motives apart from Jesus's historical purposes.

In her 2003 *Journal for the Study of the New Testament* article "A Woman's Touch,"[1] Susan Haber steers between the Scylla and Charybdis of two feminist interpretations of Mark's narrative of the so-called hemorrhaging woman. One, represented by Marla Selvidge, recognizes the purity issue in the story, but implausibly interprets the narrative as intent on the abrogation of oppressive purity legislation. The other, represented by Mary D'Angelo, interprets the narrative within the framework of Mark's christological understanding of Jesus's miracles, but dismisses the purity issue as irrelevant to the story. Haber's convincing analysis shows that both

---

This chapter was initially prepared in 2008. Some of the contents were incorporated in Kazen 2010c, chs. 5–6, but the text was originally intended in this form, as a tribute to and a dialogue in retrospect with the late Susan Haber. The chapter was slightly updated for publication in 2011 and published in *Purity, Holiness, and Identity in Ancient Judaism and Early Christianity: Essays in Memory of Susan Haber*, ed. Carl Ehrlich, Anders Runesson, and Eileen Schuller, WUNT 1/305 (Tübingen: Mohr Siebeck, 2013), 112–43. Since then it has been only marginally edited. Used by permission.

1. Haber 2008, 125–41.

interpretations disregard crucial aspects of the narrative and that neither resolves the narrative tension in the text: that between undeniable allusions to the woman's impurity—not least by expressions borrowed from the LXX text of Leviticus[2]—and the Markan rhetorical and christological emphasis on faith and healing. In Haber's reading of the narrative "it is the health of the woman and not her impurity that is the primary issue of concern."[3] Impurity is, however, by definition an essential but secondary component in the story.

Other scholars, too, have discussed faith and/or healing as the primary concern of the Markan narrative.[4] The role and place of the secondary component—impurity—is, however, a moot question. While attempting an answer, Haber's article, in fact, like all good scholarly work, raises a number of further questions. In the present chapter I would like to identify a few of these and venture their consequences. The way we interpret the narrative of Jesus and the *zābâ* affects our overall reading of Mark and our understanding of Mark's view on impurity in general. This will be demonstrated by asking some similar questions of the Markan handwashing story and employing some similar strategies for interpretation.

The present essay thus has a double goal. I wish to continue a dialogue regarding Jesus and the *zābâ* in Mark 5 that regrettably cannot have two full voices.[5] In addition, I wish to address the interpretation of the handwashing incident in Mark 7 with the help of insights from the previous *zābâ* narrative. Both tasks are carried out in three consecutive steps.

First, I would like to address the historical question raised by Haber about halakic interpretations in the Second Temple period and their

---

2. I.e., ῥύσις αἵματος (Mark 5:25; Lev 15:19, 25), which is not an ordinary Greek expression for vaginal bleeding, and the frequent use of ἅπτεσθαι both in Mark 5 and Lev 15. Cf. the expression ἡ πηγή τοῦ αἵματος (Mark 5:29), which comes from Lev 12:7 (see also Lev 20:18).

3. Haber 2008, 136.

4. Cf. Kahl 1996; Kazen 2010a, 130–33, cf. 172; Wainwright 2006, 112–23. Wainwright (2006, 98) points out that "the language of teaching and healing intertwine within or between stories throughout [Mark's] gospel (1.21, 22; 2.13; 5.35; 6.2, 6; 8.3; 9.38; 10.35)."

5. Haber's (2003) article "A Woman's Touch" was written before she came in contact with my work, and similarly, I published my *Jesus and Purity Halakhah* (2002), in which I discuss this narrative, before Haber's article went into print. Subsequently, however, Haber initiated a fruitful conversation around these matters, which was regrettably and suddenly cut short.

consequences for the status of female dischargers. In the corresponding section dealing with the handwashing incident, it will become clear that questions concerning halakic interpretations and their consequences are crucial for our interpretation of other Markan passages dealing with purity, too.

Second, I wish to comment on some literary issues of Markan language in the *zābâ* narrative that Haber discusses in her article. When we assume things about the Markan audience from the language involved, we take a risky shortcut, unless we also consider diachronic aspects of the textual tradition, that is, Markan tradition history. In the corresponding discussion about the handwashing narrative, we will find that similar considerations regarding language and audience are crucial in the current debate about the dating of Mark, particularly in the light of halakic traditions.

Third, I will attempt to deal with the effect of Mark's christological agenda on his portrait of Jesus. This point to a large extent intersects with the previous one, but has significance for our interpretation of Jesus's attitude and motives and our understanding of how such things can or cannot be traced at various levels in the development of the Jesus tradition. This last concern is not one that Haber addresses here, but belongs to my own interests. Here, too, an analysis of Mark's Christology and Jesus's motives in chapter 5 may have implications for how we separate Christology from historical motives in Mark 7, and thus it affects our interpretation of Jesus's purity conflicts in general.

My indebtedness to the three subheadings in Haber's article for my own points should be acknowledged. The present text, however, must be understood both as a continued conversation and as a contribution with its own agenda.

The *Zābâ* Narrative

Historical Considerations Regarding the *Zābâ*

The status of the *zābâ* at the end of the Second Temple period is a contested issue.[6] In the legislation of Lev 15 all dischargers are envisaged as staying within settlements. While this is not stated explicitly, it is implied

---

6. Cf. Cohen 1991; Sanders 1990; 1992; Fonrobert 1997; Maccoby 1999; Baumgarten 1999a; Kazen 2010a; Haber 2003; Wassén 2008.

by the fact that contact leading to defilement is assumed; hence, provisions are described not only for the purification of dischargers but also for the purification of those who have contacted these impurity bearers.

The legislation of Lev 15 deals with both the *zāb* and the *zābâ*, as well as with the menstruant and the semen emitter. Only for *zābîm* and *zābôt* is a seven-day purification period prescribed *after* the cessation of symptoms; during biblical and early rabbinic times menstruants counted their seven days from the *onset* of menstruation, not from its end, as later became practice.[7] The semen emitter's period of impurity is only one day, just like that of people contracting a secondary impurity by contacting one of the primary impurity bearers. Although the Qumran Temple Scroll extends this period to three days,[8] the semen emitter is nevertheless not subject to a seven-day purification period according to any known Jewish movement. When compared to *zābîm* and *zābôt*, we have to think of the semen emitter and the menstruant as subject to a lesser or an intermediate type of impurity. In their case we could in fact think of the *discharge as such* as the primary contaminant.[9]

In addition, Lev 12 provides rules for the *yôledet* (postpartum woman), which in part seem to depend on, or presuppose, the legislation of Lev 15.[10] While the second stage of the purification period of the *yôledet* is much longer than that of any discharger, it has little to do with the cessation of symptoms. The first stage is not dependent on the length of bleeding, either, but consists of seven days, counted from the birth of the child and modeled on the menstruant, although it is doubled in the case of a girl. The state of the *yôledet* is, like that of the menstruant, a regular and recurring situation. For a number of reasons, then, *zābîm* and *zābôt* stand out in their character as irregular dischargers.

---

7. The beginning of this development can be seen in b. Nid. 66a. Eventually, the menstruant was equaled with the *zābâ gədôlâh*, although this was not self-evident in Talmudic times. Cf. Meacham (leBeit Yoreh) 1999a, 29–32; Meacham (leBeit Yoreh) 1999b, 255–56.

8. 11QT[a] XLV, 7–8. The extension is probably based on Exod 19:10–15 and modeled on ideas of the war camp. Due to the utopian and nonsectarian nature of the Temple Scroll we cannot conclude that semen emitters actually were considered impure for three days at Qumran, although this might be possible. Cf. Harrington 1993, 91–94; Werrett 2007, 156–59.

9. Cf. Samaritan interpretations. See Bóid 1989a, 236–38, 335.

10. This is clear from the way in which the first period is described as compared to the second (Lev 12:2, 5).

In contrast to the legislation in Leviticus, assuming dischargers within settlements, the strict tradition of Num 5:2–3 requires the expulsion of all chronic impurity bearers: people with skin disease ("lepers"), *zābîm*, and the corpse-impure. The menstruant and the *yôledet* are not mentioned and most probably are not thought to be included in the list. The strict tradition thus singles out irregular dischargers and treats them just like Lev 13 treats people with skin disease: they are to be expelled (Lev 13:46). Hence, nothing is said in Lev 13 of contamination by touch or purification from contact with a person with skin disease. Such rules were later deduced from the rules of "leprous" houses in Lev 14.[11] The corpse-impure are never dealt with in Leviticus, except for brief instructions concerning priests (Lev 21:14); the general legislation concerning corpse impurity is found in Num 19, and from this passage we cannot say for sure whether they are envisaged within or outside the "camp." Only a short sentence (Num 19:22) states that their touch defiles items and people with an impurity that lasts until the evening. Nothing like the elaborate details of the discharge laws is to be found in the biblical texts.

Regardless of how we try to structure the biblical purity legislation, discrepancies abound. I have elsewhere discussed discrepancies within the laws on discharges,[12] as well as discrepancies between various sets of purity laws, with regard to which categories were envisaged within or outside settlements according to various pieces of textual evidence, and the possible rationale behind various views.[13] The full argument cannot be rehearsed here. Some details are, however, particularly relevant for the present issue: the historical status of the *zābâ*.

It is often asserted that the discharge laws of Lev 15 are to be read systemically and that the laws of female dischargers are modeled on those of the *zāb*. This is true to a large extent and particularly valid for the purification of the *zābâ* by washing her clothes and bathing. Although this is never explicitly said, it is probably to be assumed from the rules for the *zāb*.[14] No difference is acknowledged in rabbinic interpretation, but the

---

11. Cf. m. Neg. 12–13; Maccoby 1999, 141–48; Kazen 2010a, 112–16. This, of course, does not mean that avoidance of contact with people with skin disease was not practiced before explicit rules were formulated, since this is the point of expulsion.

12. Kazen 2007.

13. Kazen 2015c = ch. 8 in this volume. See also Kazen 2010c, 91–135.

14. This requirement is spelled out only for the *zāb* (Lev 15:13) but not for the *zābâ* (15:28). Cf. Milgrom 1991, 923–24, 934–35.

immersion of all dischargers is taken for granted (m. Nid. 4:3; m. Mikw. 8:1, 5). Other differences with regard to contamination by contact may have been intended in the text but are nevertheless read systemically and harmonized toward the end of the Second Temple period; touching and being touched were apparently seen as equally contaminating (m. Zavim 5:1, 6; 4QTohorot^a). Does a basic systemic shaping of the text then suggest a complete harmonization of *every* detail? I do not believe so. While some assume that the exception to the rule of contamination by touch, that a *zāb* contaminates other people *unless his hands are washed*, would have been equally valid for the *zābâ*,[15] we have no evidence of such an understanding or practice. Although the text of Leviticus is to some extent shaped with systemic considerations in mind, these rules are not of a piece. Some of the underlying differences between the rules for the *zāb* and the *zābâ* might, for example, be explained by the fact that the male discharge is not as visible as female blood. Others could be due to different social roles of men and women respectively. While most rules were read and interpreted systemically, some details and discrepancies could also be exploited in ways that cannot be anticipated by moderns.[16] We thus cannot presuppose that discharging women at the end of the Second Temple period could mitigate their impure status by washing their hands, too. Although handwashing before meals became a means to lessen *secondary* impurities in this period, this proves nothing concerning the use of handwashing for female discharging *impurity bearers*.[17]

Turning to discrepancies *between* rules for various types of impurity bearers, what interests us here is neither their differing backgrounds or origins, nor the order or number of varying rites of purification, but the

---

15. This is assumed by Haber, too. See Haber 2008, 128.

16. Two examples: in m. Nid. 8:1–3, Rabbi Aqiba appeals to the word *blood* (not *stain*) in Lev 15:19 for disregarding bloodstain from a *zābâ*; in b. Ker. 8b, the occasional use of "man" in Lev 13 is taken to mean that certain rules are not applicable to women but they are only included when the text talks of the person with skin disease.

17. The scant evidence we have talks only of handwashing for the *zāb*. Cf. the fragmentary text of 4Q277. The hand of a female discharger (4Q272 1 II, 8: ...הזבה דם[שבֹּ]עת—a menstruant or possibly a *zābâ* during her seven-day purification period) is probably mentioned in 4Q272 1 II, 17, but in the singular (ידה). This does not suggest the washing of hands as in the case of the *zāb* but, if one may be allowed to speculate, possibly has to do with washing off the first (*niddâ*) blood as part of a first-day purification procedure. See further below and Kazen 2010b.

actual practice of inclusion, isolation, or expulsion of certain categories and not of others at the end of the Second Temple period.

The exclusion of people with skin disease from towns and settlements is a fairly clear issue. It is demanded both by Lev 13–14 and Num 5, and the practice is attested by numerous texts: in addition to gospel evidence we can mention a number of Qumran texts as well as Josephus (Mark 1:40–45; Luke 17:11–19; Josephus, *Ag. Ap.* 1.281; *Ant.* 3.264; 4QMMT B64–72; 4Q274 1 I, 1–4; 11QT^a XLVI, 16–18; XLVIII, 14–17). Although rabbinic texts provide a leniency by applying the expulsion rule to *walled* cities only (m. Kelim 1:7),[18] this limitation cannot automatically be claimed for first-century practice. The call of the person with skin disease ("unclean, unclean") is confirmed in a number of texts, with the intent that no contact whatsoever was being considered (Lev 13:45; 4Q274 1 I, 3–4; b. Sotah 32b; b. Shabb. 67a; b. B. Qam. 92b; b. Hul. 78a; Nid. 66a; b. Mo'ed Qat. 5a);[19] even the purifying "leper," after having been readmitted to the settlement, must keep a certain distance from anything pure during the seven-day purification period, according to some traditions (Lev 14:8–9; 4QMMT B64–72; 4Q274 1 I, 1–2). Biblical law demands that the person purifying from skin disease should not enter his house during this process. There are no signs of any mitigating practices with regard to this before the fall of the temple.[20]

In spite of the clear tradition in Num 5 and the uncertainty regarding what is assumed in Num 19, the corpse-impure are, on the other hand, envisaged within ordinary cities, even by the very strict and somewhat utopian Temple Scroll.[21] The Temple Scroll expressly associates this with a command for a first-day ablution, which is an apparent innovation when compared to biblical legislation.[22] The common practice of an extra

---

18. A walled city then became defined as one surrounded by walls from the time of Joshua (m. Arakh. 9:6). A development toward an even greater leniency (restrictions only applicable during the Jubilee) is suggested by b. Arakh. 29a.

19. Many of the Talmudic references apply Lev 13:45 secondarily to other issues.

20. The rabbis later interpreted the command to stay outside one's tent leniently, as referring to sexual intercourse. See b. Ker. 8b; b. Mo'ed Qat. 15b.

21. Although envisaged outside the temple city (11QT^a XLV, 17) the corpse-impure are not mentioned among those quarantined outside ordinary cities (XLVIII, 13–17). Similarly, Philo (*Spec.* 1.261; 3.205–206) thinks of the corpse-impure staying out of sacred areas, while Josephus (*Ant.* 3.261) suggests that they were somehow isolated within Jerusalem during their purificatory period.

22. For further discussion and references, see Kazen 2010a, 185–89; 2010c,

first-day ablution in Second Temple Judaism to mitigate corpse impurity has been much discussed and is evidenced in a number of texts belonging to a diversity of contexts. It is suggested by other Qumran texts, too. Philo reflects it, and it is presupposed in Josephus as well as in the Gospel of John. Tobit assumes it, and it may be implied already in Ezekiel (1QM XIV, 2–3; 4Q414; 4Q514; Philo, *Spec.* 1.261; 3.205–206; Josephus, *Ant.* 3.261; *J.W.* 6.290; John 11:55; Tob 2:5, 9; Ezek 44:25–26). Various traditions differ as to how far such a first-day ablution goes; the Mishnah even envisages the corpse-impure in the court of gentiles (m. Kelim 1:8), but here we may suspect a more lenient view than those dominating toward the end of the Second Temple period. The strict Temple Scroll assigns a special place outside the temple city for such people (11QT^a XLV, 17).[23] In spite of conflicting views, all sources agree on the presence of the corpse-impure within ordinary cities or settlements, and this must be explained by the common practice of an extra first-day water rite, which lessened the virulence of the impurity involved, although without shortening its duration. Josephus (*Ant.* 3.261), however, seems to suggest that the corpse-impure did not stay in their houses during their seven-day purification period. This is implied in Tobit, too, and somehow corresponds to the explicit command regarding the person with skin disease.

The trickiest issue when reconstructing first-century practice is the status of various types of dischargers. According to the strict tradition, they should be excluded from settlements. According to the most probable reading, the Temple Scroll demands a similar treatment of dischargers as it does of people with skin disease, even for the ordinary city and including menstruants and postpartum women.[24] This is the most extreme among

---

97–106; 2015c = ch. 8 in this volume.

23. For discussion and further references, see Kazen 2010c, 97–98. The utopian character of the Temple Scroll and the extent of the temple city (עיר מקדש) are points under discussion. Schiffman, following Levine, suggests that it refers to the temple proper, while Milgrom follows Yadin in understanding it to include the entire city. Crawford (2000, 49), in a compromise, suggests that the temple city "is not envisioned by the author/redactor of the Temple Scroll as having permanent residents, but as a place of temporary residents." The whole city would thus be looked on as a temple area for visiting pilgrims and cultic personnel, with God as the only permanent resident.

24. XLVIII, 14–17 may possibly be read as if dischargers were supposed to be secluded within settlements, rather than expelled like people with skin disease. The most natural reading, however, is that they were supposed to stay outside, since the purpose is to prevent them from "defiling in their midst" (אשר לוא יטמאו בתוכם).

the positions that we find represented in contemporary texts and could only—if at all—have been practiced among minor groups in places where such a stance was embraced by a majority. As for general practice, we have to look for other evidence. With regard to Jerusalem, Josephus seems to make a distinction between chronic dischargers (*zābîm* and *zābôt*) on the one hand and menstruants (presumably including parturients) on the other. The former are supposed to be expelled, while some sort of isolation or quarantine is envisaged for the latter.[25] Later the Mishnah bars any discharger from the Temple Mount, but nothing is said of the temple city (m. Kelim 1:8). Conflicting definitions of how to define the temple and the temple city may be at work and confuse our attempts to compare various views.[26] When asking for actual first-century practice, however, I would rather draw details from Josephus's descriptions than from later mishnaic hierarchies of holiness and purity, in spite of the fact that Josephus at times may be idealizing. Assuming a middle way between the strictest and most lenient views, we would expect a differentiation between chronic dischargers and menstruants/parturients. We may thus suggest that while some (the strictest) thought that no dischargers should be allowed within Jerusalem, menstruants (and parturients) were accepted with varying expectations of seclusion or isolation attached to their presence.

As for the ordinary city we unfortunately have too little evidence to do anything but proceed down the treacherous road of deduction. Josephus's rules for Jerusalem are similar to the strict stance of the Temple Scroll regarding the ordinary city. Moving holiness one step further back, we would expect a less strict ruling than that of the Temple Scroll to have accepted most dischargers within ordinary cities, although subject to certain restrictions. As we have noted, people healed from skin disease were allowed into settlements after an initial purification, including bathing, at the beginning of their seven-day purification period. Likewise, the corpse-impure were not expelled thanks to an initial ablution. In both cases, how-

---

25. "[Moses] expelled [ἀπήλασε] from the city both those who were sick with *lepra* and those with genital discharges; also the women whom the natural flux came over, he set aside [μετέστησε] until the seventh day, after which he allowed [them] to live in their place [ἐνδημεῖν] as already pure. Similarly also for those attending a dead [person], after so many days [he allowed them] legitimately to live in their place [ἐνδημεῖν]" (*Ant.* 3.261). Unless otherwise noted, all translations are mine.

26. See Crawford 2000, 42–49, and n. 23 above. Cf. the ten degrees of holiness in m. Kelim 1:6–9.

ever, there are indications that they were not supposed to stay inside their homes. It is quite possible that menstruants similarly employed a first-day water rite, washing off the first menstrual *niddâ* blood, similar to what is described in Samaritan halakah. This is indicated by 4Q274 1 I, 7–8a and fits with evidence from a number of other texts of sprinkling or bathing being used for early purification not only from skin disease and corpse impurity, but from other impurities, too.[27]

As for the *zāb*, we have already mentioned the biblical provision of lessening his contamination potency by handwashing. We have also noted the lack of evidence for this provision being extended to the *zābâ*. While it is reasonable to think of an initial ablution for *zābîm* and *zābôt after* the cessation of symptoms, analogous to that of menstruants, handwashing for a *zāb during* his indefinite period of full impurity seems to be an exception allowing for temporary and limited contact only. There is no evidence that this should have affected his *general status*, whether excluded, isolated, or restricted, but it must at least have facilitated some types of social interaction. Without the possibility of taking recourse to this provision, the *zābâ* would have been the most vulnerable and serious case of all the dischargers. This is indicated in the list of impurities in Mishnah Kelim 1:4, where she is mentioned toward the end, next to the person with skin disease, the bone, and the corpse.

The status of the *zābâ* toward the end of the Second Temple period is thus to be understood as more severe than that of other dischargers, close to that of a leper. She was certainly subject to restrictions, in many instances probably in some sense isolated,[28] and in certain locations where strict interpretations were favored perhaps even excluded—although I think this would have been exceptional. Unlike the *zāb* and the menstruant, she could probably not take recourse to a mitigating water rite to lessen her contamination potency even temporarily.

Markan Language and Markan Audience

The language of the Markan narrative of the *zābâ* has been extensively discussed. Haber comments on a number of literary characteristics in the text. We have already mentioned the Greek language borrowed from the

---

27. For further evidence, see Kazen 2010b; cf. Milgrom 1995, 67; Baumgarten 2000.
28. The evidence for and arguments against a special place of seclusion for impure women cannot be discussed here. Cf. Kazen 2010a, 160, esp. n. 371.

LXX, which renders every suggestion that purity legislation is not alluded to highly implausible.²⁹ Just like Haber, "I concur with the majority of scholars who assume … that the description of the woman is intended to allude to Lev 15 and the laws concerning purity."³⁰ She observes, however, that the primary concern in the text is healing and notes that this creates a tension in the text between the woman who needs healing by touch and the healer who is implicitly defiled by the same touch. This tension is supposed to be felt by the audience, that is, those listening to the Markan narrative, and the audience is assumed to be familiar with the purity laws.

At this point, however, we must ask ourselves *at which level* we envisage this tension and whether the allusions just mentioned originate from the same level. Haber is certainly right that the abrogation of purity laws is not a concern of the Markan narrative and that this is a difference when compared to Mark 7.³¹ Mark's focus in the *zābâ* narrative is on healing. But which people constitute the audience? Is the tension really apparent for the audience of *Mark's* narrative? If so, why does he not bring it out in any way? In the narrative of the leper (Mark 1:40–45), purity language is similarly used, but here the purity issue is *explicit*, even including instructions for purification and references to the law of Moses. The additional instruction about bringing the sacrifice "for your purification which Moses stipulated" (προσένεγκε περὶ τοῦ καθαρισμοῦ σου ἃ προσέταξεν Μωϋσῆς) would not be necessary for an audience that was able to grasp the details of Jewish purity law without assistance. Since, however, the purity issue is unavoidably constitutive for this narrative—an understanding of people with skin disease as impure would have been common knowledge, and purification is used synonymously with healing—this is the sort of information that an author would need to provide for a not-too-well-informed audience, mainly consisting of gentiles with little understanding of the legal *details* of Jewish law.

Similarly, in the handwashing narrative in Mark 7, the author explains legal details for the sake of his audience. He has hardly begun his story before he interrupts himself to explain the expression "with unclean hands" (κοιναῖς χερσίν) by "unwashed." Then he inserts a lengthy explanation about Pharisaic and Jewish or Judaean purificatory water rites before

---

29. See above, n. 2.
30. Haber 2008, 132–33.
31. Haber 2008, 136.

eating (7:2–4), as if his audience would be more or less unaware of these. Later in the narrative the author finds it necessary to explain *qorban* (7:11).

In the narrative of the *zābâ*, nothing like this is present. While it is safe to say that allusions to Lev 15 exist in the Greek text, why are we to suppose that they would be apparent to *Markan* readership, or to *Mark's* audience that elsewhere needs to be informed about Jewish practices and Jewish laws?

A plausible explanation may be found by considering the *zābâ* narrative a pre-Markan tradition, incorporated by Mark. This would explain why a number of traits and details are clearly present while not exploited by the author. Furthermore, the tradition must have reached Mark in written form and in Greek. There are good arguments for assuming this. It has long been observed that the language of this narrative is somewhat exceptional; participles abound in a way that is unusual for Mark.[32] While it might be argued that this could be due to Mark's formation of a sandwich construction, the language of the middle sections of other Markan sandwiches does not support this idea. Mark's composition technique alone cannot satisfactorily explain the Greek of the *zābâ* narrative. The different character of this narrative as compared to the surrounding narrative of Jairus's daughter strongly suggests that the sandwich construction is not pre-Markan but a Markan trait. This judgment is further strengthened by the frequency of such constructions in Mark. Had Mark received this narrative as an oral tradition in Aramaic, we would have expected neither this Greek nor these allusions to purity legislation that seem redundant and risk blurring Mark's focus.

This would mean that the purity issue, including the allusions to Lev 15 (LXX), belonged to and was grasped by an *earlier* audience to a Greek pre-Markan tradition, but not necessarily by the *Markan* audience. While a pre-Markan audience would have been able to relate the narrative of the person with skin disease with the narrative of the *zābâ*—although we do not know whether they would have had access to both in close proximity to each other—a Markan audience would rather have understood other points, relating to faith and healing, just as Haber suggests. Mark in facts

---

32. Cf. Taylor 1982, 289. Taylor points out that in 5:25–27 we find a rare example in Mark of a longer Greek sentence construction, with several subordinated participles. In addition to this, the intercalation uses the past tense in contrast to the Jairus narrative, which is mainly in the present tense except for the transition passages. Cf. Theissen 1983, 180–82.

sandwiches two narratives that both have implicit purity issues, but only for the purpose of letting the *faith* of the since-twelve-years sick woman spill over onto the father of the twelve-year-old daughter, all within a *christological* framework. The question of what happened to the purity of Jesus when touched by the *zābâ* is thus to be seen as a hypothetical *pre-Markan* question, which is not further discussed or answered on the *Markan* level.

While the pre-Markan tradition can be used as a small piece of evidence for tracing the behavior of the historical Jesus, it says little about Mark and his audience. The *tension* between purity and healing may have been present in Mark's *mind*, but he does *not* expect *his* audience to become occupied with it. When he wishes them to consider purity issues, he tells them—and then usually for the explicit purpose of bringing out theological and christological points, as we will further see below. We may even question whether he explicitly wishes his audience to consider such issues, or whether it is rather the details of his tradition that force him to provide necessary explanations for a relatively uninformed audience.

Mark's Christology and Jesus's Motives

On the Markan level, the narrative of the *zābâ* has a focus on faith and healing, which is particularly brought out through the sandwich construction, relating it to the story of Jairus's daughter. As Haber puts it: "The purpose of such interpolation in the Markan narrative is always interpretive, enabling the framing story to be understood against the background of the inside narrative and vice versa."[33]

Many scholars have noted a number of similarities and contrasts between the two intertwined narratives.[34] Most of these should be taken as resulting from Markan redaction. While there is no reason to repeat all of them here, we will comment on the implicit purity issue, which is also found in the Jairus story, since the dead child would transmit corpse impurity to anyone entering the house. This is not commented on by Mark, who portrays Jesus and his disciples as entering together with the parents. In Luke's version one might even get the impression that the mourners are inside. Matthew, however, has carefully redacted the story so that only Jesus goes in after having dismissed the mourners. At the

---

33. Haber 2008, 137.
34. Cf. Kazen 2010a, 130–31; Haber 2008, 137–38.

risk of overinterpretation, I suggest that Matthew is sensitive to the purity issue in a way that Mark is not. While Mark must be aware of the potential question concerning corpse impurity, it is of no concern to him, since his audience would not raise it and his own focus is elsewhere. While the two narratives in the sandwich construction are brought together by Mark, this is not because of the purity issue, which can be found in both of them, but because of the motif of faith. The purity issue would have been relevant at a pre-Markan stage, but then the two narratives would most likely not have been intertwined in this way.

The most important motif holding the two stories together on the *Markan* level is thus the focus on faith. The faith of the *zābâ* (Mark 5:34: ἡ πίστις σου σέσωκέν σε) informs the Jairus story and spills over onto Jairus, who is admonished not to fear but to believe (5:36). "The message is clear: as the faith of the hemorrhaging woman made her well, so, too, will Jairus's faith bring about his daughter's restoration to life."[35] Haber points to Mark's emphasis on Jesus's miraculous power, which points to his divine power.[36] The christological intent of the combined narrative can be spelled out further. A number of parallels to the Elijah-Elisha tradition indicate a prophetic Christology in the pre-Markan tradition.[37] Mark, however, goes further, making the *zābâ* an example of a kind of *saving faith*—a faith that is introduced already in 1:15, results in forgiveness for the paralytic (2:5), and not only saves the *zābâ* but also leads to the resurrection of Jairus's daughter (5:34, 36). Its absence prevents miracles in Jesus's hometown (6:6), but faith saves the possessed boy in spite of his father's unbelief (9:24) and gives sight to Bartimaeus (10:52). The *zābâ* becomes not only an example for Jairus, but also a corrective to the women at the resurrection. The latter fear (16:8: ἐφοβοῦντο γάρ) in spite of the exhortation not to (16:6: μὴ ἐκθαμβεῖσθε). The Markan audience already knows, however, that courage and faith bring salvation and resurrection, and they readily see that the behavior of the women at the grave is not an appropriate response. The *zābâ* provides a pattern for their own faith, confirming the identity and power of Jesus for anyone believing in his resurrection.

---

35. Haber 2008, 138.
36. Haber 2008, 138–39.
37. I.e., Jesus lives in the desert, is served by wild animals (Mark 1:13), and raises a dead child (5:21–24, 35–43). Like Elisha, he raises a child, heals a person with skin disease (1:40–45), and performs a bread miracle (6:30–44). See Kazen 2010a, 172–74; 2005a, 58–60.

Mark's focus is thus on faith and Christology, and the narrative of Jesus and the *zābâ* is part of his wider rhetorical scheme, as Haber also points out. This is important to remember when Mark's portrait of Jesus is discussed, in particular Mark's portrait of Jesus's attitude in legal matters. One fairly common approach refers to Jesus's special authority in order to explain his relative freedom from, or liberal interpretation of, certain laws or halakic traditions. Such ideas, however, bring with them implicit—if not explicit—christological claims. While these claims fit Mark's theological agenda, they do not necessarily represent the attitudes or motives of the historical Jesus. It is important to note the level at which such ideas can be evidenced. The question of authority may be an important clue, but if this is the case, where did such authority reside? Mark's understanding is not necessarily valid for pre-Markan tradition and certainly not for the historical Jesus.

Similar considerations apply to suggestions that Jesus advocated compassion before cult, an attitude with deep roots in Israel's prophetic heritage but also liberally exploited in early Christian polemical discourse against Jewish critics and adversaries. Such an attitude can be read out of the texts, but does it represent more than secondary interpretations? The idea that Jesus defended the plain meaning of Scripture against later halakic developments is likewise theologically loaded. While in some cases it is found on the surface of the text, it may result from early Christian redactional activity, at a time when negligence of halakic observance was defended with references to the teaching of Jesus. An analysis of Markan rhetorical strategy and christological agenda, the question of Markan audience, and the level of historical development of purity halakah all have wider implications for interpreting Mark and reconstructing historical issues behind the Markan text. From the *zābâ* narrative we will thus turn to Mark 7 and the handwashing incident.

The Handwashing Narrative

Handwashing at the End of the Second Temple Era

The growth and development of purity halakah during the Second Temple period—one of Haber's main interests—cannot be adequately discussed today without considering the numerous archaeological findings of *miqwā'ôt* and stone vessels.[38] While there is no room to deal with these in

---

38. Cf. Haber 2008, 161–206.

detail here, they testify to widespread and frequent practices of purification by water and the use of preventive measures to avoid contamination, even by minor impurities, of food and drink. It seems that the "expansion of ritual washing to new uses not known in the Hebrew Bible" was a general expansionist phenomenon during this period, and a number of scholars see this as part of the development of ideas of graded impurity and graded purifications.[39]

This heightened concern for purity resulted in practical solutions, mitigating or lessening the contamination potential of a number of *impurity bearers* (including the corpse-impure and the menstruant but probably not the *zābâ*) by new and early ablutions. However, it also resulted in similar solutions for handling certain *secondary impurities*.[40] The category of *ṭəbûl yôm* must be seen in this light; it made early purification by immersion possible for those contaminated with a one-day impurity.[41] The extension of a second-degree impurity to *ḥullîn* (ordinary food), the idea of liquid being more susceptible to impurity than other substances, thus reverting to a first-degree impurity, and the increasing practice to keep full purity at ordinary meals were conspicuous developments that demanded practical solutions. Handwashing before meals was one of the most important.[42]

Following Jacob Neusner, many interpreters have understood such handwashing as an emulation of priestly practice. Even Ed P. Sanders, who opposes this view, comes very close to it by admitting that Pharisees made *minor symbolic gestures* toward living like priests.[43] This, however, is an anachronistic interpretative description and not a current *rationale* at the end of the Second Temple period. The practices in question can be satisfactorily explained as resulting from a general ambition for as high a degree of purity as possible, which was promoted

---

39. Lawrence 2006, 189. Cf. Milgrom 1978; 1991, 969–76, 991–1000; Baumgarten 1992; 2000; Eshel 1999; Regev 2000a, 177–81.

40. Kazen 2010c, 113–23; 2015c = ch. 8 in this volume.

41. Instead of waiting for sunset. Cf. Baumgarten 1980; Sanders 1990, 36–37; Schiffman 1994; Kazen 2010a, 75–81; Crossley 2004, 197–200. This is not to say that the full rabbinic concept of *ṭəbûl yôm* had evolved by the time of the Second Temple period, but some of its crucial presuppositions must have been present. See further Kazen 2013a, ch. 3.

42. Kazen 2015c = ch. 8 in this volume; cf. Kazen 2010a, 67–85; 2010c, 119–23.

43. Sanders 1990, 192.

9. Jesus and the Zābâ: Implications for Interpreting Mark   233

by expansionist interests and which won increasing acceptance among the people at large.⁴⁴

It has often been questioned whether hands were considered separately unclean at the time of Jesus. Roger Booth, after having provided a possible historical and legal context for handwashing at the time of Jesus, nevertheless ends up with conclusions similar to those of Sanders: such a practice before the eating of *ḥullîn* would have been of no use unless people practiced regular immersions, which we cannot assume since that would have been too unpractical.⁴⁵ Since then, however, a number of studies have made it very likely that an increasing number of Jews, especially in Judea, were following such customs already at the time of Jesus.⁴⁶ While some would claim that a formal ruling, declaring hands as separately unclean, only belongs to a period of heightened tension and conflict before the Jewish War, this does not mean that the idea or the actual practice was late.⁴⁷ One type of stone vessel found has been thought to have served for handwashing.⁴⁸ Although this particular identification is disputed today,⁴⁹

---

44. My stance is to a large extent supported by Furstenberg 2008. Furstenberg (191, esp. n. 38) points out that Neusner's interpretation rests on the midrash in Sifre Numbers 116 on Num 18:7 (Furstenberg mistakenly says 17:8), which should be dated to the time of Rabbi Judah the Patriarch.

45. Booth 1986, 185–87.

46. Tomson 1988; Deines 1993; Regev 2000a; 2000b; Poirier 2003; Crossley 2004, 183–205.

47. Traditionally, a decree on the separate impurity of hands has been associated with the so-called eighteen decrees, a Zealot synod in 66/67 CE, and a tumultuous meeting in the upper room of Hananiah/Hanina. Roger Booth (1986, 162–73) has suggested a dating to 51 CE, but his reconstruction is too speculative for my taste. I am more convinced by Peter Tomson's (1988) reasoning that regardless of whether or not the ten items of m. Zavim 5:12 (which include a statement on the impurity of hands) were formulated at some tumultuous gathering close to the war, the core of the saying in m. Zavim 5:12, including the separate impurity of hands, did not belong to the eighteen decrees. It rather belongs to the oldest layer of the Mishnah and was formulated by R. Joshua. Before that it must have been practiced for some time at least in the Pharisaic tradition (for further references, see Tomson 1988). Cf. Furstenberg (2008, 183–84, esp. n. 19), who finds the reconstruction of the Babylonian Talmud unreliable and asserts that the handwashing custom belonged to pre-70 Pharisaic halakah.

48. I.e., "cream pitchers" that are claimed to contain approximately the amount stipulated by the Mishnah for handwashing purposes. Cf. Magen 1994; Deines 1993, 245–46.

49. It is disputed that these vessels had a uniform volume corresponding to the mishnaic requirement for handwashing, as once supposed. See Reed 2003, 387–89;

an early understanding of the defiling force of liquids is attested already in several Qumran texts, and together with a general understanding of stone as less susceptible to impurity, this would suggest a role for stone vessels in maintaining purity. The combined evidence of archaeology, Qumran texts, the Mishnah, and Mark indicate that handwashing before common meals was advocated by expansionist groups at the end of the Second Temple period and practiced already at the time of Jesus, although certainly not by *all* Jews, as Mark would have it. What distinguished expansionists from ordinary people, however, was not necessarily observance as compared to nonobservance, but the former's consistency and strict interpretation.[50] Today such views are argued by an increasing number of scholars.

The development of (extra) water rites for early purification or the lessening of contamination potency is a crucial piece of evidence in reconstructing the state of purity halakah around the turn of the era. It is important for assessing the status of various impurity bearers and, thus, for interpreting certain gospel narratives such as the story of Jesus and the *zābâ*. This is true for interpreting the Markan handwashing narrative (Mark 7), too, although here the issues are different, focusing on secondary impurities.

Whose Audience Is Reflected in Mark 7?

Although the handwashing referred to in Mark 7 should be understood as early first-century practice, this says little about the Markan narrative. James Crossley has argued for an early dating of Mark's Gospel, based primarily on the antiquity of halakic practices reflected in a number of Markan narratives. Three of these are discussed in detail: the cornfield incident, the *Streitgespräch* over divorce, and the handwashing incident; the latter receives a chapter of its own.[51]

While I find many of Crossley's halakic analyses convincing, I cannot accept his conclusions for an early dating of Mark. The problems involved in the handwashing narrative are similar to those we encounter in the Markan story of Jesus and the *zābâ*, that is, separating levels in the text,

---

Miller 2003, 416; cf. Miller 2010. (Now see also Miller 2015.) The reconstruction is, in fact, another example of anachronistic retrojection of rabbinic evidence into the Second Temple period. However, the discussion about hand impurity in no way depends on a particular use of these particular cups.

50. Cf. Kazen 2010a, 86–87, 269–72.

51. Crossley 2004, especially 159–205.

identifying audiences, and drawing conclusions about the concerns of the author.

Crossley agrees that the Gospel of Mark is "edited in light of gentile ignorance of Jewish purity laws," but he stresses that the underlying assumptions "only make sense in a Jewish context."[52] He furthermore points out that Mark's editorial comments in 7:3–4 display a good understanding of purity law and suggests that this betrays an interest on the part of Mark for the expansion of purity halakah, all of which can help us understand Mark's motives.[53] At first sight, it may seem that Crossley differentiates between Mark and the traditions that are being used.

By a strange twist of argument, however, Crossley claims that Mark writes before any conflict regarding the keeping of biblical purity laws emerged in the early Christian movement. Mark's wish would not have been to question purity law in general, only the *expansion* of biblical law or, more precisely, the idea that secondary impurities could contaminate food through contact via hands and liquid. Since, according to Crossley, Mark consistently portrays Jesus as faithful to biblical law, his editorial comment in 7:19 should be taken to mean that all foods that the Torah permits for consumption are clean and, therefore, handwashing is unnecessary.[54] Mark's point would simply be that one could eat food with unwashed hands, but it has nothing to do with what foods Jews would eat or not; it thus has basically the same intent as Jesus's saying in 7:15.

According to Crossley, the reason why Matthew changes Mark is that food laws have now become a source of conflict, no longer being observed by all Christians, and Mark's editorial comment in 7:19 may now be misunderstood to justify such behavior. Matthew thus changes Mark's comment to "but to eat with unwashed hands does not defile the human being" (Matt 15:20), which would actually be what Mark originally meant, and by making Jesus talk of "the mouth" in the key saying, he restricts the possible meaning of Mark 7:15 to the issue of handwashing before eating.[55]

Crossley's arguments for an early dating of Mark before any dissension concerning food or purity laws would have surfaced have several flaws. Here we can only discuss the problem of the audience. If Mark's primary audience is gentile, and in addition to that a type of gentile audience that would *need*

---

52. Crossley 2004, 200.
53. Crossley 2004, 200.
54. Crossley 2004, 192.
55. Crossley 2004, 200–202, 208.

to be informed in detail of current halakic practices among Palestinian or Judean Jews, why would Mark go to such pains in order to convince them that handwashing is unnecessary, especially when nothing is at stake, that is, when they seem *unaware of the practice*? I agree with Crossley that there are assumptions in this text that belong to a Jewish context and that the traditions may be very early. I think, however, that Crossley at times confuses Mark with his source and Mark's audience with an earlier one.

Contrary to the narrative of Jesus and the *zābâ*, the handwashing incident is told in a way that *brings out* the purity issue. Mark's redactional comments (7:3-4, 19) are necessary because *his* audience would otherwise understand neither the details and purposes of handwashing, nor the relevance of this story for their own quite different problems. Furthermore, the two answers ascribed to Jesus (7:6-8, 9-13), before he actually addresses the subject matter of the accusation, have the same point of Jesus criticizing his opponents for replacing the commandment or word of God with human *paradosis* (7:8, 9, 13). The former (7:6-8) consists of a quotation from Isa 29, a passage frequently used by early Christians.[56] While a prophetic critical stance is in line with the historical Jesus, this quotation of Isaiah in a version closer to the LXX than to the MT is likely to represent the work of Mark, or at least a pre-Markan tradition in Greek. The *qorban* section (7:9-13) that follows is juxtaposed to the Isaianic citation with little redactional effort; it begins with a new introductory formula (καὶ ἔλεγεν αὐτοῖς). It could represent a separate tradition going back to the historical Jesus, and it clearly places the commandment of God against human tradition. From an editorial point of view, however, this makes it a very suitable parallel to the handwashing story, since the latter *lacks* this opposition once the Isaianic reply is removed. We could thus easily think of both of these answers as separate pieces of early polemics, inserted into a likewise pre-Markan handwashing tradition by the author. This does not mean that Mark must have created the material, but through his redaction he achieved a clear opposition between divine command and human practice. It should be noted that in the *qorban* section, too, Mark finds it necessary to translate the meaning of *qorban* for the sake of his ignorant audience.

---

56. Cf. Westerholm 1978, 76. Westerholm mentions Rom 9:20; 11:8; 1 Cor 1:19; Col 2:22. Note also how "this people" (οὗτος ὁ λαός) is used as accusation against Jews in general. The Isaianic passage was easily understood as predictive of the Jewish people.

Matthew apparently finds such explanations unnecessary in the *qorban* section as well as in the primary handwashing story. However, he reverses the order of the *qorban* section and the quotation from Isaiah, reworking the material into a counterquestion by Jesus and integrating the two with the handwashing incident into a coherent narrative. This says something about Matthew's intended audience: they are supposed to be familiar with Jewish halakah and enjoy the support of Jesus as a responsible teacher of law for their own practice of not observing handwashing before meals.

It is tempting to think of Matthew's version as more original, since it fits a Jewish audience better.[57] There is clear evidence, however, of this being the result of subsequent redaction. In addition to the integration just mentioned, we must note the introduction of "mouth," which is clearly secondary.[58] While it is possible to interpret Mark 7:15 more broadly, Matthew talks of that which enters and exits through the *mouth* (Matt 15:11). In the following explanation, the focus is on the heart, and the issues are moral. Matthew, however, retains the focus on the mouth in addition to the heart, which causes a redundant formulation in verse 18: τὰ δὲ ἐκπορευόμενα ἐκ τοῦ στόματος ἐκ τῆς καρδίας ἐξέρχεται. The list that follows is complemented with one more *spoken* sin (ψευδομαρτυρίαι) in addition to the Markan "blasphemy," which would otherwise have been the only one associated with the mouth. Although it is entirely possible that in some instances Matthew had access to oral traditions complementing Mark, in this case his *text* is nevertheless secondary in comparison to that of Mark.

It seems to me that Matthew is trying to achieve what Crossley suggests for Mark: he wants to convince his audience that handwashing before meals is unnecessary. It may also be that he is reacting to Mark and, assuming that his audience used Mark or knew a Markan version of this narrative, Matthew might be implying that taking this story as an argument for neglecting laws concerning food or purity would be a misinterpretation. I cannot see, however, why this should place the Markan audience in the late thirties or early forties, as Crossley would have it. If no conflicts regarding legal issues

---

57. Cf. Dunn 1990, 42–44, 51. Dunn's argument concern the original form of Mark 7:15, not the entire narrative. Although I originally accepted that argument in Kazen 2002, 66–67, I have changed my opinion in the corrected reprint edition (2010a).

58. This is one reason why I consider Svartvik's (2000, 375–411) interpretation of the Markan saying as focused on "evil speech" quite unlikely.

were yet on the table, are we then to assume that Mark's gentile audience followed every "biblical" command regarding Sabbath, food, and purity? Why would Mark then bring up the handwashing issue? It only makes sense if his audience was pressed to accept this practice. But could they then have been so ignorant about this halakic custom that Mark had to explain it to them? The point that handwashing before meals is unnecessary would have been relevant to Jesus's original audience, and even more so to pre-Markan audiences at a time when the idea of an opposition between human tradition and divine command was being developed. But the redacted text of Mark has to explain two halakic practices to an unknowing gentile audience in order to convey a slightly different point from that in preexisting Jesus traditions, which, if left unexplained, would remain puzzling: that inner purity is more important than outer (Mark 7:15).

Although I think that the historical Jesus expressed something similar, Mark would not need to teach his gentile audience this by elaborate explanations of foreign practices, unless he had a further purpose. That purpose is revealed "at home/in the house" (Mark 7:17–23), which is Mark's typical way of expounding the meaning and contemporary relevance of the Jesus tradition for his present audience.[59] This passage suggests that his audience is aware of outer and inner impurity, although they were perhaps ignorant of the halakic details previously explained, and that Mark invites them to recontextualize the Jesus tradition and apply it to their own situation, meaning that food impurity is now irrelevant. This interpretation is supported by the subsequent narrative of the Syro-Phoenician woman, suggesting that the present inclusion of gentiles—their purity—was foreboded already during Jesus's ministry, too.

It is not necessary to suppose that the Markan audience was discussing whether to eat pork or not; the issues at stake could have been other food- and purity-related conflicts that had to do with commensality between Jewish and gentile Christ-believers.[60] But we must suppose *some issue related to eating* as the context of the audience for which the handwashing narrative is shaped in its Markan form, and this issue is *not identical* with the historical handwashing issue behind the original tradition, since that issue has to be explained for the Markan audience. The Markan context is

---

59. Mark 7:17 uses εἰς οἶκον. See Mark 2:1; 3:20; 9:28, and the similar ἐν τῇ οἰκίᾳ in 9:33 and 10:10; cf. Hooker 1993, 180, 225, 227, 236.

60. Such as the conflict in Antioch referred to by Paul (Gal 2:11–14) or discussions about sacrificial meat (cf. 1 Cor 8; Rom 14).

one in which the Jesus tradition is being recontextualized and reapplied for a later gentile audience, which had experienced conflicts and dissensions concerning issues of food, most probably with Jewish Christ-believers.

In spite of the differences in intent between the handwashing and the *zābâ* narratives, it is reasonable to assume an earlier stage for some of the traditions in Mark 7, too, and that these would have been previously shaped in Greek with the opposition between human *paradosis* and divine command as the main point. Such arguments are most viable in contexts in which a general adherence to the details of Scripture is being presupposed and the issues at stake revolve around differences in interpretation and the question concerning which of them are truest to scriptural intent. Mark's focus is, however, elsewhere; moral matters are given priority over purity concerns, and sweeping generalizations are being made. Trying to disentangle the motives in the background is hazardous but will be attempted next.

Jesus's Motives in Purity Conflicts

Unless Mark felt bound to relate every Jesus tradition available for the mere sake of it, we must suppose that he used and shaped the handwashing tradition with a view to its relevance for his intended audience—an audience of predominantly gentile Christ-believers who needed explanations for halakic details. The polemics, accusing "this people," that is, Jews *in general*, of giving priority to human traditions over divine commands, thus *repeatedly* exhibiting lip service rather than an inner disposition (καὶ παρόμοια τοιαῦτα πολλὰ ποιεῖτε), generalizes the behavior of those whom we may envisage as opponents of the Markan audience. By implication, Mark tells his audience that *they* of course do or should do the opposite: give priority to divine commands by focusing on *inner* purity. Except for the example of honoring one's parents, the contents of the divine word are typically not identified, but can be understood negatively as the opposite of the list of vices (7:21–22) that characterizes the "others." This does not tell the Markan audience how to discriminate between Scripture and scriptural interpretation, that is, halakah or *paradosis*. It is true that the rabbis distinguish between scriptural law and tradition.[61] This distinction was, however, not easy to make, since tradition sometimes depends on interpretation, attempting to spell out

---

61. Cf. Sanders 1990, 97–130.

what is ambiguous or implicit in the law.⁶² Scholarly opinions differ as to how early a clear awareness of the difference between written text and its interpretation developed.⁶³ There are no indications that Mark expects his audience to have developed a skilled competency in this regard. They are simply assured that they do nothing wrong in not adhering to Jewish details they do not fully understand and that their behavior is more pious than that of their opponents.

On the one hand, the opposition between divine law and human tradition must be ascribed to the redactor, since it permeates the whole section (7:1–13) and unites the diverse material. On the other hand, Mark uses this opposition for general rhetorical purposes, without much concretion, giving it no role whatsoever in the exposition from verse 15 onward. This may tempt us to look for its origin prior to Mark. Does it possibly capture the historical conflict between Jesus and the Pharisees?

Friedrich Avemarie argues that Jesus would have regarded the washing of hands not as divine law but as *paradosis*, a scribal innovation, since the widespread practice was fairly recent. While the idea of unclean food

---

62. This subject is worthy of an article of its own and cannot be further discussed here. Cf. Hedner-Zetterholm 2006; Jaffee 2001, 84–99; Berger 1998, 16–25. The rabbinic concept of an Oral Torah probably arose among the Pharisees at the end of the Second Temple period, but its prominence seems to be late, when it played a role in promulgating the Babylonian Talmud and supporting central rabbinic authority. The idea that opposing groups such as Sadducees or Samaritans (and later Karaites) were literalists who did not accept any halakic interpretations is oversimplified—at times others could accuse rabbinic interpretations of being literalist, too—but they did not accept what they understood as Pharisaic or rabbinic novelties without a basis in their own traditions (cf. Josephus, *Ant.* 13:295-298). See Bóid 1989b; 1997. Bóid (1997, 104–6, and personal communication) regards the washing of hands together with the other items mentioned in Mark 7:2-4 as belonging to the seven rabbinic commandments that were added as new *mitsvot*, not to interpret the Torah but in order to assert rabbinic (or Pharisaic) authority to actually institute new practices on the same level as the Torah. The seven rabbinic *mitsvot* are summarized in Maimonides's *Book of Commandments* (washing hands before bread, *eruv*, blessing before food, Sabbath candles, Purim, Hanukkah, and *hallel* on certain occasions), but certainly have a long prehistory. I find it difficult, however, to see this concept confirmed at the end of the Second Temple period. In any case the Markan discussion makes an analogy with the *qorban* tradition, which is *not* among the seven. At the time of Jesus, I would rather understand the washing of hands before *ḥullin* as an expansionist halakic practice that was questioned as to its legitimacy and antiquity.

63. Berger 1998, 5, 159 n. 15, referring to Alon, Gilat, Neusner, Jaffee, and Kraemer.

contaminating the eater is found in rabbinic law and may well go back to the Second Temple period, it is not of biblical origin. Furthermore, Avemarie claims that neither Scripture nor "rabbinic teaching ... credit[s] the impurity of hands with sufficient intensity as to impart itself on foodstuff."[64] Jesus would thus have claimed that hands *never* contaminate ordinary food and that contaminated food in any case *never* contaminates a person; only things coming out of the mouth defile (v. 15). Avemarie takes Jesus's answer in an *absolute* rather than a relative sense,[65] claiming that here Jesus upholds Scripture against halakah.[66]

Many exegetes consider the saying in Mark 7:15 (οὐδέν ἐστιν ἔξωθεν τοῦ ἀνθρώπου εἰσπορευόμενον εἰς αὐτὸν ὃ δύναται κοινῶσαι αὐτόν, ἀλλὰ τὰ ἐκ τοῦ ἀνθρώπου ἐκπορευόμενά ἐστιν τὰ κοινοῦντα τὸν ἄνθρωπον) as originating with the historical Jesus but then assuming a *relative* reading, that is, taking the οὐ ... ἀλλά construction as reflecting a Semitic dialectic negation, meaning "not so much as" or "rather."[67] The meaning would correspond to Israelite prophetic criticism (Hos 6:6), which was meant to emphasize the *priority* of humanitarian concerns, not the abrogation of the cult. Jesus would thus have meant that inner (im)purity takes priority over outer.

In the past, the main problem with taking Mark 7:15 as originating with Jesus was seen in its lack of *Wirkungsgeschichte*; subsequent conflicts in regard to food laws in the early church would be difficult to understand if a clear saying of Jesus to this effect were to have been known. Such views, however, presuppose an absolute reading from an anti-Torah perspective. A relative reading greatly diminishes the problem, as the saying originally would not have been understood as questioning food or purity laws, only relativizing them. The lack of *Wirkungsgeschichte* can, however, also be explained by an absolute reading, restricting the issue to handwashing. Although Crossley speaks of not taking the saying literally, he comes close to Avemarie in similarly restricting its scope to defilement through handwashing, thus understanding it to criticize halakic tradition.[68]

---

64. Avemarie 2010.
65. Despite conceding that a relative sense is consistent with Markan Greek; cf. Mark 9:37.
66. In 7:19 Mark goes one step further, shifting the focus from eater to food and denying the impurity of food altogether, i.e., denying scriptural law. This is not, however, part of Jesus's argument.
67. E.g. Westerholm 1978, 83; Booth 1986, 69–71.
68. Crossley 2004, 193.

Restricting the scope of Mark 7:15 to the issue of handwashing is, however, not without problems. It is this general statement concerning that which goes in and out, which gives occasion to the explanation indoors (vv. 17–23), that represents Markan present-day application, as suggested above. This elaboration on inner (im)purity for the benefit of the Markan audience is based on a *nonliteral* understanding of the saying in verse 15; what comes out of a person is taken in an ethical sense. If, however, the saying in 7:15 is to be taken in a restricted sense, we would expect this to be valid not only for its first half but also for the second. If οὐδέν ἐστιν ἔξωθεν τοῦ ἀνθρώπου εἰσπορευόμενον εἰς αὐτὸν ὃ δύναται κοινῶσαι αὐτόν is taken absolutely and literally, that is, meaning that no contagion, no impurity, can enter the human person through the intake of common food (since contamination via hands is unscriptural and thus invalid), then what does the following ἀλλὰ τὰ ἐκ τοῦ ἀνθρώπου ἐκπορευόμενά ἐστιν τὰ κοινοῦντα τὸν ἄνθρωπον mean?

One possibility is that it refers to bodily impurities. Avemarie suggests this, but immediately retreats: genital discharge does come from within and is a biblical source of impurity, but this reasoning does not fit with other sources.[69] But perhaps it does after all? Corpse impurity was understood as some kind of death ooze, a quasi-physical miasma, coming out of dead bodies, with the ability to, among other things, fill enclosed spaces. The skin diseases subsumed under the heading *ṣāraʿat* ("leprosy") seem to have involved scales and cracking of the skin. Jesus's saying would then have expressed the view that bodily substances (death ooze, genital discharges, and "leprosy-stuff" breaching the body envelope) transmit impurity, while food does not. Alternatively, with a relative reading, the saying could have categorized these impure substances as more aggressive impurity transmitters than food. The idea is interesting, because it would represent one more stance regarding the transmission of impurity, in addition to the various noncompatible ideas of impurity transmission found in the Mishnah.[70] And it could claim scriptural support.

Yair Furstenberg has suggested a somewhat similar interpretation. Taking handwashing before eating as an originally Greco-Roman custom,

---

69. Avemarie 2010.

70. Rabbi Eliezer: connection; Rabbi Joshua: interposition of liquid; Rabbi Aqiba: hands unclean in the first degree; standard view: hands unclean only in the second degree; categorizing according to the concepts of unclean and unfit. See m. Yad. 3:1–2; m. Tehar. 2:2–7; cf. m. Ḥag. 2:5–7; m. Ohal. 1:1–3.

adopted by the Pharisees and integrated into the purity system, Furstenberg argues that the rabbinic system, originating in the Second Temple period, reverses the direction of contamination. Instead of people and vessels contaminating food and liquids as in the biblical system, we find food and liquids contaminating people and vessels. Jesus would then have reacted against these innovations, favoring a view of humans as the *source* of impurity rather than its target.[71]

While these suggestions should be seriously considered, I find it unlikely that the impurity of humans and their contaminating power should have been the *focus* of the historical Jesus, explaining his *motives* for defending his disciples' neglect to wash their hands. Narrative traditions elsewhere do not suggest that Jesus took a strict view on defilement from the main "fathers of impurity." Moreover, subsequent early Christian development would not make sense had the historical Jesus taken a clear stance, emphasizing the human body as the primary source of impurity and transmitter of bodily contact-contagion. A moral interpretation fits a continuity perspective much better.[72] While the Markan exposition is located εἰς οἶκον, and thus represents early Christian elaboration, the *impetus* for a moral interpretation is likely to have come from the Jesus tradition, as Mark 7:15 suggests.[73]

Moreover, the separation of biblical law from halakah is difficult. The idea of separate hand impurity seems to be derived from scriptural rules concerning the *zāb* and handwashing (Lev 15:11–12). As we have already mentioned, the idea of handwashing before meals may be seen as a counterpart of this provision with regard to *secondary* impurities. The idea of unclean foods contaminating the eater has some scriptural support, too. According to Lev 11, various types of "swarmers" are considered disgusting and may not be eaten, but the dead bodies of "ground swarmers" are also said to contaminate by contact, rendering not only clothes and utensils unclean, but also liquids and foodstuff (Lev 11:29–38). The implicit supposition is that unclean food that has somehow come into contact with dead ground swarmers should be discarded. When Lev 11:45 warns against making oneself disgusting and unclean through these ground swarmers, a

---

71. Furstenberg 2008, 192–98.
72. For a definition of a continuity or continuum perspective, see Holmén 2007, 1–13.
73. Furstenberg (2008, 197–98) does acknowledge that "the force of Jesus's statement lies in its ability simultaneously to rise to a moral level."

systemic reading would understand this to include a prohibition against eating such food, since it would make the eater unclean.[74] As purity rules were harmonized, this rule seems to have been applied to all sorts of ritual impurities, to the effect that they contaminated foodstuffs by contact and that such food made the eater unclean. This logical argument may be seen in Mishnah Teharot 2, in which Rabbi Eliezer argues from an idea of connection, and it would easily have been understood as scriptural law.

The attempt to read Mark 7:15 as intent on the body as a source of impurity should, however, not be too readily dismissed. Some such view could be seen as part of an ongoing inner-Jewish discussion. It is possible to think of the saying behind Mark 7:15 as a kind of slogan, an argument against expansionists such as the Pharisees and the Essenes, by nonexpansionists, perhaps Sadducees or people representing an old-fashioned Galilean type of piety, who did not accept recent innovations. This does not necessarily mean that some accepted human traditions in addition to biblical law, while others did not.[75] Interpretative activity, that is, halakic development, was necessary for anyone attempting to apply ancient law within the bounds of changing historical circumstances. This did not prevent one group from accusing another of transgressing the Torah, when the issues at stake depended on differing hermeneutics, as some contemporary texts suggest (cf. Pss. Sol. 2.3, 8.11–13; CD-A IV–V; 4QMMT B 49–72). Jesus would then have used a current argument against the requirement of handwashing that was neither his own nor unknown to his opponents, but at the same time he gave it his own slant.[76]

The reason for taking Jesus's saying in a wider sense is that the paradigm of inner and outer fits with other parts of the Jesus tradition, which is evident when we look at Q.[77] In Q 11:44 Jesus complains that the Pharisees are like unmarked graves. The point in the Lukan version is not, as in Matthew, that they are whitewashed (hypocrites), but that they are unmarked

---

74. Most of these examples are mentioned by other interpreters, too, but with differing interpretations. See, e.g., Furstenberg 2008, 195; Crossley 2004, 193–97; Sanders 1990, 199–205, 228–36. For a discussion of Lev 11, see Kazen 2008, 55–57; 2011, 72–80.

75. Cf. n. 62 above.

76. This suggestion is admittedly speculative and in need of support from an extended discussion about contemporary halakic development, in order to be further pursued, which is not possible here.

77. For a fuller discussion than the one provided below, see Kazen 2010a, 223–28.

and thus their impurity is invisible.[78] The saying could be taken to indicate that Jesus acknowledged corpse impurity and worked with a basic purity paradigm, like any Jew in the Second Temple period, but it says nothing about what significance he attributed to it. In its context, however, the saying is associated with a discussion about inside and outside, emphasizing the *relative priority of inside* over against the outside.

A similar interpretation is reasonable for the cup saying (Q 11:39–41), which reads in Luke's version: "Now you Pharisees, you purify the outside [τὸ ἔξωθεν] of the cup and the plate, but your inside [τὸ δὲ ἔσωθεν] is full of greed and evil. Fools, did not he who made the outside also make the inside? Rather give the contents [τὰ ἐνόντα] as alms, and lo, all is clean to you." For this last sentence, Matthew instead has "Blind Pharisee, purify first the inside [τὸ ἐντός] of the cup, so that also its outside [τὸ ἐκτός] may become pure."

A number of scholars have related this saying to the rabbinic tradition about the schools of Hillel and Shammai concerning the order of handwashing and blessing the cup at a meal (m. Ber. 8:2–3; cf. t. Ber. 6 [5]:2–3). This tradition, like Mark 7, presupposes the separate impurity of hands, based on the assumptions mentioned above. The saying is given a moral interpretation with the point that the inside is just as important, or even *more* important, than the outside. The bottom line is thus the *relative priority of social and ethical issues* over against purity concerns. The subsequent saying on tithing (Q 11:42), concluding that "you should have done this without neglecting the other," also suggests a relative interpretation. In the Lukan version, this priority of the inside is motivated by concern for the poor, and almsgiving seems to have a purificatory effect (Luke 11:41). This may be read as a focus on the restoration of the people and as a concern for the marginalized that is made difficult by expansionist interpretations, which in the case of purity would have affected social fellowship and food supply. Against such an interpretation, Jesus is portrayed as giving priority to moral issues for social reasons.

While the narrative context of the Lukan version is provided by Luke (11:37–38),[79] it conspicuously places traditional sayings about inside and outside in a setting that concerns ritual purification, in which Jesus's practice of purification is questioned by a Pharisee, just as his disciples' behavior

---

78. For a number of reasons Matthew must be seen as responsible for more redactional changes than Luke (Kazen 2010a, 223–28).

79. Cf. the Lukan syntax and style; Kazen 2010a, 227.

is questioned in Mark 7. Outside the canon, we find Oxyrhynchus Papyri 840 similarly locating a discussion of inside and outside, interpreted in moral terms, in a setting where the purificatory practices of Jesus and his disciples are questioned by a representative of the expansionist interpretation.[80] An inside-outside discourse is thus clearly associated with ritual purification in the Jesus tradition outside Mark, too.

Conclusions

By juxtaposing the *zābâ* narrative in Mark 5 to the handwashing story in Mark 7, we have attempted to interpret their historical purity issues, define their audiences, and disentangle Mark's agenda from that of earlier traditions and the motives of the historical Jesus.

Examining the historical status of genital dischargers at the end of the Second Temple period, we have suggested that the *zābâ* was the most vulnerable category, close to the person with skin disease, in a hierarchy of impurities. Unlike many other impurity bearers, she seems not to have had access to any extra water rite for mitigating or lessening contagion by contact, such as the first-day ablution for the corpse-impure, or handwashing for the *zāb*. Although the origin is uncertain, handwashing for secondary impurities may be seen as an extension of this type of practice for primary impurity bearers—a possibility of early purification not prescribed in the Torah but having some possible biblical precedents.

Looking at the Markan text and language, we have emphasized the importance of distinguishing between various levels and possible audiences. In the *zābâ* narrative, there is an undeniable purity issue in the Greek text, which is not made explicit or exploited by Mark. His focus is, as Haber has shown, on Jesus's divine healing power and the saving faith of the woman. The purity issue, however, was of little relevance to Mark's audience, although Mark himself was probably fully aware of it. The tension between purity and healing in the *zābâ* narrative would thus not have been readily visible for a Markan audience, but more so at a pre-Markan stage. The handwashing narrative in Mark 7 must be read with similar discrimination. The antiquity of the practice of handwashing cannot be

---

80. A case can be made for some degree of historical memory behind this tradition; see Kazen 2010a, 256–60. For a recent full-length study of P.Oxy. 840, judging it an early second century Jewish-Christian text using memories of canonical stories but *not* earlier sources, see Kruger 2005.

used for an early dating of Mark, but the ignorance in halakic matters of the obviously gentile Markan audience shows that some of the arguments contained in the redacted traditions rather belong to a pre-Markan level. Halakic detail in Mark 7 speaks only for the antiquity of pre-Markan traditions. It is unreasonable to think that Mark would have used the handwashing narrative to instruct a gentile audience, otherwise ignorant in halakic matters, that the practice of handwashing—which they did not understand—was unnecessary, and at a time before conflicts concerning food or purity laws among early Christ-believers would have emerged. Rather, the narrative is shaped to address an issue related to eating, different from the historical issue of handwashing, which was relevant to a later audience.

Asking for the motives of a historical person is by necessity a speculative enterprise. However, it may be a useful exercise for distinguishing possible motives of the historical Jesus from those of the Markan author or of the early Christ-believers who were bearers of pre-Markan traditions.

Mark's motives are at least in part christological and soteriological. In the *zābâ* narrative there is a focus on the saving faith of the woman and on Jesus as God's eschatological messenger with divine healing powers. Similarly, the handwashing story, in Mark's view, emphasizes Jesus's superiority over other Jewish teachers and his authority to interpret the divine word, taking it beyond previous limitations, eventually breaking out of—or at least expanding—ethnic limitations.

The question of Scripture versus tradition was certainly a live issue toward the end of the Second Temple period. Although Mark makes use of this opposition in his narrative framework for general purposes, the validity of biblical commands over against recent innovations or interpretations does not seem to be his prime concern in the handwashing story, since it plays no role in the subsequent interpretation. It only serves as a rhetorical tool. Mark's categories are blunt, and the fine points would not have been comprehensible for his gentile audience, except for a general assurance that they were in fact following the divine word in spite of not accommodating themselves to a Jewish lifestyle. At an earlier stage of tradition, however, Scripture against halakah could have been a main focus. Just as the purity issue in the story of Jesus and the *zābâ* would have been obvious to Greek-speaking Jewish readers at a pre-Markan level, the finer points in the traditions behind Mark 7 regarding halakic interpretation and conflicts between Scripture and tradition would have been of relevance to a pre-Markan audience. To claim the priority of Scripture over tradition would have been of prime importance in pre-Markan traditions, assuring early Christ-believers of Jewish heritage that their non-observance on a number of halakic issues was justified by the example of their master in accordance with the Jesus tradition. The priority of Scripture over against halakah also continued to be of utmost importance in later Matthean communities, in which conflicts with emerging rabbinic Judaism were accentuated.

As for Jesus's own motives, we may doubt that the Scripture versus tradition issue was the most important. It certainly belonged within the context of competing groups with opposing interpretations, and accusations of neglecting the Torah in favors of one's own ideas could always be of good value in a debate. We might even think of Jesus using a Sadducean or Galilean argument: "let's not accept this new extension of defilement from the outside—ritual impurity primarily goes the other way, it comes out of the body."[81] Jesus would then, however, have given this a wider application. And as elsewhere, his motives would probably have been tied to his eschatological kingdom vision, and the priority given to marginalized and vulnerable social categories. Inclusion of the periphery is a marked characteristic of Jesus's project of restoration. The tendency to portray Jesus as giving priority to the poor and liminal dominates the Jesus tradition to such an extent that it is difficult to dismiss. In the *zābâ* narrative, concern for one of the most vulnerable among the impurity bearers must be considered a plausible explanation on a historical level. Jesus's attitude to purity issues could profitably be understood as expressing the relative priority of social action in favor of the poor and needy in view of the eschatological restoration of the people, which provided a framework for his activity. The handwashing incident could be read into such a context, too. Jesus would then represent the rural and the poor, who could not afford discarding foodstuffs or compromising social fellowship because of expanded interpretations of purity rules.

Although we have suggested that the question of Jesus's authority belongs to Markan or pre-Markan Christology, it may in part go back to Jesus.[82] Historically, however, it is reasonable to posit that Jesus regarded his authority as eschatological rather than personal, that is, as inherent in his kingdom vision rather than in his own person. It thus had to do with the

---

81. Cf. Furstenberg's (2008) interpretation.
82. Mark repeatedly describes Jesus as one with ἐξουσία (Mark 1:22, 27; 2:10; 11:28, 29, 33; cf. his authorization of the disciples in 3:15 and 6:6).

relative priority of inside versus outside, of periphery versus center, and of common people versus establishment. These are, however, suggestions that go beyond the scope of the present chapter and need further corroboration.[83]

---

83. I have pursued these issues further in Kazen 2013a.

10
Skin-Disease Contamination and Exclusion: How Not to Reconstruct History for a Good Cause

> Certain types of skin disease were regarded as impure conditions, not only in Israel but in many parts of the ancient world, and people with skin disease were often isolated or excluded. This chapter discusses recent attempts to downplay skin-disease contamination and exclusion in early Judaism. Based on evidence from the Priestly legislation, Qumran, Josephus, and the gospels, I argue that people with skin disease were understood to transmit impurity by contact and were therefore isolated or excluded from human habitations. The fight against tendentious portrayals of Jesus against a dark foil of Second Temple Judaism is not served by improbable historical reconstructions.

Ancient texts need to be interpreted in view of their historical contexts, but reconstructing contexts is not always easy. More often than not, sources are insufficient and evidence is patchy. This forces us to make inferences and fill in gaps. As a result, historical reconstruction—by which we can never mean anything but suggesting a plausible scenario—will always remain a hypothesis, but as such it is not enough for it only to be *possible*. A plausible hypothesis must also be *probable*, in the sense that it explains more of the available evidence in a simpler way than competing alternatives do. If this is not the case, a hypothesis must be doubted. That is, at least, how history is usually carried out except when there is a definite agenda behind. Admittedly, the appraisal of what distinguishes probability from possibility is subject to human judgment, which can never be entirely free from bias. Scholars can, however, and do, indeed, present and weigh arguments

---

Thanks to Hannah Harrington and Yonatan Adler for reading and commenting on the draft.

before each other, submitting our subjective assessments to intersubjective discussion, in order to detect blind spots and avoid wishful thinking.

In the present chapter, I attempt this, on the issue of how to reconstruct the social status of people with skin disease (צָרַעַת/λέπρα, often translated as "leprosy")[1] in Jewish societies at the end of the Second Temple period. The common view has been that during the Second Temple period, people with skin disease were quarantined, isolated, and not allowed access to settled areas, since they were believed to transmit impurity by contact (touch) and by presence under a common roof ("overhang"). This understanding is based on Lev 13–14, Qumran texts, Josephus, and some New Testament gospel texts, as well as on rabbinic rules. Recently, however, such an interpretation has been questioned. In a 2018 *Journal of Biblical Literature* article, Myrick Shinall claims that "lepers had relatively unhindered social access," and some other New Testament scholars, such as John Meier, Amy-Jill Levine, and Ben Witherington, have downplayed the evidence for contamination by touch and for isolation.[2] Arguments often focus on what is perceived as a *lack of evidence* for the exclusion of people with skin disease from Jewish society during the first century CE.

This is often for a good cause: to stop New Testament scholars from using historical data for ideological reasons, in this case from portraying Jesus positively by construing Judaism negatively. Shinall objects to the picture created by New Testament scholars of Jesus interacting with people affected by skin disease "within a purity system that socially isolated lepers" and argues that "neither the gospel texts nor the available background information on Second Temple Judaism demands that we read the leprous characters of the gospels as outcasts."[3] He wants to expose scholarly tendencies to portray Jesus positively by construing Judaism negatively.

While I support any combat against stereotyping and also find a value in submitting traditional interpretations that have become established

---

1. Neither צָרַעַת nor λέπρα refers to Hansen's disease (what we generally mean by *leprosy* today), but to a variety of skin ailments with particular symptoms and generally shunned in the ancient world. For discussions regarding terminology and diagnosis, see Hulse 1975; Wilkinson 1977; 1978; Kazen 2010a, 98–99.

2. Shinall 2018, 915; Meier 2009; Levine and Brettler 2011; Levine and Witherington 2018.

3. Shinall 2018, 916.

truths to close scrutiny, I do not think that a possible but less probable revisionist interpretation of the evidence is helpful. It may, in fact, do harm to the cause. I agree with Shinall that "being impure does not per se imply being a pariah,"[4] but the issues at stake are broader and more complicated than whether people with skin disease were treated as social outcasts. If, in fact, they were considered ritually impure, how were they thought to contaminate, if not by physical contact? And if, as Shinall concedes, there was some "social exclusion," how do we envisage the physical exclusion or isolation of people with skin disease in the Jewish areas during the early Roman period? Must we not assume that the degree to which restrictions applied in a particular context varied?

The Priestly Legislation

According to Lev 13:45–46, a person with skin disease is called impure (טָמֵא) and must wear torn clothes, have disordered hair, cover the upper lip, cry "impure, impure," and live alone, outside the "camp" (מַחֲנֶה). In addition, Num 5:2 commands the Israelites to put out of the camp anyone with skin disease, discharges, or corpse impurity.

Shinall claims that Lev 13–14 says little about the social condition of people with skin disease. Rules focus on diagnosis. He claims that there is neither a prohibition against contamination by touch nor evidence for the exclusion of people with skin disease from Jewish society.[5] Meier similarly argues that Lev 13–14 has no prohibition against touching a person with skin disease and does not state that touch renders anyone impure.[6] Levine and Witherington say that the passages "are vague at best about the transmission of impurity by touch," and in *The Jewish Annotated New Testament* Levine states that "no Jewish law forbids touching a person with leprosy."[7] Shinall points out that, although rules about "leprous" clothes and buildings indicate defilement through contact, this is never explicitly said about persons with skin disease. The rules about clothes and buildings, however, are generally considered supplementary, second-

---

4. Shinall 2018, 917.
5. Shinall 2018, 918.
6. Meier 2009, 411.
7. Levine and Witherington 2018, 140; Levine and Brettler 2011, comment on Luke 5:13; cf. Aaron M. Gale's comment on Matt 8:3 in the same volume.

ary to the main laws of Lev 13–14.⁸ Which is more likely, that the idea of contact contagion regarding people with skin disease was triggered by, and developed from, rules about clothes and houses, or that these secondary instructions attest to underlying assumptions regarding defilement by physical contact? What would otherwise be the point of isolation during periods of examination (Lev 13:1–44); the instruction (13:46) to live alone, outside the camp (בָּדָד יֵשֵׁב מִחוּץ לַמַּחֲנֶה); the command to call out "impure, impure" (טָמֵא טָמֵא);⁹ and the command to the purifying person to stay out of his "tent" for seven days (Lev 14:8)? And why does the priest need to go outside the camp to examine the healed person and perform the bird rite (Lev 14:2–9)? These restrictions are extremely difficult to explain if contamination by touch or by being present in the same room as a person with skin disease was not considered problematic to begin with. The only reasonable alternative is to assume that to the Priestly writers the idea of contact contagion was taken for granted, a cultural assumption. In fact, this is supported by comparative evidence, as we shall see, and the text was understood from such assumptions by all who received it, at every stage of interpretation.

All of the mentioned authors argue in one way or another against contamination by touch by referring to the examining priest having to touch people with skin disease.¹⁰ I find the argument confusing because examination is enjoined by the law, and only afterwards is the person's

---

8. Milgrom 1991. Milgrom (808) talks of "an editorial interpolation," and based on form, structure, contents, and style he argues (886–87) for a second hand responsible for the section on mold on fabrics (Lev 13:47–59) and a third hand (which Milgrom thinks is H) for the section on "leprous" houses (14:33–53). Hieke (2014, 477–78) provides a brief overview of various scholarly views on the composition of Lev 13–14, including Seidl, Milgrom, Staubli, Elliger, and Nihan. See also Nihan 2007, 270–77.

9. Should טָמֵא טָמֵא be understood as a warning or as a lament? Although the latter interpretation does occur in the Babylonian Talmud (b. Nid. 66a), the warning aspect (to avoid contamination) is also found in the Talmud (b. Mo'ed Qat. 5b), as well as in the Sifra, and the Targum. See Milgrom 1991, 804–5; Maccoby 1999, 125–26. Both Milgrom and Maccoby understand this interpretation of the call as a cry of despair to reflect a softening of ostracism and an advance of the social status of people with skin disease in later times. On isolation during periods of examination, see further below.

10. Shinall 2018, 919; Levine and Witherington 2018, 140; Meier 2009, 412–13, referring to "the rigorous inspection of a leper by a priest demanded by the fragments of the *Damascus Document*" (413).

ritual status declared.¹¹ The whole point of the examination is to decide whether the person with skin disease should be allowed close interaction with others.

Regarding the instructions of Lev 13:45–46, Levine and Witherington suggest they were not in effect, since "Leviticus is speaking of proximity to the wilderness sanctuary, not of living somewhere between Galilee and Samaria."¹² Shinall says that the "camp" assumes the exodus setting and suggests that a strict reading could have taken the rule to apply only then, while more expansive readings could interpret the camp as Jerusalem, or even as any Jewish settlement. He points out that a number of questions remain unanswered, such as how to define a settlement and its boundaries. These are the very sort of questions that later rabbis asked themselves, questions that triggered later halakic elaborations of skin-disease rules.¹³ For purposes of historical interpretation, however, we do not need to grope completely in the dark. Some of the basic questions of textual and historical research go a long way. How are these texts structured? What is their context? When did they originate? What people did they address, what issues were assumed, and what issues needed explication for the addressees?

Let us take a brief look at the argument of Lev 13. It immediately reveals that exclusion and contact contagion are assumed. Leviticus 13:4 instructs the priest to shut up the suspect person for seven days. This period of isolation is analogous to the seven-day impurity or purification period for many dischargers (Lev 12; 15) and for the corpse-impure (Num 19). There is arguably a risk that, if this will prove to be a case of genuine skin-disease impurity, the person will contaminate others, and thus this person needs to be isolated until the opposite is proved. Even then, people have to wash their clothes to be considered fully clean (13:6; cf. 13:34). This indicates that people were regarded as being in some intermediate state of impurity during their isolation. According to Lev 13:9–11, certain changes in the skin during the quarantine period result in the person being declared

---

11. The priest admittedly also examines quarantined persons and people who have been healed, before pronouncing them clean. Although we might assume the priest to touch these people, the text never says this. In any case, priests were understood to be exempt from certain rules because of their divinely appointed tasks (cf. service on the Sabbath).

12. Levine and Witherington 2018, 470.

13. A quick look at Mishnah Nega'im suffices to illustrate this point.

impure. Then the priest must not isolate (סגר) that person. This, of course, does not mean that the impure person now may walk about anywhere, but implies that mere isolation does not suffice; more serious restrictions now apply, spelled out further in Lev 13:45–46.

The purity laws of Leviticus most probably received their present form during the early Persian period, early fifth century, many would say, as part of the establishment of a priestly and scribal elite in Achaemenid Yehud. The *narrative framework* is the wilderness camp. The *referent* is Jerusalem, as the only city to speak about in this small-scale vassal temple state. In due time there would be many towns and cities under the influence of Priestly purity law, and interpretation would go in different directions, as history shows. But a basic stance toward people with skin disease is historically undeniable as witnessed by Priestly law: they should stay outside the city, live alone, indicate their state by asocial behavior and/or behavior similar to mourning practices, and shout out their condition.

The complements in Numbers appear maybe a half-century later. While Num 5:2–4 is often discussed as a "stricter" tradition, it makes little difference for people with skin disease, who already according to Leviticus are assumed to live alone, outside the town. The fact that they are singled out for isolation together with other impure categories (dischargers and the corpse impure), for which there are numerous contamination rules, strongly suggests that they are understood to contaminate in a similar way. It takes some credulity to think that people in early Second Temple society did not understand these categories in an analogous way. Questions about how these people "are to migrate with the rest of the Israelites when it is time to move the camp"[14] betrays a lack of understanding of the literary genre, theological purpose, and historical provenance of this text. Even if various traditions may have had previous lives of their own, this particular combination is for people in early Persian-period Yehud. They would not bother about the logistics of past mythical migrations. They would, however, bother about what to do with their impure people, whose conditions would probably, in most cases, be of transient character. This applies to skin disease, too, as is evident from the numerous instructions about diagnosis.

Which is the most probable scenario? Let us consider the options. (1) The Priestly writers spend two chapters on historical curiosities: nei-

---

14. Shinall 2018, 920.

ther the elaborate instructions for diagnosis and purification nor exclusion were applied at the time of writing, but these are historical memories from the exodus. (2) The Priestly writers introduce new procedures for diagnosis and purification, as well as new rules about exclusion, in Achaemenid Yehud. (3) The Priestly writers introduce or codify new or more elaborate procedures for diagnosis and purification in Achaemenid Yehud, assuming some basic previous practices of isolation and/or exclusion of people with skin disease.[15]

The first alternative requires a naive view of history (traditions from the exodus), a deficient understanding of literary features, and a lack of respect for the historical context of the text (how and for whom was this text written and received the way it was?). The second alternative is unlikely, because of the discrepancy between the detailed rules for diagnosis and purification, and the lack of corresponding instructions for isolation and exclusion, while at the same time, isolation is clearly required. The third alternative provides explanations for all of the caveats and arguments the skeptics voice.

Comparative Evidence

There would be no reason for us to expect narrative material from the Deuteronomistic History (Naaman; the four men outside Samaria; Uzziah/Azariah; see 2 Kgs 5; 7; 15; cf. 2 Chr 26)[16] to provide any elaborate information about methods of purification, details of contamination, or length of isolation or exclusion. It would be anachronistic to expect such texts to reflect Priestly legislation; only those who believe the Priestly rules were actually delivered by Moses would come up with such an idea. Nor should we expect pentateuchal narrative traditions, such as that of Moses before Pharaoh and Miriam's punishment, to reflect Priestly legislation in detail. Both stories employ the same expression for the skin suddenly turning white: "leprous" like snow, מְצֹרַעַת כַּשָּׁלֶג. This expression does not belong to the Priestly technical terminology for diagnosing skin disease, where white color is represented by לָבָן. The Miriam story affirms a general expectation of exclusion and thus supports the Priestly legislation by reference to popular legend. Shinall argues that if Miriam was healed immediately

---

15. Cf. Nihan 2013; Kazen 2015b = ch. 4 in this volume.
16. These narratives are often referred to in the discussion.

she could have been admitted to the camp at once after having undergone the appropriate rituals, instead of staying outside for seven days, which shows this story is inconsistent with the purity laws.[17] It is not of a piece with the purity laws, however; it simply belongs to a different genre with a different purpose. What do we expect?

Except for the story about Moses's hand and the Naaman story, which belongs to the Elijah-Elisha cycle, in which ritual impurity is hardly an issue (think only of Elisha's bones [2 Kgs 13:20–21], and Naaman is a non-Israelite anyway), the narrative mentions of skin disease indicate a possibly preexilic unspecified practice of exclusion. This is as much as we can say about preexilic skin disease rules, but to argue from this that it "shows the inconstancy of this exclusion throughout the biblical tradition,"[18] as does Shinall, is confusing. The point of the Priestly purity legislation is precisely to bring together and systematize previous incongruent or diverse practices. Herodotus (*Hist.* 1.138) claims that the Persians expelled people with skin disease from towns.

> One who has the "leprous" [λέπρην] or white [λεύκην] disease, he may neither come into [κατέρχεται] a town [πόλιν], nor mingle with [συμμίγεται] the other Persians. They say one who has this [disease] has sinned against the Sun. Many expel [ἐξελαύνουσι] every stranger who has contracted this [disease].[19]

While the historical accuracy of Herodotus's reports in general can be discussed,[20] he provides here a description from the fifth century BCE—approximately the same time as the Priestly purity rules were shaped or redacted—of a general practice of expelling people with skin disease from towns and prohibiting them to mingle with others, which is congruent with similar practices known from other contexts. Jacob Milgrom refers to a Mari letter, a Šurpu incantation, and a Babylonian *kudurru* (boundary-stone) inscription, and Jean Nougayrol identifies a number of such boundary-stone inscriptions from the time of Nebuchadnezzar I, referring to *išrubu* (skin disease) covering the body of a person, who is driven out of a city and stays outside its walls so that others should not approach

---

17. Shinall 2018, 925–26.
18. Shinall 2018, 926.
19. Unless otherwise indicated, all translations are mine.
20. See, e.g., the essays in Munson 2013.

him.²¹ We are now talking of ancient West Asian evidence from the late second millennium BCE. There are simply no good historical reasons to doubt that various kinds of restrictions for people with skin disease had been common in this region for centuries. At the point in time when the Priestly purity rules were formulated, we have reason to consider Persian influences, too, in particular on some of the purification rites (smearing of body parts; Lev 14:14–18, 25–29).²² There is also reason to assume some innovative traits in the Priestly elaboration of rules for diagnosis, as all of this becomes part of priestly claims for control in an emerging temple state with a (re)new(ed) cult. However, the basic notion of expelling people with skin disease and avoiding contact with them was simply assumed, as it was long-standing tradition. This easily explains why the rules in Lev 13–14 do not elaborate on such matters.

That exclusionary practices were century old is actually acknowledged by Shinall, but the lack of "a uniform application of Levitical regulations throughout Israel's history" is appealed to in order to cast doubts on first-century CE practices, as he claims that "exclusionary practices varied over time and space and are counterbalanced by references to lepers' integration within society."²³ As we will see, there is little counterbalance, and the argument is flawed from the beginning, as it assumes Priestly purity laws through Israel's history. In actual fact, the purity laws stand at the beginning of Second Temple Judaism, and although interpretations and implementations varied, the question is whether there is continuity between the Priestly law and real-life practice during the first century CE.

If isolation of people with skin disease, as expressed in varying practices of exclusion and avoidance, was part of a broader culture for centuries, is it reasonable to question the impact of Priestly rules, based on variations or silences in Deuteronomistic or pentateuchal narratives? Should we not give more weight to texts from the latter part of the Second Temple period and look for a probable trajectory from the Priestly legislation to rabbinic halakah?

---

21. Milgrom 1991, 805, 818, 911; Nougayrol 1948, 203–8. Although the exact meaning is debated, the term seems to refer to some type of skin disease, corresponding to צרעת.

22. Kazen 2015b = ch. 4 in this volume.

23. Shinall 2018, 928–29.

Evidence from Qumran

Textual evidence relevant for the late Second Temple period is relatively simple to list. First we have texts from Qumran. The Temple Scroll prohibits any person with skin disease (כול צרוע) from entering the temple city (11Q19 XLV, 17–18) and envisages separate places east of the city, one for people with skin disease (מצורעים) and the others for dischargers and semen emitters (XLVI, 16–18). Similarly, ordinary cities[24] are supposed to seclude people with skin disease, genital dischargers, menstruants, and parturients (XLVIII, 14–17). Shinall points to the fact that it is not entirely clear whether people with skin disease are envisaged as isolated within the cities or outside (בכול עיר),[25] but I think the command "not to *enter* your cities" can hardly be misunderstood (לוא יבואו לעריכמה). Whether, when, where, or to what extent this ideal was implemented we do not know. At least with regards to genital dischargers, it seems to have been somewhat utopian.[26] The point, however, is that exclusion or isolation of people with skin disease is assumed. The discussion is about how to apply it. Meier finds the Temple Scroll more or less irrelevant for the question of contamination by touch, because it does not directly address this issue, but assumes the defilement of whole cities, he says, by the presence of people with skin disease.[27] This is a literalist reading of sorts. What understanding of contamination should we expect from authors and readers in a text describing the isolation of people with skin disease together with the isolation of various types of genital dischargers, when the latter categories are normally understood to contaminate by touch or by physical contact? What manner of contamination would we expect people to have assumed from impurity bearers who had to be isolated outside the town and were not allowed to return to their homes until all levels of the appropriate purification rites had been performed? What conclusions would we expect people to draw from the secondary rules about leprous houses that contaminated

---

24. The formulation (וכול עיר ועיר) really indicates "each and every city," as Yonatan Adler (personal communication) points out.

25. Shinall 2018, 923.

26. For discussions about the Temple Scroll's instructions in relation to first-century CE practice, in particular in relation to the practice of first-day ablutions, see Kazen 2010c, 91–111; 2015c = ch. 8 in this volume.

27. Meier 2009, 477 n. 218.

people who entered them? We know that from the rabbis: contamination by touch and by overhang. But both manners of contamination are indicated by first-century texts, too.[28]

In 4QMMT, which is usually dated to the middle of the second century BCE,[29] the authors argue with the recipients over how to apply instructions about skin disease in practice (B64–72). People purifying from skin disease should not "enter (any place) with holy purity" (B65). In the context, this most probably refers not to the temple,[30] but to pure food. They should stay outside their house for the seven days, according to Lev 14:8 (B66–67). This seems to be common ground for the authors and the recipients. The problem in the eyes of the authors is that the recipient group, or perhaps the general population, allow people purifying from skin disease to enter their houses and presumably eat pure food before the end of the purification period (B67–68). Exactly what this means is a moot point, but the authors seem to regard this transgression as unintentional. They recommend that the infringement is repaired by a חטאת sacrifice (B68–70) and explain that one must not eat sacred food until after sunset on the *eighth* day, when the final sacrifice is made (B71–72). If what their protest concerns is that some others do not wait until after sunset on the eighth day, then this seems to be a conflict concerning the exact interpretation of the stages in the purification ritual for people with skin disease. We know from later rabbinic texts how the rabbis discussed such stages and that they required the last step, the eighth-day sacrifice, before eating sacrificial meat (m. Neg. 14:2–3). Whether this corresponds exactly to the 4QMMT authors' taxonomy is not crucial for our purpose; in any case the rabbis did not seem to require sunset on the eighth day. The point is that beyond these disagreements on details, 4QMMT provides clear evidence of a general understanding

---

28. The rabbinic concept of overshadowing is more complicated and approximates that of corpse impurity (without becoming identical). Cf. Maccoby 1999, 141–48. The understanding of contamination from being in the same room would have been simpler during the Second Temple period. Cf. Kazen 2010a, 114–15.

29. For an overview of the various arguments and a discussion of the complexities involved, see von Weissenberg 2009, 15–25.

30. As Schiffman (1989, 248) suggests, reading the conjectural לבית (Qimron) as "temple." Other conjectures have been made, but since the text interprets Lev 14:8 (the purifying person should stay outside his tent), "house" is the best interpretative conjecture here; only that it refers to the purifying person's home, just as the biblical "tent" intended. See Kazen 2013a, 153–54, especially nn. 148, 150.

that people with skin disease were excluded and isolated according to the rules of Lev 13–14.³¹

In 4Q274, fragment 1 I, 1–II, 1, contamination by touch is explicitly discussed. The text focuses on purifying people and the need for various types of purifiers to keep separate during their periods of purification and neither mingle nor touch or be touched. The fragment first describes a person purifying from skin disease, who has to keep a minimum distance of twelve cubits from any dwelling-house,³² and it stipulates purification by water for all other impure people (presumably other purifying categories), who touch him (1 I, 1–4). The motivation for these instructions seems to be an interpretation of טמא טמא as "impure to the impure" (4Q274 1 I, 3).³³ The subsequent lines focus specifically on different categories touching others.

Shinall takes this fragment as contrasting evidence for "social intercourse between the leprous and nonleprous."³⁴ Meier again dismisses the text as "both fragmentary and ambiguous."³⁵ But as in 4QMMT, there is a focus in 4Q274 on the purity of food and a concern for impurity lasting *all* the days, presumably until sunset on the eighth day. While certain traits are particular to the people behind this text, the understanding of

---

31. Meier (2009, 447 n. 218) gives almost no attention to 4QMMT, which he regards as sectarian and more or less dismisses as irrelevant to the discussion, since "the precise question of an individual touching a leper is not raised."

32. Baumgarten (1995a; cf. Baumgarten 1999a) identifies the person in lines 1–4 as a *zāb*, while Milgrom (1995) thinks he is a person with skin disease. The call "impure, impure" suggests skin disease, unless the use of this phrase was extended and applied to dischargers as well. The short distance (12 cubits) would speak against a person with skin disease, who is supposed to stay outside any settlement according to biblical regulations, *unless* we assume the description to concern a person in the process of purifying from skin disease. This fits the text very well (Kazen 2010b).

33. Such an interpretation makes sense in the context of 4Q274, which arguably deals with contact between various categories of (purifying) impure people (cf. Milgrom 1995; Kazen 2010b). Some other texts from Qumran may also attest to such an understanding, e.g., when various impurity bearers are envisaged by the Temple Scroll to be kept apart not only from the clean but each category in separate places (11Q19 XLVI, 16–18; XLVII, 14–17).

34. Shinall 2018, 923.

35. Meier 2009, 412. After having discussed the problems, although not in depth, Meier (477 n. 218) concludes: "whether the text is relevant at all to our purpose remains debatable."

defilement by touch or body contact as valid for all types of impure people most probably reflects general presuppositions.[36]

Evidence from Josephus

Second, we have the evidence from Josephus. Anyone who denies or downplays skin-disease contamination by touch or contact has to labor hard to undo Josephus's clear statements. In his earliest work, *The Jewish War* (mid 70s or around 80 CE), Josephus mentions the exclusion of people with skin disease twice. The first mention is found in the midst of a description of the Jerusalem temple (*J.W.* 5.227): "For dischargers and 'lepers' [λεπροῖς] the whole city [ἡ πόλις ὅλη], and for women during their monthly period the temple [τὸ δ' ἱερὸν] was closed off [ἀπεκέκλειστο]." The second mention is similar in content, but is just an aside in an account of a Jerusalem population count by Cestius by counting Passover lambs, which is itself a digression in Josephus's (*J.W.* 6.426) description of the overthrow of Jerusalem. "Since neither for 'lepers' [λεπροῖς], nor for genital dischargers, nor for women in their monthly period, nor for any other defiled persons, was it allowed to take part in this sacrifice." In *Ant.* 3.261–262, 264 (93–94 CE), in a context of sacrifices, Josephus writes:

> He [Moses] expelled [ἀπήλασε] from the city also those afflicted by skin disease [λέπρᾳ] and those with genital discharge. And the women, whom the natural secretion came upon, he set aside [μετέστησε] until the seventh day, after which he allowed them to live at home [ἐνδημεῖν] as they were now pure. Similarly, it is also allowed for those burying a corpse to live at home [ἐνδημεῖν] after the same number of days.... The "leprous" [λεπροὺς], however, he completely expelled [εἰς τὸ παντελὲς ἐξήλασε] from the city, not to live together with [συνδιαιτωμένους] anyone and in no way different from a corpse.

Finally, we have a passage from *Ag. Ap.* 1.281–282 (94–100 CE), in a context where Josephus argues against Manetho's association of Moses and the Israelites with skin disease:

---

36. I have discussed this text first in Kazen 2010a,152–54, then suggested a reconstruction of the fragment and a full translation in Kazen 2010b, which has been well received. See Birenboim 2012; Wassén 2016b. Cf. also Holtz 2012.

> Those having "leprosy" [τοῖς γὰρ λεπρῶσιν] he has forbidden either to stay [μένειν] in a city [ἐν πόλει], or to live [κατοικεῖν] in a village [ἐν κώμῃ], but to live alone [μόνους περιπατεῖν] with their clothes rent, and the one who touches [τὸν ἁψάμενον] them or happens to come under the same roof [ὁμωρόφιον γενόμενον], he does not consider pure. And even if the disease is cured and he receives back his nature [i.e., natural condition], he [i.e., Moses] has proscribed some spring water purification rites, by washings and by shaving off all hair, and he orders performing many and all sorts of sacrifices and then to enter [παρελθεῖν] the holy city.

In order to argue that Josephus's evidence has little relevance for first-century CE practice, critics usually begin with his general unreliability and ideological bias. In the case of skin disease, skeptics focus on the passage from *Against Apion* and claim that Josephus exaggerates because he is defending Judaism against Manetho's accusations.[37] Meier says that Josephus's claims about defilement by touch and by being under the same roof are made "in the heat of the debate" and are absent from *Jewish Antiquities*. Although he suggests to leave the issue open, Meier in fact strongly insinuates that Josephus is either exaggerating or reflecting the first steps of a development later to be seen in the Mishnah.[38]

Levine and Witherington similarly blame the polemical situation in *Against Apion* and consider it an apologetic "gloss on Leviticus, say[ing] nothing about first-century practice." They even suggest that "Josephus demonstrates that not all, or even any, are banished"... "by indicating that people *do* live 'under the same roof' with those suffering from leprosy."[39] This can perhaps be argued from Thackeray's or Whiston's English translations ("live/s under the same roof with them"), but is more difficult from the Greek. Josephus actually says that Moses considers as impure one who touches or *happens to come under the same roof* as a person with

---

37. Shinall 2018, 921; Meier 2009, 412; cf. Levine and Witherington 2018, 141.
38. Meier 2009, 412.
39. Levine and Witherington 2018, 141. This is an amazing argument, considering that the authors find Josephus's "comment about forbidding leprous people to appear in public ... no more evidence of first-century practice than is Apion's own claims that the Jewish people are a leprous people" (141). (Apion was, by the way, not the one who claimed what Josephus argues against, but Manetho.) If Josephus's explicit statements have no relationship to historical practice, how can a different practice be indicated by subtle implication, based on questionable translation of the same author?

skin disease (τὸν ἁψάμενον αὐτῶν ἢ ὁμωρόφιον γενόμενον οὐ καθαρὸν ἡγεῖται).⁴⁰

Meier points out that, in *Jewish Antiquities*, Josephus does not mention contamination by touch.⁴¹ Shinall thinks *Jewish Antiquities* describes a more "limited exclusion" from Jerusalem.⁴² The aim is to question that contamination by touch and exclusion were commonly practiced during Jesus's time. I cannot understand how Josephus's statement in *Antiquities* that Moses "completely expelled [εἰς τὸ παντελὲς ἐξήλασε] the 'leprous' from the city, not to live together with [συνδιαιτωμένους] anyone" is less clear or more lenient than his statement in *Against Apion*. The differences all have to do with the context of his various statements.

In *Jewish Antiquities*, Josephus walks through the books of Moses, and his comments on various impure people all lead up to statements about their required sacrifices. Contamination by touch generally does not require a sacrifice, so why should he have mentioned that? In *Against Apion*, Josephus argues, as many have pointed out, against Manetho and thus brings up every possible argument against Moses and the Israelites being afflicted by skin disease. Hence we learn that exclusion concerns not only Jerusalem, but also other towns or villages (κώμη), and we are informed about contamination by touch and by presence in the same room

---

40. The word ὁμωρόφιος is admittedly used in the sense of "lodging under the same roof with," as in Lucian, *Phal.* 1.1 (καὶ μόνον οὐ σύνοικοι καὶ ὁμωρόφιοι τοῦ θεοῦ), or in Plutarch, *Quaest. conv.* 2.10 (οὐ μόνον ὁμεστίους οὐδ᾽ ὁμωροφίους ἀλλὰ καὶ ὁμοχοίνικας καὶ ὁμοσίτους τῷ πᾶσαν σέβεσθαι), and probably also in Strabo, *Geog.* 9.3 (ἀπὸ τῶν ὁμοτραπέζων ἀρξάμενον καὶ ὁμοσπόνδων καὶ ὁμωροφίων), but it also occurs with the simple meaning of "being under the same roof," while eating, visiting, or just happening to meet and talk to someone, as in Demosthenes, *Exord.* 21.118 (εἰ δὲ λαλῶν μὲν καὶ ὁμωρόφιος γιγνόμενος) and *Exord.* 18.287 (μήθ᾽ ὁμωρόφιον μήθ᾽ ὁμόσπονδον γεγενημένον εἶναι τοῖς πρὸς ἐκείνους παραταξαμένοις), and Antiphon, *Murder* 5.11. The last example motivates court proceedings against murder in the open air as follows: "first, that the jurors may avoid entering the same building (μὴ ἴωσιν εἰς τὸ αὐτὸ) as those whose hands are unclean [τοῖς μὴ καθαροῖς τὰς χεῖρας]: and secondly, that he who is conducting the prosecution for murder may avoid being under the same roof [ἵνα μὴ ὁμωρόφιος γίγνηται] as the murderer." Here is a vague implication of defilement by just being under the same roof as an impure person. Context is crucial for interpretation. In Lucian, ὁμωρόφιοι is paralleled to σύνοικοι, but in Antiphon, μὴ ὁμωρόφιος is paralleled to μὴ ἴωσιν εἰς τὸ αὐτό, and in Josephus τὸν ... ὁμωρόφιον γενόμενον is paralleled to τὸν ἁψάμενον αὐτῶν.

41. Meier 2009, 512.

42. Shinall 2018, 922.

(under the same roof). These are relevant details to mention in that particular context. In *Jewish War*, Josephus does not talk as explicitly about expulsion because his topic is different. When he talks about the Jerusalem temple, he differentiates between dischargers and people with skin disease, for whom the whole city is closed off, and menstruants, who cannot enter the temple area (*J.W.* 5.227). When he later talks of the Passover sacrifice, he merely lists the impure categories not allowed to take part (*J.W.* 6.426). Context does indeed provide a key to interpreting a passage.

My question to those who want to downplay or discredit Josephus's discussion in *Against Apion* is: For what reason does Josephus provide this picture of expulsion and contamination by touch and overhang?[43] Let us consider the options: (1) Josephus interprets the Bible, regardless of current practice; (2) Josephus exaggerates for apologetic reasons; (3) Josephus reflects practices after the fall of the temple, toward the end of the first century CE, which were part of rabbinic development but not current during Jesus's time; (4) Josephus reflects practices that were only cherished by the priestly elite to which he belonged; and (5) Josephus reflects fairly common practice in late Second Temple period Jewish society.

Let us take a closer look at the first option. Shinall argues that Josephus sets his discussion in the context of the exodus, without claiming it as recent practice.[44] This type of argument has been voiced several times before.[45] But a number of features are not from the biblical text. Josephus specifies both cities and villages, which is an interpretation of the biblical legislation, as are the specifications about contamination by touch and by coming under the same roof. Josephus rather interprets the Bible *in view of* current practice. The idea of contamination by touch can be assumed from Lev 13–14, and mechanisms of contagion may have been inferred from rules about other impurities. The idea of contamination by being under the same roof is reflected in Lev 14:8, which prohibits the person purifying from skin disease to enter his tent during the seven-day purification period and can be associated with the rule that a person becomes

---

43. Note that I do not imply the rabbinic elaboration of "overhang" or "overshadowing." See n. 28 above.

44. Shinall 2018, 922.

45. Maccoby (1999, 36) claims that Josephus's statement regarding menstruants in *Ant.* 3.261 refers not to his own time but to the time of Moses, and Sanders (1990, 160) says about the same issue that Josephus only reflects rules of the aristocratic priesthood. Regarding people with skin disease, however, Sanders (158) trusts Josephus.

impure by entering a leprous house (Lev 14:46–47). As Hyam Maccoby has pointed out, the notion of enclosed-space contamination is definitely prerabbinic.[46] Also, Josephus's claim that the purifying person must not enter Jerusalem before the eighth-day sacrifices is not in biblical law but attested in Qumran, although with a difference in interpretation, as we have already seen.

The convergence with evidence from Qumran also makes option two unlikely. Here we find decided views on where and how impure categories, including people with skin disease, should be isolated outside Jerusalem and other cities, prohibitions against touching, and evidence of competing views about at what point a person purifying from skin disease may enter his house. These views may have been stricter than general practice, but they assume that the details mentioned by Josephus in *Against Apion* belonged to general practice. Thus we cannot dismiss Josephus's evidence as apologetic exaggeration. The literary context does not require such an explanation, as we have seen.

Nor is it reasonable to suggest that these views were new at the time Josephus was writing, as in option 3. When historical evidence is patchy—which is more often than not the case with remains from antiquity—one way to do history is to reconstruct a plausible trajectory of development, based on the evidence we have. Meier discusses contamination by touch as a rabbinic development.[47] This is impossible; the development is much earlier, as we have seen. It is true, however, that rabbinic views on skin disease are stringent with regard to contamination, while they are lenient with regard to identification.[48] In an era without a temple and no possibilities to sacrifice as part of the purification process, this approach was functional: it prevented contamination and limited skin disease impurity to a minimum. Rabbi Judah discusses spots and skin color (m. Neg. 2:1), saying: "The shades of 'leprosy' [should be decided] for leniency [להקל], but not for stringency [להחמיר]." Except for two cases (described in m. Neg. 4:11; 5:1), any doubt regarding skin disease is considered pure (כל־ספק נגעים טהור). The rabbis also limited its effects. Expulsion only applied

---

46. Maccoby 1999, 143–44.
47. Meier 2009, 412.
48. Harrington 1993, 182, 198–213. For a somewhat different view, emphasizing leniency with regard to contagion and stringency with regard to ritual defilement, but discussing changes in rabbinic attitudes in the late Tannaitic and early Amoraic periods, see Feder 2012.

to walled cities (m. Kelim 1:7), and in another place (m. Arakh. 9:6) we learn that houses in cities not surrounded by walls in the time of Joshua ben Nun are not counted as houses in a walled city. Special arrangements for people with skin disease to attend synagogues with a special partition (m. Neg. 13:12; t. Neg. 7:11), also attest to this development, aiming at lenient practice under changed circumstances. It is this increased leniency that we find in the Tannaitic period, not the earlier stringency that Josephus reports.[49]

The fourth option is possible, but not probable. Appeals to elite practices are common among scholars who doubt that people in general would be willing, or could afford, to adhere to strict purity rules to the extent that Josephus and other people of priestly descent had wished.[50] This is part of a broader discussion concerning the general level of adherence to purity laws during the first century CE, for which there is little room here. I can only refer to the many studies during recent years that confirm widespread practicing of purity all through Judea and Galilee, not least attested by the distribution of stone vessels and *miqwā'ôt*.[51] We can discuss to what extent the views attested in texts found in Qumran represent sectarian interests or more general trends, and we can argue about what some of these texts assume as generally acknowledged. A discussion of priestly and other types of influence and efforts to have the people comply with particular interpretations and practices is very legitimate. However, a reconstruction of purity practices in the first century CE needs a plausible trajectory from preexilic practices and Persian-period purity rules to rabbinic interpretation, via the Hellenistic and early Roman periods. We must ask for the most likely scenario to explain all available evidence. In view of the trajectory that is possible to reconstruct from the combined evidence, it is historically unlikely that issues of expulsion and of contamination by

---

49. Shinall notes my arguments for rabbinic texts representing a post-70 CE development toward leniency (Kazen 2010a, 109–17) but finds it strange that I use material from the Mishnah for arguing an earlier date for contamination by touch. My argument, however, assumes the reconstruction of a trajectory that takes account of evidence from different sources and over a period of several centuries (cf. Kazen 2013a, 140–76). The problem with many arguments from scholars downplaying the role of purity in Second Temple Jewish society is that they treat various pieces of evidence in isolation.

50. Cf. Sanders 1990, 160; Wassén 2016a, 30–31.

51. A few important samples: Reich 2013 (although based on his 1990 dissertation); Magen 2002; Berlin 2005; Adler 2011; 2016; 2017.

touch or overhang were only concerns of a group of priests during the first century CE.

There remains the last option, that Josephus reflects what was fairly common practice in Second Temple Jewish society. This would represent a natural development of the skin-disease rules in Lev 13–14, together with the emphasis on exclusion in Num 5:2–4. Josephus's picture fits well enough with the available Qumran evidence; in fact, the Qumran evidence can be read as a party pleading against a general situation close to what Josephus describes. The gospel narratives mentioning people with skin disease are also simpler to read against Josephus's picture than against alternative scenarios. Finally, rabbinic halakic elaborations are usually easy to explain against the background provided by Josephus, when one considers the need to handle skin-disease impurity during a period when it became increasingly clear that the temple cult would not be readily resumed.

Skin Disease in the Gospels

The third group of evidence for purity practices at the end of the Second Temple period comes from the gospels. Behind many attempts to downplay the contagion and exclusion of people with skin disease lies a dissatisfaction with the way in which New Testament scholars often use purity rules and purity practices as a backdrop to gospel narratives, especially in their portrayal of Jesus as liberated and liberating from Jewish restrictions. It is important to keep watch over the way in which scholars of a particular confession portray "the other," both for ethical and historical reasons. For the same reasons, however, we should be careful not to disregard or diminish evidence just because it is wrongly used.

Shinall suggests that exegetes "need not, and indeed should not, read the stories of Jesus's healing of lepers in light of a general social exclusion of the leprous or a specific taboo against touching them." He argues that the evidence outside the New Testament is inconsistent, that the gospel texts at times offer counterevidence, and that reading exclusion into these narratives creates "insidious anti-Judaism."[52]

I have tried to show that the evidence we have is quite consistent if we place it along a trajectory from preexilic to rabbinic times. Practices could differ, and conflicting opinions on details of interpretation can be

---

52. Shinall 2018, 917.

found. But there are no grounds for questioning that at least from the Persian period, when the priestly elite shaped and organized earlier practices into a codified system, exclusion from settlements and contamination by touch, probably also by being in the same room as a person with skin disease, were standard views and practices. We can discuss whether at certain times and places they were compromised or disregarded, but the evidence is consistent. As for *social* exclusion in a grim and absolute sense, it perhaps depends on exactly what we mean. Considering that skin disease was not necessarily a chronic state and that people are portrayed to be isolated to a similar degree as dischargers, and also that there were degrees of isolation depending on the stage of disease and healing, there is no need to assume that ancient Jewish society abandoned their sick and let them die of starvation, and that Jesus came to rescue "the Jews" from such superstition. This type of distortion is, however, rarely found among serious scholars. As for contamination by touch, I think there is no way to come around that without evidence bending.

What about counterevidence in gospel narratives? Do these narratives provide evidence against social isolation? Shinall thinks so and accuses exegetes of "interpretive acrobatics,"[53] thereby putting himself at risk of being hit by the ricochet. He points out that the crowds following Jesus in Matt 8:1 do not react to the approach of a man with skin disease, and in Luke 5:12 the encounter takes place in a city. He even tries to argue from Mark's narrative that this happened in a populated area and questions that physical contact was prohibited in Galilee.[54] This disregards everything we know of the formation of the gospels and the ways in which Matthew and Luke use and redact Mark. In Matthew the crowds belong to the Sermon on the Mount, which is Matthew's literary construct, and they follow Jesus down from the mountain in 8:1, to provide a narrative bridge to the tradition about the man with skin disease, which Matthew has taken over from Mark. As soon as the author enters the Markan tradition, the crowd is no longer there. We are talking, of course, of the narrative world, which does not behave exactly like real ones, especially when traditions are loosely stitched together. As for Luke, his late first-century CE Hellenistic mind naturally places nonlocalized events in "a city," since the human, civilized world in which things happen basically consists of *poleis*, whether or not

---

53. Shinall 2018, 929.
54. Shinall 2018, 929–30.

they are identified. His understanding of details of law elsewhere seems fairly limited, or he finds them irrelevant for his audience, except for general law obedience as a marker of piety.[55] To distinguish between literary and historical aspects is basic. I cannot see what counterevidence these redactional items present.

Here is an issue, however: none of the gospel authors bothers much about purity in these narratives because their focus is elsewhere. The ways in which purity is read into some of the gospel authors' agendas could and should be criticized. If, however, we ask for first-century CE practice *before* the fall of the temple, we should *not* look for what the gospel authors try to *convey* but for the *traces* the tradition might have *retained* from a time before 70 CE. The Markan tradition contains several conspicuous traits that may or may not originate with Mark: Jesus's strong emotional reaction, the conspicuous language, the touch, and the "expulsion."[56] There are several possible interpretations, but the point is that the details can be very well understood against a general practice similar to that which Josephus describes.

The Synoptic Gospels narratives about people with skin disease arguably originate with the one tradition behind the Markan narrative. There is an issue, however, with Luke's second narrative, involving ten people with skin disease (Luke 17:11–19). Whether it can provide any additional historical information is a moot point. Some of the details make it difficult to believe that Luke constructed this from the Markan narrative. People with skin disease live together in a group, they meet Jesus at the entrance to the village, they stop at a distance, and Jesus does not touch them. This is probably a variant tradition with some details that reflect first-century CE practice.[57]

---

55. Luke's lack of attention to halakic detail can be argued from a number of examples: in 2:22–39 the purification of the mother after childbirth is described as a purification of both mother and child, and fused with the rite of the firstborn; the animal analogy in 13:15–16 is a popular or commonsense argument rather than a halakic one; and in 8:51–53 Luke—in contrast to Mark and Matthew—describes the scene to the effect that Jesus's interaction with the crowd takes place *inside* the house where the dead girl lies. Cf. Kazen 2010a, 120.

56. I have discussed this at length elsewhere (Kazen 2010a, 98–107). Shinall (2018, 930) says that Jesus shows no hesitation in touching the man in any of the three gospels. With regard to the Markan tradition, this can definitely be contested.

57. What is the alternative? Is it probable that people with skin disease were, in fact, allowed to dwell in towns and come close to others, they just liked to be in a

Shinall thinks I am inconsistent: "Details that counter the ostracism of lepers are secondary accretions, while details that confirm their ostracism constitute traces of the original tradition."[58] Again, however, he disregards the difference between what is obvious traditional material and what is merely redactional bridges. He also says that in spite of recognizing healing by touch as a motif in ancient miracle stories, I see "in the mention of Jesus's touching a leper an emphasis intended to highlight Jesus's rejection of purity restrictions."[59] However, I never claimed such a thing.[60]

Shinall refers to Papyrus Egerton 2 as evidence that early Jesus-followers did not understand people with skin disease to be isolated, because in this text the supplicant, at least according to Bell and Skeat's reconstruction, says: "Teacher Jesus, while traveling with lepers and eating with them in the inn I myself also became leprous" (P.Egerton 2, 1r, ll. 35–39).[61] Since unrestricted association with people with skin disease fits ill with evidence from many parts of the ancient world,[62] this reconstruction and interpretation was immediately questioned. By taking the participles [συν]οδεύων and συνεσθίω[ν] as referring to Jesus rather than to the supplicant, the meaning changes drastically. This could either be the case assuming deficient grammar (lack of definite article for the participles) or by reconstructing differently, as for example Karl Schmidt,[63] or

---

group, and Luke then added the distance and the setting at the entrance to the village, in order to emphasize respect? Or did he add all of this because in his time, Josephus wrote such exaggerated claims and Luke thought that this applied to Jesus's time, although it didn't? Why then would he place the person in 5:12 inside a city? All such questions become unnecessary if we just engage in a bit of redaction-critical work. For further discussion, see Kazen 2010a, 118–20.

58. Shinall 2018, 930 n. 44.

59. Shinall 2018, 930 n. 46.

60. I have said that "the available sources retain memories of Jesus as not conforming to, or being in tension with, the expansionist purity ideals, which were influential on the contemporary scene." I have also said that "it is highly unlikely that Jesus was directly opposed to, or attempting to do away with, Jewish law and tradition." See Kazen 2010a, 198.

61. Shinall 2018, 931–32. Shinall's rendering. Cf. Bell and Skeat 1935, 28.

62. See my discussion in Kazen 2010a, 124–26.

63. Schmidt 1936. Shinall (2018, 932) argues, referring to Tobias Nicklas, that Schmidt's reconstruction is too long for the fragment. This is a common opinion, but counting the letters and measuring the fragment proves this questionable. There are other lines in Bell and Skeat's reconstruction that would be just as long, and a glance

both. Shinall says that "Kazen, however, prefers this [Schmidt's] reading so that he can argue that Egerton does not provide evidence against the ostracism of the leprous."[64] This is misrepresenting my point. I was not arguing about Egerton as evidence against the ostracism of people with skin disease, I was asking whether Egerton possibly characterized Jesus's behavior toward people with skin disease in any way that could point to historical traces.[65] Regardless of how we reconstruct and interpret Papyrus Egerton 2, it carries little weight as an argument either for or against a commonly practiced exclusion of people with skin disease from towns in Jewish areas during the first century CE. Such arguments must rest on other evidence.[66]

One piece of possible counterevidence remains: Simon the "leper" in Bethany, who hosts Jesus for the dinner at which he is anointed (Mark 14:3; Matt 26:6). Shinall reads this as evidence that a person with skin disease could live in the town and socialize freely with others, and he dismisses the common suggestion that the epithet *lepros* reflects Simon's previous state, from which he had been healed.[67] Without evidence, we cannot know whether it was the literary-theological purpose of Mark to present Simon in this way, or whether he transmitted the designation from an underlying pre-Markan tradition. But regardless of which is the case, I find it hard to believe that Mark, who in 1:40–45 portrays Jesus as recoiling and hesitating before a person with skin disease, here assumes that an "active" *lepros* serves as the host unchallenged. It is even more difficult to understand why poor Simon is left unhealed in a gospel otherwise portraying Jesus as the supreme healer and exorcist of the messianic age. It is simply counterintuitive to think that Mark's recipients would not understand Simon as an ex-leper.

---

at the right margin in 1v and 2v reveals that it is uneven and has lots of space, which I have pointed out before (Kazen 2010a, 125 n. 205.

64. Shinall 2018, 932.

65. What I say is that whether or not we accept Schmidt's reconstruction in its details, there is the possibility, in one way or another, to read this fragment's description as referring to Jesus, thus characterizing a behavior that would, in retrospect, come to be understood as typical of him.

66. I would no longer argue strongly for the Egerton narrative reflecting an independent tradition.

67. Shinall 2018, 932.

History and Ideology

Shinall claims that the gospels "offer no compelling evidence for the social exclusion of the leprous" and that the evidential basis in general for such a practice is thin.[68] I think this can only be argued when pieces of evidence are studied in isolation, when issues of dating texts are disregarded, when textual tradition and redaction as well as literary context are neglected, and when no attempt is made to understand a developmental trajectory of thought and practice. Shinall thinks "references to the social situation of lepers are few and scattered widely over centuries" and that scholars construct a picture by assuming uniformity.[69] However, one does not need to assume uniformity to sort evidence along a trajectory; it is rather helpful with an eye for differences and an acknowledgment of competing views. And the evidence is not that disparate: most of it belongs to the Second Temple period and attests to evolving practices from the Persian to the early Roman period.

This is perhaps why Shinall, after having argued that there was no Levitical prohibition against touch, that evidence for exclusion is slim and scattered and uncertain, and that there is counterevidence that people with skin disease "had relatively unhindered social access," nevertheless in the last paragraph admits that "some level of exclusion of the leprous recurs throughout the sources."[70] Still, this does not prevent him from concluding that "the categorical isolation of the leprous does not appear in Jewish texts the way it is so often assumed and that we have very little information on what level of isolation, if any, lepers experienced in first-century Galilee."[71] Hence exegetes are called on to no longer presuppose the exclusion of people with skin disease in their interpretations. Maybe "categorical" means the idea that there would not have been any diversity, and maybe "the way it is so often assumed" includes the "insidious anti-Judaism" Shinall previously referred to and the supersessionist sentiments and interpretations that not only he but many of us combat. If so, it makes this type of interpretation of the evidence understandable, but still implausible.

---

68. Shinall 2018, 932–33.
69. Shinall 2018, 933.
70. Shinall 2018, 915, 934.
71. Shinall 2018, 934.

For dealing with the (very real) problem of overt and covert and at times unconscious anti-Jewish interpretations we need, indeed, critical awareness and historical consciousness, but we are not helped by revising history against what is a plausible interpretation of available evidence. The possible does not become probable just because the probable is at times misused. The solution to the problem of interpretations prejudiced against Judaism does not depend on whether, during the first century CE, people with skin disease were touched or not, whether they were avoided, isolated, or excluded, whether they were hated or loved, whether they were tolerated or not within settlements here or there. Anti-Jewish interpretations are based on faulty presuppositions of quite another sort and unacceptable regardless of which historical reconstructions they rest on and whether these are deemed the most probable.

Caution in interpreting evidence should always be exercised, and especially when results might be misused, but we should not refrain from historical interpretations and reconstructions just because evidence is not complete. Then we could just as well do away with history as a discipline. Diversity is found in all societies and not least in the Jewish region during the first century CE. But to suggest that people with skin disease did not contaminate by physical contact and were not excluded from human settlements, to discredit the assumptions of the priestly instructions and Josephus, to disregard the evidence from Qumran and the rabbis, in order to revise the background to the gospel narratives, is historically improbable. One should preferably not engage in such a reconstruction, not even for a good cause.

11
Purity as Popular Practice: Erasing the Anachronistic Divide between Household and Cult

Ritual purity is often seen as mainly of interest in relation to the holy and the cult, but historically people kept purity rules and engaged in purification rites in everyday life and far from the temple. This chapter discusses material (archaeological) evidence, textual evidence from the Second Temple period, and later rabbinic evidence for purity being practiced as part of ordinary life and not predicated on the temple and its cult. I argue that the temple-oriented view is not only wrong but also distorts our interpretation of related matters.

The notion that the ritual purity laws of Second Temple Judaism existed solely for the sake of the temple is a scholarly construct with little basis in reality. Unfortunately, this has not kept some from making it the central hermeneutical principle for their reconstructions of popular, Pharisaic, or tannaitic purity halakah.
—John C. Poirier, "Purity beyond the Temple in the Second Temple Era"

In this chapter I discuss the tension between views on purity being practiced for the sake of the temple or as part of everyday life. I will argue against the idea that Jewish purity practices during the Second Temple period were primarily focused on the Jerusalem temple cult and therefore of marginal concern for everyday life.[1] Such a view should long since have been abandoned because of the combined textual and archaeological evidence, which point in quite a different direction. Although texts as well as

---
1. In doing this, I follow up on a question I briefly mentioned but never pursued a decade ago in Kazen 2010c, 9–10.

archaeological remains are always subject to different interpretations, historical reconstruction is not equal to *any possible* hypothesis, but should always go for the *most plausible* one—plausible in comparison to its alternatives. It is a problem that this basic principle is not always respected in historical research where ideological bias is strong, and the topic of purity is an example of this. Besides discussing evidence-based historical arguments, we will also ask ourselves to what extent the scholarly tendency to limit purity practices to the cult reflects an anachronistically modern and secular understanding of religion as separate from life at large.

Background

The arguments I present are not necessarily new; many have been presented before in one shape or another, but here I would like to juxtapose material evidence, texual evidence from the Second Temple period, and rabbinic evidence. A seminal article was John Poirier's "Purity beyond the Temple in the Second Temple Era," published in 2003 in the *Journal of Biblical Literature*. Although it is frequently referenced, I think it deserves more attention than it has been given. The issue is of course much older than this, as it is tied up with a number of other questions: whether people actively avoided impurity; whether other people than "sectarians" or "extremists" observed particular purity practices, such as washing their hands before common meals or immersing after contact with various impurity bearers; whether people suffering from skin diseases classified as ṣāraʿat were generally avoided and barred from towns and villages; and whether menstruants were somehow isolated or restricted during their period.

The scholarly discussion about the extent to which the general population observed purity practices has been going on at least since the early twentieth century, when Adolph Büchler questioned the nineteenth-century view that rabbinic halakah basically reflected the Second Temple period and suggested many purity practices to be late Tannaitic innovations (Ushan period) and others, such as handwashing, to be extended customs with little influence outside priestly groups and a few other individuals doing it out of piety.[2] Three decades later, Gedalyahu Alon argued almost the opposite, that purity was not limited to priestly contexts and

---

2. Büchler 1968.

practiced for the sake of cultic matters only, but by a larger part of the population and especially scrupulously by the *ḥăbērîm*. He found it farfetched that Ushan sages should have invented numbers of new halakot, not rooted in earlier tradition. However, he did understand this wider observance as an extension of priestly law to the common people.[3]

Closer to our times we know the debates between Jacob Neusner and Ed P. Sanders. While Neusner described the Pharisees as a pietist pure food association, aspiring to priestly sanctity and applying priestly laws outside the temple to the meal, Sanders argued against such an "analogy between the altar and the common table," although he reluctantly ends up saying that the Pharisees made minor symbolic gestures towards living like priests.[4] Sanders offers an ambiguous picture, since on the one hand, against Neusner and others, he clearly affirms the observance of purity halakah beyond cultic (temple) concerns "for its own sake," far from Jerusalem, and regardless of any upcoming temple visits, and he argues that most Jews in Palestine kept the biblical laws.[5] On the other hand, against Alon and others, he repeatedly argues against the idea "that the Pharisees had imposed the halakah of priestly purity on all and sundry," by downplaying evidence for food purity as well as for general observance of menstrual seclusion, by commonsense arguments that certain practices would have been too complicated or too expensive.[6] Poirier suggests that Sanders "allows the view that he is challenging to determine his options" and "continues to regard the sanctity of the temple as the motivating principle behind purity in general."[7]

The last statement could probably work as an apt description of a number of scholars working on purity. Jacob Milgrom thinks the main problem with impurity is contamination of *sancta*, which logically follows from his understanding of impurity contaminating the temple from afar when people neglect to purify—a kind of airborne impurity.[8] Hannah Harrington defines purity as "a state of cleanness required for lay partici-

---

3. Alon 1977.
4. Sanders 1990, 176, 192, 232, 234. See, e.g., ch. 22 ("Summary") in Neusner 1971, 301–19.
5. Sanders 1992, 184, 188, 192, 218–19, 228–30, 236–37, 248.
6. Sanders 1990, 143–45, 149–51, 157, 160–61, 233. Even priests winked at the rules (135).
7. Poirier 2003, 248.
8. Milgrom 1976; 1991, 999. Cf. the criticism of Maccoby 1999, 165–92.

pation in the cult effected by physical purification rituals."⁹ Cecilia Wassén considers the "overarching function of purity regulations ... to prevent impurity from coming into contact with the holy; most importantly the temple in Jerusalem."¹⁰ Although she does concede that people far from the temple cared about purity and that *miqwā'ôt* and stone vessels attest to a general concern, and even references Morten Hørning Jensen's description of the development as "a purity wave," she also argues that Jews did not actively avoid impurity and that only priests, Pharisees, and Essenes, whose lifestyle was extreme, avoided unnecessary impurities.¹¹

Numerous scholars are part of this debate. Eyal Regev, for example, has argued that "non-priestly" purity was observed not only by Pharisees, but by many Jews during the late Second Temple period, and interprets this as a sign of an increasing individualism, in contrast to the priestly system, which focused on the community and the cult. Individual bodily practices filled personal spiritual needs that the institutionalized temple was unable to satisfy, especially for those living far away from Jerusalem.¹² What is interesting here, besides extending the pietism of Neusner's Pharisees to a broader segment of the population, is that Regev nevertheless assumes the cult as the default motivation for purity rules.

The double role of purity rules with regard to the cult and with regard to everyday life remains a riddle. Alon found both restrictive and expansionist tendencies in rabbinic texts supported by Scripture: on the one hand the rabbis extended holiness, including strict adherence to purity laws, to all Israel; on the other hand they interpreted laws leniently to make them livable. For Alon, the stricter laws were originally priestly. For Milgrom, this double role rather reflects different sources: the Priestly source, which

---

9. Harrington 1993, 2; cf. 2004, 8–12.
10. Wassén 2016a, 20.
11. Wassén 2016a, 20–22, 26, 31–32. Wassén's argument is theoretically possible with regard to the massive and widespread finds of *miqwā'ôt* (no one avoided impurity because purification by immersion was easily available), but it does not work with regard to stone vessels (not used primarily for purification but particularly for prevention, i.e., *avoidance* of impurity). Wassén's argument requires that stone vessels were only used by "extremists"—or that their widespread use was a matter of fashion rather than for purity purposes. The latter argument has been made, but is only reasonable for luxury stoneware, not for the large quantities of rough and fairly unsofisticated chalk-stone vessels. Cf. Zangenberg 2013, 551–54. For further discussion, see below.
12. Regev 2000a.

limits holiness to the sanctuary, and the Holiness source, which requires holiness of the whole land and its inhabitants.[13]

As already suggested, the question of purity for the sake of the cult or as popular practice is tangled up with a number of other issues. In order to visualize the problem and its repercussions I will oversimplify: if impurity is considered an issue only or mainly with regard to *sancta*, then there is little need for ordinary people (nonpriests) to observe purity practices except in preparation for temple visits and when separating priestly portions from foodstuff. There is little need to quarantine or isolate any impurity bearer except close to the temple, that is, in Jerusalem, and there is no point in avoiding contact with such people unless one is planning to shortly touch something belonging to the cultic sphere. For people outside Jerusalem, there is, in fact, most of the time no reason to avoid any impurities, or to purify after having contracted them, because one-day impurities will be long gone before the next temple visit. In sum, if purity was only kept for the sake of the temple, there would be no need to bother about impurity in everyday life. Impurity would just have been a ritual aspect of death and sex that must be kept apart from the the cult, the sphere of the holy and divine. The people who would have avoided light impurities must either have been priests or belonged to a sectarian group aiming to appropriate priestly practices for themselves, whether as a supererogatory measure to increase their own holiness or because of their interpretation of Scripture and halakah. The evidence, however, point in a different direction, to which we will now turn.

Material Evidence

Archaeological evidence for general observance of purity practices during the late Second Temple period consists mainly of stepped pools and chalkstone vessels.[14] When Ronny Reich first published on *miqwāʾôt* in the 1980s and 1990s, there was a heated debate about their identification and their spread. Reich counted around three hundred of them, half of them in Jerusalem and the other half elsewhere. The predominance of Jerusalem pools made it possible to still maintain the cult as the primary motivation

---

13. Alon 1977; Milgrom 1991, 42–51, esp. 48–49; 2000, 1711–26; cf. Harrington 1993, 3–5.

14. For a recent and accessible discussion and interpretation of the large number of finds of stepped pools and chalk-stone vessels, and their distribution, see Adler 2016.

for ritual purification. In his somewhat (but not sufficiently) updated version from 2013 of his original dissertation from 1990, Reich counts 459 stepped pools from before 70 CE, 206 of which are found in Jerusalem with surroundings and 16 in Galilee, the rest elsewhere. In addition he lists 74 pools from after 70 CE.[15] The shift in the evidence is marginal.

However, Reich did not seem to consider Yonatan Adler's dissertation from 2011, in which he lists 850 stepped pools in a detailed inventory. Of these, more than 600 are from the Hasmonean and early Roman period, about 170 in Jerusalem and almost 70 in Galilee.[16] Today the count is over 900. Adler points out the difficulty in distinguishing a pre-70 archaeological context from the subsequent period up to the Bar Kokhba revolt.[17] Hence hundreds of *miqwā'ôt* outside Jerusalem in sites not destroyed during the first war could and would have been in use up to the Bar Kokhba revolt. Of the stepped pools built after Bar Kokhba, most are found in Galilee and in the southern Hebron hills, where large Jewish populations were found.[18] Without getting bogged down by further details, we note Adler's conclusions: archaeological evidence does not indicate any decline in *miqweh* practices before 135 CE. For the period after the Bar Kokhba revolt evidence is inconclusive. Purifications in stepped pools continued, but we cannot know exactly to what extent the custom continued.[19]

Based on recent evidence, it is no longer a responsible claim that purification was mainly for the sake of the temple cult and a concern around Jerusalem. There is still a larger concentration of finds in Jerusalem and in Judea, but we cannot be certain about the reasons for fewer finds of *miqwā'ôt* in Galilee than farther south. Adler suggests that this could partly be due to less development in Galilee, with fewer salvage excavations, compared to the central part of Israel. Such excavations have provided a large number of the *miqwā'ôt* finds in recent years. Also, excavations in Galilee have often focused on monumental structures, such as potential synagogues, rather than on domestic areas. Moreover, Galilee

---

15. Reich 2013. Cf. Adler 2014a.
16. Adler 2011.
17. Adler 2017, 270–71. Pottery types from the last half of the first century continued in use during much of the second, and hardly any new vessel types were introduced between the wars. Archaeology's "Early Roman period" is often called the late Second Temple period, despite running into the first half of the second century.
18. Adler 2013, 244.
19. Adler 2017, 273.

had more access to natural spring water, and Adler speculates about natural water sources sometimes making *miqwā'ôt* less necessary.[20] Be that as it may, the finds we already have suffice to prove that ritual purification by immersion was a widespread practice in Galilee, too, and the archaeological evidence altogether attests to such practice close and far from the temple, before and after its destruction. Besides large *miqwā'ôt* in public space, close to the Jerusalem temple, stepped pools have been found all over the country in private homes as well as in shared courtyards, and in all types of settlements, from elite mansions in Jerusalem's upper city to simple settlements in the countryside. They appear adjacent to synagogues, to burial places, and to food production units, such as wine and oil presses.[21] All of this suggests that purification in water played an important role in everyday life for Jews in the early Roman period, with no signs of decrease before the Bar Kokhba revolt. While the loss of the temple had a great impact on Judaism in other regards, it seems to have changed little for the continuation of purity practices, at least for a good part of a century after the first revolt.

These are the facts on the ground, but they can of course be variously interpreted. There have always been skeptics against the identification of stepped pools as a *miqwā'ôt*, pointing out that they could have been used for a variety of purposes. Also, rabbinic requirements for valid *miqwā'ôt* (measurements, methods of filling, etc.) cannot be retrojected into the Second Temple period; that would be anachronistic.[22] While all of this is certainly true, storage pools generally seem to have much narrower steps, and industrial installations usually look quite different. Jürgen Zangenberg points to new technologies (plastering) in the Hasmonean period, when stepped pools first appear.[23] While this partially explains their construction, it says little of their motivation. Cecilia Wassén has recently questioned purity as a motivation for the construction of stepped

---

20. Adler 2017, 272.
21. Adler 2013, 244. Cf. Adler 2008a; 2008b; 2009. Whether the presence of *miqwā'ôt* in the vicinity of certain synagogues in the land of Israel indicate purification before prayer and/or Torah study is a debated issue. Cf. Reich 1995, 296; Adler 2008a. The *proximity* of a *miqweh* does not, however, necessarily prove the *purpose* of purifications and Adler is now hesitant to conclude too much regarding *miqweh* purification before synagogue prayer (personal communication).
22. Cf. Miller 2015, 32–103.
23. Zangenberg 2013, 543.

pools, basing herself on an understanding of their construction from the early first century CE and onward as triggered by Jewish encounters with Greek and Roman bathing culture.[24] Seeing stepped pools as "the result of the general bathing culture of the Greco-Roman world" and associating their emergence with new washing habits, Wassén says: "The presence of stepped pools demonstrate that people washed themselves in new ways; it does not reveal much about whether people *also* cared about purity."[25] I disagree with the last inference. We must ask ourselves why only Jews within the land of Israel were influenced to construct basins of this particular kind[26] and why none of their neighbors did. The answer is probably

---

24. Such views of the emergence of stepped pools are not new and not necessarily contrary to seeing purity as a motivation for their construction. For scholars associating the emergence of stepped pools with developments in bathing culture *and* purity observance, see, e.g., Adler 2018; Regev 2010. Cf. Fatkin (2019), who seems to agree with the Hellenistic origins, but suggests that the invention of stepped pools for purification was part of John Hyrcan's strategy to establish his authority in matters of religious practice and that, beginning with the elite, this mode of purification quickly spread among the population.

25. Wassén 2019, 58.

26. Diaspora Jews did not. Suggestions about *miqwā'ôt* in or near diaspora synagogues are not corroborated by material finds, even though proximity to water and various types of water installations may suggest purification of hands and feet; cf. Runesson 2001. The only candidate is the vaulted cistern right under a supporting wall in the building in Delos, believed to be a synagogue, which is far from sure. Although not a stepped pool, this basin has been suggested to have served the purpose of purification through immersion, the bather descending by a ladder; cf. Bruneau 1970, 490–91; Binder 1999, 306; Runesson 2001, 124. If true, this would be the only extant example of a ritual bathing pool in the diaspora and one of the oldest anywhere (second century BCE). The arguments against the cistern having ever been used for immersion are, however, overwhelming. The cistern lacked steps, was 4 m deep, and could only have been accessed from the area under the arch, which was a maximum of 32 cm above the original floor level. It was not a *miqweh*, and it cannot have been used for immersion. See Matassa 2007, 100–103; Trümper 2004, 575–78. Why, then, are there no diaspora *miqwā'ôt*? One possible explanation is that the use of stepped pools (as well as chalk-stone vessels) was thought of as a land-bound halakic practice, analogous to land-bound biblical commandments. Although a date toward the end of the Tannaitic period has been suggested for the *baraita* of the boundaries of the land of Israel (e.g., t. Shevu. 4:11), the delineated area roughly coincides (with some variations) with the distribution of *miqwā'ôt* and chalk-stone vessels before 70 CE. See Magness 2017. I do not agree with Magness (49), however, that a graded understanding of spheres of holiness implies that "cultic purity laws were originally highly localized to the Temple precincts." The underlying reasoning could be turned the other

that for ordinary bathing purposes people would prefer pools with drainage and/or smaller tubs that could easily be emptied, cleaned, and filled. If the emergence of stepped pools is understood as postcolonial mimicry of sorts, we need a plausible explanation for this peculiar hybrid. There is one, supported by slightly later rabbinic texts: purity concerns. One does not need to retroject rabbinic conditions or posit an exclusively ritual use in order to understand purification by immersion as the decisive factor behind the architecture of *miqwā'ôt*.

Even if one accepts the number and spread and locations of stepped pools as evidence for purifications being common, regular, and frequent, one could perhaps argue that most of these concerned necessary or permitted impurities related to menstruation, semen emission, sexual intercourse, and burial, as well as purification from long-term impurities caused by certain diseases. Such impurities were part of ordinary life and could not be avoided. What about other impurities that were contracted through physical contact with impurity bearers or other primary sources of impurity? Some argue that impurity was generally considered neutral to the degree that ordinary people did not even try to avoid it when they could; such scrupulousness was only for the extreme.[27] People in general did not bother to avoid impurity through contact with dischargers, people with skin disease ("lepers"), graves and burial grounds, corpse impurity from unrelated people, through overshadowing/overhang, or impurity from carcasses and from dead "swarmers" via hands, food, and liquid. Immersion was simple and would take care not only of necessary impurities but also of unnecessary contamination.

Behind such reasoning lies a spoken or unspoken assumption that purity was only or mainly understood to affect the cultic sphere, the temple. But the logic breaks down. If purity was only necessary for the sake of the cult, why bother in other contexts? If impurity was so neutral and innocuous that most people did not care about secondary contaminations, why bother about purifying from them at all—people would hardly be aware of contamination if they were not observant anyway. If such minimalist assumptions and arguments are accepted, we cannot assume that people in general purified themselves except from the most obvious and major impurities. And even then the motivation remains unclear. I would not

---

way around: that which was considered to defile people in general would have been regarded as even worse for the sanctuary.

27. This is what Wassén (2016a, 30–31) suggests.

deny that there were different levels of observance within the population. To the contrary, this is why we find dissensions, associations, and conflicts between various groups, accusing one another of flouting the law while the real issues are differences in interpretation and application.[28] But if major segments of the population neither avoided impurity nor purified, except when absolutely necessary for the sake of the cult, both the numbers and the distribution of *miqwā'ōt* seem a bit of an overkill. A minimalist and cult-centered view is neither intuitive nor plausible.

It becomes even more problematic when we bring chalk-stone vessels into the equation. These vessels, which were popular during approximately the same period, most probably had as their primary purpose to *prevent* contamination from spreading. The Torah's lack of mention of the status of stone vessels in contexts where contamination of vessels is discussed seems to lie behind the view that they were insusceptible to impurity.[29] The rabbis assume this,[30] and it is hinted at in the Gospel of John (2:6).

---

28. Disagreement regarding halakic interpretation and practice must be one important reason for the sharp conflicts between dissenting groups during the late Second Temple period, such as Sadducees against Pharisees, early Christ-believing groups against emerging rabbinic Judaism, and the people behind texts such as 4QMMT against other (mainstream?) Jews. When, for example, the covenanters accuse others of defiling the sanctuary by not separating pure from impure and sleeping with menstruants, this likely reflects differing views on contamination chains or how to count days (CD V, 7).

29. The main texts are Lev 11:32–36 and Num 31:22–23. The Leviticus text lists the type of vessels (כלים) that are defiled by a dead שרץ falling onto them and distinguishes between those vessels that can be purified by water and those that must be destroyed. The text from Numbers distinguishes between vessels of metal and other vessels: the former must be purified through fire *and* water, while those vessels that cannot withstand fire are purified by water only. Stone goes unmentioned in both texts. From a "nominalist" perspective, this could be interpreted as stone being unsusceptible to impurity, while a "realist" interpretation would probably notice generalising expressions like כל־כלי אשר־יעשה מלאכה בהם (Lev 11:32) and כל־דבר אשר־יבא באש (Num 31:23). Although no overt discussion regarding this particular issue exists in the ancient sources, according to my knowledge, this is plausible as a principled way of understanding the position seemingly taken by the covenanters and the opposite position taken by the later rabbis. Cf. the type of argument concerning halakic difference and development in Shemesh 2009; Kazen 2013a.

30. Several times in Seder Teharot, especially in m. Ohalot, vessels of stone are mentioned together with "dung" vessels and (unburned) earthen vessels (e.g. m. Ohal. 5:5; 6:1; cf. m. Kelim 10:1). The underlying assumption is that they do not contract impurity, although the discussions concern more complex issues, such as the circumstances

The sudden flourishing of a chalk-stone vessel industry during the early Roman period is a conspicuously Jewish phenomenon and only found in Jewish settlements in Roman Palestine. Many archaeologists and scholars have studied the chalk-stone vessels, beginning with Yitzhaq Magen, whose publications on industries at Ḥizma and near the Temple Mount are seminal, and Roland Deines, who brought the archeological and textual discussion together more than twenty-five years ago.³¹

In recent years some scholars have warned against drawing far-reaching conclusions from the presence of stone vessels. Stuart Miller thinks "stone vessel usage was a spin-off of the increased use of stone during the Herodian period for construction purposes" and that "scholars who regard stone vessels as Jewish identity markers may be overstating not only the origins but also the implications of stone vessel *usage*."³² Stoppers and lids could have been originally made of stone for other purposes.³³ Zangenberg mentions among other things decorated tabletops and sundials as "objects of the refined lifestyle of an increasingly prosperous elite that readily adopted elements of Hellenistic decorative language."³⁴ He does "not consider stone objects as general evidence for an all-encompassing quest for purity."³⁵ Wassén similarly claims that "stone vessels may have been popular for utilitarian reasons, as well as for fashion" and that "the presence of stone vessels does not necessarily indicate a concern for purity."³⁶ While I find certain criticisms, for example against the purported use of measuring cups for handwashing, relevant,³⁷ I think these critics

---

under which certain covered vessels protect contents against corpse impurity through overshadowing, in which case also clay vessels are included. The clearest *direct* early rabbinic evidence for the unsusceptibility of stone is probably from m. Parah, where the preparation of the purification water (מי נדה) in Jerusalem was thought to have involved children bringing water from the pool of Siloam in stone cups (כוסות של אבן) (m. Parah 3:2), priests beating up the burnt bones with stone hammers (מקבות של אבן) (m. Parah 3:11), and the water being mixed in vessels of stone (כלי אבנים), vessels of "dung," or (unburned) clay vessel (m. Parah 5:5; cf. the presupposition behind m. Mikw. 4:1), all of which are never explicitly mentioned in the biblical texts.

31. Magen 1994; 2002; Deines 1993.
32. Miller 2015, 174.
33. Miller 2015, 174.
34. Zangenberg 2013, 548, 553–54.
35. Zangenberg 2013, 554.
36. Wassén 2019, 56.
37. Cf. Miller 2015, 176.

somehow downplay the main issue, which is not about sundials or decorated items for the elite, but the fairly rough storage vessels and tableware that have been found in large quantities and hardly give an impression of being luxury goods. Their aesthetic quality is admittedly a matter of taste. We may assume that they required more labor than pottery, although we cannot know for sure.[38] Most importantly, however, these vessels, made of soft chalk-stone, were far from ideal for handling food and drink: they were porous and dusty, and it is difficult to understand their sudden popularity and distribution in Jewish areas during a limited period, unless there is some other plausible explanation.

I will not go into further detail concerning the study of stone vessels and their typology.[39] Suffice it to state that their production continued through the period between the wars, but almost ceased after the second revolt. From the period before that, vessels and fragments are found at virtually every excavated site, alongside pottery, of course. Chalk-stone vessels were widely used as a complement, and the most reasonable explanation is for purity purposes. The whole point of their use was to *prevent* the spread of impurity, that is, *avoid contagion* in everyday life. It is not reasonable to suggest that their use was limited to storing and eating *tərûmâ* only; again, their numbers and the distribution of the remains makes such a limited use quite unbelievable.[40] We must rather envisage their use by various impurity bearers in order to prevent the spread of secondary impurities to others, by purifying people in intermediate states, and by pure people in order to protect the purity of food and liquid in various contexts. To be more specific in our speculations we would need to outline, or rather reconstruct, possible types and chains of contamination during the period in question, which becomes increasingly difficult once we realize that the rabbinic "removes" are partially after-constructions and later rationalisations, that practices varied and were continuously evolving and reinterpreted, and that we need to discuss plausible trajectories of development of customs, logic, and halakic reasoning between the evidence from Qumran and other Second Temple period texts and Tannaitic elaborations. There is no room here to explore this further.[41]

---

38. Berlin (2014, 214) speculates that stone vessels were rather inexpensive.
39. Cf. Cahill 1992; Magen 2002.
40. Cf. Regev 2000a, 181–83.
41. Cf. my attempts on Sabbath, purity, and divorce halakah in Kazen 2013a.

From the material evidence, however, we must conclude that there are no indications of stone vessels being used exclusively by certain groups or sects. Hence the avoidance of impurity, and the aspiration of a high degree of purity for its own sake and with little or no relevance for the Jerusalem temple cult, cannot and should not be denied.

Textual Evidence

We should probably date the redaction of the purity laws of Leviticus to the early fifth century BCE, while the corpse-impurity laws in Numbers are part of late pentateuchal redaction in the fourth century BCE.[42] The purity laws in Leviticus certainly find their roots in earlier customs and local cultural practices, and it is reasonable to think that, for example, the lists of clean and unclean animals were formulated and expanded already during the exile, when previous customs were no longer ecologically and locally anchored, but needed support. But as I have discussed elsewhere, the evidence for preexilic purity practices only attests to very general conceptions, while many of the details in Lev 11–15 and Num 19 seem to reflect influence from Persian culture and religion (Zoroastrianism).[43] Hence we must contextualize the biblical purity legislation within Yehud, a vassal temple-state of limited scope, giving attention to the rebuilding of the Jerusalem temple and the restoration of its cult. The experiences of exile and return also nourished ideas of holiness, not only of the temple, but with regard to the population and the land—ideas that come to expression in the Holiness Code and complement and color the sacrificial and purity laws later in the fifth century BCE.[44]

In view of this context, it is conspicuous that so little in the laws about impurities of the body (Lev 12–15) reflects a concern for cultic contami-

---

42. Achenbach 2003, 499–529, 629–33. Corpse-impurity laws are seen as belonging to one of the last stages of redaction. The redaction of the purity laws of Leviticus should be dated within the framework of the composition of P, but before it was supplemented by Lev 4–5 and 6–7, around the middle of the fifth century BCE. Purity laws as well as sacrificial laws most probably have a prehistory in the form of checklists or priestly manuals. See Nihan 2007, 269–394, esp. 383–94, 614.

43. Kazen 2015b = ch. 4 in this volume.

44. For H in relation to P in general and the Holiness Code in relation to the first half of Leviticus in particular, see Nihan 2007, 395–575; cf. the seminal works of Knohl (1995) and Milgrom (1991; 2000; 2001), identifying H in the Pentateuch, although Milgrom's dating in particular is far too early.

nation. It is true that Lev 16 is all about purification of the sanctuary, and based on the literary structure of Leviticus it is possible to read previous chapters in light of this. A close reading of the texts, however, reveals astonishingly little in this regard and not enough for building global assumptions. Leviticus 12:4 prohibits the parturient to touch anything holy or enter the sanctuary before the second part of her purification period is over. Leviticus 13:46 orders persons with skin disease to stay out of the camp. Leviticus 14:8 allows such a person back in camp but not into his house during his seven-day purification period. Leviticus 14:45 orders stone and wood from a "leprous" house to be deposited outside the city. Leviticus 15:31 says, after the instructions regarding the *zābâ*: "Thus you shall keep the people of Israel separate from their uncleanness, so that they do not die in their uncleanness by defiling my tabernacle [*miškān*, tent, dwelling] that is in their midst."[45] In addition to these texts, the food laws add (Lev 11:43–45):

> You shall not make yourselves detestable with any creature that swarms; you shall not defile yourselves with them, and so become unclean. For I am the LORD your God; sanctify yourselves therefore, and be holy, for I am holy. You shall not defile yourselves with any swarming creature that moves on the earth. For I am the LORD who brought you up from the land of Egypt, to be your God; you shall be holy, for I am holy.

These verses are generally understood to come from a Holiness source, redacting the first part of Leviticus a half-century or so later.[46] The same applies to Lev 11:43–45, to Lev 15:31, and to the section in Lev 14 dealing with leprous houses. Leviticus 12 is often seen to be somewhat later than Lev 15, as it assumes the basic discharge laws. These Holiness source passages do little more than emphasize the need for the people to guard their holiness by avoiding impurity and purifying from it when contaminated. The temple is not the main motivation, however, but the holiness of God and the special status of the people. The two passages that mention the sanctuary are Lev 12:3 and 15:31. The latter has been used to argue for a concept of airborne defilement of the sanctuary from afar,[47] but I find it

---

45. Unless otherwise noted, Scripture translations in this chapter follow the NRSV; all other translations are mine.
46. See n. 44 above.
47. The idea is elaborated by Milgrom, but has been criticized. See n. 8 above.

more natural to interpret it in line with Lev 12:4. People must not enter the temple while unclean; that would be dangerous.[48] In the vulnerable context of a small, struggling temple-state, God demands holiness from the people, which includes purity, and especially not bringing impurity into the rebuilt temple that has just replaced a previous structure, which was destroyed because of the people's lack of holiness and obedience to the law. But this does not mean that purity laws had as their main focus to protect the temple. They rather reflect customary everyday behavior, codified as socioreligious law, interpreted theologically as holiness, and therefore particularly applicable in relation to the sanctuary.

To read the purity laws as temple-centered, one must first assume their temple-centeredness. In every regard, these instructions are about everyday life, about separation from impurity, avoidance, and purification when avoidance is not possible. They regulate customs for ordinary life: do not eat or touch carcasses of unclean animals and disgusting swarmers, purify vessels and protect food and liquid, purify after skin diseases and genital discharges, avoid contact contagion from all impurities and impurity bearers; if you cannot, purify immediately—these are the ways in which contamination spreads.

The alternative would be to read the rules about vessels, food, and liquids as irrelevant unless one was just about to separate *tərûmâ* and to understand the reason for expelling the person with skin disease to be protection of the temple, while others could freely interact with him or her without considering contagion. (For what reason the person with skin disease should then call out "Unclean, unclean" remains a riddle.) The elaborate discharge laws would not aim to make people avoid defilement by contact, but only to carefully identify an array of contacts that would disqualify a person from entering the sanctuary on that day. I find such an interpretation unsatisfactory.

What, then, about corpse impurity? The Holiness Code discusses it briefly with regard to priests. Priests may not touch a dead body except for close relatives (Lev 21:1–4), and the high priest is not allowed even that (21:10–12). This is motivated by the sanctity of the priest, but the

---

48. Lev 12:4 spells this out in order to make it clear that, even though the parturient's first period of impurity is seven days (fourteen after the birth of a girl), as in most other cases, she may not enter sanctuary until the lengthy second period is over. This needs to be pointed out. Purity is not for the sake of the cult, but holiness is extra sensitive to impurity.

possible contamination of the sanctuary is never made explicit. In Num 19, corpse impurity is spelled out in more detail, juxtaposed to instructions for the red-cow rite, which the priestly authors have somehow subsumed under the *ḥaṭṭ'at* sacrifice (Num 19:9). Here it is clear that corpse impurity concerns everyone and requires purification by purification water (*mê niddâ*). The person who neglects this remains impure (Num 19:12, 13), and his *nepeš* shall be "cut out [*nikrətāh*] from Israel [19:13]/the midst of the congregation [19:20]." The motivation is that "he has defiled the tabernacle of YHWH" (*'et-miškān* [tent, dwelling, 19:13]/ *miqdaš* [sanctuary, 19:20] YHWH *ṭimmē'*). In what way corpse impurity is thought to defile the temple, however, remains unexplained. Milgrom and many of his followers would say "from afar," through the air, by remaining unpurified in the camp, but the assumptions required for this interpretation cannot be verified.

The exact meaning of the phrase "he has defiled" is unclear. Is the *kārēt* penalty because, having already defiled the sanctuary by becoming impure, this person remains in an impure state and implicitly *continues* to defile (perhaps implied by the clause order of v. 20), or does the person defile only by neglecting the proper purification rituals, so that by immediate purification there will be no defilement of the sanctuary (implied by the clause order of v. 13)?[49] Or does the statement simply mean that people who do not purify within the community of the Yehud temple state also defile the sanctuary by/when coming in contact with it?

We cannot tell for certain whether Num 19 expresses a different understanding of how impurity affects the temple, when compared to Lev 11–15. In any case, the instructions about purification after war in Num 31:19-24 make no mention of the sanctuary. The warriors must stay out of the camp for seven days while purifying from corpse impurity. Similarly, the strict rule of Num 5:1-3, requiring the corpse-impure, as well as people with skin disease and with genital discharges, to be quarantined outside settlements refers to the camp and not explicly to the sanctuary building, even though the divine presence is in focus. The

---

49. The phrase כִּי אֶת־מִקְדַּשׁ יְהוָה טִמֵּא (טמא *piel* perfect) could theoretically be interpreted in a number of ways: the person has defiled the sanctuary (by neglecting purification), the person had already defiled the sanctuary (when he on top of that also neglected purification), the person has defiled and will continue to defile the sanctuary, or perhaps, by remaining in a state of impurity, the person will certainly defile/ have defiled the sanctuary.

three categories must be expelled so that "they shall not defile their camp in which I dwell among them [*'ăšer 'ănî šokēn bətôkām*]" (Num 5:3). Divine holiness is definitely incompatible with impurity and motivates the expulsion of impure categories from human dwellings.

It has been debated whether "the camp" here in the text represents the temple city only or towns and villages in general. Similar considerations apply to the expulsion of people with skin disease according to Lev 13. Do these texts intend to say that chronic impurity bearers should not dwell in Jerusalem or in any settlements? When we take a look at how these regulations were subsequently interpreted and elaborated on, we find numerous discrepancies. The Temple Scroll says of the same three categories—the corpse-impure, people with skin disease, and genital dischargers—that they must not enter the temple city until they have purified (11Q19 XLV, 15–18). Exactly how this relates to the subsequent passage about three places outside the temple city for people with skin disease, genital dischargers, and semen emitters (11Q19 XLVI, 16–18) is not entirely clear. Further on, the text instructs ordinary cities to seclude the same categories: people with skin disease, people with genital discharges, menstruants, and parturients (11Q19 XLVIII, 14–17). Josephus similarly outlines varying standards: dischargers and people with skin disease were not allowed in the temple city, he says, while menstruants were only barred from the temple itself (*J.W.* 5.227; cf. *Ag. Ap.* 2.103–104). In another place (*Ant.* 3.261) he also includes the corpse impure and makes clear that they and menstruants were set aside (*metestēse*) in contrast to dischargers and people with skin disease, who were expelled (*epēlase*).

I have discussed these texts elsewhere, in particular the role of first-day ablutions for modifying the biblical rules, which could explain some of the discrepancies,[50] but I will leave the details aside for now. Suffice it to point out that Num 5 has triggered interpretations both for the temple city and for ordinary towns. The camp in Numbers, and in Leviticus, of course represents the temple city, since these texts are shaped by the priestly elite in fifth- and fourth-century BCE Yehud, struggling to establish themselves within a small temple state centered on Jerusalem and its sanctuary. As perspectives grew wider, rules had to be adapted to a broader context.

---

50. Kazen 2010a, 156–59, 163–65, 187–189; 2010b; 2015c, 155–63, 166–67 = ch. 8 in this volume.

Ideas of gradual spheres of holiness and corresponding gradual stages of purity developed further, until they reached a stage reflected in rabbinic texts (cf. m. Kelim 1:6–9).

In almost every time and at almost every place except for the Jewish region during the Second Temple period, temples and cult places were part of everyday life. Purity customs would always and inevitably be intertwined with cultic issues. There is something anachronistic and secular about the question whether purity practices evolved for the sake of the temple or for everyday life, as if those two aspects of human culture could be separated, but the particular situation created by postexilic cult centralisation complicates matters. The way in which many of the purity laws are elaborated in detail suggest Persian influence on the priestly elite during and after the exile.[51] The Zoroastrian discharge and corpse-impurity rules, with their corresponding purification rites, as registered in Vendidād, appear to be quite unrelated to temple cult, but reflect customary behaviors and practices.[52] In Persian-period Yehud, Israelite customary behaviors and practices were further developed with regard to the cult in Jerusalem, but also with regard to everyday life. The varying and sometimes disparate traditions used and reworked only occasionally indicate a particular focus on the cult, in spite of their priestly redactors.

Rabbinic Evidence

Let us now turn to rabbinic evidence, Tannaitic texts in particular. It is quite common to regard the rabbis as innovators in comparison to the strict and conservative sectarians assumed behind the Qumran texts. Since the Pharisees are often seen as forerunners of the rabbis we regularly encounter statements about their innovations, which neither other groups, such as the Sadducees, the Essenes, and the Jesus movement, nor the general population accepted. They include practices such as handwashing before common meals and the concept of *ṭəbûl yôm*, the role of liquid in contamination, and other issues.[53] During recent years, several scholars have warned against equating the dissensions reflected in

---

51. Kazen 2015b = ch. 4 in this volume; Achenbach 2003, 500–504; Colpe 1995.
52. This is even more so with the Zoroastrian categorization of noxious animals, *khrafstra*.
53. Cf. Baumgarten 1980; Schiffman 1994.

a document such as 4QMMT with some of the rabbinic evidence and retrojecting Tannaitic definitions back into a first-century context.[54]

Aharon Shemesh and some others have partly turned the argument around. The key is to understand the character of custom and to see halakah as often reflective of popular practice. The legal interpretation found in many Dead Sea texts is based on a close reading with a realist bent, which repeatedly results in strict and sometimes innovative rulings. Written law is never equal to customary behavior but often codifies an ideal. Legal interpretation usually expounds and adapts an earlier ruling to the contemporary context, but can do so in line with, or in contrast to, current custom. In the legal texts from Qumran, there is a tendency toward stringency of a kind that extends or even goes against previous customary behavior. Some of these issues reflect current tendencies of more general acceptance, while others are innovations and become areas of conflict between competing groups. In both cases, interpretations in the halakic texts from Qumran are based on close reading and exegesis.[55]

Because of this "biblicist" approach, those who wanted to defend custom against new and often quite strict interpretations became increasingly pressed. Unless we understand the character of custom, we will easily misunderstand the process. Custom usually does not need a defense, but is understood to be in line with law by default. When custom is questioned, however, that which was assumed must now be proved. This is the probable background to the combination of an increasingly nominalist argumentation that gradually evolves in the rabbinic movement, together with exegetical justifications. In the process of defending custom from Qumran-like innovations, a text-based but increasingly nominalist approach evolves and comes to fruition with the Tannaim, eventually resulting in new types of innovation, partly related and partly unrelated to the former and now disappeared adversaries of the rabbinic predecessors. Eventually, this type of rabbinic argumentation, together with an increase in rabbinic authority, makes the rabbis see and identify their interpretations as their own decrees, even in some cases where they defend earlier practices.

---

54. See, e.g., Himmelfarb 2010; Fraade 2011, 69–91. Fraade (2011, 70 n. 4) also mentions Yaakov Elman, Lester Grabbe, and Menahem Kister among those who have questioned the extent to which we can read 4QMMT in light of later rabbinic texts.

55. Shemesh 2009; Schwartz 1992; Schremer 2001; Noam 2006; 2010b; 2010c; Kazen 2013a.

While this is all in the abstract, concrete examples can be found in various publications. An interesting example for our purposes is handwashing for common meals, often viewed as a Pharisaic innovation and a rabbinic decree. The way in which handwashing is presented in the Gospel of Mark, however, poses problems for such a view. It seems more likely that some of the Pharisees built on already-existing and more unspecific handwashing customs, as a defense against new and strict ideas regarding immersion and meals, as we find in, for example, Qumran. Also, the way in which Tannaitic texts portray Bet Hillel and Bet Shammai debating the timing of handwashing suggests that it was a common practice in the early Roman era (m. Ber. 8:2).[56] Later, the rabbis then reinterpret handwashing as a voluntary protective measure to safeguard *tərûmâ* and claim it as their own ruling. This is true of their nominalist argumentation for it, but it is not true of the earlier, underlying custom.[57] For those who assume a purity-for-the-sake-of-the-temple view, however, the rabbinic anachronism fits well.

Harrington describes the rabbinic agenda as lenience with regard to identification and stringency with regard to contamination.[58] Together these two approaches limit impurity at a time when purification of at least some types of impurity becomes difficult. This has partly to do with the loss of the temple, but the fact that rabbinic purity halakah accommodates for that, while giving so much attention to purity matters in the Tannaitic period, strongly suggests that purity did not primarily serve the cult, but was a matter of custom and identity.

Secondary or one-day impurities were hardly affected by the loss of the temple, as they could always be remedied by ablution or immersion. What about primary impurities? Corpse impurity required ashes from the red cow for the *mê niddâ*. The rabbinic list of the nine red cows that had been burned since Moses (m. Parah 3:5) is to a large extent legendary, but nevertheless shows that the ashes were considered to last for generations. Although the ritual according to Num 19 does not seem to require a temple, it was understood to be conducted by the high priest. Without the cult, the ashes would eventually not be available, and corpse impurity could then no longer be properly purified. As long as they lasted, however, purification from corpse impurity would have been possible without the temple.

---

56. Hayes 2007, 754.
57. Kazen 2013a, 171–76, 186–88, 287–88.
58. Harrington 1993, 182, 202.

Purification of people with skin disease would have been slightly more complicated. They were required to sacrifice three lambs on the eighth day of their purification, in addition to water purifications and the bird rite that by itself needed no temple.[59] Again, the situation would have been difficult to handle for people far from Jerusalem before the fall of the temple. Interestingly, however, the rabbis interpreted the purification in steps as removing layers of impurity so that the last step, sacrifice, allowed for eating holy things, *qodāšîm* (m. Neg. 14:2–3). From an earlier period, the Qumran Halakic Letter (4QMMT B64–72) reveals a similar understanding of graded impurity as it protests against people purifying from skin disease who eat *qodāšîm* before sunset on the eighth day. This last level of purity, then, would have been relevant mainly for the consumption of sacrificial meat, which would not have been an issue far from, or without, a temple. For practical purposes, purification from skin disease could do without the temple, too.

Genital discharges (except for menstruation and semen emission) probably caused most problems of the primary sources of impurity. *Zābîm* were required to sacrifice pigeons on the eighth day of their purification. This would have been a constant problem for people living far from Jerusalem already during temple times, although the number of people who needed to sacrifice at the temple as their final step of purification might have been small. However, it was still a possibility. After 70 CE it was not. Hence there would have been reason to limit the number of *zābîm* as far as possible.

This is exactly what we find in early rabbinic texts. Based on their understanding of the details in Lev 15, the rabbis developed an interpretation of pressure and location, which limited susceptible objects underneath a discharger to beds and chairs (*midrās* impurity). All other items became subject to *maddāp* impurity, a kind of overshadowing. The latter were possible to purify in a *miqweh*, and *maddāp* did not affect people. Harrington sees the development of these categories as a conscious move to limit contamination to people as far as possible.[60] Contamination

---

59. The bird rite required a priest (Lev 14:4), but this may be an addition to/modification of the rite by the priestly authors. The Mishnah assumes that the whole rite is conducted by a priest (m. Neg. 14), while the Tosefta and the Sifra restrict the role of the priest (t. Neg. 8:5; Sifra to Lev 14:2–4 [Sifra Parashat Mesora Parashah 1]); cf. Schwartz 2000, 218–22.

60. Harrington 1993, 250.

potency is, in a sense, increased, while susceptibility is constrained. This is combined with a lenient approach in defining dischargers. The Mishnah (m. Zavim 2:2) lists seven excuses for a man with discharges, which count as exemptions, including what he has eaten, drunk, or carried, whether he had jumped or been ill, and sexual arousal. Rabbi Aqiva's leniency is met by disbelief: "Rabbi Aqiva says: 'Even if he had eaten any food, bad or tasty, or had drunk any liquid.' They said to him: 'There would be no *zābîm* from now on!' He said to them: 'The responsibility for *zābîm* does not rest upon you!'"[61] According to another passage, a woman can blame bloodstains on, for example, lice or wounds (m. Nid. 8:1–3). An example story pictures Rabbi Aqiva again taking a lenient stance:

> It happened to a certain woman that she came before Rabbi Akiva and she said to him: "I have seen a stain." He said to her: "Perhaps there was a wound on you?" She said to him: "Yes, but it has healed." He said to her: "Perhaps it can open up and let out some blood?" She said to him: "Yes." And Rabbi Akiva declared her clean. He saw his disciples staring at each other. He said to them: "Why is this ruling difficult in your eyes? For the sages did not pronounce this ruling for stringency [*ləhaḥămîr*], but rather for leniency [*ləhāqēl*], as it is said [Lev 15:19]: "And a woman who is discharging and blood shall be her discharge in her body"—blood and not a stain. (m. Nid. 8:3)

Although Aqiva is sometimes particular in other regards, too, these examples show a tendency to limit definitions to the point where *zābîm* become next to nonexistent.

The rabbis also limit contamination from skin disease. In a passage (m. Kelim 1:7) counting ten spheres or degrees of holiness[62] (although they are actually eleven!), walled cities are number two, holier than the land of Israel, "because they must send away people with skin disease from their midst" (*šemmašallǝḥîm mittôkān 'et hamməṣōrāîm*). Although this is not an argument for lenience, we learn about rabbinic assumptions in passing. In another passage (m. Arakh. 9:6) we also learn in passing that houses in cities not surrounded by walls in the time of Joshua ben Nun are not counted as houses in a walled city. To this Hyam Maccoby adds a Talmudic passage about rules for walled cities being relevant only in

---

61. אין אחריות זבים עליכם. (m. Zavim 2:2).
62. Cf. n. 26.

the period when Jubilee Years were observed (b. Arakh. 29a), suggesting that according to rabbinic opinion, people with skin disease were never expelled from cities during the Second Temple period.[63] This is a good example of continued rabbinic interpretation, but historically useless. The point to make, however, is that by narrow qualifications the rabbis seem to have limited the effects of ṣāraʿat impurity, just as they limited its definition. In a discussion of spots and skin color (m. Neg. 2:1), Rabbi Judah is reported to have said: "The shades of 'leprosy' [should be decided] for leniency (ləhāqēl), but not for stringency (ləhahămîr)." Except for two cases (described in m. Neg. 4:11; 5:1), any doubt regarding skin disease is considered pure (kol-sāpēk nəgāʿîm ṭāhôr).

Examining the Mishnah's rules for skin disease, Harrington finds a restrictive interpretation with regard to the pronouncement of the disease and an expansive interpretation with regard to the contamination power. She sees a clear agenda in the Mishnah's rules for skin disease: "The Rabbis wish to reduce the incidence of ṣāraʿat as much as possible, hence their definition of the disease is very narrow. By the rules of the Mishna it would be difficult to be designated a məṣōrāʿ."[64] This applies to the Tosefta as well. A leprous house "has never come into existence and is never going to come into existence," and even if there would be some such houses, Jerusalem is exempted (t. Neg. 6:1). The possibility to pronounce garments leprous is also restricted (t. Neg. 1:5; 5:2–3). But contamination rules regarding those with skin disease who still remain are expanded, so as to ensure their isolation and protect the community.[65]

In sum: the loss of the temple affects the rabbis' attitudes to impurity, but not in the way one would expect if purity were mainly an issue in relation to the cult. Even their urge to constantly define, develop, and expand serves the function, at least during the Tannaitic period, to accommodate everyday observance to a new context, in which, among other things, possibilities for purification were circumscribed.

---

63. Maccoby 1999, 146–47.
64. Harrington 1993, 198.
65. Cf. Harrington 1993, 198–213. There are admittedly many ambiguous examples, too. According to m. Neg. 13:12 and t. Neg. 7:11, if a person with skin disease enters a synagogue he must be closed off by a wall, enter first, and exit last. The presence of a person with skin disease in a synagogue may seem surprising, but the provisions can be interpreted as simultaneously lenient toward the person and protective toward the community.

As with the material evidence, there are no signs of a decrease in purity practices in the period directly following the fall of Jerusalem. If one still wishes to cling to a temple-oriented understanding of purity, one might suggest that purity customs were retained in anticipation of a new temple and that their importance diminished when hope was gone. But all evidence suggests the opposite, that an exclusively temple-oriented understanding evolved as "part of the program of alleviating the halakic burden."[66] Poirier suggests that the principle of temple orientation was an innovation "to make the purity code more livable" and that "these decrees presuppose the obsolescence of the temple."[67] He points out that the clearest expression of such a view comes from Moses Maimonides in the twelfth century:[68]

> All that is written in the Torah and the words of Scripture concerning the laws of ritual purity and impurity apply only with regard to the Sanctuary, sacrifices consecrated for it, *terumah*, and the second tithe. For individuals who are ritually impure were warned against entering the Sanctuary or partaking of sacrificial foods, *terumah*, or the second tithe while impure. There is no prohibition at all against partaking of ordinary foods while impure. Instead, it is permitted to eat ordinary foods that are impure and partake of ordinary beverages that are impure.[69]

---

66. Poirier 2003, 263.
67. Poirier 2003, 262–63. Poirier in fact says "to make the purity code more livable (by making most of it obsolete)," but I think the bracketed explanation is misleading for the early rabbis. It is more relevant at a later stage.
68. Translations of Maimonides by Touger n.d.
69. Maimonides, *Mishneh Torah* 10 (Book of Cleanness), part 6 (The Uncleanness of Foodstuffs), 16:8. Note the subsequent motivation, based on Lev 7:19, which is a typical example of nominalist reasoning: "Behold, it is written in the Torah: 'The meat that will come in contact with any impurity should not be eaten.' It can be inferred that it is permissible to partake of ordinary foods while impure, because the verse is speaking only about sacrificial foods. If so, what is the intent of the statement: Ordinary food that is a primary derivative of impurity is impure and that which is a secondary derivative is disqualified? The intent is not that the food itself is forbidden to be eaten, instead, its status is important only when counting levels with regard to *terumah* and sacrificial foods. For if ordinary food that is a secondary derivative of impurity touches *terumah*, it disqualifies it and causes it to be considered as a tertiary derivative. Similarly, if it touches sacrificial food, it imparts impurity to it and causes it to be considered as a tertiary derivative, as we explained. Similarly, if a person who ate ordinary food that was a secondary derivative of impurity touches *terumah*, he disqualifies it."

According to Maimonides, this applies not only to food, but to all sources of impurity, with the effect that purity concerns become virtually irrelevant for ordinary people: "Similarly, it is permissible for a person to touch all sources of impurity and contract impurity from them."[70] Two centuries earlier, the Karaite al-Qirqisani had complained about rabbanite lack of observance of purity practices, saying they claim there is no such concept since the temple was destroyed, and since there is no purification from corpse impurity anymore, everyone is unclean.[71] Such views may have begun to gain ground in Amoraic times, although it took centuries before they were fully established.[72]

Conclusion: Erasing the Anachronistic Divide

Evidence do not favor an exclusively temple-oriented view of purity in Second Temple Judaism. But what about the historical origins of purity conceptions? What do earlier Israelite purity customs indicate? What is the focus of impurity in Babylonian, Hittite, Persian, Greek, and Roman cultures? These are topics on their own, which cannot be discussed now.[73] But I suggest that researchers will easily find what they look for. The evidence can point in different directions, depending on assumptions, some of which run the risk of becoming anachronistic. Impurity was always an issue for the cult. But so were building styles, construction techniques, organization, and the provision of sacrificial animals and other foods. This does not mean that all of these things were primarily oriented toward temple cults. Rather, they were intrinsic parts of human life in antiquity, in the household and in society. Temples are palaces, dwellings, households of the gods, and many of the issues that concern households and societies in general concern temples even more.[74] In the ancient world, the holy is

---

70. וכן מותר לאדם ליגע בכל הטומאות ולהתטמא בהן; Maimonides, *Mishneh Torah* 10, part 6, 16:9. Here again, the subsequent motivation is based on a nominalist exegesis and interpretation of biblical texts: "This is evident from the fact that the Torah warned a priest and a nazirite from becoming impure through contact with a human corpse. One can infer from this that all other members of the people are permitted. Moreover, even priests and nazirites are permitted to contract impurity from all other sources of impurity with the exception of a human corpse."
71. Poirier 2003, 261–62.
72. Poirier 2003, 263–64.
73. Cf. the articles in Frevel and Nihan 2013.
74. On this point, cf. Adler's (2016, 247–48) analogy with perjury: "While one

always present as part of life, and religion is often not even defined as a separate category, since it is an aspect of everything.⁷⁵ The divide between household and cult is anachronistic. Neither gods nor humans like dirt.

There are, of course, very legitimate questions to ask about developments and influences, origins and effects. But to minimize and downplay the role that Jewish purity practices played in everyday life during the early Roman period, even for the good purpose of correcting some Western interpreters' negative portraits of Second Temple Judaism, is historically dubious. And to pose "biblical" purity rules against extrabiblical innovations, as if texts were transcriptions of practice rather than contextual prescriptions and as if popular customs were biblicist and text bound rather than living and developing expressions of general concern, is a somewhat Protestant and secular anachronism. The temple-oriented view is not only wrong; it also distorts our interpretation of a number of other, associated issues.

---

should never tell a lie anywhere, uttering falsehoods in a courtroom is a particularly serious offense that carries actual penalties." Similarly, if impurity is a serious thing to be avoided in everyday life, it is even more serious to be impure in an explicitly cultic setting.

75. Cf. Nongbri 2013.

12
A Perhaps Less Halakic Jesus and Purity: On Prophetic Criticism, Halakic Innovation, and Rabbinic Anachronism

> Purity practices during the first century CE were widespread in Judea and Galilee as part of everyday life and not limited to concerns relating to the temple cult. Developments in key water rites were partly triggered by concepts of graded impurity, to which an understanding of defilement via food also belonged. Certain rabbinic characteristics represent later developments and cannot be assumed for the time of Jesus. Hand impurity did not originate as a rabbinic decree to protect *tərûmâ*, and accusations against Pharisees for setting aside Scripture in favor of their own traditions did not originate with the historical Jesus, but suggest later polemics. Jesus's stance on purity is perhaps better characterized as prophetic than halakic.

In this chapter I argue (1) that purity practices at the time of Jesus were widespread and common in Judea as well as in Galilee; (2) that purity was not observed entirely, or primarily, because of the temple; (3) that an extended use of some key water rites evolved during the late Second Temple period for practical purposes and depended on basic concepts of graded impurity; (4) that defilement via impure food was an issue; (5) that a number of rabbinic characteristics represent later developments, including the elaborate system of "removes" or degrees of impurity, an understanding of defilement of utensils and people by food and liquids as rabbinic rather than scriptural law, and claims that hand impurity originated as a rabbinic decree to protect *tərûmâ* (priestly food); (6) that the gospel accusation against the Pharisees for setting aside divine Scripture in favor of human halakah represents early Christian rhetorical polemics

---

This chapter was first published in *JSHJ* 14 (2016): 120–36. Used by permission.

rather than the historical Jesus; and (7) that Jesus's stance on purity was less halakic and more prophetic than often assumed. The arguments lean on continuing research regarding the development of halakah and halakic reasoning, and on recent studies on material finds associated with the practice of purity.[1] It draws on my previous work, including my 2013 book, *Scripture, Interpretation, or Authority?*[2]

Purity Practices Widespread

First, *there is evidence for widespread and common observance of purity*. It makes a huge difference for evaluations of Jesus's stance whether purity was observed extensively or not by Israelites in Judea and Galilee. Some scholars tend to downplay the observance of purity and purification rituals. This is done in a number of ways.

One is to claim that except for priests, purity practices such as handwashing and immersion were only practiced by small groups of sectarians and extremists, such as those in Qumran and certain voluntary associations.[3] Jacob Neusner can exemplify this: he understood the Pharisees as a "pure food association," imitating priests by eating in purity.[4] The view has been severely criticized by Ed P. Sanders, John Poirier, Eyal Regev, Yair Furstenberg, and others.[5] I have previously suggested that what might be viewed as a similarity from a later point in history did not originate for that reason.[6] Corpse-impurity rules, for example, are applied to people in general in certain parts of Numbers, while only applied to priests in the slightly earlier Holiness Code.[7] But this does not express a lay wish to play priests. There are historical and other reasons for general adherence to purity practices, not least a widespread general aspiration for a high degree of holiness.[8]

---

1. See, e.g., Schwartz 1992, 229–40; Shemesh 2009; Noam 2008; 2010b; 2010c; Adler 2008b; 2009; 2011; 2014a; 2016; Miller 2015.
2. Kazen 2013a.
3. This view was articulated already in Büchler 1968, 96–157.
4. Neusner 1971, 3:188; 1974–1977, 22:106, 108; 1979, 14.
5. Sanders 1990, 131–254; Poirier 1996; 2003; Regev 2000a; 2000b; Furstenberg 2008.
6. Kazen 2010a, 69–70; 2010c, 117–18.
7. Compare Num 19:11–19 with Lev 21:1–4, 11.
8. For a discussion of the contextualization of purity practices in Persian-period Yehud, see Kazen 2015b = ch. 4 in this volume; 2010c, 10–11. For discussions of the widespread aspiration for holiness, see Adler 2016.

Another, somewhat different downplaying attempt is exemplified by Sanders. His covenantal nomism gives room for a common observance, but although he concedes that a high level of purity was generally aspired to,[9] he makes observance almost palatable to modern Western rationality and common sense. Pharisees were not like their caricatures, not so Catholic but more Protestant.[10] Speaking of meal practices, and after having admitted that Pharisees generally did not eat with less pure people, Sanders states: "In real life, most people do not eat with most other people. In communities today where Methodists, for example, have church suppers, usually there are only Methodists there."[11] Besides being falsified by the Methodist congregations I have known, the analogy is useless. Concerning handwashing, Sanders claims that many people thought priests should wash their hands before eating tərûmâ, and some washed hands before handling priests' food, but only a small number of ḥăbērîm adopted the practice of eating ḥûllîn (ordinary food) in a state of purity. This practice, which was eventually made normative by the rabbis, was not accepted by the common people at the time of Jesus because it was impractical. Had such rules been generally followed, Sanders explains, some impure people would have starved. Sanders's stance is that people would have followed these rules had they been able, but since these were too impractical, people did not, nor did many of the Pharisees.[12] Even priests "winked at the rules."[13] They would simply not have kept their wives separate during menstruation, Sanders says, because some were poor and could not afford extra furniture and food.[14]

Others, too, emphasize issues of practicality. Cecilia Wassén points out that intercourse, childbirth, and tending the dead were considered both good and necessary activities and claims that Jews in general did not actively avoid impurity; only certain groups (priests, Pharisees, and Essenes), whose "lifestyle was quite extreme," would have done so.[15] It is

---

9. Sanders 1990, 184; 1992, 218–19, 229–30, 245–46.
10. This has been noted by a number of people commenting on and reviewing Sanders; see, e.g., the unduly harsh and highly exaggerated but nevertheless at this point relevant criticism of Neusner 1992, 166–69.
11. Sanders 1990, 441.
12. Sanders 1990, 149–51, 160–63, 174–75, 232–34.
13. Sanders 1990, 135.
14. Sanders 1990, 233.
15. Wassén 2016a, 31.

a hazardous task for modern scholars to judge what ancient peoples in various contexts would deem impractical or extreme. History is full of examples of cultures in which complex rituals and practices were commonplace, in spite of poor conditions.[16]

Purity without Temple

The downplaying of purity observance often goes together with the *untenable view that* except for sectarians, *purity practices were restricted to, or at least focused on, the temple*. Impurities from menstruation, sex, or burial would not have concerned anyone except in view of a temple visit. Jacob Milgrom suggests that a main problem with impurity was *sancta* contamination.[17] Neusner understands the Pharisees to appropriate priestly purity laws for themselves outside the temple.[18] The demand of Num 5 to quarantine severe impurity bearers is read together with the Temple Scroll as extremist.[19]

---

16. One example (without claiming any continuity with ancient practice) is the Falashas. For references, see Kazen 2010a, 72 n. 187. Cf. Milgrom 1991, 765.

17. For Milgrom (see esp. 1976) this goes together with his understanding of the sanctuary being defiled from afar by people neglecting to purify. Cf. on this point the criticism by Maccoby 1999, 165–92.

18. See above, n. 4. Sanders (1990, 173–76) shows convincingly Neusner's temple-table analogy to be untenable: (1) a number of post-70 rabbinic sayings do *not* require ordinary food to be eaten in purity; (2) the houses distinguish between priests' food and their own; (3) prohibitions against impurity bearers touching pure food are absent in the Mishnah; (4) there are no discussions about eating other types of food prohibited to priests; (5) biblical purity laws did not apply to priests and the temple only; (6) a full analogy between altar and table is nowhere implied in Leviticus or in Pharisaic material. Furstenberg (2008, 191) points out that Neusner's interpretation rests on a midrash in Sifre Numbers from the time of Rabbi Judah. See further Kazen 2010c, 117–19; 2013a. See also Poirier's (2003) argument that the idea of purity laws existing only for the sake of the temple is a scholarly construct based on Maimonides's understanding.

19. Num 5:2–3 suggests the exclusion of the skin diseased, genital dischargers, and the corpse-impure from the camp. The Temple Scroll does the same with regard to the temple city (11Q19 XLV, 15–18) and in addition has restrictions for intercourse and semen emitters (XLV, 11; XLVI, 16–18). As for the ordinary city the text, which talks of making special places in every city (XLVIII, 14–17), is open to various interpretations: the skin diseased are definitely excluded, as the purpose is said to be to prevent them from entering the cities and defiling them, but in the case of dischargers,

12. A Perhaps Less Halakic Jesus and Purity

To limit the scope of purity to the sanctuary and its observance to extreme groups is untenable for several reasons. The priestly rules for contact contagion in Lev 12–15 assume any contact with skin-diseased persons to be by all means avoided, and the details of the discharge rules are aimed at avoiding every contamination. Although the sanctuary figures occasionally,[20] it is not the focus of these rules. Neither Numbers nor the Temple Scroll is sectarian, even though the latter has utopian traits.[21] What we need is to analyze these texts as scribal elite statements within their sociopolitico-religious contexts in the Persian and Hellenistic periods, and to find out their effects on Second Temple Jewish society.[22]

As long as finds of stone vessels and *miqwā'ôt* were overrepresented in Jerusalem, which was the case when Ronny Reich and Yitzhak Magen published their seminal studies, arguments downplaying and limiting the scope of purity practices were still possible to maintain.[23] Today they are not. Stone vessels were used almost everywhere. Stepped pools are found all over—and it is becoming increasingly difficult to talk of an overrepresentation in Jerusalem. Here I can only refer to the most recent statements and interpretations by Yonatan Adler and Stuart Miller.[24] According to Adler's counts, more than 80 percent of the pools are outside Jerusalem, compared to 50 percent in earlier estimations.[25] Most of the recent finds since the

---

the purpose of preventing them from "defiling in their midst" could perhaps be read as seclusion within settlements, although this is not the most natural reading.

20. In purity rules for people in general: Lev 12:4; 15:31; Num 19:13, 20; for priests: Lev 22:2–9. See further Adler 2016.

21. Although it is highly unlikely that the utopian views of the Temple Scroll were actually practiced by the general population, it is not a sectarian document but originated before the Qumran community. Despite its utopian traits, it represents expansionist ideals of a kind that were likely increasing in influence. Cf. Crawford 2000, 24–29; 2008, 84–104.

22. Cf. Kazen 2015b, 445–60.

23. Magen 1994; 2002. Ronny Reich's (2013) major study, his dissertation from 1990, has only recently been updated and put into print, but a number of articles have since long been available in English, e.g., Reich 1988; 1989; 1993; 2000; 2002. For a thorough discussion of the history of interpretation and the present state of the evidence, see Adler 2016.

24. See n. 1 (Adler and Miller) for references.

25. Here the figures provided by archaeologists differ, less depending on what is counted and how than on how updated they are. Reich originally counted around 300 *miqwā'ôt*, half of which were found in Jerusalem. In his 2013 publication, which unfortunately does not take Adler's evidence into account, he counts 459 pre-70

1990s are rural, and in many villages there are numerous stepped pools so that many households had their own, in addition to communal pools. One conspicuous example out of many is Ḥorvat Burnat, where more or less each house or each compound had access to a pool.[26] In addition, stepped pools are found near oil and wine presses and other workshops. Although the insusceptibility of stone was *not unanimously* assumed, and although the emergence of the stone-vessel industry *might* be explained as a spinoff from Herodian building industry, and although stepped pools hewn in the bedrock *could* be used for multiple purposes, there is no way to explain the present state of these material finds except for a *widespread* and *general* observance of purity practices, including frequent, probably daily purifications, far from the temple.[27] Moreover, an earlier interpretation that these practices disappeared as a result of the fall of the temple is shown to be false. Both stone vessels and stepped pools remain in production and use for centuries. There is a marked decrease, but not until after the Bar Kokhba revolt, and then at least partly for natural reasons (abandoned settlements, etc.).[28] Purity was observed by wide circles among the general population

---

stepped pools, out of which 206 are found in Jerusalem and only 16 in Galilee (Reich 2013, 272–314). In addition to these he counts 74 later (post-70) pools (pp. 314–19). Adler, however, speaks of over 600 from the Hasmonean and early Roman periods in Judea, including about 170 in Jerusalem, plus fewer than 70 in Galilee, and lists 850 altogether in a meticulously detailed inventory. See Adler 2011, 321–43; 2013; cf. Amit and Adler 2010. Of the stepped pools built in the period after Bar Kokhba, a large number are found in Galilee, such as the more than forty baths found in Sepphoris (Adler 2013, 244). It is true, however, that regardless of how one counts, pre-70 stepped pools in Judea far surpass those in Galilee in number. Adler (243) discusses whether this reflects differences in observance or rather the fact that Judea has been much more intensively excavated. This issue simply cannot be settled until many more excavations have been carried out in Galilee.

26. Adler 2014a, 70 and 73, fig. 3, from Amit, Torgü, and Gendelman 2008. The site plan gives an excellent example of what has been found to be the case in numerous other sites as well. Another example with a large concentration of stepped pools, mentioned by Adler (2014a, 69), from the period 70–135 CE, is Shu'afat.

27. Miller 2003; 2007; 2010; 2015, 95–98, 151–83. Interestingly, Sanders (1992, 222–23) does make a similar point in his discussions about stepped pools, based on the then-available evidence, according to which only around half of the finds were situated outside Jerusalem. This makes Sanders's downplaying of evidence in other areas the more ambiguous, or even puzzling.

28. On this point Miller is more inclined to interpret the evidence as signs of continuing practices well into the Byzantine period, while Adler, after having entertained

as part of household religion, on a daily basis, unrelated to the sanctuary, and even after the fall of the temple.[29]

Extended Water Rites

New finds of stepped pools and their wide dissemination also influence judgments concerning my third point: *the extended use of water rites*. The existence of an extra first-day ablution for a seven-day corpse impurity has been observed for long, and while some of the texts referred to in this context associate such a rite with temple visits, others do not.[30] Recent finds of stepped pools in the proximity of burial places indicate that people purified immediately after burials.[31] There is little reason to under-

---

a similar view, now finds the evidence for a significant decrease in (although not the cessation of) purity practices after the Bar Kokhba revolt much more likely. Both Adler and Miller agree that there is no evidence for a decline as a result of the temple's destruction and the cessation of the sacrificial cult in 70 CE. See Miller 2015; Adler 2016; for Adler's earlier view, emphasizing continuing observance through the Byzantine period, see Amit and Adler 2010.

29. Adler 2011, 71–72.

30. First-day ablutions are discussed especially in relation to texts from Qumran; cf. Milgrom 1978, 512–18; 1995; Baumgarten 1992; 2000; Eshel 1999; Regev 2000a; 2000b. I have discussed the evidence at length in Kazen 2010c, 63–111, and in summary in 2013a, 147. Ezekiel suggests an initial purification after corpse impurity for priests (Ezek 44:25–26), Tobit specifically attests to such a practice for ordinary people (Tob 2:9), and Philo (*Spec.* 1.261; 3.205–206) suggests a first-day water rite as part of the procedures for being allowed into the temple. Josephus's (*Ant.* 3.261) distinction between dischargers and those with skin disease on the one hand being expelled from Jerusalem, while menstruants and the corpse-impure are envisaged as being contained but secluded, would fit with the practice of a mitigating first-day water rite for the two latter (not chronic but temporary) impurities. The Temple Scroll (with utopian traits but not sectarian; see n. 21 above) does not envisage the corpse-impure inside Jerusalem, but when it does with regard to ordinary cities the text explicitly requires a first-day ablution (11Q19 XLIX, 16–21; L, 13–16). A first-day ablution is also spelled out in 4Q414 and implied in 1QM XIV, 2–3 and in 4Q274 1. Texts that mention pilgrims arriving in Jerusalem a week before Passover in order to purify make sense in view of a first-day ablution (*J.W.* 6.290; John 11:55). Samaritan texts take a first-day rite for granted (*Kitâb al-Kâfi* III [43]; XIII [11–13]); texts in Bóid 1989a, 153–54, 242–43, 324. As is clear from the samples above, a first-day water rite for purification from corpse impurity (and possibly from other seven-day impurities too) is applied in relation to temple visits, but by no means exclusively or primarily.

31. Adler 2009.

stand such practice as restricted to purification after a secondary (one-day) impurity from contact with corpse-impure persons, at a time when immediate (first-day) ablutions were becoming commonplace for more severe seven-day impurities, too.[32] I have argued elsewhere that first-day ablutions were also employed in the seven-day purification process after *zābâ* impurity as part of a development based on systemic thinking, understanding impurity as multilayered.[33] For this, the seven-day purification period of the person healed from skin disease might have served as precedent, as well as the two stages of impurity for the parturient.[34] Scripture thus triggered an early understanding of impurity as graded, even though the advanced system of the rabbis did not evolve until later, as I will demonstrate in a moment.

Similar considerations apply to handwashing. Although not prescribed by biblical law, handwashing became a means for upholding a high degree of purity at meals, preventing the transference of light impurities to food that would contaminate the eater.[35] A likely scriptural precedence

---

32. For this point, see my comments on Adler 2009 in Kazen 2010c, 142–43 n. 24; 2013a, 147–48 n. 121. Adler argues that these stepped pools were only used for mourners' purification from the light one-day impurity, since he regards the first-day ablution for a seven-day corpse impurity a sectarian phenomenon. As we have seen (and as I have discussed at greater length elsewhere), there is no good reason for regarding a first-day ablution for seven-day impurities particularly sectarian, and findings of stepped pools adjacent to burial grounds in my view rather add another piece of evidence for first-day ablutions being common practice to the list presented above. The rationale for these pools is, in fact, even more plausible when we consider their function for the fully corpse-impure, who would otherwise not be able to return home and would contaminate other people, while those with a one-day impurity would be less problematic.

33. Kazen 2010b.

34. The purification rite for people healed from skin disease includes bathing on the first day, subsequent to the bird rite, after which the ex-leper is allowed into the camp, but not into the house (Lev 14:8). The two-stage purification process for parturients (Lev 12) might likewise have been suggestive for developed ideas of graded impurity, even though it does not mention washings explicitly.

35. Logically, handwashing before meals must either assume that hands can become separately impure apart from (or more impure than) the rest of the body from contact with secondary impurities, needing separate purification to return to the same level of (im)purity as the rest of the body, or assume that although impure at the same level as the rest of the body they can acquire a lighter degree of impurity than the rest of the body through separate washing. The first assumption is often implied in scholarly discussions relating to rabbinic texts and their interpretations.

is found in the discharge laws, where a *zāb* is said to contaminate anything/anyone he touches, unless he has washed his hands (Lev 15:11).[36] This again indicates an understanding of impurity as graded, though still in a fairly unqualified sense. Handwashing before meals is known from rabbinic sources, being assumed by the schools of Shammai and Hillel (m. Ber. 8:2), but it is also known from Mark 7, where the author, writing around 70 CE, assumes it as a long-standing practice.

Defilement via Food

This leads us to my fourth point, that *defilement via impure food was an issue*. Scholars have often suggested that Mark is exaggerating about the extent to which handwashing was practiced ("*all* Jews").[37] This is probably true, but it would be equally wrong to limit the practice to small groups of extremists. Some claim that eating ordinary food in purity would have been of no use, because impure hands would only defile food in the second remove and such food could not defile a person anyway. It could only, via liquid, contaminate priestly food (*tərûmâ*).[38] Hence the rabbis' claim that it was a rabbinic decree in order to safeguard the purity

---

The second assumption is implied by Lev 15:11, which is one likely background to the development of more general handwashing practices. Whether these two assumptions were formulated and whether a differentiation between them played any role for views and practices of handwashing at the end of the Second Temple period has not, to my knowledge, been subject to scholarly discussion. In any case the result is similar: handwashing prevents further spread of impurity. An additional assumption, making handwashing meaningful, is that of liquids (which hands easily come in contact with during a meal) being especially conducive to impurity. For an extended discussion of various interpretations of the problematic role of liquids in the Second Temple period and beyond, see Kazen 2010a, 81–85; 2013a, 165–76.

36. See previous note.

37. Even if Mark is exaggerating about "all Jews" following Pharisaic handwashing practice, we should read him to mean this to be an established practice at the time. Reading the Greek *ioudaioi* as "Judeans" makes no change, but only requires us to remind ourselves that Galileans were in some sense Judeans, too.

38. Cf. Sanders 1985, 297–98, 228–30; 1992, 237–38. Similarly, Avemarie (2010, 266–67) claims that impurity of hands is not strong enough to contaminate food, and that Jesus anyway does not consider defilement by impure food as existing. Zaas (1996, 224) also suggests that the chain of contagion from hands to food and eater was not biblical.

of *tərûmâ* (m. Shabb. 1:4; m. Zavim 5:12; m. Tehar. 10:4; b. Shabb. 13b, 14a-b; b. Pesah. 14b).

The fine details of this discussion would take pages to tangle out, as with the numerous suggestions about the origin of the handwashing practice. I have dealt with this in detail elsewhere.[39] We do not know the chain of tradition—the rabbinic evidence has missing links. But it is entirely unlikely that the author of Mark would grasp a recently invented rabbinic decree and present it to his readers as ancient practice.[40] Something is going on in the rabbinic defense of handwashing and eating in purity that scholars often fail to realize. Here we need to apply insights about halakic development, which leads us into my fifth point.

Rabbinic Anachronisms

A number of rabbinic characteristics commonly appealed to in discussions about handwashing practices during the Second Temple period in order to eat in purity *represent later developments*. The *elaborate system of removes* that we can deduce from rabbinic texts is a scholarly construct, incorporating or harmonizing texts that represent views and discussions from a variety of angles.[41] This system is certainly *related* to the situation during the Second Temple period, but reflects the far end of a long development. Texts such as m. Tehar. 2:2 suggest competing systems and diverging views, in particular with regard to purity of food. Rabbi Eliezer, who

---

39. Kazen 2010a, 67–85; 2010c, 113–35; 2013a, 162–76.

40. It requires a leap of faith to believe that Mark is picking up a recent practice, going to great pains to present it as ancient custom for his apparently quite ignorant gentile recipients, only to use it as an illustration in an argument that is aimed to prove to them that they can eat nonkosher food. It is much more reasonable to think that this practice is part of Mark's received tradition and the best he can offer—in spite of having to surround it with explanatory clauses—in order to argue his case (all foods clean), which is quite far from the meaning of the tradition he uses. I have similar problems with James Crossley's (2004) alternative early dating of Mark, and its concomitant result that Mark and Jesus are both protesting against handwashing before meals, since this requires that Mark's fairly ignorant gentile readers (such they are in Crossley's view, too) needed all the textual wriggling of Mark 7 in order to be convinced not to follow a peculiar practice (handwashing), the existence of which they needed to be informed of in the first place.

41. See the varying systems and charts in Wright 1987; Milgrom 1991; Harrington 1993; Kazen 2010a, 2–7, 78–81; 2010c, 168.

often reflects ancient halakah, understands the eater to share the impurity level of the food, in contrast to Rabbi Joshua, whose understanding better fits the "system."[42] The discussions in Mishnah Teharot are at the same time both extremely detailed and struggling with conflicting conceptions and perspectives of contamination. This suggests a basic but simpler and less differentiated understanding of graded impurities and contamination chains during Jesus's time, including views of secondary impurities being able to contaminate people.[43]

An early understanding of secondary impurities and food contamination would have entailed a basic understanding that *people and vessels could be defiled by food and liquids*. Although some claim this to be a rabbinic reversal of the biblical rule, I have argued that this is not the case.[44] The idea of liquid being especially conducive to impurity is old, originating with Lev 11 and attested in Qumran as well as in the Mishnah.[45] It figures in the schools' discussion about handwashing (m. Ber. 8:2).[46] Some of the rabbis claimed that impure food could not defile a person, except for the very special case of a pure bird that had died a natural death (m. Tehar. 1:1–3; Sifra Parashat Emor Pereq 4).[47] The roundabout way and nominalist exegesis by

---

42. R. Eliezer's ruling is simple: the eater shares the food's degree of impurity, whether the first, second, or third degree. This, in fact, does not fit the harmonized "system" at all, according to which people could not become impure in a third degree and hands only in a second. R. Joshua's ruling is consistent with a view of liquid reverting to the first degree, thus recontaminating with a second-degree impurity. Joshua's ruling, however, partly operates with a scale *relative* to the holiness of that which is contaminated, or blends conceptions of contamination potential with degrees of susceptibility. In any case, the point is that the eater of ordinary food impure in the first or second degree is not affected any further than by second-degree impurity (assumed to contaminate tərûmâ), while eating food in the third degree will only affect qodāšim, but not tərûmâ.

43. On the developed notion of removes being later than 70 CE, see Neusner 1974–1977, 22:62, 160–64; 1987, 171–78; 1998, 205. See also Hübner 1986, 162–64; Westerholm 1978.

44. Furstenberg 2008, 192–98; Kazen 2010c, 130–34; 2013a, 184–88.

45. 4QMMT B55–58; cf. CD XII, 15–17; m. Yad. 4:7 (referring to Pharisees and Sadducees); m. Tehar. 2:6–7; m. Parah 8:7 // m. Tehar. 8:7; t. Demai 2:11–12. Note that 4QMMT can no longer be understood to represent a narrow sectarian view only, but rather more general expansionist ideas. See further Weissenberg 2009, 19–20; Harrington 2011, 329–37.

46. Cf. the explanation of t. Ber. 6:2.

47. Neusner 1988, 3:196.

which they arrived at this conclusion reveals a late date. Leviticus 11 does suggest that impure food defiles the eater (11:39–44), although the precise relationship between the impurity of food and drink contaminated by *šereṣ* impurity via a vessel (11:32–34), and defilement from eating carcass (11:40), remains unclear. In any case later rabbis seem to argue *against* a customary understanding of food impurity contaminating the eater that had evolved during the Second Temple period, partly based on a systemic reading of Lev 11 together with the subsequent purity laws.[48]

Hence *claims that hand impurity originated as a rabbinic decree to protect* tərûmâ *are also late.*[49] Some rabbinic traditions in fact suggest that a rule of this kind originated in the late Second Temple period (m. Shabb. 1:4; m. Zavim 5:12; b. Shabb. 13b) and some ascribe it to Hillel and Shammai themselves rather than their schools (b. Shabb. 14b). In any case the practice must have been there before the rule. Later rabbis nevertheless go to great lengths in order to explain away the relevance of hand impurity for ordinary food, claiming that defilement of vessels by liquid, food impurity from liquid defiled by hands, and contamination of people via food were only safety measures to prevent contamination of *tərûmâ* and not binding in the same way as biblical rules.[50] All of this is part of an innovative tendency that creates a dichotomy between purity for the sake of the cult and as a voluntary undertaking in ordinary life, and resorts to exegetical explanations and nominalist interpretations that are extremely unlikely to have originated in the first century CE.

Scripture versus Halakah Later Polemics

This means that *the accusation against the Pharisees for setting aside divine Scripture in favor of human halakah*, which we find for example in Mark 7, *is unlikely to come from the historical Jesus*.[51] If all of the aforementioned assumptions reflect late rabbinic interpretations and rhetorics in order to limit the scope of many purity practices and restrict them to the

---

48. Part of this rabbinic discussion focuses on the capacity of liquids to defile utensils, which the Amoraim understood as a rabbinic law (cf. b. Pesah. 14b, 17b–20b; Sifra Parashat Shemini Parashah 8, CXVI:I [Neusner 1988, 2:204–5]).

49. See m. Shabb. 1:4; m. Zavim 5:12; m. Tehar. 10:4; b. Shabb. 13b, 14a–b; b. Pesah. 14b.

50. For references, see above, nn. 48 and 49.

51. Kazen 2013a, 179–82.

cultic sphere, they cannot represent the historical Pharisees. It is anachronistic to project the Talmudic denials that food is capable of defiling the eater and that impurity of ordinary food was only observed as an extra in order to safeguard *tərûmâ* onto the scene in which Jesus and the Pharisees disagree on handwashing. In an evolving and dynamic context, every practice is at some point and to some degree innovative,[52] but handwashing before meals hardly appeared suddenly, neither at the time of Jesus nor at the time of Mark. It grew organically out of a sociocultural context, from early biblical and customary roots. It is Mark who—just like other early followers of Jesus—accused his non–Christ believing Jewish opponents of neglecting Scripture in favor of their own interpretations, just like the incipient rabbinic movement accused the Jesus movement of the same thing. If we read the rhetorics in Mark 7 with its apologetic appeal to Isa 29:13, as Jesus's accusation against the Pharisees for introducing extrabiblical concepts and practices, we become guilty of double anachronisms by projecting Christian as well as rabbinic apologetics onto Jesus and the Pharisees.[53]

Prophetic or Halakic?

So what does all of this mean for our picture of the *historical Jesus and his stance on purity*? My conclusion is that he appears as *less halakic and more prophetic than sometimes assumed*. This is not to deny that he partakes in what we at least in hindsight must label halakic discourse. Nor does this statement suggest that a deep and detailed understanding of halakic development and the state of purity halakah during the first century CE would be superfluous—far from it! But Jesus did not debate with the rabbis of the Mishnah, and his opponents rarely held exactly the same assumptions as their successors. Since Jesus's voice is constantly blended with the voices of his followers, we must beware of construing anachronistic halakic conflicts based on assumptions not yet evolved. Various suggestions that Jesus

---

52. Late rabbinic attempts to limit the consequences of liquids for impurity in ordinary life by downplaying their capacity to defile are in fact more innovative than the general view of the defiling force of liquids that had become customary in the late Second Temple period.

53. Isa 29 is a common source for early Christian polemics against Judaism, as Westerholm (1978, 76) points out: examples within the New Testament are Rom 9:20; 11:8; 1 Cor 1:19; Col 2:22.

defended biblical law against Pharisaic innovations, or that he understood bodily impurity to contaminate items and food, but not vice versa, build on faulty assumptions and a state of halakic development that was not in place yet.

There have been many attempts recently to associate Jesus's central statement in Mark 7:15—that nothing from the outside, going in, can defile a human being, but that which goes out from a human being defiles the human being—with various halakic issues.[54] These attempts usually take Jesus's statement literally, or absolutely, but to avoid the impression that Jesus flouted purity practices altogether, the statement can be taken as an argument in a halakic debate, in which Jesus and his opponents disagree regarding handwashing as a halakic expansion, how food contaminates the eater, and the direction of contamination. I want to emphasize that if the central statement is read thus, it certainly does *not* represent Jesus, but someone who debates with later rabbis.

Mark, who is hardly interested in a halakic debate, instead gives the saying a moralizing interpretation, ending with a vice list typical of early Christian letters (Mark 7:17–23). The vice list can hardly represent Jesus either.[55] If the central statement in 7:15 originates with early Jesus tradition—as many scholars believe—it is more reasonable to read it as a dialectic negation, contrasting outer impurity (contagion) with inner impurity (heart), relativizing the former in order to emphasize the importance of the latter. This is not identical with Mark's moralizing expansions that follow. The mention of "heart" in verse 19, which triggers the Markan vice list, is perhaps an explanatory gloss, but the conception of inner purity, or purity of heart, is nevertheless a possible candidate for Jesus's own viewpoint.

Purity of heart may sound pietistic to Western post-Christians, but is a common metaphor in Israelite tradition, not least in the Psalms and in Proverbs.[56] However, it is also linked with prophetic rhetorics: Jeremiah

---

54. Cf. Meier 2009, 342–477; Avemarie 2010; Furstenberg 2008; Wassén 2016a.

55. The whole section is "indoors" (*eis oikon*)—an expression Mark frequently uses to provide interpretations relevant for the context of his recipients (cf. Mark 2:1; 3:20; 9:28; and the similar *en tē oikia* in 9:33; 10:10)—and can be suspected of being Markan redaction. The vice list is typical of diaspora Judaism and the early Jesus movement.

56. Cf. Ps 51:12, as well as the juxtaposition of clean hands (palms) and pure hearts in Pss 24:4; 73:13; Prov 20:9; 22:22. See also 4Q435; 4Q436; 4Q525.

(4:14) speaks of Jerusalem washing her heart from evil, and Ezekiel juxtaposes purification from idolatry to a new heart (Ezek 36:25–27).[57] Prophetic discourse often emphasizes social justice by downplaying, or even denouncing, cultic matters, such as sacrifice, incense, or fasting—the best-known examples are found in Isaiah and Amos (Isa 1:10–17; 58:1–12; Jer 6:20; Hos 6:6; Amos 5:21–27). But just as the prophets did not think of closing down the cult,[58] Jesus did not aim to abolish purity practices.

Purity language is used in Israelite tradition without halakic connotations to emphasize moral uprightness and innocence.[59] This is true regarding prophetic critique of cultic matters, too. As we have seen, the historical Jesus did discuss halakic issues with his contemporaries, but those were not the later rabbis. If Jesus addressed issues of purity—and cult—rhetorically, from the perspective of an eschatological prophet, he would have aimed at abolishing neither, but rather have looked for social justice, understood as faithfulness to God. This is exactly what the alternative purity sayings from the Q tradition imply: purification of the inside for the sake of the poor (Luke 11:39–41). Luke's rhetorics on this point is more similar to Mark's than sometimes acknowledged: "purify the inside and all will be clean." Here too, the argument is not that bodily impurity is unimportant, but that it is irrelevant compared to (i.e., less relevant than) an inside "full of greed and evil" (Luke 11:39).[60]

The relative importance of a pure inside (heart) as compared to pure food, pure hands, or pure bodies could thus have been a historical motive for Jesus's defense of his and his disciples' seemingly negligent behavior. At least the core of the human being had not been defiled. At its essence, this is not a halakic way of reasoning, but rather a prophetic stance. Purifications of the body are not denied, but placed in relation to social justice and compassionate behavior.

---

57. Cf. the purification of the innermost part of human flesh in 1QS IV, 20–21.

58. For studies emphasizing that prophetic cult criticism did not aim to abolish the cult, see Lafferty 2012; Eidevall 2012.

59. I will not here enter the discussion about "ritual" and "moral" impurity, which I consider to be highly problematic concepts; see my application of cognitive metaphor and conceptual blending theories on the use of purity language in Kazen 2014 = ch. 5 in this volume.

60. Cf. 1QS III, 4–9, emphasizing that no outer purifications or atonements are sufficient for an unrepentant sinner.

Bibliography

Abe, Chikara. 2003. *Impurity and Death: A Japanese Perspective*. Parkland, FL: Dissertation.com.

Achenbach, Reinhard. 2003. *Die Vollendung der Tora: Studien zur Redaktionsgeschichte des Numeribuches im Kontext von Hexateuch und Pentateuch*. BZABR 3. Wiesbaden: Harrassowitz.

———. 2009. "Verunreinigung durch die Berührung Toter: Zum Ursprung einer altisraelitischen Vorstellung." Pages 347–69 in *Tod und Jenseits im alten Israel und in seiner Umwelt: Theologische, religionsgeschichtliche, archäologische und ikonographische Aspekte*. Edited by Angelika Berlejung and Bernd Janowski. FAT 64. Tübingen: Mohr Siebeck.

Adler, Yonatan. "The Ritual Baths Near the Temple Mount and Extra-purification before Entering the Temple Courts: A Reply to Eyal Regev." *IEJ* 56:209–15.

———. 2008a. "The Ancient Synagogue and the Ritual Bath: The Archaeological Evidence and Its Relevance to an Early Rabbinic Enactment" [Hebrew]. *Cathedra* 128:51–72.

———. 2008b. "Second Temple Period Ritual Baths Adjacent to Agricultural Installations: The Archaeological Evidence in Light of the Halakhic Sources." *JJS* 59:62–72.

———. 2009. "Ritual Baths Adjacent to Tombs: An Analysis of the Archaeological Evidence in Light of the Halakhic Sources." *JSJ* 40:55–73.

———. 2011. *The Archaeology of Purity: Archaeological Evidence for the Observance of Ritual Purity in Ereẓ-Israel from the Hasmonean Period until the End of the Talmudic Era (164 BCE–400 CE)* [Hebrew]. Ramat-Gan: Bar-Ilan University Press.

———. 2013. "Religion, Judaism: Purity in the Roman Period." Pages 240–49 in *The Oxford Encyclopedia of the Bible and Archaeology*. Edited by Daniel Master et al. Oxford: Oxford University Press.

———. 2014a. "Tosefta Shabbat 1:14—'Come and See the Extent to Which Purity Has Spread': An Archaeological Perspective on the Historical

Background to a Late Tannaitic Passage." Pages 63–82 in *Talmuda de-Eretz Israel: Archaeology and the Rabbis in Late Antique Palestine*. Edited by Steven Fine and Aaron Koller. Boston: de Gruyter.

———. 2014b. "The Myth of the *'ôṣār* in Second Temple-Period Ritual Baths: An Anachronistic Interpretation of a Modern-Era Innovation." *JJS* 65:263–83.

———. 2016. "Between Priestly Cult and Common Culture: The Material Evidence of Ritual Purity Observance in Early Roman Jerusalem Reassessed." *JAJ* 7:228–48.

———. 2017. "The Decline of Jewish Ritual Purity Observance in Roman Palaestina: An Archaeological Perspective on Chronology and Historical Context." Pages 269–84 in *Expressions of Cult in the Southern Levant in the Greco-Roman Period*. Edited by Oren Taal and Zeev Weiss. CS 6. Turnhout: Brepols.

———. 2018. "The Hellenistic Origins of Jewish Ritual Immersion." *JJS* 69:1–21.

———. 2019. "New Insights in the Study of Roman Period Jewish Chalk Vessels" [Hebrew]. *Qad* 157:2–17.

———. Forthcoming. *The Origins of Judaism: An Archaeological-Historical Reappraisal*. AYBRL. New Haven: Yale University Press.

Adler, Yonatan, and Omri Lernau. 2021. "The Pentateuchal Dietary Proscription against Finless and Scaleless Aquatic Species in Light of Ancient Fish Remains." *Tel Aviv* 48:5–26.

Alon, Gedalyahu. 1977. *Jews, Judaism and the Classical World: Studies in Jewish History in the Times of the Second Temple and Talmud*. Jerusalem: Magnes.

Amihay, Aryeh. 2017. *Theory and Practice in Essene Law*. New York: Oxford University Press.

Amit, David, and Yonatan Adler. 2010. "The Observance of Ritual Purity after 70 C.E.: A Reevaluation of the Evidence in Light of Recent Archaeological Discoveries." Pages 121–43 in *"Follow the Wise": Studies in Jewish Culture and History in Honor of Lee I. Levine*. Edited by Zeev Weiss, Oded Irshai, Jodi Magness, and Seth Schwartz. Winona Lake, IN: Eisenbrauns.

Amit, David, Hagit Torgü, and Peter Gendelman. 2008. "Ḥorvat Burnat: A Jewish Village in the Lod Shephelah during the Hellenistic and Roman Periods." *Qad* 136:96–107.

Amit, David, Jon Seligman, and Irina Zilberbod. 2016. "Stone Vessel Production Caves on the Eastern Slope of Mount Scopus, Jerusalem."

Pages 320–42 in *New Approaches to Old Stones: Recent Studies of Ground Stone Artifacts*. Edited by Yorke M. Rowan and Jennie R. Ebeling. London: Routledge.

André, Gunnel, and Helmer Ringgren. 1986. 'טָמֵא *ṭāmēʾ*; טֻמְאָה *ṭumʾâ*'. *TDOT* 5:330–42.

Angyal, Andras. 1941. "Disgust and Related Aversions." *JAbPsy* 36:393–412.

Appelrouth, Scott, and Laura Desfor Edles. 2011. *Sociological Theory in the Contemporary Era: Texts and Readings*. Los Angeles: Pine Forge.

Attridge, Harold W. 2004. "Pollution, Sin, Atonement, Salvation." Pages 71–83 in *Religions of the Ancient World: A Guide*. Edited by Sarah Iles Johnston. Cambridge: Belknap.

Auld, A. Graeme. 2011. *I & II Samuel: A Commentary*. OTL. Louisville: Westminster John Knox.

Aune, David E. 2011. "Paul, Ritual Purity, and the Ritual Baths South of the Temple Mount." Pages 287–320 in *Celebrating Paul: Festschrift in Honor of Jerome Murphy-O'Connor, O.P., and Joseph A. Fitzmyer, S.J.*. Edited by Peter Spitaler. CBQMS 48. Washington, DC: Catholic Biblical Association of America.

Avemarie, Friedrich. 2010. "Jesus and Halakhic Purity." Pages 255–80 in *The New Testament and Rabbinic Literature*. Edited by Peter Tomson, Didier Pollefeyt, Fernando García Martínez, and Reimund Bieringer. JSJSup 136. Leiden: Brill, 2010.

Baert, Patrick, and Filipe Carreira da Silva. 2010. *Social Theory in the Twentieth Century and Beyond*. 2nd ed. Malden, MA: Polity.

Balberg, Mira. 2014. *Purity, Body, and Self in Early Rabbinic Literature*. Berkeley: University of California Press.

Barmash, Pamela. 2005. *Homicide in the Biblical World*. Cambridge: Cambridge University Press.

Baronov, David. 2016. *Conceptual Foundations of Social Research Methods*. 2nd ed. Abingdon: Routledge.

Barr, James. 1985. "The Question of Religious Influence: The Case of Zoroastrianism, Judaism, and Christianity." *JAAR* 53:201–35.

Baumgarten, Joseph M. 1967. "The Essene Avoidance of Oil and the Laws of Purity." *RevQ* 21:183–92.

———. 1980. "The Pharisaic-Sadducean Controversies about Purity and the Qumran Texts." *JJS* 31:157–70.

———. 1992. "The Purification Rituals in DJD 7." Pages 199–209 in *The Dead Sea Scrolls: Forty Years of Research*. Edited by Devorah Dimant and Uriel Rappaport. STDJ 10. Leiden: Brill.

———. 1995a. "The Laws about Fluxes in 4QTohora^a (4Q274)." Pages 1–8 in *Time to Prepare the Way in the Wilderness*. Edited by Devorah Dimant and Lawrence H. Schiffman. STDJ 16. Leiden: Brill.

———. 1995b. "The Red Cow Purification Rites in Qumran Texts." *JJS* 46:112–19.

———. 1999a. "D. Tohorot." Pages 79–122 in *Qumran Cave 4, XXV: Halakhic Texts*. Edited by Joseph M. Baumgarten et al. DJD 35. Oxford: Clarendon.

———. 1999b. "The Purification Liturgies." Pages 200–212 in vol. 2 of *The Dead Sea Scrolls after Fifty Years: A Comprehensive Assessment*. Edited by Peter W. Flint and James C. VanderKam. Leiden: Brill.

———. 2000. "The Use of מי נידה for General Purification." Pages 481–85 in *The Dead Sea Scrolls Fifty Years after Their Discovery: Proceedings of the Jerusalem Congress, July 20-25, 1997*. Edited by Lawrence H. Schiffman, Emanuel Tov, and James C. VanderKam. Jerusalem: Shrine of the Book, Israel Museum.

Beck, Roger. 2004. "Sin, Pollution, and Purity: Rome." Pages 509–11 in *Religions of the Ancient World: A Guide*. Edited by Sarah Iles Johnston. Cambridge: Belknap.

Beckman, Gary M. 1983. *Hittite Birth Rituals*. 2nd ed. Wiesbaden: Harrassowitz.

Bell, Catherine M. 1992. *Ritual Theory, Ritual Practice*. Oxford: Oxford University Press.

Bell, H. Idris, and Theodore C. Skeat. 1935. *Fragments of an Unknown Gospel and Other Early Christian Papyri*. London: Oxford University Press.

Bendlin, Andreas. 2007. "Purity and Pollution." Pages 178–89 in *A Companion to Greek Religion*. Edited by Daniel Ogden. BCAW. Oxford: Blackwell.

Berger, Klaus. 1988. "Jesus als Pharisäer und frühe Christen als Pharisäer." *NovT* 30:231–62.

Berger, Michael S. 1998. *Rabbinic Authority*. New York: Oxford University Press.

Berlin, Andrea M. 2005. "Jewish Life before the Revolt: The Archaeological Evidence." *JSJ* 36:417–70.

———. 2014. "Household Judaism." Pages 208–15 in *Life, Culture, and Society*. Edited by David A. Fiensy and James Riley Strange. Vol. 1 of *Galilee in the Late Second Temple and Mishnaic Periods*. Minneapolis: Fortress.

Berquist, Jon L. 1995. *Judaism in Persia's Shadow: A Social and Historical Approach*. Minneapolis: Fortress.

———. 2006. "Constructions of Identity in Postcolonial Yehud." Pages 53–66 in *Judah and the Judeans in the Persian Period*. Edited by Oded Lipschits and Manfred Oeming. Winona Lake, IN: Eisenbrauns.

———. 2007. *Approaching Yehud: New Approaches to the Study of the Persian Period*. SemeiaSt 50. Atlanta: Society of Biblical Literature.

Binder, Donald D. 1999. *Into the Temple Courts: The Place of the Synagogue in the Second Temple Period*. SBLDS 169. Atlanta: Society of Biblical Literature.

Birenboim, Hannan. 2012. "Expelling the Unclean from the Cities of Israel and the Uncleanness of Lepers and Men with a Discharge according to 4Q274 1 i." *DSD* 19:28–54.

Biró, Tamás. 2013. "Is Judaism Boring? On the Lack of Counterintuitive Agents in Jewish Rituals." Pages 120–43 in *Mind, Morality and Magic: Cognitive Science Approaches in Biblical Studies*. Edited by István Czachesz and Risto Uro. BibW. Durham: Acumen.

Blidstein, Moshe. 2017. *Purity, Community, and Ritual in Early Christian Literature*. OSAR. Oxford: Oxford University Press.

Blomberg, Craig. 2005. *Contagious Holiness: Jesus' Meals with Sinners*. Downers Grove, IL: InterVarsity.

Blum, Erhard. 1990. *Studien zur Komposition des Pentateuch*. BZAW 189. Berlin: de Gruyter.

Bodel, John. 2000. "Dealing with the Dead: Undertakers, Executioners and Potter's Fields in Ancient Rome." Pages 128–51 in *Death and Disease in the Ancient City*. Edited by Valerie M. Hope and Eireann Marshall. London: Routledge.

Bóid, I. Ruairidh M. 1989a. *Principles of Samaritan Halachah*. SJLA 38. Leiden: Brill.

———. 1989b. "The Samaritan Halachah." Pages 624–49 in *The Samaritans*. Edited by Alan D. Crown. Tübingen: Mohr Siebeck.

———. 1997. "L'Antiquité des Racines du Karaïsme." *JEOL* 34:101–115.

Booth, Roger P. 1986. *Jesus and the Laws of Purity: Tradition History and Legal History in Mark 7*. JSNTSup 13. Sheffield: JSOT.

Borg, Marcus J. 1984. *Conflict, Holiness and Politics in the Teachings of Jesus*. Lewiston, NY: Mellen.

Borgeaud, Philippe. 1999. "Melampous and Epimenides: Two Greek Paradigms of the Treatment of Mistake." Pages 287–300 in *Transforma-

tions of the Inner Self in Ancient Religions. Edited by Jan Assmann and Guy G. Stroumsa. SHR 83. Leiden: Brill.

Boyce, Mary. 1975. *Early Period*. Vol. 1 of *A History of Zoroastrianism*. HdO 1/8/1/2/2A. Leiden: Brill.

———. 1982. *Under the Achaemenians*. Vol. 2 of *A History of Zoroastrianism*. HdO 1/8/1/2/2A. Leiden: Brill.

Boyer, Pascal, and Pierre Liénard. 2006. "Why Ritualized Behavior? Precaution Systems and Action Parsing in Developmental, Pathological and Cultural Rituals: With Open Peer Commentary." *BehBS* 29:1–56.

Broshi, Magen. 1974. "The Expansion of Jerusalem in the Reigns of Hezekiah and Manasseh." *IEJ* 24:21–26.

———. 2006. "Qumran and the Essenes: Purity and Pollution, Six Categories." *RevQ* 22:463–74.

Bruneau, Philippe. 1970. *Recherches sur les cultes de Délos à l'époque hellénistique et à l'époque impériale*. BEFAR 2017. Paris: Éditions E. de Boccard.

Büchler, Adolf. 1926. "The Levitical Impurity of the Gentile in Palestine before the Year 70." *JQR* 17:1–81.

———. 1928. *Studies in Sin and Atonement in the Rabbinic Literature of the First Century*. London: Oxford University Press.

———. 1968. *Der Galiläische 'Am-haʾareṣ des Zweiten Jahrhunderts: Beiträge zur innern Geschichte des palästinischen Judentums in den ersten zwei Jahrhunderten*. Hildesheim: Georg Olms Verlagsbuchhandlung.

Bulbulia, Joseph. 2010. "Charismatic Signalling." *JSRNC* 3:518–51.

Burkert, Walter. 1985. *Greek Religion: Archaic and Classical*. Oxford: Blackwell.

Cahill, Jane. 1992. "Chalk Vessel Assemblages of the Persian/Hellenistic and Early Roman Periods." Pages 190–274 in *Stratigraphical, Environmental, and Other Reports*. Vol. 3 of *Excavations at the City of David 1978–1985: Directed by Yigal Shiloh*. Edited by Alon De Groot and Donald T. Ariel. Qedem 33. Jerusalem: Institute of Archaeology, Hebrew University.

Cazelles, Henri. 1977. "Pur et impur aux origines de l'Hébreu et à Ugarit." Pages 443–49 in vol. 2 of *Mélanges offerts au R. P. Henri Fleisch, S.J.*. Edited by Université Saint-Joseph, Lebanon. MUSJ 49. Beirut: Imprimerie Catholique.

Chankin-Gould, J. D'ror, Derek Hutchinson, David Hilton Jackson, Tyler D. Mayfield, Leah Rediger Schulte, Tammi J. Schneider, and Elizabeth Winkelman. 2008. "The Sanctified 'Adulteress' and Her

Circumstantial Clause: Bathsheba's Bath and Self-Consecration in 2 Samuel 11." *JSOT* 32:339–52.

Chilton, Bruce. 1996. *Pure Kingdom: Jesus' Vision of God*. Grand Rapids: Eerdmans.

Choksy, Jamsheed K. 1989. *Purity and Pollution in Zoroastrianism: Triumph over Evil*. Austin: University of Texas Press.

———. 2004. "Sin, Pollution, and Purity: Iran." Pages 505–7 in *Religions of the Ancient World: A Guide*. Edited by Sarah Iles Johnston. Cambridge: Belknap.

Cholewinski, Alfred. 1976. *Heiligkeitsgesetz und Deuteronomium: Eine vergleichende Studie*. AnBib 66. Rome: Biblical Institute.

Christiansen, Birgit. 2013. "Reinheitsvorstellungen und Entsühnungsriten der Hethiter und ihr möglicher Einfluss auf die biblische Überlieferung." *BN* 156:131–53.

Cohen, Shaye J. D. 1991. "Menstruants and the Sacred in Judaism and Christianity." Pages 273–99 in *Woman's History and Ancient History*. Edited by Sarah B. Pomeroy. Chapel Hill: University of North Carolina.

Colpe, Carsten. 1995. "Priesterschrift und Videvdad: Ritualistische Gesetzgebung für Israeliten und Iranier." Pages 9–18 in *Meilenstein: Festgabe für Herbert Donner zum 16. Februar 1995*. Edited by Manfred Weippert and Stefan Timm. ÄAT 30. Wiesbaden: Harrassowitz.

———. 2003. *Iranier – Aramäer – Hebräer – Hellenen: Iranische Religionen und ihre Westbeziehungen; Einzelstudien und Versuch einer Zusammenschau*. WUNT 154. Tübingen: Mohr Siebeck.

Coser, Lewis. 1977. *Masters of Sociological Thought: Ideas in Historical and Social Context*. 2nd ed. Fort Worth, TX: Harcourt Brace.

Coulson, Seanna, and Todd Oakley. 2000. "Blending Basics." *CL* 11.3/4:175–96.

Crawford, Sidnie White. 2000. *The Temple Scroll and Related Texts*. CQS 2. Sheffield: Sheffield Academic.

———. 2008. *Rewriting Scripture in Second Temple Times*. Grand Rapids: Eerdmans.

Crossley, James G. 2004. *The Date of Mark's Gospel: Insights from the Law in Earliest Christianity*. JSNTSup 266. London: T&T Clark.

———. 2015. *Jesus and the Chaos of History: Redirecting the Life of the Historical Jesus*. Oxford: Oxford University Press.

Curtis, Valerie. 2013. *Don't Look, Don't Touch: The Science behind Revulsion*. Oxford: Oxford University Press.

Damasio, Antonio R. 1994. *Descartes' Error: Emotion, Reason and the Human Brain*. New York: Grosset/Putnam.

Danks, David. 2009. "The Psychology of Causal Perception and Reasoning." Pages 447–70 in *The Oxford Handbook of Causation*. Edited by Helen Beebee, Christopher Hitchcock, and Peter Menzies. Oxford: Oxford University Press.

Darmesteter, James. 1895. *The Vendîdâd*. 2nd ed. Part 1 of *The Zend-Avesta*. SBE 4. Oxford: Clarendon.

Darwin, Charles. 1989. *The Expression of the Emotions in Man and Animals*. WCD 23. New York: New York University Press.

Deines, Roland. 1993. *Jüdische Steingefässe und pharisäische Frömmigkeit: Ein archäologisch-historischer Beitrag zum Verständnis von Joh 2,6 und der jüdischen Reinheitshalacha zur Zeit Jesu*. WUNT 2/52. Tübingen: Mohr Siebeck.

deSilva, David A. 2000. *Honor, Patronage, Kinship and Purity: Unlocking New Testament Culture*. Downers Grove, IL: InterVarsity.

Dhabhar, Ervad B. N. 1932. *The Persian Rivayats of Hormazyar Framarz and Others: Their Version with Introduction and Notes*. Bombay: K. R. Cama Oriental Institute.

Dietrich, Jan. 2010. *Kollektive Schuld und Haftung: Religions- und rechtsgeschichtliche Studien zum Sündenkuhritus des Deuteronomiums und zu verwandten Texten*. ORA 4. Tübingen: Mohr Siebeck.

Douglas, Mary. 1966. *Purity and Danger: An Analysis of Concepts of Pollution and Taboo*. London: Routledge & Kegan Paul.

———. 1972. "Deciphering a Meal." *Daedalus* 101:61–81.

———. 1975. *Implicit Meanings: Essays in Anthropology*. London: Routledge & Kegan Paul.

———. 1978. *Natural Symbols: Explorations in Cosmology*. Harmondsworth, UK: Penguin.

———. 1993. *In the Wilderness: The Doctrine of Defilement in the Book of Numbers*. JSOTSup 158. Sheffield: JSOT.

———. 1996. "Sacred Contagion." Pages 86–106 in *Reading Leviticus: A Conversation with Mary Douglas*. Edited by John F. A. Sawyer. JSOTSup 227. Sheffield: Sheffield Academic.

———. 1999. *Leviticus as Literature*. Oxford: Oxford University Press.

———. 2001. *In the Wilderness: The Doctrine of Defilement in the Book of Numbers*. Paperback ed. Oxford: Oxford University Press.

———. 2002. *Purity and Danger: An Analysis of Concepts of Pollution and Taboo*. London: Routledge.

———. 2004. *Jacob's Tears: The Priestly Work of Reconciliation*. Oxford: Oxford University Press.

Dunbar, Robin I. M. 1987. "Sociobiological Explanations and the Evolution of Ethnocentrism." Pages 48–59 in *The Sociobiology of Ethnocentrism*. Edited by Vernon Reynolds, Vincent S. E. Falger, and Ian Vine. London: Croom Helm.

Dunn, James D. G. 1990. *Jesus, Paul and the Law: Studies in Mark and Galatians*. London: SPCK.

———. 2002. "Jesus and Purity: An Ongoing Debate." *NTS* 48:449–67.

———. 2003. "Jesus and Holiness: The Challenge of Purity." Pages 168–92 in *Holiness Past and Present*. Edited by Stephen Barton. London: T&T Clark, 2003.

Durkheim, Émile. 1950. *The Rules of Sociological Method*. 8th ed. Translated by Sarah A. Soloway and John H. Mueller. Edited by George E. G. Catlin. New York: Free Press.

Edelman, Diana V., Philip R. Davies, Christophe Nihan, and Thomas Römer. 2012. *Opening the Books of Moses*. BM 1. Sheffield: Equinox, 2012.

Eidevall, Göran. 2012. *Sacrificial Rhetoric in the Prophetic Literature of the Hebrew Bible*. Lewiston, NY: Mellen.

Eilberg-Schwartz, Howard. 1990. *The Savage in Judaism: An Anthropology of Israelite Religion and Ancient Judaism*. Bloomington: Indiana University Press.

Ekroth, Gunnel. 2002. "The Sacrificial Rituals of Greek Hero-Cults in the Archaic to the Early Hellenistic Periods." KS 12. Liège: Centre International d'Étude de la Religion Grecque Antique.

Ellens, Deborah L. 2003. "Menstrual Impurity and the Innovation in Leviticus 15." Pages 29–43 in *Wholly Woman, Holy Blood: A Feminist Critique of Purity and Impurity*. Edited by Kristin de Troyer, Judith A. Herbert, Judith Ann Johnson, and Anne-Marie Korte. SAC. Harrisburg, PA: Trinity Press International.

———. 2008. *Women in the Sex Texts of Leviticus and Deuteronomy: A Comparative Conceptual Analysis*. LHBOTS 458. New York: T&T Clark.

Elliger, Karl. 1966. *Leviticus*. HAT 1/4. Tübingen: Mohr Siebeck.

Erbele-Küster, Dorothea. 2008. *Körper und Geschlecht: Studien zur Anthropologie von Leviticus 12 und 15*. Neukirchen-Vluyn: Neukirchener Verlag.

———. 2011. "Gender and Cult: 'Pure' and 'Impure' as Gender-Relevant Categories." Pages 375–405 in *Torah*. Edited by Irmtraud Fischer and Mercedes Navarro Puerto, with Andrea Taschl-Erber. English ed. edited by Jorunn Økland. BW 1/1. Atlanta: Society of Biblical Literature.

Eshel, Esther. 1999. "4QRitual of Purification A." Pages 135–53 in *Qumran Cave 4, XXV: Halakhic Texts*. Edited by Joseph M. Baumgarten et al. DJD 35. Oxford: Clarendon.

Eshel, Hanan. 1997. "A Note on 'Miqvaot' at Sepphoris." Pages 131–33 in *Archaeology and the Galilee: Texts and Contexts in the Graeco-Roman and Byzantine Periods*. Edited by Douglas R. Edwards and C. Thomas McCollough. SFSHJ 143. Atlanta: Scholars Press.

———. 2000. "CD 12:15–17 and the Stone Vessels Found at Qumran." Pages 45–52 in *The Damascus Document: A Centennial of Discovery*. Edited by Joseph M. Baumgarten, Esther G. Chazon, and Avital Pinnick. STDJ 34. Leiden: Brill.

Eskenazi, Tamara Cohn. 2006. "The Missions of Ezra and Nehemiah." Pages 509–29 in *Judah and the Judeans in the Persian Period*. Edited by Oded Lipschits and Manfred Oeming. Winona Lake, IN: Eisenbrauns.

Fantham, Elaine. 2012. "Purification in Ancient Rome." Pages 59–66 in *Rome, Pollution and Propriety: Dirt, Disease and Hygiene in the Eternal City from Antiquity to Modernity*. Edited by Mark Bradley with Kenneth Stow. Cambridge: Cambridge University Press.

Fatkin, Danielle Steen. 2019. "Invention of a Bathing Tradition in Hasmonean Palestine." *JSJ* 50:155–77.

Fauconnier, Gilles, and Mark Turner. 2002. *The Way We Think: Conceptual Blending and the Mind's Hidden Complexities*. New York: Basic Books.

Faulkner, Jason, Mark Schaller, Justin H. Park, and Lesley A. Duncan. 2004. "Evolved Disease-Avoidance Mechanisms and Contemporary Xenophobic Attitudes." *GPIR* 7:333–53.

Faust, Avraham, and Hayah Katz. 2016. "The Archaeology of Purity and Impurity: A Case-Study from Tel 'Eton, Israel." *CAJ* 27:1–27.

Feder, Yitzhaq. 2011. *Blood Expiation in Hittite and Biblical Ritual: Origins, Context, and Meaning*. WAWSup 2. Atlanta: Society of Biblical Literature.

———. 2013. "Contagion and Cognition: Bodily Experience and the Conceptualization of Pollution (*ṭum'ah*) in the Hebrew Bible." *JNES* 72:151–67.

———. 2014. "The Semantics of Purity in the Ancient Near East: Lexical Meaning as a Projection of Embodied Experience." *JANER* 14:87–113.

———. 2016. "Defilement, Disgust, and Disease: The Experiential Basis of Hittite and Akkadian Terms for Impurity." *JAOS* 136:99–116.

Feinstein, Eve. 2010. "Sexual Pollution in the Hebrew Bible." PhD diss., Harvard University.

———. 2014. *Sexual Pollution in the Hebrew Bible*. New York: Oxford University Press.

Feldman, Emanuel. 1977. *Biblical and Post-biblical Defilement and Mourning: Law as Theology*. LJLE. New York: Yeshiva University Press, KTAV Publishing House.

Finkelstein, Israel. 1996. "Ethnicity and Origin of the Iron I Settlers in the Highlands of Canaan: Can the Real Israel Stand Up?" *BA* 59:198–212.

———. 1997. "Pots and People Revisited: Ethnic Boundaries in the Iron Age I." Pages 216–37 in *The Archaeology of Israel: Constructing the Past, Interpreting the Present*. Edited by Neil A. Silberman and David Small. JSOTSup 237. Sheffield: Sheffield Academic.

———. 1998. "The Rise of Early Israel: Archaeology and Long-Term History." Pages 7–39 in *The Origin of Early Israel: Current Debate: Biblical, Historical and Archaeological Perspectives; Irene Levi-Sala Seminar, 1997*. Edited by Shmuel Aḥituv and Eliezer D. Oren. BS 12. Beer-Sheva: Ben-Gurion University of the Negev Press.

Fishbein, Harold D. 2012. *Peer Prejudice and Discrimination: The Origins of Prejudice*. 2nd ed. Mahwah, NJ: Routledge.

Fonrobert, Charlotte E. 1997. "The Woman with a Blood Flow (Mark 5.24–34) Revisited: Menstrual Laws and Jewish Culture in Christian Feminist Hermeneutics." Pages 121–40 in *Early Christian Interpretation of the Scriptures of Israel: Investigations and Proposals*. Edited by Craig A. Evans and James A. Sanders. JSNTSup 48. SSEJC 5. Sheffield: JSOT.

Förster, Niclas. 2015. "Kultische Reinheit und Identitätsfindung – Jesus und der jüdische Tempel nach P.Oxy. 840." Pages 85–109 in *Juden und Christen unter römischer Herrschaft: Selbstwahrnehmung und Fremdwahrnehmung in den ersten beiden Jahrhunderten n. Chr.* Edited by Niclas Förster and J. Cornelis de Vos. SIJD 10. Göttingen: Vandenhoeck & Ruprecht.

Fraade, Steven D. 2011. *Legal Fictions: Studies of Law and Narrative in the Discursive Worlds of Ancient Jewish Sectarians and Sages*. JSJSup 147. Leiden: Brill, 2011.

Frandsen, Paul John. 2004. "Sin, Pollution, and Purity: Egypt." Pages 497–99 in *Religions of the Ancient World: A Guide*. Edited by Sarah Iles Johnston. Cambridge: Belknap.

———. 2007. "The Menstrual 'Taboo' in Ancient Egypt." *JNES* 66.2:81–106.
Fredriksen, Paula. 2000. *Jesus of Nazareth, King of the Jews: A Jewish Life and the Emergence of Christianity.* London: Macmillan.
Freedman, Daniel G. 1961. "The Infant's Fear of Strangers and the Flight Response." *JCPP* 2:242–48.
Frei, Peter, and Klaus Koch. 1984. *Reichsidee und Reichsorganisation im Perserreich.* OBO 55. Freiburg: Universitätsverlag.
Frevel, Christian. 2013. "Purity Conceptions in the Book of Numbers in Context." Pages 369–411 in *Purity and the Forming of Religious Traditions in the Ancient Mediterranean World and Ancient Judaism.* Edited by Christian Frevel and Christophe Nihan. DHR 3. Leiden: Brill.
Frevel, Christian, and Christophe Nihan, eds. 2013. *Purity and the Forming of Religious Traditions in the Ancient Mediterranean World and Ancient Judaism.* DHR 3. Leiden: Brill.
Frymer-Kensky, Tikva. 1983. "Pollution, Purification, and Purgation in Biblical Israel." Pages 399–414 in *The Word of the Lord Shall Go Forth: Essays in Honor of David Noel Freedman on His Sixtieth Birthday.* Edited by Carol L. Meyers and Michael O'Connor. Winona Lake, IN: ASOR/Eisenbrauns.
Furstenberg, Yair. 2008. "Defilement Penetrating the Body: A New Understanding of Contamination in Mark 7.15." *NTS* 54:176–200.
———. 2015a. "Outsider Impurity: Trajectories of Second Temple Separation Traditions in Tannaitic Literature." Pages 40–68 in *Tradition, Transmission, and Transformation from Second Temple Literature through Judaism and Christianity in Late Antiquity: Proceedings of the Thirteenth International Symposium of the Orion Center for the Study of the Dead Sea Scrolls and Associated Literature.* Edited by Menahem Kister, Hillel Newman, Michael Segal, and Ruth Clements. STDJ 113. Leiden: Brill.
———. 2015b. "Controlling Impurity: The Natures of Impurity in Second Temple Debates." *DI* 30:163–96.
———. 2016a. *Purity and Community in Antiquity: Traditions of the Law from Second Temple Judaism to the Mishnah* [Hebrew]. Jerusalem: Magnes.
———. 2016b. "Initiation and the Ritual Purification from Sin: Between Qumran and the Apostolic Tradition." *DSD* 23:365–94.
———. Forthcoming. "The Christianization of Proselyte Baptism in Rabbinic Tradition." In *Coping with Religious Change in the Late-Antique*

Eastern Mediterranean. Edited by Eduard Iricinschi and Chrysi Kotsifou. STAC. Tübingen: Mohr Siebeck.

Gane, Roy. 2005. *Cult and Character: Purification Offerings, Day of Atonement, and Theodicy*. Winona Lake, IN: Eisenbrauns.

García Martínez, Florentino. 1988. "Les limites de la communauté: Pureté et impureté à Qumrân et dans le Noveau Testament." Pages 111–22 in *Text and Testimony: Essays on New Testament and Apocryphal Literature in Honour of A. F. J. Klijn*. Edited by Tjitze Baarda, Anthony Hilhorst, and Gerard P. Luttikhuizen. Kampen: Kok.

García Martínez, Florentino, and Eibert J. C. Tigchelaar, eds. 1998. *The Dead Sea Scrolls Study Edition*. 2 vols. Leiden: Brill.

Geertz, Clifford. 1973. *The Interpretation of Cultures: Selected Essays*. New York: Basic Books.

Gershevitch, Ilya. 1968. "Old Iranian Literature." Pages 10–28 in *Iranistik: Literatur*. Edited by Bertold Spuler. HdO 1.4.2.1. Leiden: Brill.

Gerstenberger, Erhard S. 1996. *Leviticus: A Commentary*. OTL. Louisville: Westminster John Knox.

Gibson, Shimon. 1983. "The Stone Vessel Industry at Ḥizma." *IEJ* 33:176–88.

———. 2005. "The Pool of Bethesda in Jerusalem and Jewish Purification Practices of the Second Temple Period." *POC* 55:270–93.

Gilders, William K. 2011. "Jewish Sacrifice: Its Nature and Function (According to Philo)." Pages 94–105 in *Ancient Mediterranean Sacrifice*. Edited by Jennifer Wright Knust and Zsuzsanna Várhelyi. New York: Oxford University Press.

———. 2013. "Ancient Israelite Sacrifice as Symbolic Action: Theoretical Reflections." *SEÅ* 78:1–22.

Ginsburskaya, Mila. 2009. "The Idea of Sin-Impurity: The Dead Sea Scrolls in the Light of Leviticus." *TynBul* 60:309–12.

———. 2010. "The Right of Counsel and the Idea of Purity in the *Rule of the Community* (1QS) and the *Rule of the Congregation* (1QSa)." Pages 77–90 in *Qumran Cave 1 Revisited: Texts from Cave 1 Sixty Years after Their Discovery; Proceedings of the Sixth Meeting of the IOQS in Ljubljana*. Edited by Daniel K. Falk, Sarianna Metso, Donald W. Parry, and Eibert J. C. Tigchelaar. STDJ 91. Leiden: Brill.

Goldingay, John. 2014. *A Critical and Exegetical Commentary on Isaiah 56–66*. ICC. London: Bloomsbury.

Goldstein, Elizabeth. 2015. *Impurity and Gender in the Hebrew Bible*. Lanham, MD: Rowman & Littlefield.

Grabbe, Lester L. 2004. *Yehud: A History of the Persian Province of Judah.* Vol. 1 of *A History of the Jews and Judaism in the Second Temple Period.* LSTS 47. London: T&T Clark.

Graf, Fritz. 2010. "Pollution and Purification." Pages 420–23 in vol. 5 of *The Oxford Encyclopedia of Ancient Greece and Rome.* Edited by Michael Gagarin and Elaine Fantham. Oxford: Oxford University Press.

Grappe, Christian. 2004. "Jesus et l'impureté." *RHPR* 84:393–417.

Gray, George Buchanan. 1903. *A Critical and Exegetical Commentary on Numbers.* ICC. Edinburgh: T&T Clark.

Greer, Jonathan S. 2019. "The Zooarchaeology of Israelite Religion: Methods and Practice." *Religions* 10.254. doi:10.3390/rel10040254.

Guichard, Michaël, and Lionel Marti. 2013. "Purity in Ancient Mesopotamia: The Paleo-Babylonian and Neo-Assyrian Periods." Pages 47–113 in *Purity and the Forming of Religious Traditions in the Ancient Mediterranean World and Ancient Judaism.* Edited by Christian Frevel and Christophe Nihan. DHR 3. Leiden: Brill.

Günther, Linda-Marie. 2013. "Concepts of Purity in Ancient Greece, with Particular Emphasis on Sacred Sites." Pages 245–60 in *Purity and the Forming of Religious Traditions in the Ancient Mediterranean World and Ancient Judaism.* Edited by Christian Frevel and Christophe Nihan. DHR 3. Leiden: Brill.

Haber, Susan. 2003. "A Woman's Touch: Feminist Encounters with the Hemorrhaging Woman in Mark 5.24–34." *JSNT* 26:171–92.

———. 2008. *"They Shall Purify Themselves": Essays on Purity in Early Judaism.* Edited by Adele Reinhartz. EJL 24. Atlanta: Society of Biblical Literature.

Haidt, Jonathan. 2001. "The Emotional Dog and Its Rational Tail: A Social Intuitionist Approach to Moral Judgment." *PR* 108:814–34.

———. 2003. "The Moral Emotions." Pages 852–70 in *Handbook of Affective Sciences.* Edited by Richard J. Davidson, Klaus R. Scherer, and H. Hill Goldsmith. Oxford: Oxford University Press.

Hanson, Paul D. 1979. *The Dawn of Apocalyptic.* Rev. ed. Philadelphia: Fortress.

Harrington, Hannah K. 1993. *The Impurity Systems of Qumran and the Rabbis: Biblical Foundations.* SBLDS 143. Atlanta: Scholars Press.

———. 2004. *The Purity Texts.* CQS 5. London: T&T Clark International.

———. 2006. "Purity and the Dead Sea Scrolls—Current Issues." *CurBR* 4:397–428.

———. 2008. "Keeping Outsiders Out: Impurity at Qumran." Pages 187–203 in *Defining Identities: We, You, and the Other in the Dead Sea Scrolls*. Edited by Florentino García Martínez, Peter W. Flint, and Eibert J. C. Tigchelaar. STDJ 70. Leiden: Brill.

———. 2011. "Ritual Purity." Pages 329–47 in *The Dead Sea Scrolls and Contemporary Culture: Proceedings of the International Conference Held at the Israel Museum, Jerusalem (July 6–8, 2008)*. Edited by Adolfo D. Roitman, Lawrence H. Schiffman, and Shani Tzoref. STDJ 93. Leiden: Brill.

———. 2012. "How Does Intermarriage Defile the Sanctuary?" Pages 177–95 in *The Scrolls and Biblical Traditions: Proceedings of the Seventh Meeting of the IOQS in Helsinki*. Edited by George J. Brooke, Daniel K. Falk, Eibert J. C. Tigchelaar, and Molly M. Zahn. Leiden: Brill.

———. 2019. *The Purity and Sanctuary of the Body in Second Temple Judaism*. JAJSup 33. Göttingen: Vandenhoeck and Ruprecht.

Hayes, Christine E. 2002. *Gentile Impurities and Jewish Identities: Intermarriage and Conversion from the Bible to the Talmud*. New York: Oxford University Press.

———. 2007. "Purity and Impurity, Ritual." Pages 746–56 in vol. 16 of *Encyclopedia Judaica*. 2nd ed. Edited by Michael Berenbaum and Fred Skolnik. Detroit: Macmillan Reference.

Hedner-Zetterholm, Karin. 2006. "Kontinuitet och förändring i judendomen: Den muntliga Torahs roll." *SEÅ* 71:209–30.

Henninger, Joseph, Dimitri Meeks, Marie-Joseph Seux, Henri Cazelles, and Édouard Cothenet. 1979. "Pureté et impureté." Pages 398–553 in vol. 9 of *Dictionnaire de la Bible: Supplément*. Edited by Louis Pirot, André Robert, Henri Cazelles, and André Feuillet. Paris: Letouzey & Ané.

Hesse, Brian, and Paula Wapnish. 1997. "Can Pig Remains Be Used for Ethnic Diagnosis in the Ancient Near East?" Pages 238–70 in *The Archaeology of Israel: Constructing the Past, Interpreting the Present*. Edited by Neil A. Silberman and David Small. JSOTSup 237. Sheffield: Sheffield Academic.

Heyes, Cecilia, and Ludwig Huber, eds. 2000. *The Evolution of Cognition*. Cambridge: MIT Press.

Hieke, Thomas. 2014. *Levitikus 1–15*. HThKAT. Freiburg im Bresgau: Herder.

Himmelfarb, Martha. 2001. "Impurity and Sin in 4QD, 1QS, and 4Q512." *DSD* 8:9–37.

———. 2004. "The Purity Laws of 4QD: Exegesis and Sectarianism." Pages 155–69 in *Things Revealed: Studies in Early Jewish and Christian Literature in Honor of Michael E. Stone*. Edited by Esther G. Chazon, David Satran, and Ruth A. Clements. Leiden: Brill.

———. 2010. "The Polemic against the Ṭevul Yom: A Reexamination." Pages 199–214 in *New Perspectives on Old Texts: Proceedings of the Tenth International Symposium of the Orion Center for the Study of the Dead Sea Scrolls and Associated Literature, 9–11 January, 2005*. Edited by Esther G. Chazon and Betsy Halpern-Amaru with the collaboration of Ruth A. Clements. STDJ 88. Leiden: Brill.

Hoffmann, David Z. 1905–1906. *Das Buch Leviticus übersetzt und erklärt*, 2 vols. Berlin: Poppelauer.

Hoglund, Kenneth G. 1992. *Achaemenid Imperial Administration in Syria-Palestine and the Missions of Ezra and Nehemiah*. SBLDS 125. Atlanta: Scholars Press.

Holmén, Tom. 2007. "An Introduction to the Continuum Approach." Pages 1–16 in *Jesus from Judaism to Christianity: Continuum Approaches to the Historical Jesus*. Edited by Tom Holmén. LNTS 352. London: T&T Clark.

———. 2009. "A Contagious Purity: Jesus' Inverse Strategy for Eschatological Cleanliness." Pages 199–229 in *Jesus Research: An International Perspective; The First Princeton–Prague Symposium on Jesus Research, Prague 2005*. Edited by James H. Charlesworth with Petr Pokorný. Grand Rapids: Eerdmans.

———. 2011. "Jesus and the Purity Paradigm." Pages 2709–44 in vol. 3 of *Handbook for the Study of the Historical Jesus*. Edited by Tom Holmén and Stanley E. Porter. Leiden: Brill.

Holtz, Gudrun. 2012. "Temple and Purification Rituals: From Torah to the Dead Sea Scrolls." Pages 197–216 in *The Scrolls and Biblical Traditions: Proceedings of the Seventh Meeting of the IOQS in Helsinki*. Edited by George J. Brooke, Daniel K. Falk, Eibert J. C. Tigchelaar, and Molly M. Zahn. STDJ 103. Leiden: Brill.

———. 2013. "Purity Conceptions in the Dead Sea Scrolls: 'Ritual-Physical' and 'Moral' Purity in a Diachronic Perspective." Pages 519–36 in *Purity and the Forming of Religious Traditions in the Ancient Mediterranean World and Ancient Judaism*. Edited by Christian Frevel and Christophe Nihan. DHR 3. Leiden: Brill.

Hooker, Morna D. 1993. *The Gospel according to Saint Mark*. BNTC 2. Peabody, MA: Hendrickson.

Houston, Walter. 1993. *Purity and Monotheism: Clean and Unclean Animals in Biblical Law.* JSOTSup 140. Sheffield: JSOT.
Hübner, Hans. 1986. *Das Gesetz in der synoptischen Tradition: Studien zur These einer progressiven Qumranisierung und Judaisiering innerhalb der synoptischen Tradition.* 2nd ed. Göttingen: Vandenhoeck & Ruprecht.
Hughes, Dennis D. 1991. *Human Sacrifice in Ancient Greece.* London: Routledge.
Hulse, E. V. 1975. "The Nature of Biblical 'Leprosy' and the Use of Alternative Medical Terms in Modern Translations of the Bible." *PEQ* 107:87–105.
Humbert, Paul. 1960. "Le substantif *tōʿēbā* et le verbe *tʿb* dans l'Ancien Testament." *ZAW* 72:217–37.
Hutter, Manfred. 2013. "Concepts of Purity in Anatolian Religions." Pages 159–74 in *Purity and the Forming of Religious Traditions in the Ancient Mediterranean World and Ancient Judaism.* Edited by Christian Frevel and Christophe Nihan. DHR 3. Leiden: Brill.
Ilan, Tal. 2015. "Since When Do Women Go to Miqveh? Archaeological and Rabbinic Evidence." Pages 83–96 in *The Archaeology and Material Culture of the Babylonian Talmud.* Edited by Markham J. Geller. Leiden: Brill.
Irons, William. 2001. "Religion as a Hard-to-Fake Sign of Commitment." Pages 292–309 in *Evolution and the Capacity for Commitment.* Edited by Randolph N. Nesse. New York: Russell Sage.
Jaffee, Martin S. 2001. *Torah in the Mouth: Writing and Oral Tradition in Palestinian Judaism, 200 BCE–400 CE.* Oxford: Oxford University Press.
Jensen, Jeppe Sinding. 2011. "Epistemology." Pages 40–53 in *The Routledge Handbook of Research Methods in the Study of Religion.* Edited by Michael Stausberg and Steven Engler. Abingdon: Routledge.
Jeremias, Joachim. 1949. "Proselytentaufe und des Neues Testament." *TZ* 5:418–28.
———. 1960. *Infant Baptism in the First Four Centuries.* London: SCM.
Johnston, Sarah Ihles, ed. 2004. *Religions of the Ancient World: A Guide.* Cambridge: Belknap.
Jong, Albert F. de. 1999. "Purification *in Absentia*: On the Development of Zoroastrian Ritual Practice." Pages 301–29 in *Transformations of the Inner Self in Ancient Religions.* Edited by Jan Assmann and Guy G. Stroumsa. SHR 83. Leiden: Brill.

———. 2013. "Purity and Pollution in Ancient Zoroastrianism." Pages 183–94 in *Purity and the Forming of Religious Traditions in the Ancient Mediterranean World and Ancient Judaism.* Edited by Christian Frevel and Christophe Nihan. DHR 3. Leiden: Brill.

Kahl, Brigitte. 1996. "Jairus und die verlorenen Töchter Israels: Sozioliterarische Überlegungen zum Problem der Grenzüberschreitung in Mk 5, 21–43." Pages 61–78 in *Von der Wurzel getragen: Christlich-feministische Exegese in Auseinandersetzung mit Antijudaismus.* Edited by Luise Schottroff and Marie-Therese Wacker. BibInt 17. Leiden: Brill.

Katz, Hayah. 2012. "'He Shall Bathe in Water; Then He Shall Be Pure': Ancient Immersion Practice in the Light of Archaeological Evidence." *VT* 62:369–80.

Kaufmann, Yehezkel. 1960. *The Religion of Israel: From Its Beginnings to the Babylonian Exile.* Translated and abridged by Moshe Greenberg. London: Allen & Unwin.

Kazen, Thomas. 2002. *Jesus and Purity Halakhah: Was Jesus Indifferent to Impurity?* ConBNT 38. Stockholm: Almqvist & Wiksell International.

———. 2005a. "Tidiga Jesusbilder: Om erfarenheten bakom och framför kristologin." *STK* 81:49–66.

———. 2005b. "Sectarian Gospels for Some Christians? Intention and Mirror Reading in the Light of Extra-canonical Texts." *NTS* 51:561–78.

———. 2007. "Explaining Discrepancies in the Purity Laws on Discharges." *RB* 114:348–71.

———. 2008. "Dirt and Disgust: Body and Morality in Biblical Purity Laws." Pages 43–64 in *Perspectives on Purity and Purification in the Bible.* Edited by Baruch J. Schwartz, Naphtali S. Meshel, Jeffrey Stackert, and David P. Wright. LHBOTS 474. New York: T&T Clark.

———. 2009. Review of *The Purity Texts*, by Hannah K. Harrington; and *Ritual Purity and the Dead Sea Scrolls*, by Ian C. Werrett. *SEÅ* 74:226–28.

———. 2010a. *Jesus and Purity Halakhah: Was Jesus Indifferent to Impurity?* ConBNT 38. Corrected repr., Winona Lake IN: Eisenbrauns.

———. 2010b. "4Q274, Fragment 1 Revisited—or Who Touched Whom? Further Evidence for Ideas of Graded Impurity and Graded Purifications." *DSD* 17:53–87.

———. 2010c. *Issues of Impurity in Early Judaism.* ConBNT 45. Winona Lake, IN: Eisenbrauns.

———. 2011. *Emotions in Biblical Law: A Cognitive Science Approach.* HBM 36. Sheffield: Sheffield Phoenix.

———. 2013a. *Scripture, Interpretation, or Authority? Motives and Arguments in Jesus' Halakic Conflicts.* WUNT 320. Tübingen: Mohr Siebeck.

———. 2013b. "Jesus and the *Zavah*: Implications for interpreting Mark." Pages 112–43 in *Purity, Holiness, and Identity in Judaism and Christianity: Essays in Memory of Susan Haber.* Edited by Carl Ehrlich, Anders Runesson, and Eileen Schuller. WUNT 1/305. Tübingen: Mohr Siebeck.

———. 2014. "The Role of Disgust in Priestly Purity Law: Insights from Conceptual Metaphor and Blending Theories." *JLRS* 3:62–92.

———. 2015a. "Purity/Impurity." Pages 166–70 in vol. 3 of *Vocabulary for the Study of Religion.* Edited by Robert Segal and Kocku von Stuckrad. Leiden: Brill.

———. 2015b. "Purity and Persia." Pages 435–62 in *Current Issues in Priestly and Related Literature: The Legacy of Jacob Milgrom and Beyond.* Edited by Roy E. Gane and Ada Taggar-Cohen. RBS 82. Atlanta: SBL Press.

———. 2015c. "Concern, Custom and Common Sense: Discharge, Hand-Washing and Graded Purification." *JSHJ* 13:150–87.

———. 2015d. Review of *Purity, Body, and Self in Early Rabbinic Literature,* by Mira Balberg. *HR* 55:231–35.

———. 2016. "A Perhaps Less Halakic Jesus and Purity: On Prophetic Criticism, Halakic Innovation, and Rabbinic Anachronism." *JSHJ* 14:120–36.

———. 2017. "Disgust in Body, Mind, and Language: The Case of Impurity." Pages 97–115 in *Mixed Feelings and Vexed Passions: Exploring Emotions in Biblical Literature.* Edited by F. Scott Spencer. RBS 90. Atlanta: SBL Press.

———. 2018a. "Levels of Explanation for Ideas of Impurity: Why Structuralist and Symbolic Models Often Fail While Evolutionary and Cognitive Models Succeed." *JAJ* 9:75–100.

———. 2018b. "Purification." Pages 220–44 in *The Oxford Handbook of Early Christian Rituals.* Edited by Risto Uro, Juliette J. Day, Rikard Roitto, and Richard E. DeMaris. Oxford: Oxford University Press.

———. 2019. "Purity and Impurity in Ancient Israel and Early Judaism." In Oxford Bibliographies in Jewish Studies (Oxford Bibliographies Online). https://tinyurl.com/SBL3106a.

Keady, Jessica M. 2017. *Vulnerability and Valour: A Gendered Analysis of Everyday Life in the Dead Sea Scrolls Communites.* LSTS 91. London: Bloomsbury T&T Clark.

Kekes, John. 1992. "Disgust and Moral Taboos." *Philosophy* 67:431–46.

Keltner, Dacher, and Jonathan Haidt. 2003. "Approaching Awe: A Moral, Spiritual, and Aesthetic Emotion." *CE* 17:297–314.

Kessler, John. 2006. "Persia's Loyal Yahwists: Power Identity and Ethnicity in Achaemenid Yehud." Pages 91–121 in *Judah and the Judeans in the Persian Period*. Edited by Oded Lipschits and Manfred Oeming. Winona Lake, IN: Eisenbrauns.

Ketola, Kimmo. 2007. "A Cognitive Approach to Ritual Systems in First-Century Judaism." Pages 95–114 in *Explaining Christian Origins and Early Judaism: Contributions from Cognitive and Social Science*. Edited by Petri Luomanen, Ilkka Pyysiäinen, and Risto Uro. BibInt 89. Leiden: Brill.

Klawans, Jonathan. 2000. *Impurity and Sin in Ancient Judaism*. New York: Oxford University Press.

———. 2006. *Purity, Sacrifice, and the Temple: Symbolism and Supersessionism in the Study of Ancient Judaism*. New York: Oxford University Press.

———. 2008. "Methodology and Ideology in the Study of Priestly Ritual." Pages 84–95 in *Perspectives on Purity and Purification in the Bible*. Edited by Baruch J. Schwartz, Naphtali S. Meshel, Jeffrey Stackert, and David P. Wright. London: T&T Clark International.

———. 2011. "Symbol, Function, Theology and Morality in the Study of Priestly Ritual." Pages 106–22 in *Ancient Mediterranean Sacrifice*. Edited by Jennifer Wright Knust and Zsuzsanna Várhelyi. New York: Oxford University Press.

Knohl, Israel. 1995. *The Sanctuary of Silence: The Priestly Torah and the Holiness School*. Translated by Jackie Feldman and Peretz Rodman. Minneapolis: Fortress.

Knoppers, Gary N. 2006. "Revisiting the Samarian Question in the Persian Period." Pages 265–89 in *Judah and the Judeans in the Persian Period*. Edited by Oded Lipschits and Manfred Oeming. Winona Lake, IN: Eisenbrauns.

Kolnai, Aurel. 2004. *On Disgust*. Edited by Barry Smith and Carolyn Korsmeyer. Chicago: Open Court.

Kratz, Reinhard G. 2005. *The Composition of the Narrative Books of the Old Testament*. London: T&T Clark.

Kruger, Michael J. 2005. *The Gospel of the Savior: An Analysis of P. Oxy. 840 and Its Place in the Gospel Traditions of Early Christianity*. TENTS 1. Leiden: Brill.

Kümmel, Werner G. 1973. "Äußere und innere Reinheit des Menschen bei Jesus." Pages 35–46 in *Das Wort und die Wörter: Festschrift Gerhard Friedrich zum 65. Geburtstag*. Edited by Horst Balz and Siegfried Schulz. Stuttgart: Kohlhammer.

Kunin, Seth D. 2004. *We Think What We Eat: Neo-structuralist Analysis of Israelite Food Rules and Other Cultural and Textual Practices*. JSOTSup 412. London: T&T Clark International.

Lafferty, Theresa V. 2012. *The Prophetic Critique of the Priority of the Cult: A Study of Amos 5:21–24 and Isaiah 1:10–17*. Eugene, OR: Pickwick.

Lakoff, George, and Mark Johnson. 1980a. *Metaphors We Live By*. Chicago: University of Chicago Press.

———. 1980b. "Conceptual Metaphor in Everyday Language." *JP* 77:453–86.

———. 1999. *Philosophy in the Flesh: The Embodied Mind and Its Challenge to Western Thought*. New York: Basic Books.

Lam, Joseph. 2016. *Patterns of Sin in the Hebrew Bible: Metaphor, Culture, and the Making of a Religious Concept*. Oxford: Oxford University Press.

Lambert, Wilfred G. 1959. "Morals in Ancient Mesopotamia." *JEOL* 15:184–96.

Lawrence, Jonathan D. 2006. *Washing in Water: Trajectories of Ritual Bathing in the Hebrew Bible and Second Temple Literature*. AcBib 23. Atlanta: Society of Biblical Literature.

LeFebvre, Michael. 2006. *Collections, Codes, and Torah: The Re-characterization of Israel's Written Law*. LHBOTS 451. New York: T&T Clark.

Lemos, Tracy M. 2009. "The Universal and the Particular: Mary Douglas and the Politics of Impurity." *JR* 89:236–51.

———. 2013. "Where There Is Dirt, Is There System? Revisiting Biblical Purity Constructions." *JSOT* 37:265–94.

Lennon, Jack J. 2010. "Menstrual Blood in Ancient Rome: An Unspeakable Impurity?" *CMDJPH* 61:71–87.

———. 2012. "Pollution, Religion, and Society in the Roman World." Pages 43–58 in *Rome, Pollution and Propriety: Dirt, Disease and Hygiene in the Eternal City from Antiquity to Modernity*. Edited by Mark Bradley with Kenneth Stow. Cambridge: Cambridge University Press.

———. 2014. *Pollution and Religion in Ancient Rome*. Cambridge: Cambridge University Press.

Levine, Amy-Jill, and Marc Zvi Brettler, eds. 2011. *The Jewish Annotated New Testament: New Revised Standard Version Bible Translation*. Oxford: Oxford University Press.

Levine, Amy-Jill, and Ben Witherington III. 2018. *The Gospel of Luke*. NCBC. Cambridge: Cambridge University Press.

Levine, Baruch. 2003. "Leviticus: Its Literary History and Location in Biblical Literature." Pages 11–23 in *The Book of Leviticus: Composition and Reception*. Edited by Rolf Rendtorff and Robert A. Kugler. VTSup 93. Leiden: Brill.

Levine, Lauren. 2012. "The Kegare Concept." Pages 227–38 in *Building Bridges in Anthropology: Understanding, Acting, Teaching, and Theorizing*. Edited by R. Shanafelt. Knoxville: Newfound.

Lévi-Strauss, Claude. 1963. *Structural Anthropology*. New York: Basic Books.

Lindsay, Hugh. 2000. "Death Pollution and Funerals in the City of Rome." Pages 152–73 in *Death and Disease in the Ancient City*. Edited by Valerie M. Hope and Eireann Marshall. London: Routledge.

Lipschits, Oded. 2006. "Achaemenid Imperial Policy, Settlement Processes in Palestine, and the Status of Jerusalem in the Middle of the Fifth Century B.C.E." Pages 19–52 in *Judah and the Judeans in the Persian Period*. Edited by Oded Lipschits and Manfred Oeming. Winona Lake, IN: Eisenbrauns.

Lipschits, Oded, and Oren Tal. 2007. "The Settlement Archaeology of the Province of Judah: A Case Study." Pages 33–52 in *Judah and the Judeans in the Fourth Century B.C.E*. Edited by Oded Lipschits, Gary N. Knoppers, and Rainer Albertz. Winona Lake, IN: Eisenbrauns.

Liu, Yulin. 2013. *Temple Purity in 1–2 Corinthians*. WUNT 2/343. Tübingen: Mohr Siebeck.

Lockett, Darian. 2008. *Purity and Worldview in the Epistle of James*. LNTS 36. London: T&T Clark.

Looy, Heather. 2004. "Embodied and Embedded Morality: Divinity, Identity, and Disgust." *Zygon* 39:219–35.

Maass, Fritz. 1997. "טהר *ṭhr* to be pure." *TLOT* 2:482–86.

Maccoby, Hyam. 1998. "Corpse and Leper." *JJS* 49:280–85.

———. 1999. *Ritual and Morality: The Ritual Purity System and Its Place in Judaism*. Cambridge: Cambridge University Press.

Magen, Yitzhaq. 1994. "Jerusalem as a Center of the Stone Vessel Industry during the Second Temple Period." Pages 244–57 in *Ancient Jerusalem Revealed*. Edited by Hillel Geva. Jerusalem: Israel Exploration Society.

———. 2002. *The Stone Vessel Industry in the Second Temple Period: Excavations at Ḥizma and the Jerusalem Temple Mount*. JSP 1. Jerusalem: Israel Exploration Society and Staff Officer of Archaeology.

Magness, Jodi. 2010. "Scrolls and Hand Impurity." Pages 89–97 in *The Dead Sea Scrolls: Texts and Contexts*. Edited by Charlotte Hempel. STDJ 90. Leiden: Brill.

———. 2011. *Stone and Dung, Oil and Spit: Jewish Daily Life in the Time of Jesus*. Grand Rapids: Eerdmans.

———. 2012. "Toilet Practices, Purity Concerns, and Sectarianism in the Late Second Temple Period." Pages 51–70 in *Jewish Identity and Politics between the Maccabees and Bar Kokhba: Groups, Normativity, and Rituals*. Edited by Benedikt Eckhardt. JSJSup 155. Leiden: Brill.

———. 2017. "Purity Observance among Diaspora Jews in the Roman World." *ArchT* 1:39–65.

Maier, Bernhard, Thomas Podella, Robert Goldenberg, Christian Dietzfehlbinger, and Gert Hartmann. 1997. "Reinheit." Pages 473–97 in vol. 28 of *Theologische Realenzyklopädie*. Edited by Gerhard Müller et al. Berlin: de Gruyter.

Maier, Johann. 2001. "Purity at Qumran: Cultic and Domestic." Pages 91–124 in *Theory of Israel*. Vol. 1 of *The Judaism of Qumran: A Systemic Reading of the Dead Sea Scrolls*. Part 5 of *Judaism in Late Antiquity*. Edited by Alan J. Avery-Peck, Jacob Neusner, and Bruce Chilton. Leiden: Brill.

Malandra, William W. 2006. "Vendīdād." In *Encyclopaedia Iranica*. Online ed. https://tinyurl.com/SBL3106b.

Malinar, Angelika. 2010. "Purity and Impurity." Pages 435–39 in *Brill's Encyclopedia of Hinduism*. Edited by Knut A. Jacobsen. Leiden: Brill.

Marcus, Joel. 2018. *John the Baptist in History and Theology*. Columbia: University of South Carolina Press.

Marx, Alfred. 2001. "L'impureté selon P: Une lecture théologique." *Bib* 82:363–84.

Matassa, Lidia. 2007. "Unravelling the Myth of the Synagogue on Delos." *BAIAS* 25:81–115.

McCarter, P. Kyle, Jr. 1984. *II Samuel: A New Translation with Introduction and Commentary*. AB 9. Garden City, NY: Doubleday.

McCauley, Robert N., and E. Thomas Lawson. 2002. *Bringing Ritual to Mind: Psychological Foundations of Cultural Forms*. Cambridge: Cambridge University Press.

McEvoy, Chad Joseph. 2002. "A Consideration of Human Xenophobia and Ethnocentrism from a Sociobiological Perspective." *HRR* (April–June): 39–49.

Meacham, Tirzah (leBeit Yoreh). 1999a. "An Abbreviated History of the Development of the Jewish Menstrual Laws." Pages 23–39 in *Women and Water: Menstruation in Jewish Life and Law*. Edited by Rahel R. Wasserfall. Hanover, NH: Brandeis University Press.

———. 1999b. "Appendix." Pages 255–60 in *Women and Water: Menstruation in Jewish Life and Law*. Edited by Rahel R. Wasserfall. Hanover, NH: Brandeis University Press.

Meeks, Dimitri. 1979. "Pureté et impureté: B. L'ancien Orient: I. Pureté et purification en Ègypte." Pages 430–52 in vol. 9 of *Dictionnaire de la Bible: Supplément*. Edited by Louis Pirot, André Robert, Henri Cazelles, and André Feuillet. Paris: Letouzey & Ané.

Meier, John P. 2009. *Law and Love*. Vol. 4 of *A Marginal Jew: Rethinking the Historical Jesus*. AYBRL. New Haven: Yale University Press.

Meinel, Fabian. 2015. *Pollution and Crisis in Greek Tragedy*. Cambridge: Cambridge University Press.

Menninghaus, Winfried. 1999. *Ekel: Theorie und Geschichte einer starken Empfindung*. Frankfurt am Main: Suhrkampf.

Meshel, Naphtali S. 2008. "Pure, Impure, Permitted, Prohibited: A Study of Classification Systems in P." Pages 32–42 in *Perspectives on Purity and Purification in the Bible*. Edited by Baruch J. Schwartz, Naphtali S. Meshel, Jeffrey Stackert, and David P. Wright. LHBOTS 474. New York: T&T Clark.

———. 2014. *The "Grammar" of Sacrifice: A Generativist Study of the Israelite Sacrificial System in the Priestly Writings with a "Grammar" of Σ*. New York: Oxford University Press.

Meyer, Robert. 1999. "Magical Ascesis and Moral Purity in Ancient Egypt." Pages 45–64 in *Transformations of the Inner Self in Ancient Religions*. Edited by Jan Assmann and Guy G. Stroumsa. SHR 83. Leiden: Brill.

Michaels, Axel, and Christoph Wulf, eds. 2011. *Emotions in Rituals and Performances*. London: Routledge.

Milgrom, Jacob. 1976. "The Priestly 'Picture of Dorian Gray.'" *RB* 83:390–99.

———. 1978. "Studies in the Temple Scroll." *JBL* 97:512–18.

———. 1981. "The Paradox of the Red Cow (Num xix)." *VT* 31:62–72.

———. 1989. "Rationale for Cultic Law: The Case of Impurity." *Semeia* 45:103–9.

———. 1990. *Numbers* במדבר. JPSTC. Philadelphia: Jewish Publication Society.

———. 1991. *Leviticus 1–16: A New Translation with Introduction and Commentary*. AB 3. Garden City, NY: Doubleday.

———. 1992. "First Day Ablutions in Qumran." Pages 561–70 in vol. 2 of *The Madrid Qumran Congress: Proceedings of the International Congress on the Dead Sea Scrolls; Madrid 18–21 March 1991*. Edited by Julio Trebolle Barrera and Luis Vegas Montaner. STDJ 11. Leiden: Brill.

———. 1995. "4QTohora[a]: An Unpublished Qumran Text on Purities." Pages 59–68 in *Time to Prepare the Way in the Wilderness*. Edited by Devorah Dimant and Lawrence Schiffman. STDJ 16. Leiden: Brill.

———. 2000. *Leviticus 17–22: A New Translation with Introduction and Commentary*. AB 3A. New York: Doubleday.

———. 2001. *Leviticus 23–27: A New Translation with Introduction and Commentary*. AB 3B. New York: Doubleday.

Miller, Stuart S. 2003. "Some Observations on Stone Vessel Finds and Ritual Purity in Light of Talmudic Sources." Pages 402–19 in *Zeichen aus Text und Stein: Studien auf dem Weg zu einer Archäologie des Neuen Testaments*. Edited by Stefan Alkier and Jürgen Zangenberg. TANZ 42. Tübingen and Basel: Francke Verlag.

———. 2007. "Stepped Pools and the Non-existent Monolithic 'Miqveh.'" Pages 215–34 in *The Archaeology of Difference: Gender, Ethnicity, Class and the "Other" in Antiquity: Studies in Honor of Eric M. Meyers*. Edited by Douglas R. Edwards and C. Thomas McCollough. AASOR 60/61. Boston: American Schools of Oriental Research.

———. 2010. "Stepped Pools, Stone Vessels, and Other Identity Markers of Complex Common Judaism." *JSJ* 41:214–43.

———. 2015. *At the Intersection of Texts and Material Finds: Stepped Pools, Stone Vessels, and Ritual Purity among the Jews of Roman Galilee*. JAJSup 16. Göttingen: Vandenhoeck and Ruprecht.

Miller, Susan B. 2004. *Disgust: The Gatekeeper Emotion*. Hillsdale, NJ: Analytic.

Miller, William I. 1997. *The Anatomy of Disgust*. Cambridge: Harvard University Press.

Mizzi, Dennis. 2017. "On the Ritual-Purity Status of Glass at Qumran." Pages 255–79 in *"What Mean These Stones?" (Joshua 4:6, 21): Essays on Texts, Philology, and Archaeology in Honour of Anthony J. Frendo*. Edited by Dennis Mizzi, Nicholas C. Vella, and Martin R. Zammit. ANES 50. Leuven: Peeters.

———. 2019. "Were Scrolls Susceptible to Impurity? The View from Qumran." Pages 27–64 in *Law, Literature, and Society in Legal Texts from Qumran: Papers from the Ninth Meeting of the International Organization for Qumran Studies, Leuven 2016*. Edited by Jutta Jokiranta and Molly Zahn. Leiden: Brill.

Munson, Rosaria Vignolo, ed. 2013. *Herodotus and the Narrative of the Past*. Vol. 1 of *Herodotus*. ORCS. Oxford: Oxford University Press.

Murphy, Catherine M. 2003. *John the Baptist: Prophet of Purity for a New Age*. Interfaces. Collegeville, MN: Liturgical Press.

Navarrete, C. David, and Daniel M. T. Fessler. 2006. "Disease Avoidance and Ethnocentrism: The Effects of Disease Vulnerability and Disgust Sensitivity on Intergroup Attitudes." *EHB* 27:270–82.

Netzer, Ehud. 1982. "Ancient Ritual Baths *(Miqvaot)* in Jericho." Pages 106–19 in vol. 2 of *The Jerusalem Cathedra: Studies in the History, Archaeology, Geography and Ethnography of the Land of Israel*. Edited by Lee I. Levine. Jerusalem: Yad Izḥak Ben-Zvi Institute.

Neusner, Jacob. 1971. *The Rabbinic Traditions about the Pharisees before 70*. 3 vols. Leiden: Brill.

———. 1973. *The Idea of Purity in Ancient Judaism*. HL 1972–1973. Leiden: Brill.

———. 1974–1977. *A History of the Mishnaic Law of Purities*. 22 vols. SJLA 6. Leiden: Brill.

———. 1975. "The Idea of Purity in Ancient Judaism." *JAAR* 43:15–26.

———. 1979. *From Politics to Piety: The Emergence of Pharisaic Judaism*. 2nd ed. New York: KTAV.

———. 1987. *The Mishnah before 70*. BJS 51. Atlanta: Scholars Press.

———. 1988. *The Sifra: An Analytical Translation*. 3 vols. BJS. Atlanta: Scholars Press.

———. 1992. "Mr. Sanders's Pharisees and Mine." *BBR* 2:143–69.

———. 1994. *Purity in Rabbinic Judaism: A Systematic Account*. SFSHJ 95. Atlanta: Scholars Press.

———. 1998. *From Scripture to 70: Pre-rabbinic Beginnings of the Halakah*. SFSHJ 192. Atlanta: Scholars Press.

Newman, George E. 2012. "The Bias toward Cause and Effect." Pages 69–82 in *Psychology of Bias*. Edited by Glenn W. Mills and Sarah J. Stone. Hauppauge, NY: Nova Science.

Newton, Michael. 1985. *The Concept or Purity in Qumran and in the Letters of Paul*. Cambridge: Cambridge University Press.

Neyrey, Jerome H. 1996. "Core Values: Clean/Unclean, Pure/Polluted, and Holy/Profane: The Idea and the System of Purity." Pages 80–104 in *The Social Sciences and New Testament Interpretation*. Edited by Richard L. Rohrbaugh. Peabody, MA: Hendrickson.

Nihan, Christophe. 2004. "The Holiness Code between D and P: Some Comments on the Function and Significance of Leviticus 17–26 in the Composition of the Torah." Pages 98–122 in *Das Deuteronomium zwischen Pentateuch und Deuteronomistischen Geschichtswerk*. Edited by Eckart Otto and Reinhard Achenbach. FRLANT 206. Göttingen: Vandenhoeck & Ruprecht.

———. 2007. *From Priestly Torah to Pentateuch: A Study of the Composition of the Book of Leviticus*. FAT 2/25. Tübingen: Mohr Siebeck.

———. 2013. "Forms and Functions of Purity in Leviticus." Pages 311–67 in *Purity and the Forming of Religious Traditions in the Ancient Mediterranean World and Ancient Judaism*. Edited by Christian Frevel and Christophe Nihan. DHR 3. Leiden: Brill.

Nihan, Christophe, and Thomas Römer. 2004. "Le débat actuel sur la formation du Pentateuque." Pages 101–4 in *Introduction à l'Ancien Testament*. Edited by Thomas Römer, Jean-Daniel Macchi, and Christophe Nihan. MdB 49. Genève: Labor et Fides.

Noam, Vered. 2006. "Traces of Sectarian Halakhah in the Rabbinic World." Pages 67–85 in *Rabbinic Perspectives: Rabbinic Literature and the Dead Sea Scrolls: Proceedings of the Eighth International Symposium of the Orion Center for the Study of the Dead Sea Scrolls and Associated Literature, 7–9 January, 2003*. Edited by Steven D. Fraade, Aharon Shemesh, and Ruth A. Clements. STDJ 62. Leiden: Brill.

———. 2007. "The Bounds of Non-priestly Purity: A Reassessment." *Zion* 72:127–60 [Hebrew].

———. 2008. "The Dual Strategy of Rabbinic Purity Legislation." *JSJ* 39:471–512.

———. 2009. "Corpse-Blood Impurity: A Lost Biblical Reading?" *JBL* 128:243–51.

———. 2010a. "Ritual Impurity in Tannaitic Literature: Two Opposing Perspectives." *JAJ* 1:65–103.

———. 2010b. "Qumran and the Rabbis on Corpse Impurity: Common Exegesis—Tacit Polemic." Pages 397–430 in *The Dead Sea Scrolls: Texts and Context*. Edited by Florentino García Martínez. STDJ 90. Leiden: Brill.

———. 2010c. *From Qumran to the Rabbinic Revolution: Conceptions of Impurity*. SSAPDJJL. Jerusalem: Yad Izhak ben-Zvi [Hebrew].

———. 2012. "Corpse Impurity." *EBR* 5:801–7.

Nogalski, James. 1993. *Literary Precursors to the Book of the Twelve*. BZAW 217. Berlin: de Gruyter.

Nongbri, Brent. 2013. *Before Religion: A History of a Modern Concept*. New Haven: Yale University Press.

Nougayrol, Jean. 1948. "*Sirrimu* (non **purîmu*) 'âne sauvage.'" *JCS* 2:203–8.

Nussbaum, Martha. 2004. *Hiding from Humanity: Disgust, Shame, and the Law*. Princeton: Princeton University Press.

Olyan, Saul. 2004. "Purity Ideology in Ezra-Nehemiah as a Tool to Reconstitute the Community." *JSJ* 35:1–16.

Oppenheimer, Aharon. 1977. *The 'Am Ha-Aretz: A Study in the Social History of the Jewish People in the Hellenistic-Roman Period*. ALGHJ 8. Leiden: Brill.

Paganini, Simone, and Boris Repschinski. 2012. "Kontinuität und Diskontinuität in der Reinheitsthematik vom Judentum des Zweiten Tempels zum Neuen Testament." *ZKT* 134:449–70.

Parker, Robert. 1983. *Miasma: Purification and Pollution in Early Greek Religion*. Oxford: Clarendon.

———. 2004. "Sin, Pollution, and Purity: Greece." Pages 507–9 in *Religions of the Ancient World: A Guide*. Edited by Sarah Iles Johnston. Cambridge: Belknap.

Paschen, Wilfried. 1970. *Rein und unrein: Untersuchung zur biblischen Wortgeschichte*. SANT 24. München: Kösel-Verlag.

Petrovic, Andrej, and Ivana Petrovic. 2016. *Early Greek Religion*. Vol. 1 of *Inner Purity and Pollution in Greek Religion*. Oxford: Oxford University Press.

Philip, Tarja S. 2006. *Menstruation and Childbirth in the Bible: Fertility and Impurity*. StBibLit 88. New York: Lang.

Piff, Paul K., Pia Detze, Matthew Feinberg, Daniel M. Stancato, and Dacher Keltner. 2015. "Awe, the Small Self, and Prosocial Behavior." *JPSP* 108:883–99.

Poirier, John C. 1996. "Why Did the Pharisees Wash Their Hands?" *JJS* 47:217–33.

———. 2003. "Purity beyond the Temple in the Second Temple Era." *JBL* 122:247–65.

———. 2005. "Three Early Christian Views on Ritual Purity: A Histori-

cal Note Contributing to an Understanding of Paul's Position." *ETL* 81:424–34.
Pressler, Carolyn. 1993. *The View of Women Found in the Deuteronomic Family Laws.* BZAW 216. Berlin: de Gruyter.
Preston, Stephanie D., and Frans B. M. de Waal. 2002. "Empathy: Its Ultimate and Proximate Bases." *BehBS* 25:1–72.
Preuss, Horst Dietrich. 2006. "תעב; תּוֹעֵבָה." *TDOT* 15:591–604.
Provan, Iain, V. Philips Long, and Tremper Longman III. 2003. *A Biblical History of Israel.* Louisville: Westminster John Knox.
Pury, Albert de. 2007. "P as the Absolute Beginning." Pages 99–128 in *Les dernières rédactions du Pentateuque, de l'Hexateuque et de l'Ennéateuque.* Edited by Thomas Römer and Konrad Schmid. BETL 203. Leuven: Leuven University Press.
Quack, Joachim Friedrich. 2013. "Conceptions of Purity in Egyptian Religion." Pages 115–58 in *Purity and the Forming of Religious Traditions in the Ancient Mediterranean World and Ancient Judaism.* Edited by Christian Frevel and Christophe Nihan. DHR 3. Leiden: Brill.
Quick, Laura. 2017. "Manuscripts and Their (Proof-)Texts: Paradigms for Purity and Holiness in the Community Rule and the Damascus Document." *BN* 175:35–53.
Rackham, H. 1961. *Pliny: Natural History with an English Translation in Ten Volumes.* Vol. 2, books 3–7. LCL. Cambridge: Harvard University Press.
Reardon, Timothy W. 2016. "Cleansing through Almsgiving in Luke–Acts: Purity, Cornelius, and the Translation of Acts 15:9." *CBQ* 78:463–82.
Reed, Jonathan L. 2003. "Stone Vessels and Gospel Texts: Purity and Socio-economics in John 2." Pages 381–401 in *Zeichen aus Text und Stein: Studien auf dem Weg zu einer Archäologie des Neuen Testaments.* Edited by Stefan Alkier and Jürgen Zangenberg. TANZ 42. Tübingen: Francke.
Regev, Eyal. 2000a. "Pure Individualism: The Idea of Non-priestly Purity in Ancient Judaism." *JSJ* 31:176–202.
———. 2000b. "Non-priestly Purity and Its Religious Aspects according to Historical Sources and Archaeological Findings." Pages 223–44 in *Purity and Holiness: The Heritage of Leviticus.* Edited by Marcel J. H. M. Poorthuis and Joshua Schwartz. JCPS 2. Leiden: Brill.
———. 2007. *Sectarianism in Qumran: A Cross-cultural Perspective.* RelSoc 45. Berlin: de Gruyter.

———. 2010. "Herod's Jewish Ideology Facing Romanization: On Intermarriage, Ritual Baths, and Speeches." *JQR* 100:197–222.
Reich, Ronny. 1981. "Archaeological Evidence of the Jewish Population at Hasmonean Gezer." *IEJ* 31:48–52.
———. 1984. "A *Miqweh* at 'Isawiya near Jerusalem." *IEJ* 34:220–23 and pl. 28.
———. 1988. "The Hot Bath-House (*balneum*), the Miqweh and the Jewish Community in the Second Temple Period. *JJS* 39:102–7.
———. 1989. "Two Possible Miqwa'ot on the Temple Mount." *IEJ* 39:63–65.
———. 1990. "Miqwa'ot (Jewish Ritual Immersion Baths) in Eretz-Israel in the Second Temple and the Mishnah and Talmud Period" [Hebrew]. PhD diss., Hebrew University.
———. 1993. "The Great Miqveh Debate." *BAR* 19.2:52–53.
———. 1995. "The Synagogue and the *Miqweh* in Eretz-Israel in the Second-Temple, Mishnaic, and Talmudic Periods." Pages 289–97 in *Ancient Synagogues: Historical Analysis and Archaeological Discovery*. Edited by Dan Urman and Paul V. M. Flesher. Leiden: Brill.
———. 2000. "Mikwa'ot at Khirbet Qumran and the Jerusalem Connection." Pages 728–31 in *The Dead Sea Scrolls: Fifty Years after their Discovery*. Edited by Lawrence H. Schiffman, Emanuel Tov, and James C. VanderKam. Jerusalem: Israel Exploration Society/Shrine of the Book, Israel Museum.
———. 2002. "They Are Ritual Baths: Immerse Yourself in the Ongoing Sepphoris Mikveh Debate." *BAR* 28.2:50–55.
———. 2013. *Miqwa'ot (Jewish Ritual Baths) in the Second Temple, Mishnaic and Talmudic Periods* [Hebrew]. Jerusalem: Yad Yizhak Ben-Zvi and Israel Exploration Society.
Ringgren, Helmer. 1986. "טָהַר *ṭāhar*; טָהוֹר *ṭāhôr*; טֹהַר *ṭōhar*; טָהֳרָה *ṭohorâ*." *TDOT* 5:287–96.
Robertson, Noel. 2013. "The Concept of Purity in Greek Sacred Laws." Pages 195–243 in *Purity and the Forming of Religious Traditions in the Ancient Mediterranean World and Ancient Judaism*. Edited by Christian Frevel and Christophe Nihan. DHR 3. Leiden: Brill.
Römer, Thomas C. 2005. *The So-Called Deuteronomistic History: A Sociological, Historical and Literary Introduction*. London: T&T Clark, 2005.
Ronen, Neta. 1999. "Who Practiced Purification in Archaic Greece? A Cultural Profile." Pages 273–86 in *Transformations of the Inner Self in Ancient Religions*. Edited by Jan Assmann and Guy G. Stroumsa. SHR 83. Leiden: Brill.

Rösch, Petra, and Udo Simon, eds. 2012. *How Purity Is Made*. Wiesbaden: Harrassowitz.

Rossides, Daniel W. 1998. *Social Theory: Its Origins, History, and Contemporary Relevance*. Dix Hills, NY: General Hall.

Rozin, Paul, Jonathan Haidt, and Clark McCauley. 2000. "Disgust." Pages 637–53 in *Handbook of Emotions*. 2nd ed. Edited by Michael Lewis and Jeanette M. Haviland-Jones. New York: Guildford.

Ruane, Nicole J. 2007. "Bathing, Status and Gender in Priestly Ritual." Pages 66–81 in *A Question of Sex? Gender and Difference in the Hebrew Bible and Beyond*. Edited by Deborah W. Rooke. Sheffield: Sheffield Phoenix.

———. 2015. "Pigs, Purity, and Patrilineality: The Multiparity of Swine and Its Problems for Biblical Ritual and Gender Construction." *JBL* 134:489–504.

Runesson, Anders. 2001. "Water and Worship: Ostia and the Ritual Bath in the Diaspora Synagogue." Pages 115–29 in *The Synagogue of Ancient Ostia and the Jews of Rome: Interdisciplinary Studies*. Edited by Birger Olsson, Dieter Mitternacht, and Olof Brandt. AIRRS 4/57. Stockholm: Åströms.

Safrai, Ze'ev, and Chana Safrai. 2011. "Papyrus Oxyrhynchus 840." Pages 255–82 in *Halakhah in Light of Epigraphy*. Edited by Albert I. Baumgarten et al. JAJSup 3. Göttingen: Vandenhoeck & Ruprecht.

Sanders, Ed P. 1977. *Paul and Palestinian Judaism: A Comparison of Patterns of Religion*. London: SCM.

———. 1985. *Jesus and Judaism*. London: SCM.

———. 1990. *Jewish Law from Jesus to the Mishnah: Five Studies*. London: SCM.

———. 1992. *Judaism: Practice and Belief 63 BCE–66 CE*. London: SCM.

———. 1993. *The Historical Figure of Jesus*. London: Penguin.

Sapir-Hen, Lidar, Guy Bar-Oz, Yuval Gadot, and Israel Finkelstein. 2013. "Pig Husbandry in Iron Age Israel and Judah: New Insights Regarding the Origin of the 'Taboo.'" *ZDPV* 129:1–20.

Sapir-Hen, Lidar, Meirav Meiri, and Israel Finkelstein. 2015. "Iron Age Pigs: New Evidence on Their Origin and Role in Forming Identity Boundaries." *Radiocarbon* 57:307–15.

Schart, Aaron. 2000. "Reconstructing the Redaction History of the Twelve Prophets: Problems and Models." Pages 34–48 in *Reading and Hearing the Book of the Twelve*. Edited by James Nogalski and Marvin A. Sweeney. SymS 15. Atlanta: Society of Biblical Literature.

Scheve, Christian von. 2011. "Collective Emotions in Rituals: Elicitation, Transmission, and a 'Matthew Effect.'" Pages 55–77 in *Emotions in Rituals and Performances*. Edited by Axel Michaels and Christoph Wulf. London: Routledge.

Schiffman, Lawrence H. 1989. "The Temple Scroll and the Systems of Jewish Law of the Second Temple Period." Pages 239–55 in *Temple Scroll Studies*. Edited by George J. Brooke. JSPSup 7. Sheffield: JSOT.

———. 1994. "Pharisaic and Sadducean Halakhah in Light of the Dead Sea Scrolls: The Case of Ṭevul Yom." *DSD* 1:285–99.

Schmid, Konrad. 2012. *The Old Testament: A Literary History*. Translated by Linda M. Maloney. Minneapolis: Fortress.

Schmidt, Karl F. W. 1936. "Ein bisher unbekanntes Evangelienfragment: Einblicke in die Arbeitsweise eines alten Evangelisten." *TBl* 15.2:34–38.

Schremer, Adiel. 2001. "'[T]he[y] Did Not Read in the Sealed Book': Qumran Halakhic Revolution and the Emergence of Torah Study in Second Temple Judaism." Pages 106–26 in *Historical Perspectives: From the Hasmoneans to Bar Kokhba in Light of the Dead Sea Scrolls; Proceedings of the Fourth International Symposium of the Orion Center for the Study of the Dead Sea Scrolls and Associated Literature, 27–31 January, 1999*. STDJ 37. Leiden: Brill.

Schwartz, Daniel R. 1986. "Viewing the Holy Utensils (P. Ox. V, 840)." *NTS* 32:153–59.

———. 1992. "Law and Truth: On Qumran-Sadducean and Rabbinic Views of Law." Pages 229–40 in *The Dead Sea Scrolls: Forty Years of Research*. Edited by Devorah Dimant and Uriel Rappaport. STDJ 10. Leiden: Brill.

Schwartz, Joshua. 2000. "On Birds, Rabbis and Skin Disease." Pages 207–22 in *Purity and Holiness: The Heritage of Leviticus*. Edited by Marcel J. H. M. Poorthuis and Joshua Schwartz. JCPS 2. Leiden: Brill.

Seidl, Theodor. 1997. *Untersuchungen zur Valenz althebräischer Verben: 3. ṬHR—"Rein Sein."* ATSAT 57. St. Ottilien: EOS.

Selvidge, Marla J. 1990. *Woman, Cult, and Miracle Recital: A Redaction Critical Investigation on Mark 5:24–34*. Lewisburg, PA: Bucknell University Press.

Shaked, Saul. 1984. "Iranian Influence on Judaism: First Century B.C.E. to Second Century C.E." Pages 308–25 in vol. 1 of *The Cambridge History of Judaism*. Edited by William D. Davies and Louis Finkelstein. Cambridge: Cambridge University Press.

Shellberg, Pamela. 2015. *Cleansed Lepers, Cleansed Hearts: Purity and Healing in Luke–Acts*. ES. Minneapolis: Fortress.
Shemesh, Aharon. 2009. *Halakhah in the Making: The Development of Jewish Law from Qumran to the Rabbis*. TLJS 6. Berkeley: University of California Press.
Shinall, Myrick C., Jr. 2018. "The Social Condition of Lepers in the Gospels." *JBL* 137:915–34.
Shiota, Michelle, Dacher Keltner, and Amanda Mossman. 2007. "The Nature of Awe: Elicitors, Appraisals, and Effects on Self-Concept." *CE* 21:944–63.
Shively, Elizabeth E. 2020. "Purification of the Body and the Reign of God in the Gospel of Mark." *JTS* 71:62–89.
Ska, Jean-Louis. 2006. *Introduction to Reading the Pentateuch*. Winona Lake, IN: Eisenbrauns.
Smith, Paul A. 1995. *Rhetoric and Redaction in Trito-Isaiah: The Structure, Growth and Authorship of Isaiah 56–66*. VTSup 62. Leiden: Brill.
Smith, William Robertson. 1927. *Lectures on the Religion of the Semites: The Fundamental Institutions*. 3rd ed. London: A&C Black.
Snyder, Benjamin J. Forthcoming. *Ritual Purity and the Origin of John's Βάπτισμα Μετανοίας*. WUNT 2. Tübingen: Mohr Siebeck.
Spencer, Herbert. 1906. *The Principles of Sociology*. 3rd ed. New York: Appleton.
Sperber, Dan. 1975. *Rethinking Symbolism*. Cambridge: Cambridge University Press.
Sperber, Dan, David Premack, and Ann James Premack, eds. 1995. *Causal Cognition: A Multidisciplinary Debate*. New York: Oxford University Press.
Staal, Frits. 1979. "The Meaninglessness of Ritual." *Numen* 26:2–22.
Stausberg, Michael, Hubert Cancik, Theodor Seidl, Bernd Kollman, Gury Scheider-Ludorff, Irina Wandrey, and Dagmar Börner-Klein. 2011. "Purification." *RPP* 10:554–57.
Stausberg, Michael, Theodor Seidl, Bernd Kollman, Gury Scheider-Ludorff, Irina Wandrey, Dagmar Börner-Klein, and Birgit Krawietz. 2011. "Pure and Impure." *RPP* 10:548–52.
Stemberger, Günter. 2012. "Forbidden Gentile Food in Early Rabbinic Writing." Pages 209–24 in *Jewish Identity and Politics between the Maccabees and Bar Kokhba: Groups, Normativity, and Rituals*. Edited by Benedikt Eckhardt. JSJSup 155. Leiden: Brill.

Stol, Marten. 2000. *Birth in Babylonia and the Bible: Its Mediterranean Setting*. CM 14. Groningen: Styx.

Sturrock, John. 1993. *Structuralism*. 2nd ed. London: Fontana.

Svartvik, Jesper. 2000. *Mark and Mission: Mk 7:1–23 in Its Narrative and Historical Contexts*. ConBNT 32. Stockholm: Almqvist & Wiksell International.

Sweetser, Eve. 2000. "Blended Spaces and Performativity." *CL* 11:305–33.

Taylor, Joan E. 1997. *The Immerser: John the Baptist within Second Temple Judaism*. SHJ. Grand Rapids: Eerdmans.

Taylor, Vincent. 1982. *The Gospel according to St. Mark: The Greek Text with Introduction, Notes and Indexes*. 2nd ed. London: Macmillan.

Teehan, John. 2003. "Kantian Ethics: After Darwin." *Zygon* 38:49–60.

Theissen, Gerd. 1983. *The Miracle Stories of the Early Christian Tradition*. Edinburgh: T&T Clark.

Thiering, Barbara. 1980. "Inner and Outer Cleansings at Qumran as a Background to New Testament Baptism." *NTS* 26:266–77.

Thiessen, Matthew. 2020. *Jesus and the Forces of Death: The Gospels' Portrayal of Ritual Impurity within First-Century Judaism*. Grand Rapids: Baker Academic.

Tiemeyer, Lena-Sophia. 2014. "The Lament in Isaiah 63:7–64:11." Pages 52–70 in *The Book of Isaiah: Enduring Questions Answered Anew; Essays Honoring Joseph Blenkinsopp and His Contribution to the Study of Isaiah*. Edited by Richart J. Bautch and J. Todd Hibbard. Grand Rapids: Eerdmans.

Tigay, Jeffrey H. 1996. *Deuteronomy*. JPSTC. Philadelphia: Jewish Publication Society.

Toews, Casey. 2003. "Moral Purification in 1QS." *BBR* 13:71–96.

Tomson, Peter. 1988. "Zavim 5:12—Reflections on Dating Mishnaic Halakha." Pages 53–69 in *History and Form: Dutch Studies in the Mishnah; Papers Read at the Workshop "Mishnah."* Edited by Annelies Kuyt and Niek A. van Uchelen. Amsterdam: J. Palache Instituut.

Toorn, Karel van der. 1985. *Sin and Sanction in Israel and Mesopotamia: A Comparative Study*. SSN 22. Assen: Van Gorcum.

———. 1994. *From Her Cradle to Her Grave: The Role of Religion in the Life of the Israelite and the Babylonian Woman*. BibSem 23. Sheffield: JSOT.

———. 2004. "Sin, Pollution, and Purity: Mesopotamia." Pages 499–501 in *Religions of the Ancient World: A Guide*. Edited by Sarah Iles Johnston. Cambridge: Belknap.

Touger, Eliyahu. N.d. Chabad.org. https://tinyurl.com/SBL3106c.

Trevaskis, Leigh M. 2011. *Holiness, Ethics and Ritual in Leviticus*. HBM 29. Sheffield: Sheffield Phoenix.

Trümper, Monika. 2004. "The Oldest Original Synagogue Building in the Diaspora: The Delos Synagogue Reconsidered." *Hesperia* 73:513–98.

Tsumura, David Toshio. 2007. *The First Book of Samuel*. NICOT. Grand Rapids: Eerdmans.

Uro, Risto. 2016. *Ritual and Christian Beginnings: A Socio-cognitive Analysis*. Oxford: Oxford University Press.

Vuong, Lily C. 2013. *Gender and Purity in the Protevangelium of James*. WUNT 2/258. Tübingen: Mohr Siebeck.

Wahlen, Clinton. 2005. "Peter's Vision and Conflicting Definitions of Purity." *NTS* 51:505–18.

Wainwright, Elaine M. 2006. *Women Healing/Healing Women: The Genderization of Healing in Early Christianity*. London: Equinox.

Wassén, Cecilia. 2008. "Jesus and the Hemorrhaging Woman in Mark 5:24–34: Insights from Purity Laws from the Dead Sea Scrolls." Pages 641–60 in *Scripture in Transition: Essays on Septuagint, Hebrew Bible, and Dead Sea Scrolls in Honour of Raija Sollamo*. Edited by Anssi Voitila and Jutta Jokiranta. JSJSup 126. Leiden: Brill.

———. 2016a. "The Jewishness of Jesus and Ritual Purity." *SIDA* 27:11–36.

———. 2016b. "The (Im)purity Levels of Communal Meals within the Qumran Movement." *JAJ* 7:102–22.

———. 2019. "Stepped Pools and Stone Vessels: Rethinking Jewish Purity Practices." *BAR* 45.4–5:53–58.

Watts, James W., ed. 2001. *Persia and Torah: The Theory of Imperial Authorization of the Pentateuch*. SymS 17. Atlanta: Society of Biblical Literature.

———. 2007. *Ritual and Rhetoric in Leviticus: From Sacrifice to Scripture*. Cambridge: Cambridge University Press.

Webb, Robert L. 1991. *John the Baptizer and Prophet: A Socio-historical Study*. JSNTSup 62. Sheffield: JSOT.

Weiss, Daniel H. 2017. "Born into Covenantal Salvation? Baptism and Birth in Early Christianity and Classical Rabbinic Judaism." *JSQ* 24:318–38.

Weissenberg, Hanne von. 2009. *4QMMT: Reevaluating the Text, the Function, and the Meaning of the Epilogue*. STDJ 82. Leiden: Brill.

Wenham, Gordon J. 1979. *The Book of Leviticus*. NICOT. London: Hodder & Stoughton.

Werman, Cana. 2011. "The Price of Mediation: The Role of Priests in the Priestly Halakhah." Pages 377–409 in *The Dead Sea Scrolls and Contemporary Culture: Proceedings of the International Conference Held at the Israel Museum, Jerusalem (July 6–8, 2008)*. Edited by Adolfo D. Roitman, Lawrence H. Schiffman, and Shani Tzoref. STDJ 93. Leiden: Brill.

Werman, Cana, and Aharon Shemesh. 2011. *Revealing the Hidden: Exegesis and Halakah in the Qumran Scrolls* [Hebrew]. Jerusalem: Bialik.

Werrett, Ian C. 2007. *Ritual Purity and the Dead Sea Scrolls*. STDJ 72. Leiden: Brill.

West, Edward W. 1885. *Dînâ-î Maînôg-î Khirad, Sikand-Gûmânîk Vigâr, Sad Dar*. Part 3 of *Pahlavi Texts*. SBE 24. Oxford: Clarendon.

Westerholm, Stephen. 1978. *Jesus and Scribal Authority*. ConBNT 10. Lund: Gleerup.

Whitehouse, Harvey. 2002. "Modes of Religiosity: Towards a Cognitive Explanation of the Sociopolitical Dynamics of Religion." *MTSR* 14.3:293–315.

Wildberger, Hans. 2002. *Isaiah 28–39: A Continental Commentary*. Translated by Thomas H. Trapp. Minneapolis: Fortress.

Wilkinson, John. 1977. "Leprosy and Leviticus: The Problem of Description and Identification." *SJT* 30:153–69.

———. 1978. "Leprosy and Leviticus: A Problem of Semantics and Translation." *SJT* 31:153–66.

Williamson, Hugh G. M. 2015. "Idols in Isaiah in the Light of Isaiah 10:10–11." Pages 17–28 in *New Perspectives on Old Testament Prophecy and History: Essays in Honour of Hans M. Barstad*. Edited by Rannfrid I. Thelle, Terje Stordalen, and Mervyn E. J. Richardson. VTSup 168. Leiden: Brill.

Wilson, E. Jan. 1994. *"Holiness" and "Purity" in Mesopotamia*. AOAT 237. Neukirchen-Vluyn: Neukirchener Verlag.

Wöhrle, Jakob. 2006. *Die frühen Sammlungen des Zwölfprophetenbuches: Entstehung und Komposition*. BZAW 360. Berlin: de Gruyter.

Wright, Benjamin G., III. 1997. "Jewish Ritual Baths—Interpreting the Digs and the Texts: Some Issues in the Social History of Second Temple Judaism." Pages 190–214 in *The Archaeology of Israel: Constructing the Past, Interpreting the Present*. Edited by Neil A. Silberman and David Small. JSOTSup 237. Sheffield: Sheffield Academic.

Wright, David P. 1987. *The Disposal of Impurity: Elimination Rites in the Bible and in Hittite and Mesopotamian Literature*. SBLDS 101. Atlanta: Scholars Press.

———. 1991. "The Spectrum of Priestly Impurity." Pages 150–81 in *Priesthood and Cult in Ancient Israel*. Edited by Gary Anderson and Saul Olyan. JSOTSup 125. Sheffield: JSOT.

———. 1992. "Unclean and Clean (Old Testament)." *ABD* 6:729–41.

———. 2012. "Ritual Theory, Ritual Texts, and the Priestly-Holiness Writings of the Pentateuch." Pages 195–216 in *Social Theory and the Study of Israelite Religion: Essays in Retrospect and Prospect*. Edited by Saul M. Olyan. RBS 71. Atlanta: Society of Biblical Literature.

Yale Perception & Cognition Laboratory Reference Guide: Causal Perception. https://tinyurl.com/SBL3106d.

Yamauchi, Edwin M. 1990. *Persia and the Bible*. Grand Rapids: Baker.

Yee, Gale A. 1987. *Composition and Tradition in the Book of Hosea: A Redaction Critical Investigation*. SBLDS 102. Atlanta: Scholars Press.

Zaas, Peter S. 1996. "What Comes Out of a Person Is What Makes a Person Impure: Jesus as Sadducee." Pages 217–26 in *Jewish Law Association Studies VIII: The Jerusalem 1994 Conference Volume*. Edited by Edward A. Goldman. Atlanta: Scholars Press.

Zaehner, Robert C. 1961. *The Dawn and Twilight of Zoroastrianism*. London: Wedenfeld & Nicolson.

Zangenberg, Jürgen. 2013. "Pure Stone: Archaeological Evidence for Jewish Purity Practices in Late Second Temple Judaism (Miqwa'ot and Stone Vessels)." Pages 537–72 in *Purity and the Forming of Religious Traditions in the Ancient Mediterranean World*. Edited by Christian Frevel and Christophe Nihan. DHR 3. Leiden: Brill.

Ancient Sources Index

Hebrew Bible/Old Testament

Genesis
  31:34–35   85

Exodus
  19:10–15   220

Leviticus   2–4, 10, 54, 63, 79–82, 88–89, 91–92, 96–100, 105, 167, 208, 218, 221–22, 255–56, 264, 286, 289–90, 293, 306
  1–3   177
  1–10   2
  3:16b–17   80
  4–5   159, 289
  4:3   177
  5:15   177
  6–7   289
  6:12–18a   80
  7:19   300
  7:22–29a   80
  7:38b   80
  9:17b   80
  10:1–7   86
  11   2, 6, 24, 49, 65, 70, 72, 77, 87–89, 99–100, 109, 113, 122, 126–28, 141, 147, 314, 210, 243–44, 313–14
  11–15   69, 71, 86, 88, 129, 171, 190, 206, 289, 292
  11:7   73
  11:8   70
  11:9–12   74
  11:11   70
  11:10   100
  11:20–23   74
  11:24–40   70
  11:29–30   100
  11:29–38   74, 243
  11:31   100
  11:32   286
  11:32–34   314
  11:32–35   98
  11:32–36   286
  11:32–38   87, 208
  11:36   84
  11:39–44   313
  11:40   314
  11:41–44   74
  11:43–45   80, 290
  11:44–45   103
  11:45   243
  12   2, 68, 74, 77, 94–95, 115, 128–30, 148, 166, 187, 190, 204, 220, 255, 290, 310
  12–15   48, 70, 83, 98, 99, 108–9, 141, 159, 171, 188, 289, 307
  12:1–5   68
  12:2   220
  12:3   290
  12:4   70, 102, 162, 290–91, 307
  12:5   220
  12:7   218
  12:8   80
  13   92, 221–22, 255, 293
  13–14   2, 83, 85, 91–92, 162, 167, 186, 223, 252–54, 259, 262, 266, 269
  13–15   76, 121
  13:1–44   254
  13:1–46   70

13:2–44	74	15:16–17	94
13:4	255	15:16–24	187
13:6	255	15:17	77
13:9–11	255	15:18	68
13:33	121	15:19	218, 222, 298
13:34	255	15:19–24	68, 70, 83
13:45	223	15:24	94, 110
13:45–46	70, 253, 255–56	15:25	68, 218
13:46	221, 254, 290	15:26–27	70
13:47–59	254	15:28	221
14	91–92, 124, 221, 290	15:29–30	187
14:1–7	97, 187	15:31	81, 102, 162, 189, 290, 307
14:1–32	167	16	2, 159, 170, 175, 290
14:2	83	16:2b	81
14:2–4	297	16:20–22	163
14:2–7	163	16:27	162
14:2–9	70, 254	16:29–34a	81
14:4	297	17–26	2, 71, 80, 108, 115, 121, 146
14:8	102, 133, 188, 254, 261, 266, 290, 310	17–27	81
		18	70, 115, 142, 148
14:8–9	98, 223	18:19	94, 110
14:8–17	92	18:22	122
14:9	133	18:24–30	115, 142, 170
14:10–31	187	18:29	94
14:14–17	98	19:20–22	159
14:14–18	259	20	70, 115–16, 148
14:25–29	259	20:13	122
14:29–45	163	20:18	94, 110, 207
14:33–53	10, 21, 254	20:21	141
14:34–53	81	21	108
14:36	70, 187	21:1–3	208
14:45	290	21:1–4	70, 86, 96–97, 169, 206, 291, 304
14:46	70		
14:46–47	92, 187, 267	21:6	102
14:54–57	81	21:10–12	206, 291
15	2, 29, 68, 74, 85, 93–95, 130, 141, 162, 166, 186, 190, 209, 218–21, 227–28, 255, 290, 297	21:11	70, 304
		21:14	221
		22:2–9	307
15:2–3	68	22:4	86
15:4–12	70	22:4–9	206
15:11	94, 102, 204, 210, 243, 311	23:37	83
15:12	94, 98, 243	23:42–43	64
15:13	83, 93, 221	26	148
15:14–15	187		
15:16	68, 82		

Ancient Sources Index

Numbers	2, 10, 79, 81–82, 86, 96–97, 100, 105, 167, 189, 256, 286, 289, 293, 304, 307
5	2, 105, 188–89, 191–93, 197, 204, 223, 293, 306
5:1–3	292
5:2	253
5:2–3	167, 221, 306
5:2–4	70, 86, 95–96, 102, 189, 256, 269
5:3	102, 293
5:15	18
10:10	82
12:10–13	72, 141
12:12	93
16	86
17:8	233
19	2, 69, 71, 96, 103, 105, 124, 159, 169, 171, 188, 206, 221, 223, 255, 289, 292, 296
19:2–10	97, 188
19:7	188
19:9	292
19:10	188
19:11–19	304
19:11–20	86
19:11–22	187
19:12–13	292
19:13	102, 162, 307
19:13–16	70
19:15	98
19:16	188
19:17–19	97–98
19:19	188
19:20	102, 162, 292, 307
19:21	188
19:21–22	70
19:22	98, 221
28:11–15	82
31	2, 105
31:19–24	86, 189, 292
31:22–23	286
35	105
35:9–34	121, 146, 169
35:33–34	70, 116, 169–70

Deuteronomy	10, 13, 88, 100, 113, 115–16, 141–42
14	2, 49, 65, 88–89, 99, 109, 113, 126–27, 141
14:3	72, 113, 128
14:3–21	88
14:9–10	89
19	108
19:1–13	121, 146, 169
21	108
21:1–9	121, 169, 146
21:8	169–70
23:12–14	144
24:1–4	122

Judges	
13:4	87

1 Samuel	
20:26	82

2 Samuel	
3:29	72, 82, 115, 141
11:2	83
11:4	83

1–2 Kings	87, 115

2 Kings	
5	257
5:10	84
5:12	84
5:14	84
7	257
7:3–20	84
10:27	144
13:20–21	86, 258
15	257
15:1–7	84
21	122
23:13–14	86
23:15–16	86

1–2 Chronicles	87

2 Chronicles		58:1–12	317
26	257	63:7–64:11	150
26:16–21	84	64:5 (Eng. 6)	150
29:5	141	65:4	88
		66:17	88
Ezra	2, 8, 10, 69, 109, 131, 148–49, 152		
6:21	77	Jeremiah	2, 115
9	49, 148	4:14	316–17
9–10	71, 122, 131, 149	6:20	317
9:1–2	131	44	122
9:2	77, 131		
9:11	72, 141, 152	Lamentations	116
9:11–14	131	1:8–9	72
10–14	77	1:17	72
Nehemiah	2, 10, 69, 109, 131, 148–49	Ezekiel	2, 10, 82, 86–87, 115–17, 131–
9:2	71	32, 134, 141–42, 148, 188, 224, 309,	
10:30	71	317	
13	49, 149	4:12–15	144
13:23–30	71	16	49, 71, 122, 131
		16:17–22	133
Job		16:51	134
18:13	93	22	148
		22–23	71
Psalms	108, 316	22:10	141
24:4	316	23	49, 77, 122, 131
51	48, 76, 125, 147	23:16–17	134
51:4 (Eng. 2)	124	23:29–30	134
51:9 (Eng. 7)	17, 124	23:37–39	134
51:12	316	36	71, 77, 122, 131–32, 148, 151
73:13	316	36:16–18	72, 131, 151
106:34–41	70, 116	36:17	85, 115
		36:25–27	317
Proverbs	116, 142, 316	43:7–9	87, 188
20:9	316	44:25–26	98, 196, 224, 309
22:22	316		
		Hosea	
Isaiah	89, 115, 148, 236–37, 317	2	
1:10–17	317	6:6	241, 317
1:16	17	9:3–4	87, 122
29	236, 315		
29:13	315	Amos	
30	148	5:21–27	317
30:19–26	150	7:17	87, 122
30:22	142, 150		

Zechariah		8:40–71	91
3	144	8:71	99
13:1	85, 152	8:97–103	97
		9	98

Ancient Near Eastern Texts

		9:15–26	93, 167
		9:26	99
Hittite Laws		10	90
HL 44b	162	12	97
		14:5	99
Persian Rivayats	95–96, 113	16:1	93, 165
H.F. f. 129	95	16:1–18	91
H.F. f. 382	95	16:6	94, 165
MU. 1.223, ll. 2–5	95	16:12	93, 99, 165
MU. 1.223, ll. 7–12	95	16:17–18	94, 165
		17:3	99
Qissa-i Sanjan	95	18:2	99
		18:65	99
Ṣad dar e-nasr	95		
76	95	Vendidād Sādah	94
76:1, 5	95		
		Yashna	99
Vendidād	10, 79, 90–99, 160, 163,		
165–67, 294,			

Deuterocanonical Books

3:15–21	91		
5–8	91	Judith	2
5:27–28	97		
5:27–62	91	Tobit	2, 224, 309
5:59	93–94, 165	2:5	196, 224
6:1–9	99	2:9	98, 196, 224, 309
6:44–51	97, 99		
7:1–3	97		

Pseudepigrapha

7:2–5	99		
7:4–5	96	Psalms of Solomon	
7:6–7	97	2.3	244
7:10–19	94, 165	8.11–13	244
7:19	94, 165		
7:73–75	94, 98, 165		

Dead Sea Scrolls

8:11–13	98		
8:16–18	99	1QM	36
8:23–25	91	XIV, 2–3	196, 224, 309
8:26	94, 165		
8:32	94	1QS	2, 13, 15–16, 77
8:35–72	93, 97, 167	III, 4–5	201
8:36	98	III, 4–9	317
8:37–71	98	IV, 20–21	317

4Q51	83	4QMMT (4Q394–399)	2, 11, 206, 261–62, 286, 295, 313
4Q266		B49–72	244
6 I, 14–6 II, 13	202	B55–58	313
		B64–72	96, 223, 261, 297
4Q272	201	B65	261
1 II, 3–18	202	B66–67	261
1 II, 8	222	B67–68	261
1 II, 17	202, 222	B68–70	261
		B71–72	261
4Q274	14–15, 202–203, 222, 262		
1	15, 86, 98, 309	11Q19	11–12, 36, 192–94, 196–99, 203–4, 220, 223–25, 260, 262, 293, 306–7, 309
1 I	96		
1 I, 1–2			
1 I, 1–4	223	XLV, 7–8	220
1 I, 1–9	202	XLV, 11	192, 306
1 I, 1–II, 1	262	XLV, 15–18	96, 192, 293, 306
1 I, 3	262	XLV, 17	223–24
1 I, 3–4	223	XLV, 17–18	260
1 I, 7–8	202, 226	XLVI, 16–18	96, 192, 223, 260, 262, 293, 306
2 I	201		
		XLVII	193
4Q277	201, 204, 222	XLVIII, 10–14	193
1 II, 8–9	201	XLVIII, 13–17	223
1 II, 10–11	204	XLVIII, 14–17	96, 193, 223–24, 260, 262, 293, 306
4Q278	201	XLIX	193
		XLIX, 16–21	98, 309
4Q284	14	L, 13–16	98, 194
1	201		
		CD	2, 11, 13, 254
4Q414	14, 98, 196, 224, 309	A IV–V	244
		A V, 7	286
4Q435	316	A XII, 15–17	313
4Q436	316	Ancient Jewish Writers	
4Q512	14, 16, 77	Josephus, *Against Apion*	
1–3	201	1. 281	223
		1.281–282	183, 263
4Q514	14, 196, 200, 224	2.103	198
		2.103–104	293
4Q525	316		
		Josephus, *Jewish Antiquities*	
		3.261	197–98, 266, 293, 309

3.261–262	185, 263	1:21–22	218
3.261–268	183	1:22, 27	248
3.264	93, 223–25, 263	1:22, 27	248
13.295–98	240	1:40–45	40, 223, 227, 230, 273
		2:1	238, 316
Josephus, *Jewish War*		2:5	230
5.227	198, 263, 266, 293	2:10	248
6.290	197, 224, 309	2:13	218
6.426	263, 266	3:15	248
		3:20	238, 316
Letter of Aristeas	55, 60, 110	5	29, 218, 246
139–169	60	5:21–24	230
		5:25	218
Philo, *Quod Deus sit immutabilis*	55	5:25–27	228
127–130	61	5:25–34	217
131–135	61	5:29	218
		5:34	230
Philo, *De migratione Abrahami*		5:35	218
89	61	5:35–43	230
		5:36	230
Philo, *De specialibus legibus*	55	6:2	218
1.206	61	6:6	218, 230, 248
1.261	98, 195–96, 223–24, 309	6:30–44	230
1.261–266	61	7	27, 30, 183, 211, 218–19, 227, 231, 234, 239, 245–47, 311–12, 314–15
3.63	201		
3.205–206	98, 195, 223–24, 309	7:1–13	240
		7:1–23	217
New Testament		7:2–4	228, 240
		7:3–4	235–36
Matthew	26, 28, 229–30, 235, 237, 244–45, 270–71	7:6–8	236
		7:8	236
8:1	270	7:9	236
8:3	253	7:9–13	236
15:11	237	7:11	228
15:20	235	7:13	236
19:12	26	7:15	24, 27–28, 235, 237–38, 241–44, 316
22:30	26		
26:6	273	7:16–23	28
		7:17	238
Mark	27, 30, 38, 40, 184, 211, 216–219, 226–31, 234–44, 246–48, 270–71, 273, 296, 311–12, 315–17	7:17–23	238, 242, 316
		7:19	27, 235–36, 241, 316
		7:21–22	239
1:4	17	8:3	218
1:13	230	9:24	230
1:15	230	9:28	238, 316

Mark (cont.)		1 Corinthians	
9:33	238, 316	1:10–17	177
9:37	241	1:19	236, 315
9:38	218	8	238
10:10	238, 316		
10:35	218	Galatians	
10:52	230	2:11–14	238
11:28	248		
11:29	248	Colossians	
11:33	248	2:22	236, 315
14:3	273		
16:6	230	James	7, 31
16:8	230		

Rabbinic Works

Q	244, 317	b. Arakhin	
11:39–41	245	29a	223, 299
11:42	245		
11:44	244	b. Bava Qamma	
		92b	223
Luke	31, 229, 244–45, 270–72, 317		
2:22–39	271	b. Eruvin	
5:12	270, 272	4b	84
5:13	253		
8:51–53	271	b. Hullin	
11:37–38	245	78a	223
11:39	317		
11:39–41	317	b. Keritot	
11:41	245	8b	222–23
13:15–16	271	9a	18
17:11–19	223, 271		
		b. Mo'ed Qatan	
John	224	5a	223
2	21	5b	254
2:6	286	15b	223
11:55	197, 224, 309		
		b. Nedarim	
Acts	31	64b	93
15:9	31		
21	31	b. Niddah	
		66a	220, 223, 254
Romans			
9:20	236, 315	b. Pesahim	
11:8	236, 315	14b	211, 312, 314
14	238	17b–20b	211, 314

b. Shabbat		m. Nega'im	
13b	314	2:1	267, 299
13b–14b	211, 312, 314	4:11	267, 299
13b–17b	207	5:1	267, 299
14b	314	12–13	221
67a	223	13:7	93
		13:11	93
b. Sotah		13:12	268, 299
32b	223	14	297
		14:2–3	212–13, 261, 297
b. Yoma		14:3	212
31a	84		
		m. Niddah	191
Baraita de Maseket Niddah	201	4:3	222
		7:4	204
m. Arakhin		8:1–3	222, 298
9:6	223, 268, 298	8:3	298
		10:6	213
m. Bava Batra		10:6–7	212–13
2:9	188		
		m. Ohalot	286
m. Berakhot		1:1–3	242
8:2	207, 296, 311, 313	5:5	286
8:2–3	245		
		m. Parah	287
m. Hagigah		3:2	287
2:5–6	210	3:5	296
2:5–7	211, 242	3:7	206
2:7	209, 212	3:11	287
		5:5	287
m. Kelim	191	8:7	214, 313
1	199, 204		
1:4	93, 204, 226	m. Shabbat	
1:6	199	1:4	207, 211, 312, 314
1:6–9	199, 225, 294		
1:7	199, 223, 268, 298	m. Tevul Yom	205
1:8	199, 224–25	2:2	214
10:1	286		
20:2	209	m. Teharot	313
26:6	209	2	244
m. Mikwa'ot		m. Yadayim	
4:1	287	3:1–2	242
8:1, 5	86, 222	4:6–7	36
		4:7	313

m. Zavim	191
2:2	298
3:1	209
5:1, 6	222
5:10	213
5:12	207–8, 211, 214, 233, 312, 314

Maimonides, *Book of Commandments*
240

Maimonides, *Mishneh Torah*
10.6.16:8	300
10.6.16:9	301

Pesiqta of Rab Kahana	36
4:7	97

Sifra	2, 254, 297
Emor Pereq 4	313
Mesora Parashah 1	297
Shemini Parashah 8	211, 314

Sifre Numbers	2, 306
116	233

Sifre Zuta Numbers	201

t. Bava Batra	
1:11	188

t. Berakhot	
6 [5]:2–3	245, 313

t. Demai	
2:11–12	313

t. Nega'im	
1:5	299
5:2–3	299
6:1	299
7:11	268, 299
8:5	297

t. Niddah	191

t. Shabbat	
1:14	19
1:16–21	207

t. Shevu'ot	
4:11	284

t. Tevul Yom	
1:3, 6	207

t. Zavim	191

y. Shabbat	
1, 3c–d [V. 1, 7]	207

Samaritan Works

Kitâb al-Kâfi	
III [43]	196, 309
XI [48–60]	202
XI [84–87]	202
XIII [11–13]	196, 309
XIII [13–18]	202

Kitâb aṭ Ṭubâkh	
[2–15]	202

Early Christian Writings

Barnabas	
10	61

Gospel of Thomas	
14	28

Origen, *Homiliae in Leviticum*	61

Papyrus Oxyrhynchus 840	32, 246

Protevangelium of James	31

Greco-Roman Literature

Antiphon, *On the Murder of Herodes*	
5.11	265

Ancient Sources Index

Aristotle, *De somniis*
   459b–460a   164

Censorinus, *De die natali*
   11.7   165

Demosthenes, *Exordia*
   21.118   265

Euripides, *Alcestis*
   98–100   168, 175

Euripides, *Orestes*
   48   174

Festus, *De verborum significatione*
   161.1   168

Herodotus, *Historia*
   1.64   165
   1.138   84, 91, 167, 258
   2.37   161
   2.41   161

Lucian, *Phalaris*
   1.1   265

On the Sacred Disease   167, 176
   1.3–4   176
   4.36–40   176

Pliny the Elder, *Naturalis Historia*
   7.63–64   165
   7.63–66   86
   7.64   115
   28.70–82   165

Plutarch, *Quastionum convivialum libri IX*
   2.10   265

Plutarch, *Quaestiones romanae et graecae*
   (Aetia romana et graeca)
   280b–c   174

Strabo, *Geographica*
   9.3   265

Thucydides, *Historia*
   3.104   165

Modern Authors Index

Abe, Chikara 44
Achenbach, Reinhard 10, 69, 82, 86, 91, 96, 189, 289, 294
Adler, Yonatan 20–23, 74, 162, 169, 182, 185, 192, 196–97, 207, 211, 251, 260, 268, 281–84, 301, 304, 307–10
Alon, Gedalyahu 5, 19, 143, 182, 207–8, 240, 278–81
Amihay, Aryeh 14, 36
Amit, David 22, 182, 308, 309
André, Gunnel 3, 44, 75, 120, 144, 157
Angyal, Andras 112, 139
Appelrouth, Scott 56
Attridge, Harold W. 169
Auld, A. Graeme 83
Aune, David E. 31
Avemarie, Friedrich 28, 182, 183, 240–42, 311, 316
Baert, Patrick 59
Balberg, Mira 34, 143
Barmash, Pamela 169
Baronov, David 56
Barr, James 90
Baumgarten, Joseph M. 11, 13–15, 182, 194, 197, 199–202, 205–6, 219, 226, 232, 262, 294, 309
Beck, Roger 158
Beckman, Gary M. 164
Bell, Catherine M. 110
Bell, H. Idris 272
Bendlin, Andreas 161
Berger, Klaus 25
Berger, Michael S. 240
Berlin, Andrea M. 268, 288
Berquist, Jon L. 70, 101
Binder, Donald D. 284
Birenboim, Hannan 15, 263
Biró, Tamás 175
Blidstein, Moshe 10, 33, 158, 165, 168
Blomberg, Craig 67
Blum, Erhard 101
Bodel, John 168
Bóid, I. Ruairidh M. 35, 86, 196, 202, 220, 240, 309
Booth, Roger P. 28, 182, 207–8, 233, 241
Borg, Marcus J. 24
Borgeaud, Philippe 176
Boyce, Mary 90
Boyer, Pascal 179
Brettler, Marc Zvi 252, 253
Broshi, Magen 11, 86, 188
Bruneau, Philippe 284
Büchler, Adolf 5, 19, 35, 109, 111, 143, 182, 207, 278, 304
Bulbulia, Joseph 178
Burkert, Walter 170
Cahill, Jane 21, 207, 288
Carreira da Silva, Filipe 59
Cazelles, Henri 10
Chankin-Gould, J. D'ror 83
Chilton, Bruce 24, 25
Choksy, Jamsheed K. 44, 90, 99, 113, 158, 162, 168, 175
Cholewinski, Alfred 81, 88
Christiansen, Birgit 10
Cohen, Shaye J. D. 219
Colpe, Carsten 10, 90, 91, 294
Coser, Lewis 57
Coulson, Seanna 48, 76, 118–19, 146, 172

Modern Authors Index

Crawford, Sidnie White   192, 194, 224, 225, 307
Crossley, James G.   67, 182, 206, 211, 232–37, 241, 244, 312
Curtis, Valerie   47, 71, 112, 113, 138, 139, 149
Damasio, Antonio R.   112, 138, 139
Danks, David   52
Darmesteter, James   90, 94
Darwin, Charles   112, 138, 139
Deines, Roland   21, 182, 205, 207, 233, 287
Desfor Edles, Laura   56
deSilva, David A.   30
Dhabhar, Ervad B. N.   95, 99, 113
Dietrich, Jan   169
Douglas, Mary   6–8, 30–31, 45, 46, 54–55, 58–60, 63, 64, 106, 107, 173
Dunbar, Robin I. M.   149
Dunn, James D. G.   24, 28, 38, 237
Durkheim, Émile   56–58
Edelman, Diana V.   81
Eidevall, Göran   317
Eilberg-Schwartz, Howard   62, 65, 107
Ekroth, Gunnel   168
Ellens, Deborah L.   29, 68, 166
Elliger, Karl   94, 254
Erbele-Küster, Dorothea   29
Eshel, Esther   194, 232, 309
Eshel, Hanan   12, 21, 205
Eskenazi, Tamara Cohn   101
Fantham, Elaine   158, 160
Fatkin, Danielle Steen   21, 284
Fauconnier, Gilles   48, 76, 118, 146, 172
Faulkner, Jason   149
Faust, Avraham   23
Feder, Yitzhaq   9–11, 44–45, 47, 144, 157, 267
Feinstein, Eve   9, 62, 75, 109, 114, 120, 128, 143–44, 168
Feldman, Emanuel   36
Fessler, M.T.   47, 113, 138, 149
Finkelstein, Israel   23, 60, 88, 114
Fishbein, Harold D.   149
Fonrobert, Charlotte E.   29, 219
Förster, Niclas   32, 33

Fraade, Steven D.   11, 295
Frandsen, Paul John   157, 160, 164
Fredriksen, Paula   183
Freedman, Daniel G.   149
Frei, Peter   101
Frevel, Christian   10, 46, 69, 81, 86, 102, 189, 301
Frymer-Kensky, Tikva   8, 63, 109
Furstenberg, Yair   15–17, 19, 28, 35, 36, 182, 233, 242–44, 248, 304, 306, 313, 316
Gane, Roy   54, 79
García Martínez, Florentino   11, 194, 200–202
Geertz, Clifford   54
Gendelman, Peter   308
Gershevitch, Ilya   90
Gerstenberger, Erhard S.   3, 91
Gibson, Shimon   21–22
Gilders, William K.   64–65
Ginsburskaya, Mila   9, 16, 143
Goldingay, John   150
Goldstein, Elizabeth   29, 142, 152
Grabbe, Lester L.   90, 295
Graf, Fritz   160, 162, 168, 170, 175
Grappe, Christian   25
Gray, George Buchanan   82
Greer, Jonathan S.   23
Guichard, Michaël   157, 160, 164, 175
Günther, Linda-Marie   35, 161, 165
Haber, Susan   29, 30, 67, 182, 192, 217–19, 222, 226–31, 246
Haidt, Jonathan   47, 71, 112, 114, 138–40, 180
Hanson, Paul D.   150
Harrington, Hannah K.   11–13, 32, 131, 143–44, 182, 191, 202, 205, 210, 220, 251, 267, 279–81, 296–97, 299, 312, 313
Hayes, Christine E.   8–9, 69, 71, 110, 131, 143, 296
Hedner-Zetterholm, Karin   240
Henninger, Joseph   3, 10
Hesse, Brian   23, 60, 88, 114
Heyes, Cecilia   52

Hieke, Thomas 3–4, 68, 166, 254
Himmelfarb, Martha 11–13, 16, 47, 77, 117, 206, 295
Hoffmann, David Z. 45, 109, 110
Hoglund, Kenneth G. 101
Holmén, Tom 25, 243
Holtz, Gudrun 47, 263
Hooker, Morna D. 238
Houston, Walter 7
Huber, Ludwig 52
Hübner, Hans 3, 24, 27, 182, 313
Hughes, Dennis D. 174
Hulse, E. V. 252
Humbert, Paul 142
Hutter, Manfred 162
Ilan, Tal 29
Irons, William 178
Jaffee, Martin S. 240
Jensen, Jeppe Sinding 53, 280
Jeremias, Joachim 17
Johnson, Mark 48, 76, 117–18, 145, 171
Johnston, Sarah Ihles 44
Jong, Albert F. de 90, 95, 160–61, 175
Kahl, Brigitte 218
Katz, Hayah 23
Kaufmann, Yehezkel 4, 59, 79, 80
Kazen, Thomas 1, 10, 12–15, 23, 26–28, 32–34, 38–40, 47–48, 67–68, 70–77, 81, 83–87, 89, 92–99, 102, 105–7, 109–15, 117, 121, 126, 128, 130, 138, 141–46, 148, 159–62, 166, 169, 172–73, 181–89, 192–95, 198, 202, 204–7, 209–11, 213, 215, 217–19, 221–24, 226, 229–30, 232, 234, 237, 244–46, 249, 252, 257, 259–63, 268, 271–73, 277, 286, 288, 289, 293–96, 304, 306, 307, 309–14, 317
Keady, Jessica M. 12
Kekes, John 140
Keltner, Dacher 180
Kessler, John 101
Ketola, Kimmo 175
Klawans, Jonathan 7–9, 15–17, 47, 55, 58, 63–64, 70–71, 106, 109–11, 116–17, 124, 142–44, 159

Knohl, Israel 4, 80–81, 289
Knoppers, Gary N. 101
Koch, Klaus 101
Kolnai, Aurel 112, 114, 139
Kratz, Reinhard G. 81
Kruger, Michael J. 32, 246
Kümmel, Werner G. 24, 27
Kunin, Seth D. 7
Lafferty, Theresa V. 317
Lakoff, George 48, 76, 117–18, 145, 171
Lam, Joseph 9, 72, 150, 151
Lambert, Wilfred G. 47
Lawrence, Jonathan D. 11, 20, 201, 232
Lawson, E. Thomas 47, 71, 112, 114, 138, 174, 175
LeFebvre, Michael 101
Lemos, Tracy M. 7–8, 46, 57–60, 62–64, 71, 106–10, 116, 131, 144, 163, 173
Lennon, Jack J. 10, 158, 160, 165, 170
Lernau, Omri 23
Levine, Amy-Jill 252–55, 264
Levine, Baruch 81, 192, 224
Levine, Lauren 44
Lévi-Strauss, Claude 56
Liénard, Pierre 179
Lindsay, Hugh 168
Lipschits, Oded 101
Liu, Yulin 31
Lockett, Darian 7, 31
Long, V. Philips 88, 114
Longman III, Tremper 88, 114
Looy, Heather 112, 138
Maass, Fritz 3
Maccoby, Hyam 6–7, 19, 36, 152, 189, 198, 208, 219, 221, 254, 261, 266–67, 279, 298–99, 306
Magen, Yitzhaq 11, 22, 205, 207, 233, 268, 287–88, 307
Magness, Jodi 12, 22, 144, 284
Maier, Bernard 3
Maier, Johann 20
Malandra, William W. 90
Malinar, Angelika 44
Marcus, Joel 17, 24
Marti, Lionel 157, 160, 164, 175

Marx, Alfred 8
Matassa, Lidia 284
McCarter, P. Kyle Jr. 83
McCauley, Clark 47, 71, 112, 114, 138
McCauley, Robert N. 174-75
McEvoy, Chad Joseph 149
Meacham, Tirzah (leBeit Yoreh) 220
Meeks, Dimitri 157
Meier, John P. 27, 33, 38, 110, 183, 252-54, 260, 262, 264-65, 267, 316
Meinel, Fabian 10
Menninghaus, Winfried 112
Meshel, Naphtali S. 56, 66, 88
Meyer, Robert 160, 161
Michaels, Axel 179
Milgrom, Jacob 3-4, 6-7, 10, 14-15, 46, 55, 59-60, 62, 64, 79-81, 84-86, 88, 91, 96, 98, 103, 106-7, 115, 128, 166-67, 182, 185, 188-89, 192, 194, 199-200, 202, 210, 221, 224, 226, 232, 254, 258-59, 262, 279-81, 289-90, 292, 306, 309, 312
Miller, Stuart S. 21-22, 74, 162, 182, 185, 205, 207, 211, 234, 283, 287, 304, 307-9
Miller, Susan B. 112, 114
Miller, William I. 112, 114, 139
Mizzi, Dennis 12
Mossman, Amanda 180
Munson, Rosaria Vignolo 258
Murphy, Catherine M. 7
Navarrete, C. David 47, 113, 138, 149
Netzer, Ehud 21
Neusner, Jacob 4-7, 19, 33-34, 58, 61, 71, 111, 114, 182, 208-9, 232-33, 240, 279-80, 304-6, 313-14
Newman, George E. 52
Newton, Michael 11, 31
Neyrey, Jerome H. 7, 30, 38
Nihan, Christophe 4, 10, 46, 54, 69, 81, 85-86, 88, 94, 102, 113, 128, 189, 254, 257, 289, 301
Noam, Vered 12, 14, 36, 37, 295, 304
Nogalski, James 87
Nongbri, Brent 302
Nougayrol, Jean 91-92, 167, 258, 259
Nussbaum, Martha 112, 140
Oakley, Todd 48, 76, 118-19, 146, 172
Olyan, Saul 69
Oppenheimer, Aharon 35-36
Paganini, Simone 25
Parker, Robert 10, 44, 108, 158-59, 162, 165, 170, 174
Paschen, Wilfried 4, 44, 120, 144, 157
Petrovic, Andrej 10
Petrovic, Ivana 10
Philip, Tarja S. 29, 152, 164
Piff, Paul K. 180
Poirier, John C. 19, 20, 30, 67, 182, 185, 192, 194, 211, 233, 277-79, 300-301, 304, 306
Premack, David 52
Premack, Anne James 52
Pressler, Carolyn 122
Preston, Stephanie D. 71, 112, 138
Preuss, Horst Dietrich 116
Provan, Iain 88, 114
Pury, Albert de 81
Quack, Joachim Friedrich 161, 163-64, 167-68, 170
Quick, Laura 13
Rackham, H. 115
Reardon, Timothy W. 31
Reed, Jonathan L. 233
Regev, Eyal 15, 20-21, 30, 182, 185, 194, 196, 211, 232-33, 280, 284, 288, 304, 309
Reich, Ronny 20, 21, 268, 281-83, 307-8
Repschinski, Boris 25
Ringgren, Helmer 3, 44, 75, 120, 144, 157
Robertson, Noel 46, 161
Römer 81, 87
Ronen, Neta 176
Rösch, Petra 10
Rossides, Daniel W. 57
Rozin, Paul 47, 71, 72, 112-15, 138
Ruane, Nicole J. 29, 59, 65-66
Runesson, Anders 217, 284
Safrai, Chana 32

Safrai, Ze'ev	32	Theissen, Gerd	228
Sanders, Ed P.	5–6, 19, 178, 181–86, 190, 195–98, 203–4, 206–9, 212, 213, 216, 219, 232–33, 239, 244, 266, 268, 279, 304–6, 308, 311	Thiering, Barbara	15
		Thiessen, Matthew	25–28, 38
		Tiemeyer, Lena-Sophia	150
		Tigay, Jeffrey H.	113
Sapir-Hen, Lidar	23	Tigchelaar, Eibert J. C.	194, 200–202
Schart, Aaron	87	Toews, Casey	15, 17
Scheve, Christian von	180	Tomson, Peter	182, 207, 211, 233
Schiffman, Lawrence H.	11, 192, 206, 224, 232, 261, 294	Toorn, Karle van der	44, 144, 157, 160, 164
Schmid, Konrad	81	Torgü, Hagit	308
Schmidt, Karl F. W.	272, 273	Touger, Eliyahu	300
Schremer, Adiel	14, 295	Trevaskis, Leigh M.	63
Schwartz, Daniel R.	14, 32, 206, 295, 304	Trümper, Monika	284
		Tsumura, David Toshio	83
Schwartz, Joshua	297	Turner, Mark	48, 76, 118, 146, 172
Seidl, Theodor	3, 254	Uro, Risto	16, 155, 177, 179–80
Seligman, Jon	22	Vuong, Lily C.	31, 32
Selvidge, Marla J.	29, 217	Waal, Frans B. M. de	71, 112, 138
Shaked, Saul	90	Wahlen, Clinton	31
Shellberg, Pamela	31	Wainwright, Elaine M.	218
Shemesh, Aharon	14, 36, 206, 286, 295, 304	Wapnish, Paula	23, 60, 88, 114
		Wassén, Cecilia	24, 29–30, 67, 182–83, 192, 202, 204, 219, 263, 268, 280, 283–85, 287, 305, 316
Shinall, Myrick C., Jr.	40, 252–60, 262, 264–66, 268–74		
Shiota, Michelle	180	Watts, James W.	4, 51, 59, 63–64, 66, 101, 173
Shively, Elizabeth E.	27, 38–39		
Simon, Udo	10	Webb, Robert L.	16–18
Ska, Jean-Louis	101	Weiss, Daniel H.	19
Skeat, Theodore C.	272	Weissenberg, Hanne von	261, 313
Smith, William Robertson	16, 43, 46, 150	Wenham, Gordon J.	185
		Werman, Cana	12, 14
Snyder, Benjamin J.	13, 16–18	Werrett, Ian C.	13, 202, 220
Spencer, Herbert	56–57, 137	Westerholm, Stephen	24, 38, 182, 236, 241, 313, 315
Sperber, Dan	52, 64		
Staal, Frits	66	Whitehouse, Harvey	174
Stausberg, Micahel	3	Wildberger, Hans	150
Stemberger, Günther	35	Wilkinson, John	252
Stol, Marten	164	Williamson, Hugh G. M.	150
Sturrock, John	56	Wilson, E. Jan	11
Svartvik, Jesper	27, 237	Witherington III, Ben	252–55, 264
Sweetser, Eve	119	Wöhrle, Jakob	87
Tal, Oren	101	Wright, David P.	3, 8, 10, 21, 46, 62–63, 81, 86–87, 107, 109, 141, 163, 166, 188, 191, 210, 312
Taylor, Vincent	17, 228		
Teehan, John	140		

Wulf, Christoph	179
Yale Perception & Cognition Laboratory Reference Guide	52
Yamauchi, Edwin M.	90
Yee, Gale A.	87
Zaas, Peter S.	28, 182, 311
Zaehner, Robert C.	90
Zangenberg, Jürgen	280, 283, 287
Zilberbod, Irina	22

Subject Index

ablution, 14–15, 74, 98, 102, 141, 156, 169, 172, 177, 188, 194–97, 199–201, 203, 205–6, 210, 215–16, 223–26, 232, 246, 260, 293, 296, 309, 310
abomination, 58, 63, 107, 113, 115, 126, 131, 133–34, 141–42, 151–52, 164
Achaemenid, 79, 81, 90–91, 100–101, 160, 256, 257
adultery, 77, 133–34
airborne impurity (from afar), 4, 6, 189, 279, 290, 292, 306
allegory, 45–46, 55, 58, 60–62, 110, 173
altar, 86, 170, 208, 279, 306
am-ha'areṣ, 5, 35, 210, 324
anachronism, 13, 33, 40, 46, 52, 63, 162, 185, 206, 215, 232, 234, 257, 277–78, 283, 294, 296, 301–3, 312, 315
ancient West Asia, 3–4, 10, 23, 59, 75, 80, 92, 97, 129, 164, 170–71, 189, 259
anthropology, 6, 34, 45, 54, 56
anti-Judaism, 37, 159, 269, 274–75
apologetics, 6, 64, 79, 107, 264, 266–67, 315
Aqiva, 222, 242, 298
Aramaeans, 84
archaeology, 10, 19–23, 162, 234, 282, 287, 307
Aristeas, 55, 60, 110
āšām, 2, 159, 177, 187
ashes, 15, 61, 96, 97, 197, 210, 296
Assyria, 87
aversion, 43–44, 47–49, 72–73, 75–76, 111, 115, 130, 141–42, 147–49, 151–53, 172

Babylonia, 18, 32, 65, 69, 84, 91–92, 115, 134, 163–64, 167, 233, 240, 254, 258, 301
baptism, 16–19, 33, 176, 177
barashnum ritual, 90, 92–93, 97–98, 161, 168, 175–76, 178
bathing, 20, 29, 49, 83, 92, 98, 166, 188, 194–96, 200, 221, 225–26, 284–85, 310
Bathsheba, 83, 85, 93
Bethany, 273
Bethel, 86
blood, 10, 18, 29, 77, 85–86, 90, 92, 94–95, 97–98, 107, 115, 121, 125, 128–29, 131–34, 146, 150–51, 156, 158, 164–65, 167, 169–70, 174, 176, 180, 190, 202, 212, 222, 226, 298
bloodshed, bloodguilt, 44, 77, 108, 116, 121, 132, 142, 146, 151, 157–59, 169–71, 176
bones, 23, 86–88, 99, 114, 204, 226, 258, 287
boundary stone, 91, 167, 258
carcass, 2, 26, 45, 88–89, 99–100, 109, 121–22, 126–27, 156, 171, 180, 285, 291, 314
chalk-stone vessels, 21–22, 207, 280–81, 284, 286–88
childbirth, 26, 62, 68, 90, 95, 107, 128, 158–60, 162–66, 183, 187, 202, 271, 305
Christ-believers, early Christians, 9, 11, 16, 26, 30, 33, 34, 61, 235–36, 238–39, 247–48, 286

Subject Index

circumcision, 18, 176
clean, 1–3, 27, 44–45, 47, 60, 65, 82, 84, 92, 124, 141, 144, 157, 195, 212, 214, 235, 245, 255, 262, 279, 289, 298, 312, 316, 317
cleaning, 179, 285. *See also* purification, purify
cleansing, 17, 30, 31, 94, 98, 124, 147, 151, 157, 160, 170, 200
clothes, 85, 92, 94, 95, 125, 150, 166, 179, 188, 194, 195, 200, 209, 211, 221, 243, 253–55, 264
commitment signaling, 178–79
conceptual blending, 43, 47–49, 74, 76–77, 105, 117–19, 123–32, 134–35, 137, 145–53, 155, 160, 172, 313, 315, 317
conceptual metaphor, 1, 9, 16, 48, 74–75, 105, 117, 120, 122, 130, 135, 137, 145, 153, 171
contagion, 2, 17–18, 24–25, 28, 39, 44–45, 48, 62, 70–73, 76, 87, 90–91, 96–97, 99, 108–10, 113, 115–16, 123–24, 144, 147, 156–57, 162, 168, 171, 186, 197, 242, 246, 254–55, 266–67, 269, 288, 291, 307, 311, 316
contamination, 30, 48, 71, 76, 85–87, 91–96, 98, 100, 112, 121–22, 124–26, 129, 138, 145, 147, 155, 162, 165, 168–69, 175, 181, 187–89, 191–93, 197, 199, 202–5, 207–11, 213–16, 220–22, 226, 232, 234–35, 241–44, 251–57, 260–63, 265–68, 270, 275, 279, 285–86, 288, 290–92, 294, 296–99, 306–7, 310–11, 313–14, 316
corpse, corpse contamination, 2, 10, 12, 14–15, 31, 33, 35–36, 45, 47–48, 61, 69, 71–72, 86–87, 89–91, 94–99, 102–3, 108, 112, 114, 124, 138, 142, 144, 156, 158–62, 165, 168–69, 171, 175, 187–95, 197–201, 203–4, 206, 208, 210, 21–13, 221, 223–26, 229–30, 232, 242, 245–46, 253, 255–56, 261, 263, 285, 287, 289, 291–94, 296, 301, 304, 306, 309–10

corpse demoness (*drug nasu*), 93, 96, 160, 168
cow's urine (*gomez*), 93, 165, 175
custom, 13–14, 19, 22, 26, 40, 69, 90, 173, 181, 192, 205–7, 209, 211–12, 215–16, 233, 238, 242, 278, 282, 288–89, 291, 294–96, 300–302, 312, 314–15
dakhma, 98–99, 168
Damascus Document, 2, 11, 13, 254
dāwâ, 142, 150
decay, 44, 47–48, 72, 113–15
defilement, 4, 6, 8, 12, 15, 17, 19, 27–28, 32–33, 36, 73–74, 84, 86–87, 90, 97, 99, 102, 107, 109, 111, 116, 120–21, 131, 134, 141–42, 144–45, 150–51, 160, 169–70, 193, 207, 210–15, 220–21, 224, 227, 234–35, 241, 243, 248, 253–54, 260, 263–65, 267, 285–86, 290–93, 303, 306–7, 311, 313–17
Delos, 165, 168, 284
demon, demonic, 4, 36, 39, 44, 59, 79–80, 90, 96–97, 99, 103, 158–60, 168
Deuteronomist, Deuteronomistic, 79, 82, 84, 86–89, 93, 113, 132, 257, 259
diagnosis, 74, 85, 92, 102, 252–53, 256–57, 259
dialectic negation, 241, 316
dirt, 1, 6, 44, 47–49, 58, 75–76, 106, 111, 120–26, 143–51, 155, 157, 161, 171, 179, 214, 302
discharge, discharger, 2, 14–15, 25, 27–29, 35, 41, 45–46, 48, 58, 62, 67–68, 72, 74–75, 83–86, 89, 91, 93–95, 98–99, 106–8, 114–15, 121, 123, 125, 129–32, 141–42, 144, 148–51, 159, 162, 164–67, 181–82, 185–94, 196–205, 209–10, 212, 216, 219–22, 224–26, 242, 246, 253, 255–56, 260, 262–263, 266, 270, 285, 290–91, 293–94, 297–98, 306–7, 309, 311
disgust, 9, 41, 43, 47–49, 71–73, 75–77, 85, 105, 111–17, 120–23, 126–32, 134–35, 137–53, 171–72, 243, 291
divorce, 122, 234, 288

dog, 97, 98, 168, 174
drink, 155, 191, 200, 232, 288, 298, 314
drug nasu, 44, 93, 96, 98, 158, 160, 168
Durkheim, 56–58, 173
Egypt, 9, 10, 44, 115, 120, 143, 155, 157, 160–61, 163–64, 167–68, 170, 290
eighth-day sacrifice, 212, 261, 267
embodiment, 12, 27, 116, 137, 179, 180
emotion, 9, 16, 43, 47–49, 52, 71–73, 75–78, 105, 111–12, 114–17, 128, 132, 134–35, 137–45, 148–50, 152–53, 156–57, 179–80, 271
Epimenides, 176
Essenes, 11, 197, 205, 244, 280, 294, 305
evolutionary, 9, 41, 49, 51, 53, 59, 70, 73–74, 77–78, 135, 137–38, 140, 144, 149–51, 153, 172, 178–80
exclusion, 12, 24, 40, 84, 91, 95, 102, 125, 188, 194, 197, 199, 223–24, 226, 251–53, 255, 257–60, 262–63, 265, 269–70, 273–75, 306
exorcism, 25–27, 39, 90, 97, 158, 160, 273
expansionist, 19, 38, 194, 197, 201, 204, 208, 210–11, 216, 232–34, 240, 244–46, 272, 280, 307, 313
expulsion, 70, 86, 91, 120–21, 146, 158, 174, 181–82, 187–91, 193–94, 198, 203–5, 221, 223–25, 258–59, 263, 265–68, 271, 291, 293, 299, 309
Falashas, 96, 186, 306
first-day ablution, 14–15, 98, 102, 169, 188, 194–97, 199–200, 203, 205–6, 210, 215, 222–24, 246, 260, 293, 309–10
fluids, 45, 47, 77, 120, 131, 144–45, 156, 161–62, 164
food avoidances, 43, 45, 62, 70, 72–73, 76–77, 126–28, 156
food impurity, 2, 211, 238, 313–14, 316
food laws, 3, 6–8, 23, 33, 45–46, 48, 58, 60, 63, 67, 70, 87–89, 99, 100, 107, 109–10, 113, 116, 141, 161, 171, 235, 241, 279, 290
functionalism, 51, 55–56, 58, 173–74

Galilee, 22, 35, 184, 197, 211, 216, 244, 248, 255, 268, 270, 274, 282–83, 303–4, 308, 311
genealogical impurity, 8, 110, 142, 143
genital discharge, 2, 15, 26, 27, 29, 35, 41, 48, 67–68, 72, 74–75, 77, 84–86, 93, 98, 108, 114–15, 121, 129–32, 141–42, 144, 148–52, 159, 164, 166, 185–86, 190–92, 197–98, 225, 242, 246, 260, 263, 291–93, 297, 306
gentiles, 8, 18, 31, 35, 68, 143, 199, 211, 224, 227, 235, 238–39, 247, 312
gonorrhea, 68, 130, 131
graded impurity, 14–15, 35, 90, 92, 98, 181–82, 194, 197, 201, 203, 212–13, 215–16, 232, 284, 294, 297, 303, 310, 313
graves, 72, 99, 114, 168, 188, 193, 230, 244, 285
Greco-Roman, 10, 28, 31, 33–34, 60, 90, 242, 284
Greece, 3, 9–10, 30, 33, 44, 65, 108, 115, 155, 158–62, 164, 168, 170, 174, 176, 196, 218, 226, 228, 236, 239, 241, 246, 264, 284, 301, 311
ḥăbērîm, 279, 305
halakah, halakic, 11–14, 16, 22, 27–28, 30, 32, 34–38, 40–41, 117, 185–87, 202, 206, 216, 218–19, 226, 231, 233–41, 243–44, 247–48, 255, 259, 269, 271, 277–79, 281, 284, 286, 288, 295–97, 300, 303–4, 312–17
hand impurity, 12, 27, 28, 73, 95, 191, 207, 211, 213–15, 227, 233–35, 241–43, 245, 265, 285, 303, 310–11, 313–14, 316–17
handwashing, 5, 19, 21, 28, 30, 35, 41, 94, 102, 175, 178, 181–83, 203–5, 207–8, 210–19, 222, 226–27, 231–44, 246–48, 278, 284, 287, 294, 296, 304–5, 310–13, 315–16
ḥaṭṭā't, 2, 159, 177, 187–89, 209, 292
healing, 25–27, 84, 92, 98, 155, 167, 218, 225, 227–30, 246–47, 254–55, 257, 269–70, 272–73, 298, 310

heifer's neck, 121, 146
hemorrhaging woman, 29, 217, 230
hierarchy, 6–7, 52, 54, 63, 66–67, 70, 173, 225
high-frequency rituals, 174
high-sensory stimulation, 174–75
Hillel, 209, 212, 245, 296, 311, 314
Hillelites, 207, 213
holiness, 11, 24–25, 27, 31–32, 39, 43–44, 70, 97, 102–3, 157, 192, 199, 209, 225, 280–81, 284, 289–91, 293–94, 304, 313
Holiness Code/source, 2, 4, 71, 73, 80–81, 86, 94, 96, 102–3, 108, 115–16, 121, 142, 146, 148–49, 170, 206, 281, 289–91, 304
homicide, 169, 174
household religion, 162, 192, 211, 309
ḥullîn, 5, 28, 182, 191, 207–8, 210, 213–16, 232–33, 240, 305
hybridity, 79, 101, 103
hygiene, 71–72, 86, 112, 114, 129, 138
hyssop, 77, 97, 124–26, 147
idol worship, idolatry, 6, 46, 70–71, 77, 85, 108, 111, 115–16, 122, 131–34, 142, 150–52, 317
immersion, 14, 16, 18, 21, 29, 31–32, 40, 67, 74, 84, 156, 161–62, 166, 169, 173, 177–80, 182, 195–96, 201, 203, 205–6, 208, 210–15, 222, 232–33, 278, 280, 283–85, 296, 304
immoral behavior, 44, 48, 70, 71, 113, 115–16, 158, 160
impure foods, 22, 47, 303, 311, 313–14
incense, 133, 156, 180, 317
indifference, 24–25, 27, 37–40, 216
innate, 52, 62, 71, 112, 138–39, 153, 172
insects, 72, 88–89, 91, 100, 113–14, 126–28
intercourse, 26, 29, 68, 77, 83, 94, 110, 122, 130–31, 166, 183, 192, 223, 262, 285, 305–6
intermarriage, 8, 12, 46, 49, 70–71, 77, 109, 131
inventions, 16, 69, 197, 211, 279, 284, 312

išrubu, 91, 167, 258
Jairus, 29, 228–30
Jerusalem, 19, 21–22, 82, 86, 100–102, 133, 161–62, 188, 197–99, 203–4, 223, 225, 255–56, 263, 265–67, 277, 279–83, 287, 289, 293–94, 297, 299–300, 307–9, 317
Jesus, 1, 3, 5, 12, 16, 19, 21, 23–33, 37–41, 177, 180–84, 210–11, 216–19, 229–31, 233–48, 251, 252, 265–66, 269–73, 294, 303–5, 311–17
John the Baptist, 7, 16–17
Josephus, 2, 12, 17, 36, 93, 181, 183, 185, 197–99, 203–4, 223–25, 240, 251–52, 263–69, 271–72, 275, 293, 309
Karaites, 35, 96, 186, 196, 240, 301
kārēt penalty, 121, 146, 292
khrafstra, 72, 91, 99, 100, 113, 128, 294
kipper, 2, 159, 167
kudurru inscription, 84, 91, 167, 258
laundering, 125–26, 156, 166–67, 177
legal essentialism, 14, 36. See also realism
legal formalism, 14, 36. See also nominalism
leniency, 12, 36, 185, 189, 191–93, 199, 203, 215, 223–25, 265, 267–68, 280, 296, 298–99
leprosy, 31, 40, 83–84, 91, 108, 141, 162–63, 167, 183, 187–93, 197–99, 204–5, 212–13, 221, 223, 225–27, 242, 252–54, 257–60, 262–65, 267, 269, 272–74, 285, 290, 299
liquids, 191, 207, 210–11, 213–15, 232, 234–35, 242–43, 285, 288, 291, 294, 298, 303, 311, 313–15
loathing, 71, 111, 141–42, 151
low-frequency rituals, 174
magic, 49, 79, 121, 124, 129, 146, 160, 177
Maimonides, 20, 240, 300–301, 306
Manetho, 263–65
mê niddâ, 292, 296
meals, 19, 59, 67, 82, 83, 95, 175, 178, 203, 207–8, 211, 216–17, 222, 232, 234, 237–38, 243, 245, 278–79, 294, 296, 305, 310–12, 315

menstrual blood, 77, 83, 85, 90, 107, 115, 128, 131–32, 150, 165, 190, 226
menstrual cloth, test rag, 150–51
menstruation, 26, 29, 44, 47, 62, 68, 85–86, 90, 93–96, 102, 107, 110, 115, 128–29, 132, 141, 150–51, 161, 163–66, 178, 185–87, 190–91, 193, 197–99, 202–5, 220–22, 224–26, 232, 260, 266, 278, 285–86, 293, 297, 305–6, 309
Mesopotamia, 9–11, 108, 155, 157, 160, 164, 168–69, 175
miasma, 44, 158–59, 176, 242
mimicry, 79, 101, 103, 285
minimalist, 6, 19, 20, 285–86
miqweh, 19–21, 31, 74, 83–84, 162, 231, 268, 280–86, 297, 307
Mishnah, 2, 5, 34, 36, 181, 183, 191, 203, 205, 207–8, 210–11, 213, 224–26, 233–34, 242, 244, 255, 264, 268, 297–99, 306, 313, 315
mold, 48, 121, 141–42, 254
moral impurity, 8–9, 15, 17–18, 28–31, 43, 45–47, 63, 71, 73, 75, 109–11, 117, 121, 124–25, 142, 146, 171, 317
mothers, 73–74, 77, 90, 95, 102, 115, 128–29, 148–49, 271
mourning, 36, 87, 168, 229, 256, 310
murder, 8, 46, 48, 83, 96, 111, 116, 121–22, 124, 126, 146, 151, 156, 160, 169–70, 195, 265
maṣorā, 186–87, 190, 299
Naaman, 84, 257, 258
niddâ, 29, 141–42, 152, 187, 191, 201–2, 222, 226, 292, 296
nominalism, 14, 36, 209, 211, 286, 295–96, 300–301, 313–14. See also legal formalism
ôṣār, 21
overhang, 187, 252, 261, 266, 269, 285, 287, 297
paradosis, 236, 239–40
parturient, 2, 68, 95, 102, 149, 165–66, 187, 190, 193, 199, 204, 212, 225, 260, 290–91, 293, 310
patriarchy, 134, 149, 151

Persian influence, 10, 81, 82, 89–93, 96, 99, 103, 130, 187, 259, 294
Persian period, 4, 68–69, 81–82, 85–86, 89, 91, 100, 162, 189, 256, 268, 270, 294, 304
Persians, 90–91, 100, 167, 258
Pharisees, 5, 11–13, 19, 24–25, 28, 32, 35–36, 182, 184, 205–6, 208–11, 227, 232–33, 240, 243–45, 277, 279–80, 286, 294, 296, 303–6, 311, 313–16
pharmakos, 158, 162, 170, 174, 180
pig, 23, 59, 60, 65–66, 72–73, 77, 88–89, 107, 114, 126–28, 147–48, 174. See also pork
pollution, 8–9, 30, 44, 54, 63, 109, 128, 134, 141, 143, 155, 157–61, 163–73, 176–77, 179, 191
popular practices, 14, 101, 206, 277, 281, 295, 302
pork, 23, 77, 88, 114, 148, 238. See also pig
postcolonial, 70, 79, 101, 103, 285
pre-Markan tradition, 228–31, 236, 246–48, 273
priest, 6–7, 12, 19, 32, 54, 61, 64, 69, 86, 90, 92, 96–97, 101–3, 108, 161, 169, 176–78, 185, 188, 198, 206–10, 212, 216, 221, 232, 254–56, 266, 269, 279–81, 287, 291, 296, 297, 301, 304–7, 309
priestly authors, 68–70, 72–73, 88, 96, 99, 100, 103, 107, 113–14, 127, 166, 187–88, 254, 256–57, 292, 294, 297
priestly elite, 12, 32, 101, 189, 266, 270, 278, 293–94
priestly law, 23, 29, 34, 59, 67–68, 81, 105, 107–8, 113, 135, 144, 148, 162, 166–67, 185–86, 251, 253, 256–57, 259, 279, 289, 307
priestly texts, 4, 13, 59, 62, 76, 80–82, 85, 105, 171, 190, 280
prostitution, 77, 133–34
purificants, 97, 156, 158, 167, 176–77, 262
purification, 2–5, 8, 10, 12, 14–21, 23, 25–27, 31, 33–34, 39, 44, 47, 49, 51,

Subject Index

purification (cont.) 52, 54, 61, 63–64, 74–75, 77–78, 80, 83, 85–87, 90–98, 102, 108–10, 122, 124–26, 129–30, 141, 143, 147, 152, 155–74, 176–83, 186–89, 192, 194–97, 199–203, 206, 209–10, 212–13, 215–16, 220–27, 232, 234, 245–46, 255, 257, 259–62, 264, 266–67, 271, 277, 280, 282–85, 287, 290–92, 294, 296–97, 299, 301, 304, 308–10, 317. *See also* cleansing
purify, 15, 18, 33, 49, 83, 93–94, 96–97, 102, 109, 120, 142, 145, 147, 151–52, 157, 160, 162–63, 165, 167, 169–70, 172, 176–80, 187, 192, 195, 200–202, 210, 223, 245, 254, 261–62, 266–67, 279, 281, 285–86, 288, 290–93, 296–97, 306, 309, 317
purity, 1–14, 16–41, 43–48, 51–55, 58, 60–65, 67–71, 73–84, 86, 88, 90–92, 96–97, 100–103, 105–13, 116–17, 122, 129, 137, 141, 143–46, 148–49, 152, 155–64, 166, 170–73, 178, 181–85, 187, 192–94, 196, 203, 205–12, 215–19, 221, 225, 227–32, 234–39, 241–48, 252, 256, 258–59, 261–62, 268–69, 271–72, 277–81, 283–85, 287–89, 291, 294, 296–97, 299–312, 314–17
qodāšim, 191, 210, 212–14, 297, 313
Qumran, 2–4, 8, 10–16, 19–20, 25, 30–31, 35–36, 47, 77, 86, 96, 117, 144, 186, 194, 197, 199–201, 208, 220, 223–24, 234, 251–52, 260, 262, 267–69, 275, 288, 294–97, 304, 307, 309, 313
rabbinic anachronism, 296, 303, 312
rabbinic innovation, 35, 240, 266
rabbinic Judaism, 4–5, 9, 33–34, 37, 175, 184, 248, 286
rabbinic legislation, 12, 21, 34, 84, 208, 211, 240–41, 252, 259, 269, 278, 283, 296, 303, 311–12, 314
rabbinic traditions, 14, 19, 33, 35–37, 241, 245, 306, 314
rape, 83, 124, 126
realism, 14, 36, 206, 209, 211, 286, 295. *See also* legal essentialism

recontamination, 214, 313
red heifer, 12, 15, 86, 96–97, 102, 159, 188, 197, 292, 296
removal, 2, 18, 26, 47–49, 76, 102, 109, 120–25, 141, 146–47, 155–56, 159, 166–67, 169–72, 177, 179, 188, 201, 206, 297, 313
removes, 18, 191, 192, 207, 210, 213–15, 288, 303, 311–13
ritual impurity, 1, 8, 15, 18, 26, 38, 45, 47–48, 53, 66, 75, 109–11, 117, 124–25, 143–44, 147, 244, 248, 258, 267
ritual purification, 16, 18, 20–21, 23, 29, 110, 157, 179, 195, 201, 232, 245–46, 282–84
ritual purity, 1, 14, 18, 25–26, 35, 38, 51–52, 58, 68, 111, 141, 155, 277, 300
roman period, 5, 20, 253, 268, 274, 282–83, 287, 296, 302, 308
Sabbath, 134, 184, 238, 240, 255, 288
sacrifice, 2, 8, 18, 31, 46, 49, 63–65, 77, 82–83, 87, 92, 95, 107, 116, 122, 133–34, 156, 158–59, 161, 166–67, 170–71, 176–77, 183, 187–90, 193, 195, 212, 227, 261, 263–67, 292, 297, 300, 317
Sadducees, 11, 28, 206, 240, 244, 248, 286, 294, 313
sag-did rite, 98, 168
sanctuary, 3–4, 6, 20, 32, 81, 102, 134, 156, 158, 162–63, 188–89, 255, 281, 285–86, 290–93, 300, 306–7, 309
scaliness, 72, 114, 120, 144–45, 162, 242
scapegoat, 10, 158, 162, 176, 180
scraping, 48, 120–21, 124, 141, 146, 179
seclusion, 185–86, 190, 193, 197–99, 204, 224–26, 260, 279, 293, 307, 309
Second Temple Judaism, 4, 9–10, 25, 32–33, 37, 75, 97, 145, 155, 162–63, 166, 169, 175, 178, 181, 183–84, 224, 251–52, 259, 277, 301–2
Second Temple period, 4–6, 10–11, 14–15, 19, 22, 29, 31–37, 67, 83–84, 98–99, 175, 182, 185–88, 190, 192, 194–97, 201–4, 206–8, 211, 215–16,

380 Impurity and Purification in Early Judaism and the Jesus Tradition

Second Temple period (cont.) 218–19, 222–24, 226, 231–32, 234, 240–41, 243, 245–47, 252, 259–61, 266, 269, 274, 277–78, 280–83, 286, 288, 294, 299, 303, 311–12, 314–15
sectarians, 5, 7–8, 12, 15, 161, 194, 197, 202, 210, 262, 268, 278, 281, 294, 304, 306–7, 309–10, 313
semen, 26, 62, 68, 74, 82, 90, 94, 107, 130–31, 164–66, 187, 190–92, 201–2, 220, 260, 285, 293, 297, 306
šereṣ, 113, 126, 141, 314
seven-day impurity, 169, 187, 189, 193, 196–97, 200–202, 220, 222–25, 255, 266, 290, 309, 310
sexual pollution, 9, 33, 109, 143
Shammai, 209, 213, 245, 296, 311, 314
Shammaites, 5, 35, 207, 213
skin disease, 85, 91, 92, 144, 162, 167, 186, 251, 255, 263, 269, 307
smell, 45, 71, 72, 112, 114–15, 129, 139, 144, 151, 157, 179
spring, 84, 200, 264, 283
sprinkling, 12, 18, 49, 61, 74, 91, 93, 96–98, 124, 151–52, 156, 169, 173, 175, 179–80, 194–96, 201, 226
status, 29, 31, 35, 39, 46, 55, 67, 69, 88, 101–2, 148, 176, 179, 190, 202, 219, 221–22, 224, 226, 234, 246, 252, 254–55, 286, 290, 300
stepped pools, 20–21, 74, 162, 169, 196, 281–85, 307–10
stone vessels, 12, 19, 21–22, 186, 205, 207, 216, 231, 233–34, 268, 280, 286–89, 307–8
stringency, 14, 215, 267–68, 295–96, 298–99
structuralism, 6–8, 43, 45, 46, 51, 55–56, 58–59, 61–62, 65–66, 78, 105, 173
sunset, 194, 196, 206, 208, 212, 232, 261–62, 297
susceptibility, 12, 132, 168, 177, 191–92, 207, 209–11, 213–14, 232, 234, 297–98, 313

swarmers, 2, 72, 74, 84, 88–89, 98–100, 103, 113–14, 126–28, 141, 148, 212, 243, 285, 290, 291
symbolism, 7, 32, 34, 43, 45–46, 51–52, 54–55, 58–66, 72, 78, 106, 110, 147, 173–74
synagogue, 268, 282–84, 299
Synoptic, 25–27, 184, 271
taboo, 7–8, 23, 30, 43, 45–46, 48, 58, 87–89, 100, 122, 127, 137, 145, 157, 161, 171, 269
ṭāhôr, 44, 144, 157, 299
Talmud, 4, 18, 65, 207, 211, 233, 240, 254
ṭāmē, 44, 75, 120–25, 128–29, 131–32, 143–45, 150, 157
Tannaim, Tannaitic, 33–34, 36, 207, 209–10, 215, 267–68, 277–78, 284, 288, 294–96, 299
tombs, 86, 168, 197
Tosefta, 2, 19, 191, 204, 214, 297, 299
ṭəbûl yôm, 11, 12, 205–6, 208, 212–15, 232, 294
tərûmâ, 191, 207–15, 288, 291, 296, 303, 305, 311–15
uncleanness, unclean, 2–3, 60–61, 65, 72, 82, 84, 86–89, 92, 97, 100, 107, 113, 116, 122, 126–28, 131, 141–42, 144, 164, 205–6, 213–15, 223, 227, 233, 240, 242–44, 265, 289–91, 300–301
unfit, 122, 146, 207, 213–14, 242
unicycle, 37
unwashed hands, 204, 214–15, 235
vassal, 69, 100–101, 162, 256, 289
Vendidād, 10, 79, 90–99, 113, 160, 163, 165–67, 294
voluntary associations, 203, 304
waiting period, 94, 165–68, 197, 206, 212, 232, 261
washing, 15–16, 18–21, 30, 41, 48–49, 84–86, 92–95, 97–98, 120–21, 123–26, 145–46, 151, 157, 165, 167–68, 170–71, 174, 179–80, 188, 194–96, 200–202, 204–8, 210–11, 214, 221–22, 226, 232, 240, 243, 255, 264, 278, 284, 305, 310–11, 317

water rituals, 14, 16, 23, 48–49, 74, 124–25, 155, 158, 171–72, 177, 179–81, 197, 224, 226–27, 234, 246, 264, 297, 303, 309
whore, whorings, 133–34
wilderness, 162–63, 255–56
woman, 29, 30, 67–68, 83, 93–94, 96, 122, 128–29, 131–34, 142, 149–51, 164–65, 185–86, 192, 198, 200, 202, 216–18, 220, 222, 224–27, 229–30, 238, 246–47, 263, 298
xenophobia, 6, 149
Yehud, 4, 54, 69, 100–101, 162, 189, 256–57, 289, 292–94, 304
yôledet, 129, 187, 189–91, 204, 212–13, 220–21
zāb, zābîm, 130–31, 187, 189, 190–91, 198–99, 201–2, 204–5, 210, 220–22, 225–26, 243, 246, 262, 297–98, 311
zābâ, zābôt, 149, 183, 185, 187, 189, 190–91, 199, 202, 204–5, 216–22, 225–32, 234, 236, 239, 246–46, 290, 310
Zoroastrianism, 11, 72, 74, 79, 90, 92–93, 95–97, 99–100, 103, 113, 160, 162–63, 165–68, 175, 178, 189, 289, 294

www.ingramcontent.com/pod-product-compliance
Lightning Source LLC
Chambersburg PA
CBHW032147010526
44111CB00035B/1238